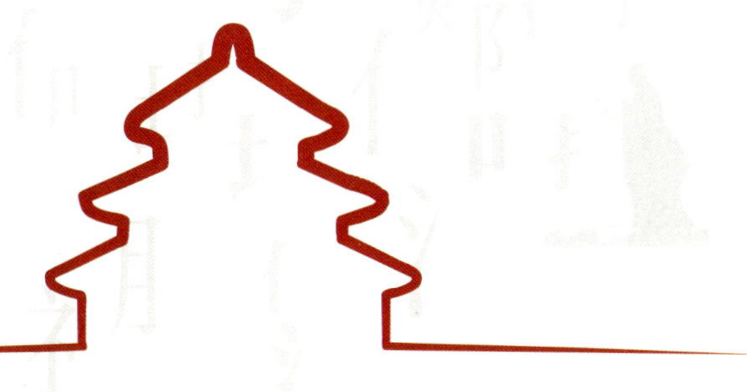

汉语心桥

——汉语在印度的传播与发展

Bridging Hearts Through Chinese Language:

The Dissemination and Development of Chinese Language Education in India

中华人民共和国驻印度共和国大使馆文化处◎汇编

四川大學出版社
SICHUAN UNIVERSITY PRESS

图书在版编目（CIP）数据

汉语心桥 ：汉语在印度的传播与发展 = Bridging Hearts Through Chinese Language: The Dissemination and Development of Chinese Language Education in India ：汉、英 / 中华人民共和国驻印度共和国大使馆文化处汇编． — 成都 ：四川大学出版社，2022.7

ISBN 978-7-5614-9476-9

Ⅰ．①汉… Ⅱ．①中… Ⅲ．①汉语－对外汉语教学－教学研究－汉、英②中华文化－文化传播－研究－印度－汉、英 Ⅳ．①H195.3 ②G125

中国版本图书馆 CIP 数据核字（2021）第 039681 号

书　　名：汉语心桥——汉语在印度的传播与发展
Hanyu Xinqiao—Hanyu zai Yindu de Chuanbo yu Fazhan
汇　　编：中华人民共和国驻印度共和国大使馆文化处

选题策划：王　军　张　晶　刘　畅
责任编辑：刘　畅
责任校对：于　俊
装帧设计：墨创文化
责任印制：王　炜

出版发行：四川大学出版社有限责任公司
地址：成都市一环路南一段 24 号（610065）
电话：（028）85408311（发行部）、85400276（总编室）
电子邮箱：scupress@vip.163.com
网址：https://press.scu.edu.cn
印前制作：成都墨之创文化传播有限公司
印刷装订：成都市金雅迪彩色印刷有限公司

成品尺寸：170mm×240mm
印　　张：24
字　　数：491 千字

版　　次：2022 年 8 月 第 1 版
印　　次：2022 年 8 月 第 1 次印刷
定　　价：238.00 元

本社图书如有印装质量问题，请联系发行部调换

四川大学出版社
微信公众号

序

作为世界文明古国，中国和印度之间有着悠久的友好交往历史。2000 多年来，中印人文交流延绵不绝。历史上，中印两国有众多僧侣、商贾沿着丝绸之路来来往往，推动了佛教东传和商贸联通，谱写了两国友好交流波澜壮阔的史诗。法显、玄奘西行求法，著有鸿篇巨制；竺法兰、摄摩腾白马驮经，开启释门正宗；菩提达摩一苇渡江，立少林禅宗祖庭。近代以来，中印在争取民族解放和国家独立的斗争中守望相助，结下了深厚友谊。泰戈尔、柯棣华、谭云山等先贤续写了中印人文交流、团结互助的佳话。新中国成立后，中印共同倡导的和平共处五项原则已成为国际关系的基本准则，这是中印两国共同向世界贡献的智慧结晶。

中印作为两大新兴经济体，在全球化浪潮中把握机遇，双双实现快速增长。两国合作带动中印人员往来增多，助推彼此互学互鉴、取长补短。印度朋友学习中文的需求不断增长，掀起一轮“汉语热”。现在印度有 20 多所大学开设中文课程，提供学历和非学历教育；各种语言培训机构雨后春笋般涌现，很多中小学，乃至幼儿园都开办汉语学习班，许多印度青年朋友走进汉语课堂学习汉语；一些商务人士也开始学习汉语会话，以便能够更好地同中国商人做生意。

随着印度高校设立专业的汉语教育机构——孔子学院 / 课堂、汉语教学中心，印度国内汉语学习者的规模逐渐扩大，在印汉语教育的教师、教材和教法问题也越来越受到汉语教育专家们的重视。为了更好地促进在印汉语教育的发展，满足越来越多的印度汉语学习者的需要，有必要对在印汉语教育经验进行梳理和总结，特别是倾听汉语教育一线教师的意见，整理他们在从事汉语教学中所遇到的问题，总结解决方案，找到行之有效的教学方法；梳理在印度汉语教育的发展历程和脉络，分析在印汉语教育的现状、存在问题和解决办法，为今后在印汉语教育发展提供切实可行的指导。

《汉语心桥——汉语在印度的传播与发展》一书，正是适应了这种形势的需要。书中汇集了很多在印度汉语教学一线的教师和学者及两国的中国学和印度学专家的文章。他们中有高校中文系的教师、从事中国学研究的专家学者，也有语言培训机构的教师；有曾经在华留学的学者，也有长期在印度孔子学院和汉语教学中心工作的中方教师，以及长期从事印度研究的中国专家学者。他们围绕在印汉语教育问题提出意见建议，汇集了一线汉语教学好的做法和经验，特别是对汉语教育在印发展的思考，以及如何发挥中印人文交流中汉语教育的作用等，为从事在印汉语教学的教师和研究者提供了很好的参考。

“国之交在于民相亲，民相亲在于心相通。”语言是文化的桥梁，是开启两国民众沟通了解之门的钥匙。语言学习对促进双方人文交流的作用不可或缺。中文是世界上使用人数最多的语言，在印推广中文教育有利于促进双方对彼此的认识和理解，构筑起一座沟通中印两国人民心灵的友谊桥梁。

作为相邻的两大文明古国，中印始终本着包容开放的态度交流互鉴，促进东方文明的繁荣进步，也为人类文明增光添彩。作为世界上人口最多的两大新兴经济体，中印需要聚焦合作，增进互信，管控分歧，共谋发展。我期待中印延续两国友好交流传统，增进相互了解和友谊，为中印关系长远发展奠定坚实的民意基础。

是为序。

中华人民共和国驻印度共和国特命全权大使

孙卫东

2020年11月

Preface

China and India, as two ancient civilizations in the world, have recorded a long history of friendly exchanges. People-to-people and cultural exchanges between the two countries have enjoyed continuous development for over two thousand years till today. In history, many monks and merchants traveled to the other country along the Silk Road, which promoted the eastward spread of Buddhism and the connectivity of commerce and trade and left a magnificent epic of friendly exchanges between China and India. For instance, famous Chinese monks Faxian and Xuanzang traveled to the West to seek Buddhist Dharma, with masterworks left behind. Dharmaratna and Kasyapa Matanga, two eminent Indian monks, brought Buddhist scriptures and statues on white horses and introduced Buddhism to China. Monk Bodhidharma, according to a legend, crossed the Yangtze River on a reed to found Chan Buddhism at Shaolin Temple in China. Since modern times, China and India have helped each other in their struggle for national liberation and independence and forged a profound friendship. Sages like Rabindranath Tagore, Dwarkanath Kotnis and Prof. Tan Yunshan continued the tales of people-to-people and cultural exchanges, solidarity and mutual support between the two countries. The Five Principles of Peaceful Coexistence, jointly initiated by China and India after the founding of the People's Republic of China, has become the basic norms of the international relations, which is the crystallization of wisdom that China and India have jointly contributed to the world.

As two major emerging economies, China and India have seized opportunities in the trend of globalization, and both achieved rapid growth. Cooperation between the two countries has led to an increase in personnel exchanges, enabling the two countries to learn from and complement each other. The increasing demand of Indian friends to learn Chinese has set off a "Mandarin Wave". Now more than 20 colleges and universities in India offer Chinese courses with academic or non-academic education. Various language training institutions have sprung up and many primary and secondary schools and even kindergartens have opened Chinese language classes. Many young Indians friends take Chinese language classes, while some business people are also starting to learn Chinese in order to do business better with China.

With the establishment of professional Chinese language education institutions in Indian colleges and universities like Confucius Institutes or Classrooms and Chinese Teaching Centers, the number of Chinese learners in India has gradually expanded. Chinese language education experts have also begun to pay more attention to issues related to teachers, teaching materials and teaching methods of Chinese education in India. It is necessary to sort through and summarize Chinese education experience in India in order to better promote the development of Chinese education and meet the needs of increasing Chinese learners in India. In particular, it needs to listen to the opinions of teachers in Chinese education, summarize problems they encountered and their solutions to find effective teaching methods. There is also a need to review the development trajectory of Chinese education in India, analyze its current status and problems, and explore solutions. The above will provide practical guidance for further development of Chinese language education in India.

The book *Bridging Hearts Through Chinese: The Dissemination and Development of Chinese Language Education in India*, is precisely born to meet those needs. This book collects articles written by teachers and scholars on the front line of Chinese teaching in India and experts in Chinese and Indian studies in both countries. Among them are teachers from the Chinese language departments of colleges and universities, experts and scholars in Chinese studies, and teachers from language training institutions. They also include scholars who have studied in China,

Chinese teachers who have been working in Confucius Institutes and Chinese Teaching Centers in India, and Chinese experts and scholars who have long been engaged in Indian studies. They put forward opinions and suggestions on Chinese education in India and brought together good practices and experiences in Chinese teaching, especially reflections on the development of Chinese education in India, and how to give full play to Chinese education in people-to-people and cultural exchanges between China and India. This book provides a good reference for teachers and researchers who are engaged in Chinese teaching in India.

As a Chinese saying goes, "Friendship, which derives from close contact between the people, holds the key to sound state-to-state relations." Language is the bridge of culture and the key to communication and understanding between the two peoples. Language learning plays an indispensable role in promoting people-to-people and cultural exchanges between the two sides. Chinese is the most spoken language in the world. Promoting Chinese language education in India will help enhance mutual understanding between the two sides and build a bridge of friendship between the Chinese and Indian people.

As two neighboring ancient civilizations, China and India have always engaged in exchanges and followed the principles of openness and inclusiveness, which have fostered the prosperity and progress of eastern civilizations and also contributed to human civilizations. As the two most populous emerging economies, China and India need to focus on cooperation, enhancing mutual trust, managing differences, and seeking common development. I hope China and India will maintain the tradition of friendly exchanges, enhance mutual understanding and friendship, and build strong public support for the long-term development of China-India relations.

For this purpose, I made the preface.

Sun Weidong

Ambassador of the People's Republic of China

to the Republic of India

目　录

CONTENTS

Part 1

第一部分 在印汉语教育的历史与现状

The History and Current Situation of Chinese Language Teaching in India

百年未有之变局下的在印汉语教学
——困境与破局

包吉氢[1]

摘要 20 世纪 80 年代起，随着中印之间经贸和人员往来日益增多，汉语教学在印度逐渐形成规模，中文曾一度被印度教育政策纲要列为中学可选修的外语之一。两国高层领导人的互访以及中国的开放和快速发展，在印度掀起了“汉语热”。2020 年是中国和印度建交 70 周年，全世界遭遇突如其来的新冠疫情，中印发生涉边事件，双边关系遭遇困难，在印汉语教学受到冲击。在此背景下，汉语教学是否还能继续前行？是否能克服困难找到应对之策？这些是本文要回答的问题。笔者总结过去 40 多年在印汉语教学得失提出，在印汉语教学不能因暂时困难而前功尽弃，为增进两国民众相互了解、推动中印关系继续向前发展，在印汉语教学需要通过创新来破局。

关键词 在印汉语教学；立体型国际汉语教材；“互联网 +”国际汉语教学模式；新时代在印汉语教师

0 绪言

中国与印度，作为两个有着几千年文明延续的邻国，相互往来、交流互鉴的历史源远流长。20 世纪 80 年代以来，伴随着中国的改革开放和国际汉语教学的兴起，以及印度自由经济改革的进行，汉语教学在印度逐步发展。印度从零星的几所大学开设中文系，到全印超过 30 所正规大学开设中文课程以及各种非学历教育的中文

1 博士，清华大学国际关系研究院南亚研究中心特聘研究员。

培训[1]，学习汉语人数超过 2 万[2]，汉语教学在印度蓬勃发展。尤其在 21 世纪的第二个 10 年，中印两国高层互访不断，民间交往日益频繁，经贸关系愈发密切。2011 年印度人力资源发展部（现更名为“教育部”）与中国国家汉办（现更名为“中外语言交流中心”）宣布双方合作在印度初高中开办汉语课程，2014 年 4 月实施；印度教育政策纲要最初版本将中文列为中学生可选的外语之一，一时间“汉语热”风靡这个南亚大国。2020 年是中印建交 70 周年，两国原本计划共同庆祝并举办 70 场活动作为纪念，以便更好地总结过去、展望未来。然而，突如其来的新冠疫情肆虐全球，加快了百年未有之大变局。中印发生涉边事件，双边关系遭遇困难，在印汉语教学受到冲击。

国之交在于民相亲，在印的汉语教学是民之相亲的重要途径。一方面，全球化趋势继续发展，中国坚定走改革开放之路，倡导各文明交融互鉴，构建人类命运共同体；另一方面，印度有舆论炒作“中国威胁论”和“中印经济脱钩”。在当前困境之下，如何使在印汉语教学所受影响程度降到最低？如何在新冠疫情依旧肆虐的情况下继续开展汉语教学？如何继续以汉语教学促进中印民间交往？以上都是本文想回答的问题。本文分为五个部分：第一部分，厘清在印汉语教育的基本概念，划定研究范围；第二部分，文献综述，回顾既往研究成果；第三部分，分析当前的困境；第四部分，提出破局的对策；第五部分，得出结论。本文希望总结过去 40 多年在印汉语教学经验，顺应时代发展，利用数字技术，结合在线教学的最新成果，以创新的理念和实践，为目前困境下的在印汉语教学扬长避短，抛砖引玉，建言献策。

1　在印汉语教学的概念

汉语国际教育在中国成为一门学科，从 1978 年中国改革开放之后逐渐兴起，最初被称为对外汉语，是“对外国人汉语教学”的简称[1]63，其实质是将汉语作为外语进行教授。在过去的 40 多年中，中国学界不断探索和建立起了汉语国际教育

1　https://www.shiksha.com/humanities-social-sciences/languages/colleges/chinese-mandarin-colleges-india, 访问时间：2020 年 10 月 22 日。

2　《汉语热持续在印度升温》, http://in.china-embassy.org/chn/gyyd/t1554853.htm，访问时间：2020 年 10 月 22 日。

图 1　包吉氢（右四）陪同孙卫东大使（中）访问印度国际大学

学科的理论和实践[2-11]。在开始讨论在印汉语教学之前，需要先厘清容易混淆的概念。

本文讨论的是在印度对非母语学生教授汉语的情况。由于印度学生通常已经有双语或三语背景，汉语是学生的第二、第三或第四语言。笔者认为，在印汉语教学理论上属于应用语言学的二语习得范畴，与心理学、认知心理学、教育学密切相关。在国际汉语教学成为一门独立学科之前，在印度的汉语教学通常是中文专业学历教育的一部分课程，设在印度大学的外语学院或东亚研究所之下。作为研究中国或汉学的基础课程，目的是培养精英人才，未来研究中国语言、历史、宗教、文化或中国问题的专家、汉学家。本文研究的范围集中在汉语语言作为外语的教学，其目的不仅仅是培养未来的汉学家，更重要的是培养大量具有汉语听说能力，能够进行中印两国人民日常交流和商业往来的人员。正如中国对外汉语教学界多数专家的意见："把培养汉学家作为汉语教学的目标是不现实的。不同的汉学家有各自不同的研究领域，因此，培养汉学家要靠我国整个教育界和学术界共同努力，不是对外汉语教学可以单独完成的任务。汉语教学可以为培养用汉语工作的汉学家服务，但是它本身的目标不是培养汉学家。”[12]10

所以，本文中的在印汉语教学指汉语作为外语的教学，包括学历和非学历教育。同时，在印度的汉语教学，从理论和实践上既适用于教授非母语学生汉语（二语习得）的一般规律，又适用于国别特殊性规律，即在印度教授汉语，需要符合印度学生的特殊性。

图 2　包吉氢（前排左四）与金德尔大学师生

2　在印汉语教学文献回顾

中印交往历史悠久，随着中国的改革开放、印度的经济改革，以及中印两国关系的持续改善，20 世纪 80 年代后，汉语教学在印度重拾发展势头，积累了一些经验和教训，不少学者及一线教师对在印汉语教学的理论、教材、教法和师资等教学实践问题和案例进行了总结，提出了建议。

1984 年在德里召开的全印汉语教学研讨会上，谭中非常全面地总结了在印汉语教学的历史，阐述了汉语词汇与佛教及梵文的紧密联系，还总结了汉语四声、笔画、语法的教学方法，建议对汉语教师进行培训，按照印度学生的语言习惯编写相应的汉语教材，针对中印商贸往来编写商务汉语，还提出利用好现代工具进行汉语教学。[13]一些印度的汉学家在1988年和2013年的全印汉学研究年会上提出，印度大学培养的中文专业学生并不能阅读汉语原版资料，汉语教师来自研究中国问题的学者；部分开设中文专业的大学设施不完备，图书馆缺乏中文资料，缺少赴华留学奖学金等。[14-15]古俊、杨文武全面回顾了中印文化、宗教、语言交往，特别是在印度汉语的教学历史，面临的政治、文化挑战，并提出中国应对策略的建议。[16]

留学中国的印度硕士毕业生阿西具体分析了在印汉语教学的现状，包括教学阶段与教学层次、师资情况与区域分布、教材的利用等，指出印度汉语教学存在的问题，提出对策。[17]也有印度硕士毕业生从教学法实践及案例入手，分析在印度的汉语教学，比如将尼赫鲁大学[18]、杜恩大学[19]、德里大学[20]作为具体实例进行详细分析，总结得失成败，提出对策意见。有汉语教师通过具体的教学法研究在印度大学的课堂中如何教授汉语中的副词[21]，以及课堂上使用肢体语言教授汉语词汇[22]。还有研究者从在印汉语教材入手，分析印度大学如何选择典型的中文现代文学作品，帮助学生理解中国文化。[23]

通过文献回顾发现，已有的文献对中印语言文化交流历史回顾详尽，提出在印汉语教学特殊性的理论研究，对汉语在印度的教材、教法、教师问题（以下简称“三教”）做了不少总结，也提出了改进的建议，但对于在印汉语教学特殊性的理论研究深入性不够，尤其是跨学科研究缺乏，如缺乏教育心理学、语言心理学、对比语言学、语言社会学与在印汉语教学相结合的课题。未来可以考虑中印联合进行学术研究，可从教学媒介语的对比入手，比如使用学生母语（印地语、泰米尔语、乌尔都语、泰卢固语）教授汉语与使用英语教授汉语的对比；也可以做母语与汉语的对比研究，总结印度学生母语的发音和语法结构在学习汉语时的困难所在，在理论上找出一些在印汉语教学的特殊规律；还可以结合社会学理论，研究在印学习汉语学生的社会阶层分布，跟踪学生学成后的职业和经济地位，考察掌握汉语技能对学生的收入及职业升迁的影响等，这些都可作为未来的研究课题。对于在印汉语教学遇到的“三教”问题如何解决，尤其对于汉语教学在印发展是否会受到世界格局、国际关系、中印双边关系及其他非传统安全因素的影响，上述文献没有论及。尽管文献都提出了对策，但总体都比较笼统，没有具体可实施的建议，且文献都囿于年代。在2020年新冠疫情暴发及中印关系受挫之后，在印度的汉语教学应何去何从，应该怎样办？本文将在以下部分进行论述。

图3 包吉氢（右五）访问印度社会研究中心

3 当前的困境

世界处于百年未有之大变局[1]，其实质就是国际力量对比发生重大变化，导致世界秩序大调整。新冠疫情加速了这一过程，使世界政治、经济和社会的各种矛盾凸显，在印汉语教学面临前所未有的困难，其中包括美国、印度和疫情因素，然而在中印经贸和印度教育转型上又有一线转机。

3.1 美国因素

美国因素是世界大变局中最重要的因素之一。美国为遏制中国发展，通过贸易、

1 《习近平：努力开创中国特色大国外交新局面》，http://politice. people. com.cn/n1/2018/0623/c1001-30078644.html, 访问时间：2020年10月22日。这是习近平总书记在2018年6月23日在中央外事工作会议上做出的一个重大论断，之后在许多场合多次提及。

科技、舆论和外交等手段不断打压中国。美国重拾“冷战”思维，用意识形态划线抹黑中国，阻断中美教育合作、学术交流和人员往来，最突出的例子是封杀作为中美人文交流重要平台的孔子学院及孔子课堂。2017 年，特朗普政府上台后开始不断污蔑孔子学院使美国大学面临间谍活动和知识产权失窃的威胁。2020 年 8 月美国国务院宣布将孔子学院美国中心列为“外国使团”后，蓬佩奥 9 月 1 日又提出希望美国大学在 2020 年年底之前关闭所有孔子学院。[1] 美国还不断鼓动其他国家向它看齐，这种做法开了一个极其恶劣的先例，为国际汉语教学蒙上一层阴影。

3.2 印度因素

在印汉语教学受印度因素影响明显。2020 年中印边境事件使双边关系遭遇困难。2020 年 8 月 2 日，印度高等教育部要求审核 4 个在印的孔子学院及 3 个孔子课堂，另外还要审查印度与中国大学合作的 54 份备忘录；9 月初印外交部被要求对中国签证做额外的安全审核。[2] 这使汉语教师获得赴印签证更加困难。据印媒报道，此前印度多家安全机构就中国在印度高等教育中日益增长的影响力发出警告。[3] 印度教育部将核查与孔院合作的印度大学是否获得预先核准，[4] 引发担忧。印在 2020 年先后三次总计禁用 224 款中国手机应用软件（App），其中包括中文学习软件，如：Learn Chinese AI-Super Chinese。[5] 印度对中印教育合作人为设置重重障碍，使得在印汉语教学雪上加霜。

1 《威胁关闭美国所有孔子学院并继续打压华为 蓬佩奥扬言要与十四亿人打“经济冷战”》，https://www.sohu.com/a/416176834_119038，访问时间：2020 年 10 月 22 日。

2 “India slaps new curbs on visas, schools to stem China’s influence”, https://timesofindia.indiatimes.com/india/india-slaps-new-curbs-on-visas-schools-to-stem-chinas-influence/articleshow/77675489.cms，访问时间：2020 年 9 月 23 日。

3 “Chinese firms, mobile apps blocked, India could next target university tie-ups”, https://www.hindustantimes.com/india-news/china-confucius-institutes-face-heat-over-propaganda/story-AZCHG9fp66KxXnHCF56JeO.html，访问时间：2020 年 9 月 23 日。

4 “Foreign institutes set up without govt nod under scanner: MEA”, https://indianexpress.com/article/education/foreign-institutes-set-up-without-govt-nod-under-scanner-mea-6543218/，访问时间：2020 年 10 月 22 日。

5 “PUBG, Ludo World among 118 more Chinese apps banned by IT ministry”, https://www.hindustantimes.com/india-news/118-more-chinese-apps-banned-including-pubg-here-is-the-full-list/story-Cr39p0cGAQWrMCrpYrQY7J.html，访问时间：2020 年 11 月 1 日。印政府 2020 年 6 月 29 日宣布禁用 59 款中国 App，7 月 23 日宣布禁用 47 款中国 App，9 月 2 日宣布禁用 118 款中国 App（笔者注）。

3.3 疫情因素

新冠疫情对印度造成巨大的影响，据印度联邦统计和计划执行部（MOSPI）数据，2020 年第二季度印度国内生产总值（GDP）下降了 23. 9%。[1] 国际货币基金组织（IMF）预测 2020 年印度经济增速为 -10. 2%。[2] 截至本文截稿之日，印度感染新冠病毒人数已超过 810 万[3]，有超过 3 亿名学生、140 万所学校和 5. 1 万个学院受疫情影响[4]。自 2020 年 3 月起师生一直不能到校上课，印度大学教育资助委员会（UGC）修订大学新生开学时间为 11 月，如疫情仍使学生无法到校，课程将改为线上。[5] 线上课程所要求的互联网连接，在印度城市家庭接入比例只有 42%，农村仅 24%，接入家庭中有超过 50% 信号连接不畅；同时，只有 8% 的印度家庭既有电脑又有互联网；另外，各地还不同程度地受到停电困扰。[6] 尽管印各方面条件不完善，但是印政府、大学及线上教育公司尽力发展线上课程，在印汉语教学虽受疫情打击，却仍有可以在线进行的希望。

3.4 中印经贸因素

中印经贸因素是黑暗困境中的一点亮光。即使印经济下行、疫情持续、中印双边关系遇阻，然而印度商务部数据显示，2020 年 5 至 8 月印度对中国出口一直处于增长态势。截至 2020 年 8 月，中国占印度出口总额的 9. 1%，仅次于美国（17%）。在印度的五个最大出口伙伴中，中国是增长最快的国家。[7] 印度对中国出口在二、三

1 "India's economy contracts by 23.9%, worst in decades", https://www.hindustantimes.com/india-news/india-s-gdp-growth-rises-falls-by-23-9-per-cent-in-april-june-quarter/story-Yj1GGTR7fuHAQ6QNL0jpBL.html，访问时间：2020 年 9 月 23 日。

2 https://www.imf.org/en/Countries/IND#countrydata，访问时间：2020 年 10 月 30 日。

3 https://www.mohfw.gov.in/，访问时间：2020 年 11 月 1 日。

4 Anushruti Singh, "Coronavirus lockdown: Indian online education gets a shot in the arm", April 9, 2020，https://smefutures.com/coronavirus-lockdown-indian-online-education-gets-a-shot-in-the-arm/，访问时间：2020 年 11 月 1 日。

5 "UGC now says first year classes will start in November, there will be no winter, Summer breaks", https://theprint.in/india/ugc-now-says-first-year-classes-will-start-in-november-there-will-be-no-winter-summer-breaks/507929/，访问时间：2020 年 11 月 1 日。

6 "India education can't go online—only 8% of homes with young members have computer with net link", https://scroll.in/article/960939/indian-education-cant-go-online-only-8-of-homes-with-school-children-have-computer-with-net-link，访问时间：2020 年 11 月 1 日。

7 印对华出口额在 2020 年 8 月份增长 15%，6 月高达 78%，5 月和 7 月分别增长 48% 和 23%（笔者注）。"Double-digit rise in exports helps India nearly halve trade gap with China", https://www.business-standard.com/article/economy-policy/double-digit-rise-in-exports-helps-india-nearly-halve-trade-gap-with-china-120100801594_1.html，访问时间 2020 年 10 月 13 日。

季度较前一年同期增长26.3%。[1] 尽管莫迪总理2020年4月开始提倡“自力更生”（Atmanirbhar Bharat[2]），印度自中国进口比例却从上个财年的14%，增长到本财年的19%[3]。数据给了我们不少信心，说明政治操弄并不能轻易使中印经贸脱钩，而这就是中印民间继续交往的动力，在印汉语教学也因此有继续发展的理由。

图4　笔者（左二）访问德里小珍珠幼儿园

面对上述困境和挑战，我们不能被暂时的困难吓倒，唯有突破固有思维模式，拓宽与印企业、行业协会、非政府组织等的合作渠道，顺应在线课程的发展，加速在印汉语教学理念和实践的改革与创新。

4　破局的对策

尽管疫情加速世界格局变化，中印关系遇到半个多世纪以来最艰难的局面，但中印是伙伴，不是对手。正如中国驻印度大使孙卫东所说：

> 中方对中印关系的基本判断没有变。中印是伙伴而不是对手，是机遇而不是威胁。……中印作为相邻的两个最大发展中国家的基本事实没有变，互为合作伙伴的方向没有变，谁也离不开谁的大格局没有变。……双边关

1　“Indian exports to US, China on rise in 2020”, https://www.livemint.com/news/india/indian-exports-to-us-china-on-rise-in-2020-11603238950035.html，访问时间：2020年10月22日。
2　https://en.wikipedia.org/wiki/Atmanirbhar_Bharat，访问时间：2020年10月14日。
3　“To outrun China, India must reform”, https://epaper. livemint. com/ Home/Article View, 访问时间: 2021年3月28日。

> 系要向前走，而不要后退或逆转。中印不要互相消耗，更不应互相对立，而应相向而行，推动双边关系早日重回正轨。[1]

在中印两国领导人的引领下，中印应达成共识，克服中印教育交流合作中暂时出现的困难，发挥中印双方有识之士的能力和优势，逆势而上。

疫情加速改变人类生活的方式，助推数字技术和互联网普及，在印汉语教学须乘势而为，突破创新。通过教材的立体化，教学模式的数字化、网络化，汉语教师的与时俱进，在印汉语教育应摆脱困扰多年的“三教”问题，提高教学效率和印度学生汉语习得的水平，增加汉语对印度学生的吸引力，扩大学习人群，为中印两国人民的相互理解和交往打下语言基础，为中印文明相互学习、共同发展贡献力量。

4.1 母语及国别化

我们对印度有个模糊的概念，印度曾是英殖民地，所以印度人大多讲英语，2000—2011 年间，全世界一半的呼叫中心（call center）都设在印度。2006 年的数据显示，呼叫中心雇用了 200 万印度人 [24]29，因为呼叫中心需要用英语工作，看上去这印证了印度人都说英语的说法。然而英语是印度学生的母语吗？据 2001 年印度人口普查数据，以英语为第一语言的人口仅有 226 449，以英语为第二语言的为 86 125 221 人，以第三语言的为 38 993 066 人 [2]。但是，正如英国广播公司（BBC）记者扎里尔・马萨尼（Zareer Masani）指出的，印度英语使用者达 1. 25 亿，位居世界第二。 英语教育的拼凑状态意味着许多印度人说的是“印式英语”（Hinglish）。[3] 印度得益于将英语作为官方语言以及商务语言，但令人大跌眼镜的是，印度工科学生中有 67% 英文不流利，约 3/4 的工科生缺乏知识经济所需的英语口语技能。[4]

我们还可以从印度教育部 2020 年的统计数据中观察印度高中及以下学生讲英

1 《驻印度大使孙卫东接受印电视台专访》，https://www.fmprc.gov.cn/ce/cein/chn/sgxw/t1810230.htm，访问时间：2020 年 9 月 24 日。

2 https://en.wikipedia.org/wiki/List_of_countries_by_English-speaking_population, 访问时间：2020 年 9 月 20 日。

3 https://k-international.com/blog/countries-with-the-most-english-speakers/ , 访问时间：2020 年 9 月 20 日。

4 “Most of engineering students lack employability skills, say experts”, https://www.thehindu.com/news/national/andhra-pradesh/most-of-engineering-students-lack-employability-skills-say-experts/article8319173.ece, 访问时间：2020 年 9 月 20 日。

语的情况（见表 1）。

表 1 印度高中以下在校生使用的教学媒介语言分布[1]

（城市/农村、男/女，所有目前学前、初小、高小、初中、高中学生平均值）

（以百分比计）

家庭语言	教学媒介语			
	家庭语言	非家庭语言		
		印地语	英语	其他语
印地语	79. 2	—	18. 9	1. 9
英语	67. 1	24. 3	—	8. 6
阿萨姆语	89	0. 7	10. 0	0. 3
孟加拉语	83. 5	4. 2	6. 9	5. 4
古吉拉特语	85. 3	1. 7	12. 7	0. 3
卡纳达语	66. 9	0. 1	39. 1	1. 9
马拉雅拉姆语	36. 6	0. 3	61. 4	1. 7
曼尼普尔语	7. 7	0. 8	75. 5	16. 0
马拉地语	73. 1	1. 5	23. 7	1. 7
奥里亚语	87. 4	1. 6	10. 2	0. 8
旁遮普语	38. 9	6. 8	53. 9	0. 4
泰米尔语	55. 5	0. 2	43. 9	0. 4
泰卢固语	37. 8	0. 2	59. 3	2. 7
乌尔都语	12. 2	13. 2	53. 8	20. 8
尼泊尔语	19. 4	7. 1	59. 5	14. 0
博多语	17. 5	12. 5	8. 2	61. 8
信德语	32. 1	1. 5	62. 9	3. 5
总平均	64. 7	7. 6	24. 4	3. 3

从这份最新的调查数据得出，超过六成印度高中以下学生的教学媒介语言为家庭语言或称母语。同样，被误以为印度普及程度高的英语，在印度高中以下作为教学媒介语言的情况还不到 1/4。

1 笔者根据印度官方统计数据整理。http://www.mospi.gov.in/sites/default/files/publication_reports/Report_585_75th_round_Education_final_1507_0.pdf, “NSS Report No. 585: Household Social Consumption on Education in India”, P.A-849, 访问时间：2020 年 9 月 17 日。

目前在印教授汉语的媒介语皆为英语，换句话说，印度学生在学习汉语之前，首先要先学会英语，才能间接地学习汉语。上述数据表明，英语只是印度学生的第二、第三，甚至第四语言，不排除有些学生英语不过关或多为印式英语，直接造成学习汉语的困难。国内出版社正努力策划出版多媒介语版本的汉语教材，比如人民教育出版社出版的《快乐汉语》有英、俄、法、德版本[1]。目前以南亚主要母语为媒介的汉语教材只有北京语言大学出版社出版的《汉语乐园》（包括45种语言的版本），含印地语、孟加拉语、乌尔都语、尼泊尔语等。[2]但《汉语乐园》仍有不足：统一教材的不同教学媒介语翻译版本，对于英文媒介的英美文化有相对较多的考量，而对小语种媒介语所代表的历史、文化、宗教背景没有进行国别化特殊处理，也没有考虑到语言结构和发音习惯对学生习得汉语的影响，尤其对于印度的多语言、多宗教特点，没有针对性。

笔者建议，未来要为印度不同母语的学生，包括印地语、泰米尔语、孟加拉语等，编写有针对性的教材。一是需要对这些母语学生做更深入细致的调查、分析和研究，在汉语习得理论层面发现规律。比如，研究印度学生母语语法结构、发音与汉语的对比，为编写印度国别汉语教材打下坚实的基础。二是摒弃统一教材的媒介语翻译版本，在已有教材编写大纲的指导下，结合印度的文化背景的认知[3]，组织中印专家编纂专供印度学生使用的汉语教材，以适合印地语、泰米尔语、孟加拉语等不同母语的印度学生。三是印度各母语师资力量比较有限，主要表现为讲印地语、孟加拉语、泰米尔语的汉语教师基本没有，可考虑以多种方式鼓励来华印度留学生学成归国从事汉语教学工作，或聘请学习小语种的中国学生以网络或访学形式教授汉语课程。既能加强中印青年交流，又可为学汉语的印度学生提供语言便利。

1 https://old.pep.com.cn/xgjy/hyjx/dwhyjx/jcjf/klhy/dyz/，访问时间：2020年9月25日。

2 https://www.ctmlib.com/search?keyword=%E6%B1%89%E8%AF%AD%E4%B9%90%E5%9B%AD&desc=1&r_per_page=10&page=1&order=full_name&sum=intermediate_language&verify_stage=&intermediate_language=%E5%8D%B0%E5%9C%B0%E8%AF%AD, 访问时间：2020年9月25日。

3 笔者注意到，印度学者把印度的种姓制度与中国的“户口”行政管理进行对比，认为两者都是划分等级。这是认知错误，因为人类对新事物的认识，总是要通过与自己熟悉的事物进行对比来实现。如果对印的国际汉语教材中可以专门用一个小节介绍“户口”这两个简单汉字组成的意义，那就是从源头向印度学生介绍正确的概念。

4.2 立体化教材[1]

立体化教材是多介质、多形式、时空融合的教材。随着技术进步和互联网普及，汉语国际教学的教材不再局限于纸质教材和教具。笔者认为，教材的概念应该是立体化教材，具体而言，应该包括汉语的传统纸质教材、CD、DVD、电子书、直播课、慕课、情景剧、短视频、微课、手机应用程序（App）等（见表 2）。未来在 VR 技术发展与普及的基础上，汉语教材一定会包括 VR 体验式教材。

表 2　汉语国际教育立体教材分类表

名称	特点	具体教材（举例）
电子书	1. 环保：节省纸张，节省印刷费和时间 2. 提高效率：教材运输和分发效率高，可根据师生对教材使用的反馈，快速及时地对内容进行更新或修改	北京语言大学出版社出版教材[2]
直播课	1. 网络学习平台开设 2. 具有录制和回放功能 3. 方便缺课学生补习 4. 教师之间互相学习	钉钉，Zoom，Google Classroom，Microsoft Teams，Blackboard Collaborate，Moodle，WebEx
慕课	1. 集中各学校的优秀教师为学生授课 2. 不受空间和时间的限制 3. 系列课程或专题讲座 4. 课程全面、完整，学习过程较长	国际汉语慕课中心[3]
微课	1. 以短视频介绍某一主题 2. 做汉语辅助教材 3. 生动活泼，简单明了 4. 既有专业老师讲解，也有外国学生的演绎	国际汉语微课中心[4] 全球孔子学院原创微课[5]
手机应用程序（App）	1. 技术的最新发展，在智能手机上下载 2. 利用碎片化的时间学习或巩固知识 3. 学习更个性化，提高学习兴趣和效率	中文联盟（Chinese Plus） 长城汉语 汉雅国际

1　参考初天斌、李少明，《移动互联网背景下立体化教材出版的应用研究》，载《出版发行研究》，2015 年第 2 期，第 39-42 页；藏文强，《汉语国际教育教材编写“立体化原则”的理论内涵》，载《现代语文》，2017 年第 11 期，第 27-30 页，笔者重新定义立体化教材。
2　https://www.blcup.com/PList/index/1426?pid=1，访问时间：2020 年 9 月 25 日。
3　https://www.blcup.com/DicCourse，该网站的慕课试运营，免费，访问时间：2020 年 9 月 25 日。
4　https://www.blcup.com/MicroVideo，在该网站下播放免费，下载收费，访问时间：2020 年 9 月 25 日。
5　http://wz.chinesecio.com/?cat=10，访问时间：2020 年 9 月 25 日。

续表 2

名称	特点	具体教材（举例）
中文教学视频	1. 个人或机构上传到视频网站平台 2. 学生可以通过视频网站获取 3. 多为免费 4. 丰富了印度学生学习汉语的素材	中国中央电视台 CCTV-4 录制的《快乐汉语》1-110 集（*Happy Chinese* Episode 1-110）

面对如此之多的立体化的教材，在印汉语教师需要根据印度学生的学习目的、学习阶段来确定。立体化的汉语教材可以提高印度学生学习汉语的兴趣和学习效率，使他们更进一步。

考虑到印度政府自2020年6月起对中国手机应用程序（App）和部分网站的禁令，笔者建议可以使用海外一些成熟的网络汉语教学工具软件。有些慕课平台上的汉语基础和中国文化课程由分别由清华大学、北京大学、上海外国语大学等中国著名高校提供，可在电脑、平板电脑和智能手机上运行。如表3所列，可帮助克服目前的困难，减少学生流失，提高学习效率和兴趣。

表 3 汉语教学慕课资源表（以英语为媒介）

网站名称及地址	慕课内容
edx https://www. edx. org/learn/chinese	1. 丰富的汉语基础课程 2. 中国文化课程 3. 免费 4. App
Future learn https://www. futurelearn. com/subjects/language-courses	1. 汉语发音 2. 中国文化短期课程 3. 免费
Open Culture https://www. openculture. com/free_mandarin_chinese_lessons	1. 汉语发音 2. 中国文化短期课程 3. 免费
Alison https://alison. com/courses/chinese	1. 汉语会话短期课程 2. 免费
Yabla https://chinese. yabla. com/	1. 汉语拼音注音，字词解释 2. 现实中国视频、音乐、新闻等 3. 付费网站

注：笔者根据网络整理。

1 https://www.youtube.com/watch?feature=youtu.be&v=eH_j2vJfic0&app=desktop，访问时间：2020 年 10 月 12 日。

4.3 “互联网 +” 教学

“互联网 +”教学是与时俱进的国际汉语教学模式和方法。该模式从传统的课堂教学转变为“互联网 +”教学的模式，转变了教师的课堂主角地位，以学生为中心、教师为主导。这个方法是通过互联网授课，师生互动、教学成果评价，充分利用网上软件工具，实现教学目的。“互联网 +”教学在 2020 年之前仍属学界讨论的最新趋势，是教师们试验阶段的教法 [25-26]，自新冠疫情之后，成为世界各国学校普遍接受的模式和方式。

“互联网 +”教学对在印的汉语教学有着直接而深远的影响。疫情对传统课堂教学模式形成较大冲击，倒逼在印汉语教学形式一步进入“互联网 +”时代。“互联网 +”教学模式和方法不仅是形势所迫也是势在必行。从印度当前防疫的状况来看，网课仍将持续相当长的时间。尽管印度各地硬件条件不同，网络覆盖及网速差异较大，目前在印汉语教学还是基本以网课形式进行。师生使用个人电脑、平板电脑和手机上网，借助远程学习平台、网络汉语教学工具软件和资料库进行教学。具体而言，远程学习平台，如钉钉、Zoom、Google Classroom、Microsoft Teams、Blackboard Collaborate、Moodle、WebEx 等，可参与直播课程，教师在线上授课、有针对性地答疑，师生或学生之间讨论，网上提交作业和批改作业；教学工具软件和资料库，比如 Pear Deck、HSK 动态作文语料库等，教师可以用来备课、出题，教学演示，设计学生互动游戏或者知识点小测验等。

笔者总结了部分网络国际汉语教学工具软件（如表 4 所示），供在印汉语教师参考。这些软件都可在电脑、平板电脑、手机上运行，与 Google Classroom、Microsoft Teams、Zoom 平台系统兼容。老师们只要挑选其中一个学习平台、几款教学工具软件熟练使用，就会对自己的教学起到事半功倍的作用。

表 4　网络国际汉语教学工具软件（英语媒介）

软件名称	用途
Pear Deck （Joinpd. com）	网课上的师生互动
Duolingo	汉语小测试

续表 4

软件名称	用途
Quizlet	网课互动测试，付费（有 7 天免费试用期）
Quizizz	网课互动测试
Skritter（https://skritter. com）	学习汉字笔画
Written Chinese（https://www. writtenchinese. com）	汉语发音、基础课程
Purple Culture https://www. purpleculture. net	汉语拼音转换、汉字笔画、汉语发音、英汉 / 汉英字典等工具（部分免费）
Arch Chinese https://www. archchinese. com	汉字笔画练习、发音，字典，教师备课工具，学生作业，游戏练习
Fast Fingers https://10fastfingers. com/typing-test/simplified-chinese	练习汉语打字，简单汉语写作
Classkick	课堂管理，给学生打分、签到等
Liveworksheets	给学生布置作业、评分、评语

注：笔者根据网络整理。

中国作为汉语母语国，中国教育部以及部分中国高校投入了相当多人力和资源建立了汉语国际教学案例及语料库[27]并向社会公开，方便汉语教师备课和出题，对印汉语教师应充分利用这些网上资源，提高教学质量。笔者整理了国际汉语教学案例及语料库列表（如表 5 所示）供参考。

表 5　国际汉语教学案例及语料库网站列表

名称	主办单位	网址	内容
网络孔子学院资源库	中国国际中文教育基金会	http://www. chinesecio. com/	教学资源案例，中外文化差异案例库
国际汉语教学助手网	北京师范大学中文信息处理研究所	www. aihanyu. org	动态语料库、备课助手、作文助手
HSK 动态作文语料库	北京语言大学语言资源高精尖创新中心	www. hsk. blcu. edu. cn	高等汉语水平考试作文考试的答卷语料库
国际汉语教学数据库	中央民族大学国际教育学院	https://cie. muc. edu. cn/xsky/gjhyjxsjk. htm	教案、教例（须注册登录）
中山大学留学生汉字偏误语料库	中山大学国际汉语学院	http://cilc. sysu. edu. cn/	汉字偏误标注版和字词句偏误标注版

中国籍汉语教师申请赴印签证困难，从某种程度上要求我们转变传统汉语教学模式，以“互联网 +”教学来应对这样的现实。笔者建议，国内仍可招募对印的汉语教师，以“互联网 +”教学的模式，为印度学生在网上答疑解惑，组织印度学生间的讨论，在网上批改作业和对学生进行测评。中印大学或机构之间可以以互联网为依托进行交流和教学。此外，中印间有商务往来的印度企业或行业协会（如印对华进出口商会等）、印度互联网教育平台、非政府组织亦可通过“互联网 +”教学模式，继续拓展民间交流。

总之，“互联网 +”教学是在数字、网络技术蓬勃发展的支撑下，以学生为中心的教学理念与方法的转变，是困境下在印汉语教学的一种积极应对方式。

4.4 在印汉语教师的新挑战

2020 年，全球遭遇突如其来的新冠疫情，单边主义、保护主义、逆全球化倾向凸显，中国率先控制疫情、重启经济，积极构建国内国际互促的双循环新格局。这就意味着，中国将继续深度融入世界，同时也为各国发展带来了机遇。国际汉语教学是中国融入世界的途径之一，在增进理解、凝聚共识、促进合作、深化友谊上具有独特的作用。当今世界处于百年未有之大变局下，笔者认为，在印汉语教师必须与时俱进，树立新时代的中国视角、印度视角和时代视角。

4.4.1 中国视角

国际汉语教师树立中国视角，第一要从汉语语言出发，教授学生汉语知识；第二从中国悠久历史和传统文化出发，教授学生中华文化的基本常识，特别要强调中国圣哲先贤的教诲，比如“和为贵”“和而不同”“四海之内皆兄弟也”，以及“天道无亲，常与善人”“天下一家”的思想，传递人类命运共同体的理念；第三，从中国的现实出发，向学生讲好中国故事，展现改革开放的成就，比如介绍中国的“新四大发明”，讲述武汉抗疫中普通人的故事，以体现中国人民的集体主义精神和中国社会制度的优势。对印汉语教师的中国视角应该立足于汉语语言，弘扬优秀传统文化，展现文化自信。

4.4.2 印度视角

对印汉语教师一定要牢固树立跨文化意识的“印度视角”。第一，印度是一个多语言、多宗教、多习俗的国家，宪法规定的官方语言就有22种之多，文化习俗印度东西南北差异非常大。除印度教之外，印度还有伊斯兰教、基督教、耆那教、佛教等宗教，所以不能错误地将印度简化为讲英语的印度教国家。对印汉语教学中，不仅要意识到中印文化之间的差异，还要意识到印度学生亦有不同，跨文化以及印文化多元必须作为重要的考量因素纳入对印汉语教学的全过程。第二，要有中印对比意识，即汉语与学生母语的对比，中国文化与学生文化的对比，从对比中更易找出差异和学习难点，跨越文化障碍，提高学习效率。第三是要找到中印文化的相通之处，比如中国古典思想中有“世界大同、天下一家”，印度人信“Vasudhaiva Kutumbakam”（世界是一家）；中国有“天人合一”的哲学思想，印度也有“Brahmatmaikyam”（梵我合一，“Brahma”指宇宙的原理，汉译“梵”，“atma”指的是自我的本质、自我的实体），简言之，中国与印度都把宇宙（自然）当作自己亲密的朋友。[28]1 对印汉语教师的印度视角应该是多元包容、文明互鉴、和谐共处。汉语教师以传播汉语为方式，作为民间的和平使者，达致民之相亲、民心相通的美好愿景。

4.4.3 时代视角

互联网+时代首先要求对印汉语教师有数字化的时代视角，适应数字时代的发展。汉语教师角色已经不仅是在传统课堂上的讲课人，还必须承担起“网课设计者”“网红主播”“网课技术达人”的任务，即懂得利用网络资源和立体化教材，主导互联网课程，引导学生在网课中讨论，在网上批改作业和给学生测评。其次，对印汉语教师需要对千禧新生代印度学生有更深入的了解，调查研究，从教育学、二语习得、社会语言学、认知心理学等理论角度发现和认识印度学生学习汉语的规律，从而提高汉语教学的质量和效率。最后，汉语教师须加强对中印关系的时代观，即了解印度政治、经济及中印关系的最新发展，在中印双边关系出现困难的情况下，在印汉语教师应继续传达友好的声音。对印汉语教师的时代观体现在教学上跟上技术发展的步伐，不断学习理论，创新教学实践，具备中印关系意识。

在印汉语教学的“三教”问题中，教师是主导性因素，需要发挥主观能动性，树立新时代的中国观、印度观和时代观，为中印两国人民之间架设沟通理解的语言桥梁，为两国的文明互鉴以及地区和平尽一份力，做一份贡献。

5 结语

本文总结了过去40多年在印汉语教学的经验教训，分析当前汉语教学在印度遇到的困难，客观理性地认清形势，认为不能因一时、一事而使多年的积累损失殆尽。为应对可能长期肆虐的新冠疫情，为推动中印关系继续向前发展，在印汉语教学需要通过创新汉语教材、教学方法和模式，培养适应网络时代的国际汉语教师来破局。“互联网+”远程教育平台、汉语教学应用软件、慕课、手机App、短视频、直播课、网络学习社区等，都将成为对印汉语教育的创新手段，克服疫情、双边关系、签证限制等困难，使汉语教学在印度继续发扬光大，为中印民之相亲打好语言沟通的基础，构筑中印文明互通的桥梁。

印度前总统K. R. 纳拉亚南[1]曾说：

> 从历史上看，我们两国文明、文化的亲属性为无数世纪的印中关系打下了基础，提供了活力，使它具有一定程度的永恒性。这种亲属性在我们遇到困难、产生误解的时期使两国的双边交往不至于僵持、死板。我们应该把两大文明从远古开始的对话恢复、重振起来，以加强两国友谊的力度。实际上，我们两国过去死灰中埋藏的火花必然会熊熊燃烧，照亮未来陌生的道路。[29]2

尽管我们处在百•年未有之大变局之下，但中印两国人民向往和平美好生活的

1 科切里尔•拉曼•纳拉亚南（Kocheril Raman Narayanan，1921年2月4日—2005年11月9日），1992年至1997年任副总统兼联邦院议长，1997年7月当选为第10任印度总统，2002年卸任。享有印度“平民总统”和“工作总统”美誉，是印度第一位“贱民”（达利特人）种姓出身的总统。

期望没有变，两国人民千年友好没有变，两国是邻居的事实也不会变，中国“天下大同”与印度的“Vasudhaiva Kutumbakam”（世界是一家）如出一辙。中印都应坚信，两国关系在风雨之后将重见阳光和彩虹，作为世界上人口超十亿的两个发展中邻国，走和平、合作、共赢之路才是奔向光明未来的康庄大道。

参考文献

[1] 吕必松. 对外汉语教学概论（讲义）（续十七）第八章 对外汉语教学的学科性质和学科建设 [J]. 世界汉语教学，1997（1）：63-67.

[2] 吕必松. 加强对外汉语教学的理论研究 [J]. 语言教学与研究，1988（4）：4-19.

[3] 吕必松. 谈谈对外汉语教学的性质和特点 [J]. 语言教学与研究，1988（7）：4-24.

[4] 刘珣. 迈向 21 世纪的汉语作为第二语言教学 [J]. 语言教学与研究，2000（1）：55-60.

[5] 施家炜. 跨文化交际意识与第二语言习得研究 [J]. 世界汉语教学，2000（3）：64-73.

[6] 张德鑫. 润物细无声——论对外汉语教学与汉学 [J]. 语言文字应用，2001（1）：33-45.

[7] 张和生. 对外汉语教师素质与培训研究的回顾与展望 [J]. 北京师范大学学报（社会科学版），2006（3）：108-113.

[8] 朱志平，江丽莉，马思宇. 1998—2008 十年对外汉语教材述评 [J]. 北京师范大学学报（社会科学版），2008（5）：131-137.

[9] 杨小彬. 我国对外汉语教材编写的成就与问题 [J]. 湖北大学学报（哲学社会科学版），2011（4）：31-34.

[10] 郑海龙，李彦涛. 基于中国式幕课视域下教师角色转型策略 [J]. 继续教育研究，2017（5）：79-81.

[11] 赵金铭. 汉语国际教育的两个研究系统——语言教学与师资培养 [J]. 国际汉语教育（中英文），2020（1）：3-9.

[12] 中国对外汉语教学学会，《世界汉语教学》编辑部，《语言教学与研究》编辑部 . 对外汉语教学的定性、定位、定量问题座谈会纪要 [J]. 世界汉语教学，1995（1）：4-12.

[13] TAN C. Teach Chinese language in India [J]. China report, 1986, 22(2):163 -194.

[14] BHATTACHARJEA M S, DESHINGKAR G, et al. Chinese studies in India: perspective and programmes[J].China report, 1988(24):4.

[15] UBEROI P. China studies in India-3[J]. China report, 2013, 49(2):185-196.

[16] 古俊，杨文武 . 印度汉语教学的发展状况、问题及对策思考 [J]. 南亚研究季刊，2011（1）：102-108.

[17] 阿西. 印度汉语教学历史与现状分析 [D]. 上海：上海师范大学，2012.
[18] 张燕玲. 尼赫鲁大学汉语教学现状调查与分析 [D]. 苏州：苏州大学，2015.
[19] 木克士. 印度汉语教学的问题及对策研究——以 Doon 大学为例 [D]. 济南：山东师范大学，2012.
[20] 岳亚骏. 印度大学汉语教学的“三教”问题及对策研究——以德里大学初级综合课为例 [D]. 大连：辽宁师范大学，2015.
[21] 潘典. 印度学生常用时间副词偏误调查分析——以印度国际大学中国学院为例 [D]. 昆明：云南大学，2015.
[22] 唐汉明. 肢体语言在印度新 HSK1 级词汇教学中的运用 [D]. 天津：天津师范大学，2017.
[23] 智辉. 印度大学选用的中国现代文学作品中呈现出来的中国文化 [D]. 沈阳：沈阳师范大学，2014.
[24] POONAM S. Dreamers: how young indians are changing their world[M]. Viking: Penguin Random House India, 2018.
[25] 刘雯. 美国堪萨斯大学孔子学院远程互动式教学模式研究 [D]. 武汉：华中师范大学，2016.
[26] 陈楠楠 . 对外汉语网络教学的介绍、问题及对策 [D]. 大连：辽宁师范大学，2015.
[27] 周小兵，薄巍，王乐，等. 国际汉语教材语料库的建设与应用 [J]. 语言文字应用，2017（1）：125-135.
[28] 季羡林. 序 [M] // 谭中，耿引曾. 印度与中国——两大文明的交往和激荡. 黄绮淑，译. 北京：商务印书馆，2006：1-2.
[29] 纳拉亚南. 祝词 [M] // 谭中，耿引曾. 印度与中国——两大文明的交往和激荡. 黄绮淑，译. 北京：商务印书馆，2006：3.

Chinese Language Teaching in India under Unseen Changes in a Hundred Years: Dilemma and Breakthrough

Bao Jiqing[1]

Abstract Since the 1980s, with the increasing economic, trade and personnel exchanges between China and India, teaching Chinese as a foreign language (TCFL) has gradually formed a scale in India. Chinese language was once listed as a selected foreign language for secondary schools in the draft of Indian National Education Policy. High-level visits of leaders between the two countries, and China's opening up and rapid development have also brought a "Mandarin Wave" in India. 2020 marks the 70th anniversary of the establishment of diplomatic relations between China and India, when the world encountered a sudden COVID-19 pandemic. Standoff at boarder areas between China and India put bilateral relations in a difficult situation, and TCFL in India has been hit by impact. In this context, can TCFL continue to move forward? Can we overcome the difficulties? How to find a way out? These are the questions this thesis wants to answer. The author summarizes the gains and losses of TCFL in India over the past four decades and proposes that TCFL in India should not be abandoned by temporary difficulties. In order to enhance mutual understanding between the two peoples and promote the continuous development of China-India relations. TCFL in India shall break through with innovation.

1 Ph.D., Non-resident Research Fellow, Center for South Asian Studies, Institute of International Relations, Tsinghua University.

Key Words TCFL in India; Three-dimension TCFL teaching materials; Internet+TCFL teaching model; New era TCFL teachers in India

0 INTRODUCTION

China and India, as two neighboring countries with civilizations that lasted for thousands of years, have a long history of mutual exchanges and mutual learning. Since the 1980s, with China's reform and opening up, the rise of teaching Chinese as a foreign language (TCFL) and India's free economic reforms, TCFL has gradually developed in India. Chinese language departments have been established from a few sporadic universities to over 30 formal universities with diploma courses and various non-academic training,[1] totaling more than 20,000 students,[2] which marks the highlight on TCFL in India. Especially in the second decade of the 21st century, high-level visits between China and India had been continuing, people-to-people exchanges had become increasingly frequent, and economic and trade relations had become closer. In 2011, the Ministry of Human Resource Development, Government of India (now the Ministry of Education, Government of India) and Hanban of P. R. China (now China International Language Exchange Center) announced that the two sides would cooperate to hold Chinese courses in Indian middle and high schools, which was to be implemented in April 2014. The initial version of the Indian National Education Policy listed Chinese as one of the foreign language courses available for middle school students to select. For a time, the "Mandarin Wave" swept this south Asian major country. The year 2020 witnesses the 70th anniversary of the establishment of diplomatic relations between China and India. The two countries originally planned to jointly celebrate and hold 70 events as a commemorative in order to better summarize the past and look forward to the future. However, the sudden

1 https://www.shiksha.com/humanities-social-sciences/languages/colleges/chinese-mandarin-colleges-india, accessed: 2020-10-22.
2 “汉语热持续在印度升温”，http://in.china-embassy.org/chn/gyyd/t1554853.htm, accessed: 2020-10-22.

COVID-19 ravaged the world and accelerated major changes unseen in a century. As a result of the standoff in the border areas, TCFL in India will inevitably be affected.

The friendship between the nations lies in the friendship between the peoples; TCFL in India is an important way for peoples to get to know each other better through language. On the one hand, the trend of globalization continues to develop. China firmly follows the path of reform and opening up, advocates the integration and mutual learning of civilizations, and builds a community with a shared future for mankind. On the other hand, there are some Indian public opinions hyping "China Threat Theory" and "China-India economic decoupling". In the current predicament, how to minimize the impact on TCFL? How to continue TCFL under the conditions of the pandamic still raging in the future? How to continue to promote people-to-people exchanges between China and India with TCFL? These are all questions that this thesis wants to answer. This article will be divided into five parts. The first part clarifies the basic concepts of TCFL in India and delimits the research scope; the second part reviews the literature of TCFL in India; the third part analyzes the current dilemma; the fourth part proposes countermeasures to break through the situation; the fifth part draws a conclusion. This thesis hopes to summarize TCFL in India in the past forty years, conform to the development requirements of the times, to use digital technology and the latest development of online teaching, and to promote with innovative concepts and practices the strengths and avoid weaknesses of TCFL in India against the current backdrop of difficulties and to provide suggestions as well.

1 THE CONCEPT OF TCFL IN INDIA

Teaching Chinese as a foreign language (TCFL) has become a discipline in China. It has gradually emerged since China's reform and opening up in 1978. It was originally called Dui Wai Han Yu (Chinese as a foreign language), abbreviation of "Teaching Chinese to Foreigners"[1]63. The essence is to teach Chinese as a foreign language. In the past 40 years, Chinese academia has been continuously exploring and has established the theory and practice of TCFL.[2-11] Before we start discussing TCFL in India, we need to clarify the confusing concepts.

Picture 1 Bao (the fourth from right) accompanied Chinese Ambassador Sun Weidong (the middle) to visit Visva-Bharati University

This article discusses teaching Chinese to non-native speakers in India. Because Indian students usually already have a bilingual or tri-lingual background, Chinese is the second or third or even fourth language of the students. The author believes that TCFL in India theoretically fills within a second language acquisition category under applied linguistics and is closely related to psychology, cognitive psychology and pedagogy. Before TCFL became a discipline, Chinese language was one of the courses for Chinese majors in Indian universities for academic education. It was set up under the Institute of Foreign Languages or East Asian Studies of Indian Universities as a basic course for studying China or Sinology. The purpose was to cultivate elite talents, future experts and sinologists who study Chinese language, history, religion, culture or Chinese issues. The scope of this article focuses on the teaching Chinese as a foreign language. The purpose is not only to train future sinologists, but more importantly, to train a large number of people who have the ability to speak Chinese and can conduct daily exchanges or business contacts between the Chinese and Indian peoples. Just as the opinion of most TCFL experts in China: "It is unrealistic to train sinologists as the goal of TCFL. Different sinologists have their own different research fields. Therefore, training sinologists depends on the joint efforts of the entire academia in our country, not a task that can be accomplished by TCFL alone. TCFL can serve to cultivate sinology partly, however, its general goal is not to train sinologists."[12]10

Therefore, TCFL in India in this article refers to teaching of Chinese as a foreign language, including academic education and non-academic language training. At the same time, TCFL in India applies both theoretically and practically to the general rules of second language acquisition to non-native speakers, as well as country-specific rules, that is, TCFL in India needs to meet the requirements of particularities of Indian students.

Picture 2　Bao (The fourth from left in the front row) and the teachers with students of OP Jindal Global University

2 REVIEW OF TCFL LITERATURE IN INDIA

China and India enjoy a long history of exchanges. With China's reform and opening up and India's economic reforms, the relationship between China and India has continued to improve. After the 1980s, TCFL has regained its momentum in India and has accumulated some experience and lessons. Many scholars and teachers have summarized and put forward suggestions on the theories, textbooks, teaching methods and TCFL teachers' training in India.

At All India Chinese Teaching Seminar held in Delhi in 1984, Tan Chung comprehensively summarized the history of exchanges between the two cultures, including the start and development of TCFL, listing the Chinese vocabulary whose meaning were from Buddhism or Sanskrit. He also generalized the teaching methods on character strokes and Chinese grammar, suggested to train TCFL teachers and compile the corresponding Chinese textbooks with media of Indian students' mother tongues. He proposed to compile Chinese language textbooks for the business purpose, and to use of modern tools for teaching.[13] Some Indian sinologists pointed out at All India Sinology Conference in 1988 and 2013 that Chinese majors trained by Indian universities couldn't read the original Chinese materials, and Chinese teachers usually come from scholars who study Chinese issues. They commented that some universities offering Chinese majors had incomplete facilities, lack of Chinese materials in libraries, and lack of scholarships to study in China.[14-15] Gu Jun and Yang Wenwu comprehensively reviewed the cultural, religious and linguistic exchanges between China and India, especially the history of TCFL in India, the political and cultural challenges they faced, and suggestions for China's strategies.[16]

Indian postgraduate Asi who studied in China specifically analyzed the situation of TCFL in India, including teaching stages and levels, teachers' qualification and regional distribution, use of teaching materials, etc., pointed out the problems of TCFL in Indian, and proposed countermeasures.[17] Others analyzed TCFL in India through the practice of teaching methods and cases, such as Jawaharlal

Nehru University[18], Doon University[19] and University of Delhi[20] for case studies. Some Chinese teachers used specific teaching methods to study how to teach Chinese adverbs in Indian university classrooms[21] and using body language to teach Chinese vocabulary in the classrooms[22] as specific examples for detailed analysis. Also, from the perspective of Chinese textbooks in India, one analyzed how Indian universities chose typical Chinese modern literary works to enable students to understand Chinese culture.[23]

Through literature review, it is found that the existing literature reviews the history of Sino-India language and cultural exchanges in detail, proposes theoretical research on the particularity of TCFL in India, and discusses the three points of TCFL in India (teaching materials, teaching methods, teachers, hereinafter referred to as "San Jiao Wen Ti"). Though a lot of summaries have been made and suggestions for improvement been put forward, the theory of the particularity of TCFL in India has not been researched deeply enough. In particular, there is a lack of interdisciplinary research, such as educational psychology, language psychology, comparative linguistics and language sociology to applied with TCFL in India. In the future, Sino-India joint research topic could start with comparison of TCFL teaching media, such as the comparison between using students' mother tongue (Hindi, Tamil, Urdu, Telugu) and using English. Comparative study between mother tongue and Chinese could also be done to summarize the difficulties of Indian students, including native pronunciation and grammatical structure for Chinese learning, in order to find out some special laws of TCFL in India theoretically. Sociological theories could also be applied to study the social status distribution of students studying Chinese in India, track their occupations and economic status after they have completed their studies, and examine the impact of speaking Chinese skills on students' income and professional promotion. All the above could be used as future research agendas. As to how to solve the problems encountered in TCFL in India ("San Jiao Wen Ti"), especially whether the development of TCFL in India will be affected by the world order, international relations, Sino-India bilateral relations and other non-traditional security factors, the above literature didn't discuss. The literature has proposed some countermeasures; however, they are relatively general, without specific recommendations that can be implemented, and the literature is limited to its age. After the outbreak of COVID-19 in 2020 and the setback of Sino-India relations, what should be the course of TCFL in India? Where and how to go? These will be discussed in the following sections.

Picture 3 Bao (the fifth from right) visited the Indian Social Research Center

3 THE CURRENT DILEMMA

The world is undergoing major changes unseen in a century,[1] whose essence is a major change in the international balance of power, leading to a major adjustment in the world order. The COVID-19 pandemic has accelerated this process, highlighting various contradictions in world politics, economy, and society. TCFL in India is facing unprecedented difficulties, including the United States, India, and pandemic factors. At the same time, there is also a silver lining of TCFL due to China-India trade and Indian education transformation.

1 "习近平：努力开创中国特色大国外交新局面", http://politics.people.com.cn/n1/2018/0623/c1001-30078644.html. This is a major conclusion made by General Secretary Xi Jinping at the Central Foreign Affairs Working Conference on June 23, 2018, and has been mentioned on many occasions since then.

3.1 AMERICAN FACTOR

The American factor is the most important in the world's great changes. In order to prevent the development of China, the United States has continuously suppressed it through trade, technology, public opinion, and diplomacy. The United States has regained its "Cold War" mentality, used ideological lines to smear China, and blocked Sino-US educational cooperation, academic exchanges and personnel exchanges. The most prominent example is banning Confucius Institutes (CIs) and Confucius Classrooms (CCs) , which are important platforms for Sino-US cultural exchanges. After the Trump administration came to power in 2017, it began to defame CIs continuously by lying that American universities were exposed to the threat of espionage and intellectual property theft. After the US State Department announced in August 2020 that the CIUS was listed as a "foreign mission", US Secretary of State Pompeo again expressed the hope on September 1st that US universities would close all CIs before the end of 2020.[1] This practice of the United States has set an extremely bad precedent, and it continues to advocate that like-minded countries should follow it, casting a shadow on TCFL.

3.2 INDIAN FACTOR

TCFL in India is significantly affected by Indian factor. In 2020, The standoff between China and India has made bilateral relations difficult. On August 2nd, 2020, the Ministry of Higher Education of India requested the review of four CIs and three CCs in India, as well as the review of 54 memorandums on cooperation between India and Chinese universities. In early September, Ministry of External Affairs, India was required to conduct additional security checks on Chinese visas.[2] All the above makes it more difficult for Chinese teachers to obtain visas to India. According to Indian media reports, many Indian security agencies have issued warnings about China's growing influence in Indian higher education.[3]

1 "威胁关闭美国所有孔子学院并继续打压华为 蓬佩奥扬言要与十四亿人打'经济冷战'", https://www.sohu.com/a/416176834_119038, accessed: 2020-10-22.

2 "India slaps new curbs on visas, schools to stem China's influence", https://timesofindia.indiatimes.com/india/india-slaps-new-curbs-on-visas-schools-to-stem-chinas-influence/articleshow/77675489.cms, accessed: 2020-9-23.

3 "Chinese firms, mobile apps blocked, India could next target university tie-ups", https://www.hindustantimes.com/india-news/china-confucius-institutes-face-heat-over-propaganda/story-AZCHG9fp66KxXnHCF56JeO.html, accessed: 2020-9-23.

The Ministry of Education of India will verify whether the Indian universities that cooperate with CIs are pre-approved.[1] These caused concern. In 2020, the Indian government has banned 224 Chinese mobile phone applications (App) altogether, including Chinese learning software such as Learn Chinese AI-Super Chinese.[2] The artificial setup of numerous obstacles to securitize Sino-Indian educational cooperation has made TCFL in India even worse.

3.3 PANDEMIC FACTOR

COVID-19 has had a huge impact on India. According to the statistics of the Ministry of Statistics and Planning and Implementation of India (MOSPI), India's gross domestic product (GDP) plummeted by 23.9% in the second quarter of 2020.[3] The International Monetary Fund (IMF) predicts that India's economic growth rate in 2020 will be −10.2%.[4] As of the deadline for this article, the number of people infected with COVID-19 in India has already exceeded 8.1 million,[5] There are more than 300 million students, 1.4 million schools and 51,000 colleges affected in India,[6] teachers and students have been unable to attend classes since March, and this will continue for some time. The University Grants Committee (UGC) of India revised the start date for freshmen to November. If the pandemic still prevents students from physically coming to campus, the course will be online.[7] The Internet connection required for online courses is only 42% of households in Indian cities and 24% in rural areas. More than 50% have poor signal connections. At the same time, only 8% of Indian households have both computers and the Internet. All regions are also plagued by power outages

1 "Foreign institutes set up without govt nod under scanner: MEA", https://indianexpress.com/article/education/foreign-institutes-set-up-without-govt-nod-under-scanner-mea-6543218/, accessed: 2020-10-22.

2 PUBG, Ludo World among 118 more Chinese apps banned by IT ministry. https://www.hindustantimes.com/india-news/118-more-chinese-apps-banned-including-pubg-here-is-the-full-list/story-Cr39p0cGAQWrMCrpYrQY7J.html, accessed: 2020-11-1.The Indian government announced the ban on 59 Chinese apps on June 29, 2020, 47 Chinese apps on July 23, and 118 Chinese apps on September 2.

3 "India's economy contracts by 23.9%, worst in decades", https://www.hindustantimes.com/india-news/india-s-gdp-growth-rises-falls-by-23-9-per-cent-in-april-june-quarter/story-Yj1GGTR7fuHAQ6QNL0jpBL.html, accessed: 2020-9-23.

4 https://www.imf.org/en/Countries/IND#countrydata, accessed: 2020-10-20.

5 https://www.mohfw.gov.in/, accessed: 2020-11-1.

6 Anushruti Singh, "Coronavirus lockdown: Indian online education gets a shot in the arm", April 9, 2020, https://smefutures.com/coronavirus-lockdown-indian-online-education-gets-a-shot-in-the-arm/, accessed: 2020-11-1.

7 "UGC now says first year classes will start in November, there will be no winter, summer breaks", https://theprint.in/india/ugc-now-says-first-year-classes-will-start-in-november-there-will-be-no-winter-summer-breaks/507929/, accessed: 2020-11-1

to varying degrees.[1] In spite of the imperfect conditions in India, the Indian government, universities and online education companies have tried their best to develop online courses. Although TCFL in India has been hit by COVID-19, there is still hope that it can be conducted online.

3.4 SINO-INDIA TRADE FACTOR

The Sino-Indian trade factor is a light in the darkness of dilemma. Even when India's economy falls, the epidemic continues, and Sino-India relations are hindered. Data from the Ministry of Commerce of India show that India's exports to China have been on the rise from May to August 2020. Up till August, China accounted for 9.1% of India's total exports, second only to the United States (17%). Among India's five largest export partners, China is the only country with the fastest growth.[2] Indian exports to China increased by 26.3% in the second and third quarters of 2020 compared to the same period last year.[3] Although Prime Minister Modi started to advocate "self-reliance" in April (Atmanirbhar Bharat[4]) the proportion of India's imports from China has increased from the previous 14% to 19% in the current fiscal year.[5] The data also give us a lot of confidence. It shows that

Picture 4　Bao (the second from left) visited The Little Pearl Kindergarten in Delhi

1 "Indian education can't go online—only 8% of homes with young members have computer with net link", https://scroll.in/article/960939/indian-education-cant-go-online-only-8-of-homes-with-school-children-have-computer-with-net-link, accessed: 2020-11-1.

2 India's exports to China increased by 15% in August 2020, up to 78% in June, and 48% and 23% in May and July, respectively. "Double-digit rise in exports helps India nearly halve trade gap with China", https://www.business-standard.com/article/economy-policy/double-digit-rise-in-exports-helps-india-nearly-halve-trade-gap-with-china-120100801594_1.html, accessed: 2020-10-13.

3 "Indian exports to US, China on rise in 2020", https://www.livemint.com/news/india/indian-exports-to-us-china-on-rise-in-2020-11603238950035.html, accessed: 2020-10-22.

4 https://en.wikipedia.org/wiki/Atmanirbhar_Bharat, accessed: 2020-10-14.

5 "To outrun China, India must reform", https://epaper. livemint. com/Home/Article View, accessed: 2021-03-28.

political manipulation cannot easily decouple China-India economics and trade, and this is where the motive force for continued people-to-people exchanges. Therefore, TCFL in India has reasons for its continued development.

Facing the above-mentioned dilemma and challenges, we cannot be intimidated by temporary difficulties. We shall break through the inherent thinking mindset, broaden cooperation channels with Indian enterprises, industry associations, and NGOs, follow the development of online courses, and accelerate reform and innovation of idea and practices with TCFL in India.

4 COUNTERMEASURES TO BREAK THROUGH

Although the epidemic has accelerated changes in the world landscape and China-India relations have encountered the most difficult situation in more than half a century, China and India are partners, not rivals. As Sun Weidong, Chinese Ambassador to India said:

> China's basic judgment on China-India relations remains changed. China and India are partners rather than rivals to each other, and opportunities rather than threats.... The basic fact of China and India as the two largest neighboring developing countries remains unchanged. The orientation of China and India as partners remains unchanged. The general landscape that China and India are inter-dependent for common development remains unchanged.... Our relationship should move forward, rather than backward or reverse. China and India should avoid mutual attrition, nor be opposed to each other. Instead, we should meet halfway to bring our relationship back on the right track at an early date.[1]

Under the guidance of the consensus reached by the leaders of China and India, both sides should overcome the temporary difficulties in educational exchanges and cooperation between the two countries, give full play to the respective capabilities and advantages of the insightful talented people of China and India,

1 "Chinese Ambassador to India H.E. Sun Weidong Gave Interview to CNBC-TV18", https://www.fmprc.gov.cn/ce/cein/chn/sgxw/t1810230.htm, accessed: 2020-9-24.

and go against the adversity.

The pandemic is accelerating the change in the way of human life and boosting the popularization of digital technology and the Internet. TCFL in India should take advantage of the trend and make breakthroughs in innovation. Through the three-dimensionalization of teaching materials and the digitization of teaching models on the Internet, Chinese teachers can keep up with the times, get rid of the problems ("San Jiao Wen Ti") that have plagued them for many years, improve teaching efficiency and the level of Chinese language acquisition of Indian students, and increase attractiveness of Chinese to Indian students and expand the number of learners. In this way, TCFL in India can lay a language foundation for mutual understanding and exchanges between the two peoples and contribute to mutual learning and common development of Chinese and Indian civilizations.

4.1 MOTHER TONGUE AND NATIONALIZATION

We have a vague concept of India. India was a British colony, so Indians speak English. Between 2000 and 2011, half of the world's call centers were located in India. Data in 2006 shows that call centers employed 2 million Indians[24]29, because the call center needs to work in English, which seems to confirm all Indians speak English. However, is English mother tongue of Indian students? According to the 2001 census of India, the population with English as the first language was only 226,449, the second language was 86,125,221, and the third language was 38,993,066.[1] There are 125 million English speakers in India, ranking the second in the world. However, as BBC reporter Zareer Masani noted in a 2012 article, the patchwork state of English education means that many Indians speak "not so much English as Hinglish".[2] India has benefited from the use of English as an official language and a business language, but what is surprising is that 67% of Indian engineering students are not fluent in English, and about three-quarters of engineering students lack the oral English skills

1 https://en.wikipedia.org/wiki/List_of_countries_by_English-speaking_population, accessed: 2020-9-20.
2 https://k-international.com/blog/countries-with-the-most-english-speakers/, accessed: 2020-9-20.

required by the knowledge economy.[1]

We can also observe English speaking among Indian high school students and below via the statistics in 2020 from the Ministry of Education of India(See Table 1).

Table 1 Percentage of students with medium of instruction as English, or Mother Tongue (the language spoken at home)[2]

(Urban/rural, male/female, all current pre-school, junior primary, senior primary, junior high and high school students average)

(Calculated in %)

Mother Tongue	Media of Instruction			
	Mother Tongue	Non Mother Tongue		
		Hindi	English	Other language
Hindi	79.2	–	18.9	1.9
English	67.1	24.3	—	8.6
Assamese	89	0.7	10	0.3
Bengali	83.5	4.2	6.9	5.4
Gujarati	85.3	1.7	12.7	0.3
Kannada	66.9	0.1	39.1	1.9
Malayalam	36.6	0.3	61.4	1.7
Manipuri	7.7	0.8	75.5	16
Marathi	73.1	1.5	23.7	1.7
Odiya	87.4	1.6	10.2	0.8
Punjabi	38.9	6.8	53.9	0.4
Tamil	55.5	0.2	43.9	0.4
Telugu	37.8	0.2	59.3	2.7
Urdu	12.2	13.2	53.8	20.8
Nepali	19.4	7.1	59.5	14
Bodo	17.5	12.5	8.2	61.8
Sindhi	32.1	1.5	62.9	3.5
Total Average	64.7	7.6	24.4	3.3

1 "Most of engineering students lack employability skills, say experts", https://www.thehindu.com/news/national/andhra-pradesh/most-of-engineering-students-lack-employability-skills-say-experts/article8319173.ece, accessed: 2020-9-20.

2 The author sorted out based on official Indian statistics, http://www.mospi.gov.in/sites/default/files/publication_reports/Report_585_75th_round_Education_final_1507_0.pdf, 'NSS Report No. 585: Household Social Consumption on Education in India', P.A-849. accessed: 2020-9-17.

It is concluded from this latest survey that more than 60% medium languages of instruction for Indian students below high school are home languages or mother tongues. Meanwhile, it is mistaken that English is the most popular language in India, and it is only less than a quarter of the medium of instruction below high school in India.

The current medium for TCFL in India is English. In other words, Indian students must first learn English before they can learn Chinese. The above statistic shows that English is only the second, third or even fourth language of Indian students. It is not ruled out that some students are not good at English or mostly use Hinglish, which directly causes difficulties in learning Chinese. China's domestic publishing houses are working hard on multi-language Chinese textbooks, for example: *Happy Chinese*, published by Renjiao, has English, Russian, French, and German versions.[1] At present, the only Chinese textbooks that use the main mother tongues of South Asia as the medium are *Chinese Paradise* published by Beijing Language and Culture University Press (including 45 languages), including Hindi, Bengali, Urdu and Nepali.[2] But the defect of *Chinese Paradise* is the different translated medium of translation used for one textbook, which relatively take more considerations of the British and American culture from English media. However, the historical, cultural, and religious backgrounds represented by non-English mediums have not been treated in a specific manner. Nor did it consider the influence of language grammar structure and pronunciation habits on students' Chinese acquisition, especially for India's multilingual and multi-religious characteristics, and there were no targeted teaching materials.

The author suggests, firstly, it is necessary to conduct more in-depth and detailed investigations among students of different mother tongues in India, including Hindi, Tamil, Bengali, etc., to analyze and discover the laws of Chinese acquisition in terms of theory in the future, for example, the grammatical structure of

1 https://old.pep.com.cn/xgjy/hyjx/dwhyjx/jcjf/klhy/dyz/, accessed: 2020-9-25.
2 https://www.ctmlib.com/search?keyword=%E6%B1%89%E8%AF%AD%E4%B9%90%E5%9B%AD&desc=1&r_per_page=10&page=1&order=full_name&sum=intermediate_language&verify_stage=&intermediate_language=%E5%8D%B0%E5%9C%B0%E8%AF%AD, accessed: 2020-9-25.

the mother tongues of Indian students and their respective comparison of pronunciation with Chinese, so that it can lay a solid foundation for compiling Chinese textbooks for Indian students. Secondly, to abandon the media-language translation version of the unified textbook. Under the guidance of the existing textbook compilation outline, combined with the cognition of the Indian cultural background[1], organize Chinese and Indian experts to compile Chinese textbooks for Indian students to suit Indian students of different mother tongues, such as Hindi, Tamil and Bengali. Thirdly, the number of teachers in each mother tongue of India is relatively limited, and there are basically no Chinese teachers who speak Hindi, Bengali, and Tamil. Various ways can be considered to encourage Indian students who finish their studies in China and to return to India to engage in Chinese language teaching, or to hire Chinese students who learn Hindi, Bengali and Tamil to teach Chinese courses online or in the form of academic visits. This can not only strengthen the exchanges between Chinese and Indian youths, but also serve as a learning tool and provide language convenience for Indian students.

4.2 THREE-DIMENSION TEACHING MATERIALS[2]

The three-dimension textbook is a multi-media, multi-form and time-space blended textbook. With the advancement of technology and the popularization of the Internet, textbooks for TCFL are no longer limited to paper textbooks and teaching aids. The author believes that the concept of textbooks should be three-dimension teaching materials. Specifically, it includes traditional Chinese paper textbooks, CDs, DVDs, e-books, live lessons, screen lessons, Massive Open Online Course (MOOC), episodes, short videos, micro lectures, and mobile applications (App)(See Table 2). In the future, based on the development and popularization of Virtual Reality (VR) technology, Chinese textbooks will definitely include

1 The author has noticed that some Indian scholars compare the Indian caste system with China's "hukou" administration and believe that both are hierarchical. This is a cognitive error, because human beings' knowledge of new things is always achieved by comparing things they are familiar with. If a section can be used to introduce the meaning of the two simple Chinese characters "户口" in the international Chinese textbooks for India, then from the original source, give Indian students the correct concept.

2 初天斌、李少明，"移动互联网背景下立体化教材出版的应用研究"，in "出版发行研究"，2015, vol.2, pp.39-42; 臧文强."汉语国际教育教材编写'立体化原则'的理论内涵", in "现代语文"，2017, vol.11, pp.27-30. Referred to the above, the author redefines three-dimensional teaching materials.

VR experiential textbooks. Currently, although traditional paper-based teaching materials, CDs and DVDs are still useful, three-dimension teaching materials are in the ascendant.

Table 2　Classification of Three-dimension Teaching Materials for TCFL

Name	Features	Examples
E-book	1. Environmental protection: saving paper, saving printing costs; 2. Efficiency: saving time of print and delivery, and content can be updated or modified quickly and timely based on the feedback from teachers and students.	E-books issued by Beijing Language and Culture University Press[1]
Live lesson	1. Set up through online learning platform; 2. With recording and playback functions; 3. Convenient for students who are absent to catch up; 4. Allow teachers to learn from each other.	DingDing, Zoom, Google Classroom,Microsoft Teams, Blackboard Collaborate, Moodle, WebEx
MOOC	1. Outstanding teachers from different school to teach students; 2. Not limited by space and time; 3. Series of courses or lectures on specific topics; 4. The course is comprehensive and complete, and the learning process is longer.	TCFL MOOC Center[2]
Micro Lectures	1. Introduce a topic with a short video; 2. TCFL auxiliary materials; 3. Lively,simple and clear; 4. Both professional teachers and foreign students can present.	TCFL Micro Lectures Center[3] Confucius Institute Online[4]
App	1. Latest development of technology, download through smart phones; 2. Use fragmented time to learn or consolidate knowledge; 3. Learning is more personalized, improves students' learning interest and efficiency.	Chinese Plus, Great Wall Chinese, Han Ya Guo Ji

To be continued

1 https://www.blcup.com/PList/index/1426? pid=1, accessed: 2020-09-02.
2 https://www.blcup.com/DicCourse, MOOC is on trial, free of charge, accessed: 2020-09-25.
3 https://www.blcup.com/MicroVideo, it needs to pay when downloads, accessed: 2020-09-25.
4 http://wz.chinesecio.com/? cat=10, accessed: 2020-09-25.

Continued

Name	Features	Examples
TCFL teaching videos	1. Upload to the video website platform by individuals or institutions; 2. Students can get it through the video website; 3. Mostly are free; 4. Enriched materials for Indian students to learn Chinese.	Happy Chinese (Episodes 1-110), by CCTV-10

How do Chinese teachers in India choose among so many three-dimension teaching materials? It needs to be determined according to the learning objectives and learning stages of Indian students. I believe that three-dimension TCFL teaching materials can improve Indian students' interest in learning Chinese and their learning efficiency and help them make progress.

Taking into account the Indian government's ban on Chinese Apps and certain websites since June 2020, the author suggests that some mature online Chinese language teaching tools can be used overseas. Among them, the MOOC of basic Chinese and Chinese culture on some online platforms are provided by provided by famous universities in China, such as Tsinghua University, Peking University, Shanghai International Studies University, etc. They can run on computers, Pads and smartphones, as listed in the following table, and can help overcome current temporary difficulties, reducing student loss, and improving learning efficiency and interest.

Table 3 List of MOOC on Chinese teaching (using English as the medium)*

Website address	Content of MOOC
Edx https://www.edx.org/learn/chinese	1. Abundant basic Chinese courses; 2. Chinese culture courses; 3. Free; 4. App.
Future learn https://www.futurelearn.com/subjects/language-courses	1. Chinese pronunciation; 2. Short Courses on Chinese Culture; 3. Free.

To be continued

Continued

Website address	Content of MOOC
Open Culture https://www.openculture.com/free_mandarin_chinese_lessons	1. Chinese pronunciation; 2. Short Courses on Chinese Culture; 3. Free.
Alison https://alison.com/courses/chinese	1. Chinese Conversation Courses; 2. Free.
Yabla https://chinese.yabla.com/	1.Chinese pinyin phonetic notation, word explanation; 2. Live Chinese videos, music, news, etc.; 3. Paid websites.

*The author's self-made.[1]

4.3 INTERNET+ TEACHING MODEL

Internet+ teaching is a TCFL teaching model and method that keeps pace with the times. The model has changed from traditional classroom teaching to the Internet+ teaching model. This model changes from the teacher-centered in the classroom to a student-centered and teacher-led one. Online lectures are conducted, teachers and students interact and teaching results are evaluated through the Internet. Online software tools are made full use of to achieve teaching goals. Internet+ teaching was still the latest trend discussed in the academic circle and was a teaching method used by teachers at the experimental stage[25-26] before 2020. Since the COVID-19 outbreak, it has become a generally accepted model and method in schools around the world.

Internet+ teaching has a direct and far-reaching impact on TCFL in India. The pandemic has had a great impact on the traditional classroom teaching model, and forced TCFL teaching method in India to enter the Internet+ era. The Internet+ teaching model and method are not only compelled by the situation, but also imperative. According to the current situation of pandemic prevention in India, online courses will continue for a long time. Although the hardware

1 https://www.youtube.com/watch? feature=youtu. be&v=eH_j2vJfic0&app=desktop, accessed: 2020-10-12.

conditions in various parts of India are different, the network coverage and network speed vary greatly. At present, TCFL in India is basically conducted in the form of online courses. Teachers and students use personal computers, Pads and mobile phones to access the Internet, and use distance learning platforms, online Chinese teaching tool software and database to teach. Specifically, distance learning platforms such as DingDing, Zoom, Google Classroom, Microsoft Teams, Blackboard Collaborate, Moodle, WebEx, etc., can function live courses, including online lectures by teachers, Q&A, discussions between teachers and students or among students, online submission of homework and correction of homework; teaching tool software and database, such as: Pear Deck, HSK Dynamic Composition Corpus and etc., are used as lecture and examinations preparation, teaching demonstrations, students interactive games or quizzes, etc.

The author has summarized some online TCFL teaching tool software (shown in Table 4) for reference for Chinese teachers in India. Those softwares can run on computers, Pads, and mobile phones, and are compatible with Google Classroom, Microsoft Teams, and Zoom platform systems. Teachers only need to choose one of the learning platforms and several teaching tool software and learn to use them proficiently. For TCFL teaching, it will do more with less.

Table 4　Online TCFL Teaching Tool Software (with English as medium)*

Name of software	Application
Pear Deck (Joinpd.com)	Online Interaction between teachers & students
Duolingo	Chinese tests (App)
Quizlet	Online tests (App), charged(7-day trial)
Quizizz	Interactive tests (App)
Skritter (https://skritter.com/)	Learn Chinese character strokes
Written Chinese (https://www.writtenchinese.com/)	Chinese pronunciation, basic courses
Purple Culture https://www.purpleculture.net/	Chinese pinyin conversion, Chinese character strokes, Chinese pronunciation, English -Chinese/Chinese-English dictionary, etc. (partially free)

To be continued

Continued

Name of software	Application
Arch Chinese https://www.archchinese.com/	Chinese character stroke practice, pronunciation, dictionary, teacher preparation tools, student homework, game practice
Fast Fingers https://10fastfingers.com/typing-test/simplified-chinese	Practice Chinese typing, simple Chinese writing
Classkick	Classroom management, grading students, sign in, etc.
Liveworksheets	Grades and comments on student work

*The author's self-made.

As China is the mother tongue country of Chinese, China's Ministry of Education and some Chinese universities have invested a lot of manpower and resources to establish TCFL teaching cases database and corpora[27] and make them available to the public to facilitate Chinese teachers to prepare lessons and tests. TCFL teachers in India should be able to make full use of these online resources to improve teaching quality. The author has compiled a TCFL teaching cases database and corpora for reference (as shown in Table 5).

Table 5 List of TCFL teaching case database and corpus website*

Name	Organized by	Website	Content
Online Confucius Institute Resource	China International Chinese Language Education Foundation	http://www.chinesecio.com/	Teaching resource case database, cases of Chinese and foreign cultural differences
Ai Han Yu	Institute of Chinese Information Processing, Beijing Normal University	www.aihanyu.org	Dynamic corpus, lesson preparation assistant, composition assistant
HSK Dynamic Composition Corpus	Language Resources Advanced Innovation Center, Beijing Language and Culture University	www.hsk.blcu.edu.cn	The answer corpus of the composition test of the Advanced Chinese Proficiency Test
International Chinese Teaching Database	School of International Education, Minzu University of China	https://cie.muc.edu.cn/xsky/gjhyjxsjk.htm	Teaching cases, Need registration

To be continued

Continued

Name	Organized by	Website	Content
Chinese Character Error Corpus for International Students of Sun Yat-sen University	International School of Chinese, Sun Yat-sen University	http://cilc.sysu.edu.cn/	Chinese Character Error Marked Version, Words and Sentences Error Marked Version

*The author's self-made.

It is difficult for Chinese teachers of Chinese nationality to get visas to India. To a certain extent, we are required to change the traditional Chinese teaching method and use Internet+ teaching to deal with this reality. The author suggests that Chinese teachers in China can use the Internet+ teaching model to answer questions for Indian students online, organize discussions among Indian students, correct homework and test students online. Chinese and Indian universities or institutions can conduct communications and TCFL through the Internet. In addition, Indian companies or industry associations (such as the Indian Chamber of Commerce for Import and Export to China, etc.) , Indian online education platform and NGOs that have business contacts between China and India can also use the Internet+ teaching model, continue non-governmental exchanges.

In short, Internet+ teaching is a change in student-centered teaching concepts and methods under the support of the flourishing development of digital and network technologies. It is an active response to TCFL in India under difficult circumstances.

4.4 NEW CHALLENGES FOR TCFL TEACHERS IN INDIA

In 2020, the world encountered a sudden COVID-19 pandemic, which makes tendencies of unilateralism, protectionism and anti-globalization prominent. China is the first to control the pandemic and restart the economy, and actively build a new dual-cycle pattern of domestic and international mutual promotion. China will continue to reform and open up. This means that China will continue to deeply integrate into the world, and it will also bring opportunities for the development of all countries. TCFL is one of the ways for China to integrate into the world. It has a unique role in enhancing understanding, building consensus, promoting cooperation, and deepening friendship. The world today is undergoing major changes unseen in a century. The author believes that TCFL teachers in India must keep pace with the times and establish the "Three Views": view on China, view on India and view on times.

4.4.1 VIEW ON CHINA

Regarding the view on China established by TCFL teachers, firstly, we should start from the Chinese language and teaching students the knowledge. Secondly, starting from China's long history and traditional culture, we should teach students the basic knowledge of Chinese culture, with special emphasis on the teachings of Chinese sages, such as: "Harmony is precious", "Harmony with differences", "All peoples in the world (within four seas) are brothers", "The ways of heaven are impartial, it only sides with good man" and "One family in the world", to convey the idea of a community with a shared future for mankind. Thirdly, proceeding from the reality of China, we should tell Chinese stories well and introduce the achievements of reform and opening up, such as China's four new inventions, the stories of ordinary people in Wuhan's fight against the pandemic, reflecting the collective spirit of the Chinese people and the advantages of the Chinese social system. TCFL teachers' view on China should be based on the Chinese language, promote excellent traditional culture, and show cultural confidence.

4.4.2 VIEW ON INDIA

Teachers of TCFL in India should firmly establish views on India in terms of cross-cultural and inter-culture awareness. First of all, India is a country with many languages, religions and customs. There are as many as 22 official languages stipulated by Indian Constitution. There are great differences in cultural customs between the east and west, the north and south in India. In addition to Hinduism, India also has religions such as Islam, Christianity, Jainism, and Buddhism. Therefore, India cannot be mistakenly reduced to an English-speaking Hindu country. It is necessary not only for TCFL teachers in India to be aware of differences between Chinese and Indian cultures, but also of differences between Indian students. Cross-cultural and inter-culture awareness must be included as an important consideration in the whole process of TCFL in India. Secondly, there must be a sense of comparison between China and India, that is, the comparison between Chinese and the students' mother tongue, and the comparison between Chinese culture and students' culture. From the comparison, it is easier to find differences and learning difficulties, overcome cultural obstacles, and improve learning efficiency. The third is to find the similarities between Chinese and Indian cultures. For example, in Chinese classical thought, there is "the world is of great harmony, all under the heaven is one family", and India believes "Vasudhaiva Kutumbakam" (the world is a family); China has the philosophical thought of "the harmony between man and nature", India also has Brahmatmaikyam (Brahma refers to the principle of the universe, Chinese translation"梵", atma refers to the essence of the self, the entity of the self). In short, both China and India regard the universe (nature) as their close friends.[28]1 TCFL teachers' view on India should be diverse and inclusive. We should bear in mind that civilizations learn from each other and live in harmony. TCFL teachers, as civil ambassadors, use Chinese as a means of spreading peace and achieve the beautiful vision of peoples' friendship.

4.4.3 VIEW ON TIME

The Internet Plus era first requires TCFL teachers in India to obtain a view of the digital age and adapt to its development. The role of a TCFL teacher is not only a lecturer in a traditional classroom, but he must also act as an "online class designer", "internet celebrity anchor", and "online class tech savvy", that means, he knows how to use online resources and three-dimension teaching materials, operate Internet courses, guide students' discussion, correct homework and give students assessments online. Secondly, TCFL teachers in India need to have a deeper understanding of Indian millennials through investigation and research to discover the laws of Chinese learning for Indian students, in terms of pedagogy, second language acquisition, socio-linguistics, and cognitive psychology, so that quality and efficiency of Chinese language teaching can be improved. Thirdly,

TCFL teachers should strengthen their sense on China-India relations, that is, understand the latest developments in Indian politics, economy and Sino-Indian relations. In the case of difficulties in Sino-Indian relations, TCFL teachers in India should continue to convey friendly voices. The view on time is to keep up with the pace of technological development in teaching, to continuously learn theories, to innovate in teaching practice, and to have a sense of Sino-Indian relations.

Teachers are the dominant factor in the issue ("San Jiao Wen Ti") of TCFL in India. Teachers need to give full play to their subjective initiative to establish view on China, view on India and view on time in a new era. They should contribute to establish a language bridge for communication and understanding between the people of China and India, for the mutual learning of civilizations and regional peace as well.

5 CONCLUSION

This article summarizes the experience and lessons of TCFL in India over the past 40 years, analyzes the current difficulties encountered in India, and understands the situation objectively and rationally. In order to cope with the prolonged COVID-19 pandemic and to continue the development of China-India relations, TCFL in India needs to break through the situation with innovative TCFL materials, teaching methods and models, and training of TCFL teachers who adapt to the internet age. Innovations, including Internet Plus online platform + TCFL application software, screen lessons, mobile apps, short videos, live online classes, online learning communities, etc., will all become means of TCFL in India to overcome difficulties of the pandemic, bilateral relations and visa restrictions. TCFL will continue to develop in India, laying the foundation for language communication between Chinese and Indian people, and to build a bridge between Chinese and Indian civilizations.

Former Indian President KR Narayananlm once said:

> Historically, our two civilizations and cultural affinity have laid the foundation

> for countless centuries of India-China relations, provided vitality and made it a certain degree of eternity. When we encounter difficulties and misunderstand, this kind of pro-affiliation prevents the bilateral exchanges between the two countries from becoming deadlocked or rigid. We should restore and revitalize the dialogue between the two civilizations that began in ancient times to strengthen the friendship between the two countries. In fact, the sparks buried in the ashes of our two countries in the past will inevitably burn and illuminate the strange road in the future.[29]2

Although we are experiencing major changes unseen in a century, the expectations of the Chinese and Indian peoples for a peaceful and beautiful life have not changed. The friendship between the two peoples has not changed for thousands of years, and the fact that the two countries are neighbors will not change, just like Chinese saying: "Tianxia Datong (天下大同)" is exactly the same as India's "Vasudhaiva Kutumbakam". Both China and India, as two developing neighboring countries with a population of over one billion, should firmly believe that the relationship between the two countries will see the sun and the rainbow again after the storm, the road to peace and win-win cooperation is the broad way to a bright future.

(Proofread by Bhavana Kumari)

REFERENCES

[1] 吕必松. 对外汉语教学概论（讲义）（续十七）第八章 对外汉语教学的学科性质和学科建设 [J]. 世界汉语教学，1997（1）：63-67.

[2] 吕必松. 加强对外汉语教学的理论研究 [J]. 语言教学与研究，1988（4）：4-19.

[3] 吕必松. 谈谈对外汉语教学的性质和特点 [J]. 语言教学与研究，1988（7）：4-24.

[4] 刘珣. 迈向 21 世纪的汉语作为第二语言教学 [J]. 语言教学与研究，2000（1）：55-60.

[5] 施家炜. 跨文化交际意识与第二语言习得研究 [J]. 世界汉语教学，2000（3）：64-73.

[6] 张德鑫. 润物细无声——论对外汉语教学与汉学 [J]. 语言文字应用，2001（1）：33-45.

[7] 张和生. 对外汉语教师素质与培训研究的回顾与展望 [J]. 北京师范大学学报（社会科学版），2006（3）：108-113.

[8] 朱志平，江丽莉，马思宇. 1998—2008 十年对外汉语教材述评 [J]. 北京师范大学学报（社会科

学版），2008（5）：131-137.

[9] 杨小彬. 我国对外汉语教材编写的成就与问题 [J]. 湖北大学学报（哲学社会科学版），2011（4）：31-34.

[10] 郑海龙，李彦涛 . 基于中国式幕课视域下教师角色转型策略 [J]. 继续教育研究，2017（5）：79-81.

[11] 赵金铭. 汉语国际教育的两个研究系统——语言教学与师资培养 [J]. 国际汉语教育（中英文），2020（1）：3-9.

[12] 中国对外汉语教学学会，《世界汉语教学》编辑部，《语言教学与研究》编辑部 . 对外汉语教学的定性、定位、定量问题座谈会纪要 [J]. 世界汉语教学，1995（1）：4-12.

[13] TAN C. Teach Chinese language in India [J]. China report, 1986, 22(2):163 -194.

[14] M S BHATTACHARJEA, DESHINGKAR G, et al. Chinese studies in India: perspective and programmes[J].China report, 1988(24):4.

[15] UBEROI P. China studies in India-3[J]. China report, 2013, 49(2):185-196.

[16] 古俊，杨文武 . 印度汉语教学的发展状况、问题及对策思考 [J]. 南亚研究季刊，2011（1）：102-108.

[17] 阿西. 印度汉语教学历史与现状分析 [D]. 上海：上海师范大学，2012.

[18] 张燕玲. 尼赫鲁大学汉语教学现状调查与分析 [D]. 苏州：苏州大学，2015.

[19] 木克士. 印度汉语教学的问题及对策研究——以 Doon 大学为例 [D]. 济南：山东师范大学，2012.

[20] 岳亚骏. 印度大学汉语教学的“三教”问题及对策研究——以德里大学初级综合课为例 [D]. 大连：辽宁师范大学，2015.

[21] 潘典. 印度学生常用时间副词偏误调查分析——以印度国际大学中国学院为例 [D]. 昆明：云南大学，2015.

[22] 唐汉明. 肢体语言在印度新 HSK1 级词汇教学中的运用 [D]. 天津：天津师范大学，2017.

[23] 智辉. 印度大学选用的中国现代文学作品中呈现出来的中国文化 [D]. 沈阳：沈阳师范大学，2014.

[24] POONAM S. Dreamers: how young indians are changing their world[M]. Viking: Penguin Random House India, 2018.

[25] 刘雯. 美国堪萨斯大学孔子学院远程互动式教学模式研究 [D]. 华中师范大学，2016.

[26] 陈楠楠 . 对外汉语网络教学的介绍、问题及对策 [D]. 辽宁师范大学，2015.

[27] 周小兵，薄巍，王乐，等 . 国际汉语教材语料库的建设与应用 [J]. 语言文字应用，2017（1）：125-135.

[28] 季羡林. 序 [M] // 谭中，耿引曾. 印度与中国——两大文明的交往和激荡. 黄绮淑，译. 北京：商务印书馆，2006：1-2.

[29] 纳拉亚南. 祝词 [M] // 谭中，耿引曾. 印度与中国——两大文明的交往和激荡. 黄绮淑，译. 北京：商务印书馆，2006：3.

A Review of the Chinese Language Teaching at Visva-Bharati Cheena-Bhavana: Centre for Promoting India-China-Educational and Cultural Exchanges

Avijit Banerjee[1]

Abstract This age-old friendship between India and China was resumed in 1924 when Indian Nobel laureate Rabindranath Tagore visited China. Tagore was a pioneer for successfully founding Visva-Bharati University in 1921, a university that was truly international in its philosophy, goals and curriculum which later became the first central university of India in 1951. Tagore sought to revive and strengthen the historical relationship between the people of both these Trans-Himalayan ancient countries through various academic research projects on "India-China Cultural Studies" collectively undertaken by the scholars of India and China and by scholars of many other countries. It was Tagore's global vision that led to the establishment of the Department of Chinese language & Culture (Cheena-Bhavana, 中国学院) in 1937, the earliest institute of Chinese language teaching and Chinese studies not only in India but also in this subcontinent. This article will try to focus on the evolution and progress of Chinese language teaching in Cheena Bhavana. It will also try to throw light on how through various activities the Centre has contributed in promoting India China educational and cultural exchanges in a true sense.

Key Words Tagore; Cheena-Bhavana; Chinese language teaching

1 Head, Department of Chinese Language and Culture (Cheena Bhavana) Visva-Bharati University.

India and China, the two-ancient civilizations of the world have a long traditional friendship. The culture of a country develops and flourishes during the exchange and blending with the culture of the other country. The cultural exchanges between India and China can be traced back to very early times.

This old friendship was not resumed until 1924 when Nobel Laureate Rabindranath Tagore visited China. Tagore was a forerunner in envisioning a globalized world community. He was a pioneer for successfully founding Visva-Bharati University in 1921, a university that was truly international in its philosophy, goals and curriculum. The awakening of India-China cultural renaissance in the 20th century was mainly due to the vision and effort of Rabindranath Tagore. Tagore's visit to China not only brought home to the Chinese the high attainments of Indian civilization but also awakened in the Chinese minds the greatness of the Eastern Civilization. In Tagore's view, the cooperation between the two great oriental civilizations was not only related to the future development of India and China, but also related to the future of Asia and of the world at large. Tagore sought to revive and strengthen the historical relationship between the people of both these Trans-Himalayan ancient countries through various academic research projects on "Sino-Indian Cultural Studies" collectively undertaken by the scholars of India and China and by scholars of many other countries.

After his return from China, Tagore started the programme for Chinese language in Visva-Bharati in 1926 with the help of the French savant Prof. Sylvian Levi and a Chinese scholar Lin Wojiang. Prof. Tan Yunshan, the Founder Director of Cheena-Bhavana came to Santiniketan in the year 1928 at the invitation of Tagore and made tireless efforts in setting up a Department of Chinese language and Culture in Visva-Bharati. Tan Yunshan went back to China and discussed the ideas and objectives of Tagore with the then chancellor of Peking University Dr. Cai Yuanpei and other relevant people. All these Chinese personalities enthusiastically responded to the ideas and in the year 1933, the Sino-Indian cultural society was formally established in Nanjing with Cai Yuanpei as its first president and Tan Yunshan as its first secretary. One of the main objectives of the society was to promote educational and cultural exchanges and friendship between the people of India and China. The society also planned to donate books and manage funds for building Cheena-Bhavana. In 1934, the Sino-Indian Cultural society was set up in Santiniketan. The work of the Sino-Indian cultural society during that time was concentrated on the establishment of a Chinese language and China Study Centre, finally the Department of Chinese Language & Culture (Cheena-Bhavana), the first institute of Chinese language teaching and studies in this subcontinent, came into existence with the following objectives[1]:

i. To conduct research studies in Indian and Chinese Learning;

ii. To promote interchange of Indian and Chinese cultures;

iii. To cultivate friendship and fraternity between India and China;

iv. To join and unite the people of India and China;

v. To promote jointly, universal peace and harmony of humanity;

vi. To help in building up "The Great Unity" of the world.

Picture 1 Chinese language major students at Cheena Bhavana

However, it may be noted that before Chinese language programme started in Visva-Bharati University in Santiniketan, the University of Calcutta in 1918 introduced a course on Chinese language but unfortunately the course could not continue due to lack of adequate Chinese language instructors.[2]

While talking about Cheena-Bhavana we must take into account the association of a number of renowned scholars who contributed immensely in the development of India-China education and cultural exchanges. The inspiration and the soul behind the establishment of Cheena-Bhavana was of course Rabindranath Tagore. Two other person who were instrumental in the development of Chinese language and studies programme at Cheena-Bhavana were Prof. Tan Yunshan and renowned India-China expert Prof. PC. Bagchi. Besides Prof. Bagchi, some other renowned scholars who were associated with Cheena-Bhavana were Pandit Vidusekhara Sashtri, P. V. Bapat, V. V. Gokhale, Sujit Kumar Mukhopadhyaya, Santi Bhikksu Sastri, N. Aiyaswami Sastri, Prahlad Pradhan and others. Some other scholars who were also there during the initial phase of Cheena Bhavan were Krishna Kinker Sinha, Amitendranath Tagore, Satiranjan Sen, K. Venkataramanan, V. G. Nair and many more.

Chinese language courses at Cheena-Bhavana before 1970 were mainly Certificate, diploma and post graduate diploma and there were no undergraduate or post graduate courses in Chinese. During this period, Prof. Tan and his colleagues carried out the Chinese language and Chinese Studies programme at Cheena Bhavana. However, the unfortunate border conflict between India and China in 1962 resulted in a sharp deterioration of the Chinese language programme at Cheena Bhavana and Prof. Tan also retired from active service in 1971. Another important development in the Chinese language programme at Cheena-Bhavana was the introduction of the undergraduate and post graduate course in Chinese language and culture in 1970. During this period the number of students pursuing Chinese language course were very few in number. What was the reason behind this? The two main reasons are as follows:

i. Deterioration in India-China relation;

ii. Lack of knowledge of the results of studying Chinese language.

Under this circumstance, there was no noteworthy development in Chinese language teaching and Chinese Study programme at Cheena Bhavana from 1970 to 1990. The Chinese language teaching programme slowly continued with one native faculty Prof. Wei Kuisun and few other Indian faculties. Academic exchange between Cheena Bhavan and the institutes in China was almost negligible.

1 DEVELOPMENT OF CHINESE TEACHING AT CHEENA-BHAVANA SINCE 1990

Prime Minister Rajiv Gandhi's visit to China in 1988 was a significant move towards normalization of ties between the two neighbours. Moreover, since the 1990s, the rise of China on the global, economic and political stage has spurred increasing interest in its language and culture. Thus it became extremely essential to understand China and the people of China. As a result, with the improvement of India-China relations and the growth of China, many Indians felt the urge to study the Chinese language. In 1993, China for the first time sent a native Chinese teacher Prof. Zhao Shouhui from Renmin University of China to Cheena Bhavana under the agreement between China's Ministry of Education and India's erstwhile Ministry of Human Resource Development (presently Ministry of Education) . The curriculum settings at Cheena Bhavana in the 80's and 90's follow the tradition of Sinology, the direction of student training was research-oriented, and course material on Chinese language was less. Some of the courses taught at Cheena-Bhavana during that period was modern Chinese Reading, Ancient Chinese Geography, Modern Chinese History (1840-1911), Chinese to English Translation from Chinese Newspaper (*People's Daily*, *Guangming Daily*). Another important aspect of Chinese language teaching at Cheena Bhavan was learning Classical Chinese Characters as selected chapters from *Analects* and *Mencius* was taught to the final year graduation and Masters Degree students. China's relation with neighbouring countries was also a vital part of Cheena-Bhavana's curriculum.

The total number of students studying Chinese language in the 80's and 90's was about forty. During that time, Cheena-Bhavana did not possess any language laboratory, and there even was no multimedia classroom. Thus it can be said that in comparison to other foreign languages, Chinese teaching in India was at a relatively backward stage.

Since 2000, there has been an upsurge of studying Chinese language in India. Many central, state and private universities started offering Chinese language in its undergraduate and postgraduate programmes. Chinese language teaching at Cheena-Bhavana also witnessed an upswing. In 2011 an MOU (Memorandum of Agreement) was signed between Visva-Bharati University and Yunnan University. This was a turning point in the teaching and learning activities of Cheena-Bhavana. In this year, Yunnan University started sending Chinese teacher volunteers to Cheena-Bhavana for imparting Chinese language training to the students. Most of these teachers were relatively young and their teaching styles became popular among students. The Chinese teachers from Yunnan University mainly assisted the students in analyzing Chinese vocabulary, Comprehension Classes, and teaching idioms and phrases which was a bit difficult for the Indian teachers. They also helped the students in improving their spoken ability. Besides

Picture 2　Chinese teacher from Yunnan University, taking class at Cheena Bhavana

this, Chinese teachers also taught students Tai Chi, Chinese songs, how to use Chinese websites. They show them Chinese movies and documentaries, and organize Chinese cultural knowledge contests and Chinese music contests. This provided the students with a good Chinese learning environment which resulted in increasing the interest of Chinese learning. During the period from 2011 to 2015 about eleven teacher volunteers came to Cheena-Bhavana from Yunnan University and contributed in improving the teaching learning environment of Cheena Bhavana.

2 MEMORANDUM OF UNDERSTANDING BETWEEN VISVA-BHARATI CHEENA-BHAVAN WITH CHINESE UNIVERSITIES AND INSTITUTES

Rabindranath Tagore dreamt of Cheena-Bhavan not only as a seat of learning but also as a centre of cultural amalgamation. With the increase in cultural exchanges between India and China, Cheena-Bhavan took the initiative to carry forward the people-to-people exchange between the two countries. In order to encourage people-to-people contact and educational cooperation between the two countries, Visva-Bharati University signed three MOUs and one Memorandum of Agreement with various Chinese Universities and Library. The first MOU was signed between Visva-Bharati University and Yunnan University, Kunming, in 2011. I have already mentioned about this MOU earlier.

Under this programme, besides sending teacher volunteers, till date about five hundred students from both the universities have visited each other's university. Especially for Indian students, the mutual visits provide them with a good language environment, which helps to stimulate their enthusiasm for learning Chinese and improving their Chinese proficiency. The realization of this programme may be attributed to the lifelong scholarly devotion and contribution of many academicians associated with Cheena-Bhavana. Visva-Bharati Cheena Bhavana Library also signed MOA with Shanghai Library, People's Republic of China in November 2016. Under this MOA, Shanghai Library provided 500 copies of books in the first year of MOA. This enriched the Cheena Bhavana Library, and improved the teaching standard of the department. This MOA between the two libraries possess important significance for India China educational exchanges. Visva-Bharati University signed an MOU with Yunnan Minzu University, Kunming, in December 2016 to push forward academic objectives of each institution and to promote better understanding between the faculty and students of Visva-Bharati University with the faculty and students of Yunnan Minzu University.

In 2017, Visva-Bharati University signed a tripartite agreement with Hanban (now renamed as into Center for Language Education and Cooperation) and Peking University. Under this MOU from 2018, selected students from undergraduate and post graduate courses are going to Peking University and pursuing a one semester language course, where the credits are transferred to Visva-Bharati University. This is a major step forward in Chinese teaching programme at Cheena-Bhavana. In addition to this, Cheena-Bhavana, has been organizing Teacher's Training Course where eminent faculties from Peking University delivers lecture on the new techniques of teaching Chinese language. Teachers and research scholars from various parts of India engaged in teaching and research of Chinese language are also sometimes invited to attend these programmes. Besides this, in order to improve the listening ability of the students, a language laboratory and multimedia room was set up in Cheena-Bhavana with the help of the Consulate Office of the People's Republic of China in Kolkata.

Picture 3　Students attending classes at language laboratory at Cheena Bhavana

3 CHEENA-BHAVANA LIBRARY—A RARE TREASURE FOR CHINESE LANGUAGE SCHOLARS

The library of Visva-Bharati Cheena-Bhavana is a special feature, a rare treasure not only to the Visva-Bharati University but also to the other universities and institutes pursuing research work on Chinese language and Chinese Studies. Some of the collection of the library is as follows[1]:

i. *A Collection of Commentaries on Chinese Canons of the Qing Dynasty* (1644 – 1911) containing 186 works consisting of 1,478 fascicles in 360 folio volumes.

ii. The Imperial Edition of the 24 Histories, consisting of 3,268 fascicles in 538 folio volumes.

iii. A Complete Collection of Chinese prose of the Three Ancient Periods-The Chin, the Han and the Six dynasties, containing works of 3,495 authors.

iv. A complete collection of the prose and poetry of the Tang Dynasty.

In addition, Cheena-Bhavana library also has a special collection of works of different kinds and of different times called "Congshu"（丛书）in Chinese, meaning "Collected Works" and the famous great Chinese Encyclopaedias. Another very important and valuable collection of the Chinese Buddhist scriptures called Tripitaka in Sanskrit and Tsang Ching in Chinese are also preserved in Cheena-Bhavana library. There are also several hundred selected books of special importance on Chinese Buddhism, Buddhist Philosophy and religion. Thus the library possesses almost a complete collection of books on Chinese Buddhism which help the scholars in pursuing their studies. In the later period, apart from the books on Buddhism, books on Chinese linguistics, politics, literature etc., are being procured for the library. Hanban, Yunnan University, Chinese Embassy in India also provided books to Cheena-Bhavana which is very useful in carrying out Chinese language teaching programmes.

4 RECENT DEVEAOPMENT IN CHEENA-BHAVANA FOCUSING ON SOME PROBLEMS AND SOLUTION TO CHINESE LANGUAGE TEACHING

In the last ten years, there has been a steady rise in the number of students showing interest in learning Chinese at Cheena-Bhavana. Internationally, the economic prosperity and rising influence of China have strengthened the appeal of the Chinese language to the outside world. Accordingly, Chinese has been increasingly considered as a language of instrumental value which can provide jobs or business opportunities and enable greater international mobilities. Thus, the entire world is under Mandarin Wave and Cheena-Bhavana is also no exception. Recently, there are not only students from West Bengal who are taking admission in Cheena-Bhavana but there are also a number of students coming from Bihar, Jharkhand and many other states and even few are from Nepal, Bangladesh and also from China. Since 2017, Hanban (presently Center for Language Education and Cooperation) is sending volunteer teachers according to the agreement between Visva-Bharati University and Hanban. This is also an important step in pushing forward the Chinese language programme at Cheena-Bhavana. The teachers besides teaching the nuances of Chinese language to the students also provide training to the students, on the various level of HSK exams.

The first specific problem encountered in the practice of Chinese teaching at Cheena-Bhavana is a serious shortage of teaching materials. In recent years, the number of Indian students learning Chinese has increased rapidly, but there is a dearth of Chinese textbooks, not to mention Chinese learning resources such as multimedia video teaching materials. As Chinese language learning requires a certain environment, many initial language learners hope to read some Chinese reading materials after class, especially Chinese books with *pinyin*, but in Indian bookstores, it is difficult to find Chinese books, let alone Chinese books with *pinyin*.

Secondly, there is a lack of Chinese teaching methods suitable for the needs of Indian students. India has many ethnic groups and complex languages. In Cheena-Bhavana there are students with different background, and their mother tongues also vary, even Hindi and Bengali are very different from Chinese. The major bottleneck in Chinese teaching is the teaching of Chinese characters. As Hindi, Bengali and even English scripts are all very different from the Chinese chracters, therefore it is sometimes difficult for the students to recognize the pictographic characters.

Thirdly, serious differences in dialects, and large differences in written and spoken Chinese, coupled with the large number of Chinese characters, difference between traditional and simplified characters, difficulties in Chinese grammar and intonation sometimes affect the enthusiasm of the students to learn Chinese.

Traditional Chinese language teaching at Cheena-Bhavana is focussed on cultivating students' reading and writing skills. In addition to emphasizing students' writing skills, modern Chinese language teaching also requires students' listening and speaking skills. Without strong listening and speaking skills, they cannot use relevant information on new media, such as television, radio, and the Internet. Only by letting the students love to watch Chinese shows and use the language can they increase their interest in learning and achieve good learning effect. Of course, how to use these new technologies in teaching needs to be guided by teachers.

In view of the above-mentioned problems and with an eye to compete with the institutes and universities offering Chinese language courses in the world, Cheena Bhavana has also made certain changes in the syllabus to improve students' ability to master Chinese language. A number of new courses like Business Chinese, Simultaneous Interpretation, Learning Chinese through watching Chinese movies and Chinese TV programmes have been incorporated into the syllabus along with some earlier courses focusing on Chinese history, literature, foreign relations, newspaper Chinese etc. The books used for classes and references are published by presses of Peking University, Beijing Language and Culture University, Yunnan University etc.

Moreover, in the last few years Cheena-Bhavana has been instrumental in organizing many international conferences on multidisciplinary topics where a number of prominent scholars from China and India participated in these conferences. In this way Cheena-Bhavana is still continuing to act as a meeting place of Indian and Chinese scholars just as Tagore visualized. In recognition of Cheena-Bhavana's contribution in upholding the Five Principles of Peaceful Co-existence, strengthening people-to-people friendship and promoting world peace and development Xi Jinping, President of People's Republic of China, conferred upon Visva-Bharati Cheena-Bhavana the "Five Principles of Peaceful Coexistence Friendship Award" in September 2014[1].

5 CONCLUSION

In view of the increasing popularity of Chinese language teaching in India, it is high time to explore more new avenues of academic and cultural cooperation between Cheena-Bhavana and the universities of China. The painstaking effort of Rabindranath Tagore and Tan Yunshan that opened up a new area of Chinese language teaching in India and India-China cultural fellowship needs to be continued.

The achievement of Cheena Bhavana thus can be summarized in four ways:

i. Cheena Bhavana acts as the foundation stone for initiating Chinese language programme not only in India but also in this subcontinent;

ii. Cheena-Bhavana serves as the place of India-China cultural dialogue, making ideas flow, resulting in India-China mutual understanding;

iii. Cheena Bhavana functions as the cradle of India-China affection. This affection started from Cheena Bhavana and spread to other parts of India;

1 "习近平会见印度友好人士、友好团体代表并颁发和平共处五项原则友谊奖", http://www. gov. cn/xinwen/2014-09/19/content_2753300. htm, accessed on 2020-10-22.

iv. Cheena Bhavana acts as the link between India-China cultural and educational interactions.

The establishment of Cheena-Bhavana is a major event in the history of India-China educational and cultural exchange. Since its foundation, Cheena-Bhavana has provided a stable platform for India-China exchanges which helped in the strengthening of bilateral relations in various fields. It has already attracted scholars and students from all corners of the world. As an integral part of Visva-Bharati University, Cheena-Bhavana is destined to play a very pioneering role in promoting India-China educational and cultural exchanges.

REFERENCES

[1] TAN Y. Twenty years of the Visva-Bharati Cheena Bhavana:1937-1957[J]. The Sino-Indian cultural society of India, 1957.

[2] RAY H P. Indian research programmes on China[M]. China Report (A Journal of East Asian Studies) New Delhi: Sage Publications,1992, 28:4.

国际大学中国学院的汉语教学反思：中印教育文化交流促进中心

阿维杰特·巴纳吉[1]

摘要　1924 年，印度诺贝尔奖获得者拉宾德拉纳特·泰戈尔（Rabindranath Tagore）访华，印度与中国之间的古老友谊得以恢复。1921 年，泰戈尔成功创办了国际大学（Visva-Bharati University），这所大学的办学思想、办学目标和课程设置都具有真正的国际性意义。1951 年，该大学成为印度第一所中央大学。中印两国与其他多国学者共同开展"印度－中国文化研究"的学术研究项目，泰戈尔希望通过这些项目让中印这两个跨喜马拉雅的古代国家可以重温两国历史渊源，加深人民间的深厚情谊。1937 年，在泰戈尔全球化视野的指导下，中国语言文化学院（Cheena-Bhavana，中国学院）成立。这不仅是在印度，在整个次大陆上都是最早的汉语教学和汉语研究学院。本文将着眼于中国学院汉语教学的发展和进步，阐明该学院是如何通过各种活动在真正意义上促进中印两国的教育和文化交流的。

关键词　泰戈尔；中国学院；汉语教学

作为世界上两大文明古国，印度和中国的友谊历史悠久。两国文明在彼此交流与融合中实现繁荣发展。中印两国的文化交流可以追溯到很早之前。

1924 年，诺贝尔奖获得者、印度诗人泰戈尔访华让这段古老的友谊重新恢复。泰戈尔是主张建立全球化地球共同体的先驱者。1921 年，泰戈尔作为奠基人，成功

1　国际大学中国学院院长。

创办国际大学，这是一所在办学思想、办学目标和课程设置上真正体现国际化的大学。正是由于泰戈尔的国际化视野和他本人的不懈努力，中印文化复兴在20世纪觉醒。泰戈尔访华不仅让中国人深刻认识到印度文化的高深造诣，而且引起了中国人对东方伟大文化的关注。泰戈尔认为，中印两大东方文明的合作不仅和两国的未来相关，和整个亚洲，乃至全世界的未来都息息相关。中印两国与其他多国学者共同开展“印度－中国文化研究”的学术研究项目，泰戈尔希望通过这些项目让中印这两个跨喜马拉雅的古代国家可以重温两国历史渊源，加深人民间的深厚情谊。

泰戈尔从中国回去后，在法国学者西尔万·列维（Sylvain Lévi）教授和中国学者林沃江（Lin Wojiang，音译）的帮助下，于1926年在国际大学创立汉语项目。1928年，在泰戈尔的邀请下，中国学院创始人谭云山教授来到和平乡（Santiniketan），为建立中国文化和汉语学院辛勤工作。回到中国后，谭云山与北京大学校长蔡元培等人共同商讨办学理念和宗旨。相关人士对这些想法做出积极回应，1933年在南京正式建立中印学会，由蔡元培担任第一届会长，谭云山担任秘书长。学会主要目标之一就是促进中印两国人民的教育文化交流，增强两国人民友谊。学会积极筹备建立中国学院，如捐赠图书和筹募资金等。1934年，中印学会在和平乡建立。当时学会的主要工作是建立汉语和中国研究中心，并最终建成中国文化和汉语学院（中国学院）。次大陆首家汉语教学和研究机构的主要目标[1]是：

（1）开展中印语言学习研究工作；

（2）促进中印文化交流；

（3）培养中印两国深厚友谊；

（4）团结中印两国人民；

（5）促进全人类的和平与和谐发展；

（6）帮助建立世界“大团结”。

但其实早在国际大学提出汉语项目前，加尔各答大学在1918年就推出汉语课程，但由于汉语老师短缺，课程无法进行下去。[2]

谈到中国学院，就不得不提为中印教育文化交流做出巨大贡献的一些知名学

图 1　印度中文专业学生在中国学院

者。在中国学院建立的背后，主要精神支柱和灵魂领袖当然是泰戈尔。其他对中国学院汉语研究项目发展做出指导性贡献的还有谭云山教授和著名的中印专家师觉月教授。除此以外，还有很多学者为中国学院的建设做出了重要贡献，其中包括梵学家撒哈提（Vidusekhara Sashtri）、贝皮特（P. V. Bapat）、哥哈尔（V. V. Gokhal）、库马尔（Sujit Kumar Mukhopadhyaya）、贝卡苏（Santi Bhikksu Sastri）、安亚苏瓦米（N. Aiyaswami Sastri）、哈德汉（Prahlad Pradhan）等。在中国学院的初创时期，很多学者予以支持，包括施纳哈（Krishna Kinker Sinha）、阿米泰德纳（Amitendranath Tagore）、三提哈彦（Satiranjan Sen）、万卡特马南（K. Venkataramanan）、奈尔（V. G. Nair）等众多学者。

1970 年前，中国学院主要提供证书、普通文凭和高级文凭的汉语课程，没有开设本科和研究生阶段的汉语课程。在此期间，谭教授和他的同事积极推动中国学院汉语教学和研究项目的发展。然而，1962 年中印边境发生摩擦，中国学院的汉语项目受到冲击，谭教授也于 1971 年从一线工作岗位退休。1970 年，中国学院引入本科和研究生汉语和中国文化的课程，汉语项目又一次迎来重大发展。但是在这期间学习汉语课程的人数寥寥无几。那么这背后的原因是什么呢？以下是两大主要原因：

（1）中印关系恶化；

（2）对学习汉语的前景认识不足。

在这种情况下，从1970年到1990年，中国学院的汉语教学和汉语研究项目一直没得取得突破性进展，仅在唯一的中国教授魏奎孙（Wei Kuisun，音译）和少数印度教员的支撑下缓慢前行。至于中国学院和中国各机构之间的学术交流更是少之又少。

1　1990年后中国学院汉语教学的发展

1988年，印度总理拉吉夫·甘地访华，中印邻国关系正常化迈出了重要一步。再加上20世纪90年代后，中国在世界政治经济舞台上的崛起让越来越多的人开始对汉语和中国文化感兴趣，了解中国和中华民族变得愈发重要。因此，随着中印关系改善和中国崛起，很多印度人认为学习汉语刻不容缓。1993年，中国教育部和印度人力资源发展部（现更名为“教育部”）签订协议，中国将派中国人民大学的赵守辉教授前往国际大学的中国学院，这是中国首次向印度高校派遣中国教师。80年代到90年代，中国学院的课程设置遵循汉学传统，学生培养的方向为研究型，汉语课程的材料较少。当时中国学院的一些课程主要是当代汉语阅读、中国古代地理、现代中国历史（1840—1911）、中文报刊英译（《人民日报》和《光明日报》）。在中国学院，汉语教学还有一个重要的课程就是学习中国经典人物，这些人物选自《论语》和《孟子》，这一课程面向的是本科最后一学年和攻读硕士学位的学生。同时，中国与邻国关系也是中国学院课程的重要内容。80年代到90年代，学习汉语的学生人数在40人左右。那时，中国学院没有语言研究室，甚至没有多媒体教室。可以说与其他外语相比，印度的汉语教学处于相对落后的阶段。

自2000年起，印度掀起学习汉语热潮。很多中央大学、州立大学、私立大学纷纷推出本科和研究生阶段汉语课程。中国学院的汉语课程也赶上了这波热潮。2011年，国际大学与云南大学确立合作关系，这是中国学院教学研究的重要转折点。云南大学派出多名中国教师志愿者前往国际大学任教，多为年轻教师，教学风格也深受学生喜爱。这些中国教师主要是在分析汉语词汇、阅读理解、学习成语和习惯用

图 2 来自云南大学的老师正在中国学院授课

语等一些对印度教师来说相对比较困难的课程上帮助学生，还可帮助学生提高汉语口语。除此之外，中国老师还教学生打太极、唱中国歌、上中国网站，给学生播放中国电影和纪录片，组织中国文化知识竞赛和中文歌曲大赛，为学生营造了良好的汉语学习氛围，大大提高了学生的汉语学习兴趣。2011 年至 2015 年，约 11 位汉语教师志愿者从云南大学来到国际大学中国学院，为改善学院的汉语教学环境做出较大贡献。

2 国际大学中国学院与中国各大学和机构的学术合作

泰戈尔希望中国学院不仅可以用于学习研究，还可以成为文化融合的中心。随着中印文化交流的不断深入，中国学院率先推动两国的人文交流。为了鼓励人文交流和教育合作，国际大学与中国三所大学、一所图书馆签署合作协议。第一所与国际大学合作的是位于昆明的云南大学，两所大学于 2011 年确立合作关系，笔者在上文已经介绍过该合作项目。

在这个项目中，除了向印度派遣老师外，截至目前，已经有来自两所大学的约 500 名学生到对方学校进行交流访问。对印度学生来说，这样的交流访问为他们提供了良好的语言环境，激发学习汉语的热情，提高他们的汉语水平。也正是众多学者对中国学院的长期学术奉献才让这个项目顺利实现。2016年11月，国际大学中国学院图书馆与中国上海图书馆签署合作协议，协议中提到，上海图书馆在协议第一年要向国际大学中国学院图书馆提供500册图书以丰富图书馆资源，提高教学质量。这一协议对中印两国的教育交流起到了至关重要的作用。2016年12月，国际大学与位于昆明的云南民族大学达成合作，双方积极推动各自学术目标的完成，促进双方教职员工和学生的交流互鉴。

2017年，国际大学与国家汉办（现更名为“中外语言交流合作中心”）、北京大学签署了三方协议。协议规定，自2018年起，国际大学可从研究生和本科课程中选取部分学生到北京大学进行一学期的语言学习，所修学分可转回国际大学。这是中国学院汉语教学项目向前迈进的重要一步。另外，中国学院还组织了教师培训课程，来自北京大学的名师亲自授课，为汉语教学传授最新教学技巧。参与汉语教学与研究的印度学者也受邀参加这些项目。此外，中国驻加尔各答总领事馆还帮助中国学院建成语音教室和多媒体教室，提高学生的汉语听力水平。

图3　学生们在中国学院的语言实验室上课

3　中国学院图书馆——汉语学者的宝库

国际大学的图书馆是其一大特色。图书馆不仅是国际大学的稀有宝库，对于其他所有进行汉语研究和中国研究的大学来说，都是不可错过的珍贵资源书库。该图书馆藏有以下图书[1]：

（1）清朝（1644—1911）《四库全书》经史子集类丛书，共 186 部 1 478 卷 360 册；

（2）钦定二十四史，共 3 268 卷 538 册；

（3）中国古代秦、汉和魏晋六朝三个时期的散文集，包括 3 495 位作者的作品在内；

（4）唐代的散文和诗歌集。

除了上述图书，国际大学图书馆还藏有不同时期、不同种类的作品集，中文称之为“丛书”（意思是“文集”）和著名的中国百科全书。该图书馆还藏有一本具有重要价值的中国佛教经文、梵文版的《三藏经》和中文版的《后藏经》，馆内还有其他几百本重要的中国佛教书籍。可见，该图书馆这些关于佛教的丰富藏书可以在很大程度上帮助学者进行深入研究。除了佛教书籍，该图书馆后来还采购了大量汉语语言学、政治、文学等门类的书籍。不仅如此，国家汉办、中国驻印度大使馆和云南大学向中国学院提供各类书籍，共同推动汉语教学项目的发展。

4 中国学院最近主要关注汉语教学存在的问题和解决方案

近十年来，越来越多的印度学生来到中国学院学习中文。中国经济繁荣发展，国际影响力不断提高，越来越多的国家对学习中文表现出浓厚的兴趣。汉语越来越被认为是一种具有工具价值的语言，可提供就业或商业机会，增强国际流动性。国际社会掀起中国热，中国学院也不例外。最近，不仅有来自西孟加拉邦的学生，还有很多比哈尔邦和贾坎德邦的学生，甚至还有从尼泊尔、孟加拉国和中国慕名而来的学生。自 2017 年起，根据国际大学和国家汉办签署的协议，汉办向国际大学派遣志愿教师。这也是中国学院推动汉语项目发展的重要一步。除了教汉语，这些教师还会指导学生参加汉语水平考试。

中国学院在实际的汉语教学中遇到的首要问题就是教学资料的短缺。近几年来，学习汉语的印度学生数量激增，但是汉语教材短缺，更不必说多媒体视频学习资料等汉语学习资源了。汉语学习要求有语言环境，很多初学者都希望在课后可以读到一些汉语材料，特别是有汉语拼音注音的中文书籍。

第二个问题是缺少适合印度学生的教学方法。印度种族群体众多，语言系统庞杂。在中国学院学习的学生背景不同，母语也不同，特别是北印度语和孟加拉语与中文语言体系完全不同。汉语教学的主要瓶颈是汉字教学。由于北印度语、孟加拉语，甚至是英语的书写方式和汉字完全不同，学生学习汉字有些困难。

第三个问题是方言系统不同，汉语书写和口语表达存在差异，汉字数量庞大，繁体字和简体字的书写方式也不相同，再加上汉语语法和语调这些因素有时候会影响学生学习汉语的热情。

中国学院的传统汉语教学主要培养学生的阅读和写作能力。除了重视学生的写作能力，现代汉语教学还对学生的听力和口语提出了新要求。没有良好的听力和口语能力，学生就无法在电视、广播、网络等媒体上获取相关知识。只有让学生爱看中文节目，习惯自己说汉语，才能提高学习兴趣，收到更好的学习效果。当然，教会学生如何利用新科技达到学习目的也是老师的职责之一。

为了解决上述问题，更好地和世界上其他提供汉语课程的机构和大学竞争，中国学院在教学大纲上做出了一些改变，其目的是提高学生的中文能力。中国电影和电视节目也被融入商务汉语、同声传译和汉语学习等新课程中，这些新课程与教学大纲上的中国历史、中国文学、中外关系和中文报刊等早期课程相融合。教学和参考所用的书籍由北京大学、北京语言大学、云南大学等高校的出版社出版。

在过去的几年里，中国学院多次成功组织以多学科为主题的国际会议，吸引很多中印两国的知名学者参会。正如泰戈尔设想的那样，中国学院一直以来都是中印学者的交流中心。2014 年 9 月，为表彰中国学院坚持和平共处五项原则，在增进两国人民情谊，推动世界和平发展上做出的重要贡献，中国国家主席习近平授予国际大学中国学院“和平共处五项原则友谊奖”。[1]

5 总结

要普及印度的汉语教学，还需不断开拓中国学院与中国各高校学术文化合作的

1 《习近平会见印度友好人士、友好团体代表并颁发和平共处五项原则友谊奖》，http://www.gov.cn/xinwen/2014-09/19/content_2753300.htm，访问时间：2020 年 10 月 22 日。

新途径。泰戈尔和谭云山的坚持和付出为印度汉语教学开创了新时代，中印文化情谊还将继续延续下去。

中国学院的成就可总结为以下四个方面：

(1) 中国学院为印度乃至整个次大陆建设汉语项目打下了坚实基础；

(2) 中国学院为中印文化对话提供场所，促进了思想传播，加深了中印两国之间的互相理解；

(3) 中国学院是中印情谊的摇篮，这份情谊始于中国学院，后又传播至印度的其他地方；

(4) 中国学院是中印文化和教育交流的纽带。

中国学院的建立是中印教育文化交流史上的重要事件。自成立起，中国学院为中印交流提供固定平台，加强双方在多领域的交流合作，吸引了无数来自世界各地的学者专家和莘莘学子。作为国际大学的一部分，中国学院一定会在促进中印教育文化交流方面继续做好开拓者和先锋者的角色。

（孙美幸 / 翻译，蔡育靓 / 校对）

参考文献

[1] TAN Y. Twenty years of the Visva-Bharati Cheena Bhavana:1937-1957[J]. The Sino-Indian cultural society of India,1957.

[2] RAY H P. Indian research programmes on China[M]. China Report (A Journal of East Asian Studies) New Delhi: Sage Publications,1992, 28:4.

印度汉语教学研究历史浅析

爱 德[1]

摘要 中印两国都是拥有2000多年历史的文明古国，两国之间也有约两千年的交往史。佛教作为印度本土的宗教，在东汉时期传入中国并自然而然地在中国传统文化中慢慢扎根。佛教是中印文学交流的良好基础。从古代开始，两国学者及僧人就开始积极研究对方的语言，做了大量的翻译工作。21世纪的中国和印度是两个新兴经济体，两国人口占全球人口总数的三分之一。中国也是印度最大的贸易合作伙伴。在此背景下学习中文，语言不仅是了解中国的工具，更是增加信任、减少误解并使贸易便利的最好方式。本文对印度汉语教学研究的历史进行浅析，展望该学科的未来发展趋势，提出建设性建议。

关键词 印度；中国；佛教；语言；中文；汉语教学

1 古代中印文学交流：以佛教为基础的友好交流

作为两个接壤的国度，中国和印度之间的交往历史超过了世界上其他任何两个国家。在佛教传入中国之前，中国和印度就有了初步接触。印度的两本史诗《罗摩衍那》和《摩诃婆罗多》当中也有关于中国的记录。有的学者还认为中国在全世界的英文名称“China”也是来自古印度对中国的称呼。[1] 佛教在东汉时期沿丝绸之路进入中国，并跟中国已有的本土学派，如道家和儒家，在经过一段时间的磨合之后本土化了。两国之间不少佛教学者和僧人进行了交流访问。公元4世纪，中国僧人法显徒步到印度，公元399—412年间他拜访了印度次大陆的各个王国并收集了大量

1 博士生，SRF奖学金获得者，2018年青年汉学家，尼赫鲁大学中国与东南亚研究中心。

的佛经书籍。返回中国后，在古都南京，法显在已在中国生活多年的印度和尚佛陀跋陀罗（Buddhabhadra）的帮助下做了大量的翻译工作并写下《佛国记》一书。公元5世纪，南印度的菩提达摩到了中国河南洛阳的少林寺。他不仅把许多梵文佛经翻译成了中文，而且还创造了禅宗佛教。到了唐朝时期，佛教成为中国的主流宗教，中印之间的人文交流也更为频繁。公元629—645年间，中国僧人玄奘到印度各个王国进行访问。那时候印度已经有了比较完整的教育体系，位于印度比哈尔邦的那烂陀大学有上万的学生，课程丰富，包括佛学、天文学、数学、医学、美术学等。玄奘在那烂陀寺待了两年，在著名的戒贤老师（Shilabhadra）的指导下掌握了佛学、逻辑和古梵文方面的知识。根据当地文献记载，玄奘在那烂陀寺期间还获得“留校任教”的资格，给其他学生开设了古汉语课程。回中国以后他把在印度的经历编写成了《大唐西域记》，后来还影响了吴承恩的《西游记》。11世纪之后，由于外来势力的侵略，印度的佛经和记载基本上被销毁或遗失了，玄奘的记录便成了研究古印度的最佳资料。明朝时期，公元1405—1433年间郑和七次下西洋，访问了印度东部和南部的一些城市，如多摩梨帝（现今西孟加拉邦的塔姆卢克市）、吉大港（现今在孟加拉国）、科钦和卡利卡特。[2]40 他同当地国王会面，还与民众做一些中国产品的买卖。这个历史事件现今仍然有迹可循。

这些僧人和学者的翻译工作及记载进一步推动了中国和印度之间的人文交流，为后代研究提供了非常宝贵的资料。值得一提的是，长期的文学交流以及双边贸易对两国的语言体系也产生了一定的影响。汉语中吸纳了很多梵语词汇，例如，“刹那”源于古梵文词“क्षण”（kshan），“比丘”源于“भिक्षु”（bhikshu）等。在印度各地的方言中我们也能找到跟中国相关的词汇。如表示该产品源于中国，如印度北方地区把花生叫作“Chiniya Badam”；南印度马拉雅拉姆语中把渔网叫作“Chinavala”，把煎锅叫作“Chinachatti”，说明这两种物品最早是郑和带到印度的。[2]45-46 这种中印之间的交流在一定程度上反映了两国人民对彼此的尊重和互学互鉴的精神。

2 殖民时期印度汉语教学：汉语教学在印度的萌芽

17 世纪，中印两国发生了翻天覆地的变化。公元 1636 年中国清朝建立，清政府前期实行闭关锁国政策。公元 1600 年英国东印度公司以贸易为由来到印度，不久便不择手段把印度大多数地区占为英国殖民地。公元 1772 年英国殖民政府在印度最大的港口城市加尔各答建立了首都，该城市当时成为印度最发达的工业城市，印度最早的汉语教学也是在加尔各答诞生的。英国及其他西方国家的传教士和学者也陆陆续续到了加尔各答，在当地参与各种教育和文化改造方面的工作。其中有个叫约翰内斯·拉撒尔（Johannes Lassar）的人在 1805 年前后在加尔各答的英国殖民政府建立的威廉堡学院（College of Fort William）开办了印度第一个现代意义的中文课堂。[3]173 拉撒尔原来是亚美尼亚人，曾经在澳门接受过教育，一直参与《圣经》的翻译工作。关于为什么英国殖民政府在加尔各答开办中文课堂的说法不一。有的学者认为，因为当时东南亚很多国家，如缅甸、越南、老挝、菲律宾等都流行用汉字，了解汉字会让英国殖民政府更好地巩固在此类国家的影响力以及更方便地传播基督教。另一个说法是，1792 年到达中国的第一个英国外交使团马戛尔尼使团的谈判失败了，英国政府就更加留心，希望通过学习中文更好地了解中国的风土人情。[3]172

与拉撒尔在加尔各答从事汉语教育工作同时，有位叫约书亚·马什曼（Joshua Marshman）的传教士也开始参与汉语教学工作。1799 年，马什曼带妻子和两个孩子来到加尔各答附近的塞兰普尔（Serampore）。受英国殖民政府的指令，马什曼进行了大量翻译工作，如把《圣经》译成孟加拉文和梵文，把《罗摩衍那》译成英文等。1806 年，马什曼认识了已参与汉语教学的拉撒尔并请他教自己汉语。同年，马什曼跟他的两个儿子，约翰·克拉克·马什曼（John Clark Marshman）和本杰明·威克·马什曼（Benjamin Wickes Marshman），及其他传教士的孩子开始上拉撒尔的汉语课。三年之后，1809 年，马什曼在拉撒尔和他的两个中国助理的指导下出版了《论语》的英文译本。接下来的几年当中，马什曼和拉撒尔共同出版了很多作品，如《汉语研究》（*Dissertation on the Chinese Language*，1810）、《汉语语法纲要》（*Elements of Chinese Grammar*，1814）、《汉语入门》（*Clavis Sinica*）、《汉字研究》（*Dissertation on Chinese*

Characters，1814）等。[4]61 1822年，马什曼出版了《圣经》的完整中文译本，该书被认为是历史上第一本完整的《圣经》中文译本。[5]62 这些传教士的努力及刻苦耐劳的精神是英国殖民时期早期印度汉学界的楷模。

图1 约翰·克拉克·马什曼

3　20世纪上半叶的印度汉语教学：学科的创立和发展

19世纪末印度最大港口城市加尔各答跟东亚的贸易交流变得更加频繁。许多来自中国广东和福建地区的华人也来到了加尔各答，在加尔各答的郊外建立了印度历史上第一条唐人街。这座城市很快成为印度第一个汉语教学中心。1918年加尔各答大学设立了东方学研究所，该所进行汉语、日语等的研究。[6]121 为了创造优秀的教学和科研环境，加尔各答大学特请世界各地的学者来此任教。1922年，两位日本教授——增田教授（Prof. Masuda）和木村教授（Prof. Kimura）——来到加尔各答大学并开设了日语和汉语课程。[7]52 他们培养的第一批学生当中最杰出的一位是师觉月（Prabodh Chandra Bagchi，1898—1956）。同一年，师觉月被大学安排到诺贝尔文学奖获得者印度诗翁泰戈尔在加尔各答附近的和平乡新建的国际大学（Visva-Bharati University）做研究。当时泰戈尔邀请了巴黎大学著名的印度学和东方学专家列维（Prof. Sylvain Lévi）来国际大学任教。[8]72 师觉月在列维的指导下在藏传佛教、汉文、巴利文和古梵文等领域展开研究曾经陪列维夫妇去尼泊尔考察。1923—1926年间，师觉月获得政府的奖学金，到法国进行研究学习并获得了博士学位，他的代表作《印度与中国：千年文化关系》

（*India and China: A Thousand Years of Cultural Relations*）至今被认为是一本全面的参考书。

虽然 20 世纪二三十年代汉学在印度开始受到欢迎，可是还存在一些限制因素。第一个限制因素是凡是印度的汉学研究都围绕佛学展开，学者们大多把汉语当作研究佛学的工具。第二个限制因素是在印度从事汉语教育的师资不足，且大多数东方

图 2　师觉月先生

学研究者来自西方国家。1924 年，泰戈尔的首次访华是中印文学交流的重大突破，中国文学界掀起了一阵“泰戈尔热”。当时不少中国文人受到了泰戈尔的影响，如徐志摩、陈独秀、郭沫若、胡适、冰心。之后，许多中国学者陆续到印度国际大学求学，如曾圣提、徐悲鸿、魏风江、金克木等。当时在湖南就读的谭云山就是在报刊上看到了泰戈尔的讲话稿和介绍印度文化的文章才对印度产生了极大的兴趣。[9]74

泰戈尔访华期间去了上海、北京、杭州、南京、济南、太原、武汉等城市，中国的风土人情及博大精深的文化给他留下了深刻的影响。他在临终前写的一首诗中仍旧怀念此次中国之行。为了推动中印两个伟大民族之间的文学交流，泰戈尔一直

梦想在国际大学建立中国学院，可是由于各种原因他的梦想直到 1937 年才实现。1927 年泰戈尔访问新加坡，正在参与新加坡汉语教学工作的谭云山第一次见到了他。泰戈尔邀请谭云山到国际大学任教，谭云山毫不犹豫地答应了。1928 年谭云山到了国际大学的所在地和平乡（Shantiniketan），开办了中文教学班。他的第一批学生一共有五位，其中两位是国际大学教授，三位是做研究工作的学者。[10]55 他们分别是慕克吉（Prabhat K. Mukherjee）、贝诺（F. Benot）、苏季子（Sujit Mukherjee）、乔杜星（Chowdhury）和斯星・佩特（Sri Pate）。其中慕克吉是著名的孟加拉语作家，也是当时国际大学图书馆馆长，后来撰写了泰戈尔的第一本传记。

在接下来的约十年当中，谭云山全身心收集图书和筹集资金。1935 年，中印学会在南京成立，该学会的成立对印度汉语教学的发展发挥了重要作用。在谭云山和许多中印友好使者的努力下，1937 年"中国学院"（Cheena-Bhavana）、中文图书馆在国际大学落成。中国学院培养了不少人才，包括白春晖（Vasant V. Paranjpe）、南希珍（K. Vankataramanan）、泰无量（Amitendranath Tagore）等，其

图 3　国际大学中国学院

中白春晖先生于1955—1957年间任印度驻华大使。[9]73 在谭云山的努力下，1943年中印两国政府商定互设留学生奖学金，同年11月，第一批印度学生共10名赴中国留学。[11]380 交换留学生的举措进一步推动了印度汉学界的发展。

20世纪三四十年代，除国际大学的中国学院外，印度其他学校的汉语教学几乎是一片空白。40年代，位于印度西部城市浦那的弗古森学院（Fergusson College）成立了一个小型的中国研究中心。该中心的巴帕特（P. V. Bapat）博士和戈哈理（V. V. Gokhale）博士对巴利文、梵文和汉语佛教典籍进行比较研究。[12]10 除此之外，著名的印度学者拉古·维拉（Raghu Vira，1902—1963）也在建立以佛教为基础的中印友好关系中做了不少工作，他于1932年以研究印中关系史为宗旨创办了“印度文化国际研究院”（International Academy of Indian Culture）。1938年发表的《罗摩衍那在中国》（“Ramayana in China”）一文中，维拉研究了印度史诗《罗摩衍那》对中国文化的影响。1955—1956年期间，他到敦煌莫高窟考察，受到了中印学术界和高级领导的高度重视。他的儿子罗凯什·钱德拉（Lokesh Chandra）成为他的接班人，继续展开有关敦煌莫高窟和中印关系史方面的研究。如今，90多岁的钱德拉先生被认为是世界汉语教学界的传奇人物。另外，1943年建立的印度国际研究学院（Indian School of International Studies）也开设了东亚研究部，该部主任杜特（V. P. Dutt）曾经在斯坦福大学和北京大学做过有关中国历史方面的研究，通晓汉语的他注重语言在国际研究中的重要性。该学院于1947年3月至4月在新德里举办了“亚洲关系会议”（Asian Relations Conference）。

虽然独立之前印度的汉语教学已经取得了初步成就，但是总体上仍然缺乏完整性和系统性。沦为殖民地和半殖民地后印度和中国交流极少，大多数学者主要关注中印关系中的佛教成分。师资和教材的欠缺以及学术范围的狭窄成为印度20世纪上半叶汉语教学发展的制约因素。1947年8月15日印度独立，1949年10月1日中华人民共和国成立，两国于1950年4月1日正式建立外交关系，印度是第一个跟中国建交的非社会主义国家。建交之后，两国关系迅速发展，印度的汉语教学也进入了新的历史阶段。

4　20 世纪下半叶的印度汉语教学：政治的动荡和考验中站稳脚跟

自从两国建交之后，印度和中国之间的交往取得了前所未有的进步。随着中国印度友好协会 1952 年在北京成立、1954 年两国之间"和平共处五项原则"的签订，中文系 / 中国研究中心在印度各地的大学里如雨后春笋般出现了。1948 年由印度国防部设立的外国语学院（School of Foreign Languages，简称 SFL）在 50 年代初专门为印度军事人员开办了中文班，此后位于印度西部浦那市的印度国防学院（National Defence Academy，简称 NDA）也启动了汉语教学。1956 年在纪念"佛陀诞生 2 500 周年"时，位于印度首都新德里的德里大学成立了佛学系（Department of Buddhist Studies），巴帕特担任该系第一任系主任。[1] 从严格意义上来讲，该系是 1964 年在德里大学所建的"中国研究中心"（1969 年更名为"中日研究系"）的前身。1961 年，位于印度北方邦古城瓦拉纳西的贝拿勒斯印度教大学（Banaras Hindu University）开设了外语系，汉语是该系最早开设的七门课程之一。20 世纪 50 年代末以来，英国殖民政府留下来的边界问题使中印两国之间产生了很多矛盾和对抗。1962 年的中印边境冲突后，双边关系日益恶化，印度的汉语教学也受到了影响。

1962 年的边境冲突之后，印度汉语教学的发展方向发生很大的转变。历来注重中印关系史、佛教、文化等的印度汉语教学由于政治和战略原因转化为围绕着中国政治、经济、外交、军事等领域的研究。1955 年到印度读书的谭中毕业后即子承父业，与他的父亲谭云山一样，成为印度汉语教学领域的重要人物。在印度获得本硕博学位之后，谭中开始在浦那（Pune）的印度国防学院教授中文。1963—1964 年被辞退以后，他到了德里大学，在新设的中文系担任副教授。[13]8 该系后期增加了日语和韩语研究，目前更名为"东亚研究系"（Department of East Asian Studies）。虽然 20 世纪 60 至 80 年代中印两国关系面临了前所未有的低潮期，可是由于印度政府对高等教育的关注，以及许多名牌大学的建立，使得该时期印度在汉语教学上获得了一定的成就。

1　参考网站：http://du.ac.in/du/index.php?page=buddhist-studies.

5 当代印度汉语教学：学科的体系化与印度的“中文热”

为了实现印度成为“有声有色”的大国的梦想，印度政府自20世纪60年代开始高度重视国家高等教育。1969年，尼赫鲁大学的创办给予印度高等教育极大的推动力。建立该学校的目的是为有高尚的思想和社会贫困阶级的学生提供高等教育。从建校开始，国际关系学和语言文学专业就成为尼赫鲁大学的王牌专业。该大学最早开办的国际关系学院（School of International Studies）有东亚研究中心（Centre for East Asian Studies），主要研究领域为中国及其他东亚国家的政治、经济、外交等。除国际关系学院外，语言文学和文化学院（School of Language, Literature and Culture Studies）1973年设立的亚非语言中心（Centre for Afro-Asian Languages）开办了中文项目。[1]随着对东亚语言需求的激增，东亚语言中心（CEAL）于20世纪80年代成立，中国和东南亚研究中心（CCSEAS）则于1996年成立。哈拉普拉萨德·雷易（Haraprasad Ray）从事该中心的汉语教学工作。1978年谭中从德里大学来到尼赫鲁大学培养中文人才。

1978年当时的印度外交部部长瓦杰帕伊（Atal B. Vajpayee）访华，为中印关系正常化铺平了道路。20世纪80年代，两国开始恢复学术交流，这个时期涌现出尼赫鲁大学首批汉语教学人才，其中墨普德教授（Prof. Priyadarsi Mukherji）、狄伯杰教授（Prof. Bali R. Deepak）、邵葆丽教授（Prof. Sabaree Mitra）、马尼克教授（Prof. Manik Bhattacharya）等人已经成为当今印度汉语教学领域的传奇人物。狄伯杰和墨普德分别于2011年和2014年获得了中华图书特殊贡献奖。墨普德是谭云山在中国学院培养的第一批学生中慕克吉（Probhat K. Mukherji）的孙子，从小就学习汉语、阅读中国文学作品。1988年印度总理拉吉夫·甘地访华之后，中印关系得到了突飞猛进的发展，两国开始了交换学生的项目，重视学习彼此的语言和文化。1990年中国研究所（Institute of Chinese Studies）在新德里的成立扩大了印度的中国研究领域。该研究所在某种意义上是第一个专门研究中国问题的智库，其刊物《中国报导》（*China Report*）是社会科学与国际关系领域的权威期刊。

1 参考网站：https://www.jnu.ac.in/sllcs/cc%26seas.

1991 至 1992 年这段时间对中印两国的经济发展同样重要，印度经济的对外开放和中国邓小平南行成为两国经济发展的主要动力。过去以外交、战略和军事为集中点的印度汉语教学领域又找到了新的发展方向。印度各地大学里的汉语教学也与时俱进，除尼赫鲁大学外，国际大学中国学院的那吉世教授（Prof. Arttatrana Nayak）、李纳教授（Prof. Reena Ganguli）和阿维杰特·班纳吉教授（Dr. Avijit Banerjee），德里大学东亚研究系的阿妮达·舍尔马教授（Prof. Anita Sharma）和瓦拉纳西的贝纳拉斯印度教大学的卡莫尔·希尔教授（Prof. Kamal Sheel）在汉语教学研究方面也取得了一定的成就。

中国经济实力的增长，双边贸易的增加，以及到印度的中国游客数量的增加给 20 世纪 90 年代末的印度带来了第一波“中文热”。2001 年中国加入世界贸易组织之后，中国的龙头企业，如华为、海尔、中兴等陆续进入印度市场，并开始招聘懂中文的人才。2005 年，中国国务院总理温家宝访问印度，两国宣布建立面向和平与繁荣的战略合作伙伴关系。[1] 2006 年，中国国家主席胡锦涛访问印度，在两国签订的一系列备忘录中教育文化交流合作是其中一项重要内容。从 2006 年起，印中两国开启了一年一度的青年代表互访项目。2009 年，印度南部的韦洛尔科技大学（Vellore Institute of Technology）与中国郑州大学签署协议并创建了印度第一个孔子学院。近几年来该学院为南印度汉语教学的发展以及在印度举办汉语水平考试起到了重要作用。同一年，印度的高等教育政策有了翻天覆地的变化，通过实施《2009 年中央大学法》，中央政府在印度各地新建了 20 所中央大学，其中至少三所大学开办了中文系。新建的大学中古吉拉特邦中央大学（Central University of Gujrat）和恰尔肯德邦中央大学（Central University of Jharkhand）都位于二、三线城市。2010 年，位于印度北阿肯德邦（Uttarakhand）的杜恩大学（Doon University）也在本科和硕士研究生中开设了中文课。这些大学汉语课程的开办在很大程度上打破了印度以大城市为中心的汉语教学现象，为来自落后地区的贫困生提供了学习汉语的

1　参考网站：https://www.indiatoday.in/magazine/diplomacy/story/20050425-chinese-premier-wen-jiabao-visit-paves-way-for-sino-indian-strategic-partnership-787893-2005-04-25.

机会。

最近几年来，随着两国关系的缓和，在两国政府和相关部门的努力下，印度的汉语课已经成为家喻户晓的学科。2011 年，印度中等教育中央委员会把汉语作为外语列入中学课程，两国共同宣布把 2011 年作为中印交流年。2013 年，印度第二个孔子学院在印度经济中心孟买建立，进一步促进了印度西部的汉语及中国文化的传播。在印度“中文热”的影响下，不少私立大学也开办了中文课程，其中曼加拉姆大学（K. R. Mangalam University）、金德尔全球大学（O. P. Jindal Global University）和拉夫里科技大学（Lovely Professional University）的汉语教学成果得到了中印学术界的普遍认可。近年来在印度大城市提供中文培训的私立机构也增加了不少，其中有些是华人开办的。印度当今汉语教学概况如表 1 所示：

表 1　印度开设汉语教学的学校及概况 *

编号	学校名称	类型	所在地	学位	使用教材或开设课程
01	尼赫鲁大学	中央公立大学	新德里	本科、硕士、副博士、博士	本科：《基础汉语课本》（1 ～ 4）（华语教学出版社）；《桥梁》（上、下）（北京语言大学出版社）；《汉语口语教程》（北京语言大学出版社）；《现代汉语高级教程》（北京语言大学出版社）；《话说中国》（华语教学出版社）；《汉语写作指导》（北京大学出版社）；《发展汉语》（北京语言大学出版社）；《漫谈中国》等 硕士：《中国文学史》（印度 GBD 出版社）；中国报刊 / 新闻短片；中国经典小说；介绍中文；中国政治概况
02	德里大学	中央公立大学	新德里	文凭、证书	《基础汉语课本》（1 ～ 4）（华语教学出版社）；《话说中国》（华语教学出版社）等

续表

编号	学校名称	类型	所在地	学位	使用教材或开设课程
03	国际大学	中央公立大学	和平乡	本科、硕士、博士	本科：《使用初级汉语教程》（北京语言大学出版社）；《外国人使用汉语语法》（华语教学出版社）；《新闻汉语导读》（北京语言大学出版社）；《唐诗鉴赏辞典》（崇文书局）；《中国概况》（北京大学出版社）等 硕士：《中国现代作品选编》（外文出版社）；《文学艺术》（外文出版社）；《中华人民共和国史》（北京理工大学出版社）等
04	贝拿勒斯印度教大学	中央公立大学	瓦拉纳西	文凭、硕士、博士	文凭：《基础汉语课本》（华语教学出版社）； 硕士：《高级汉语教程》（北京语言大学出版社）；《中国现代作品选编1919—1949》（外文出版社）；《中国新文学作品选》(北京语言大学出版社)；《鲁迅全集》（人民文学出版社）等
05	阿里格尔穆斯林大学	中央公立大学	阿里格尔	本科、硕士	本科：《基础汉语课本》（华语教学出版社）；《话说中国》（华语教学出版社）；《现代汉语高级教程》（上、下）（北京语言大学出版社）；《汉语写作指导》（北京大学出版社）等 硕士：《中国现代文学史》；《高级口译教程》；《季羡林全集》；《中国文学史》（印度GBD出版社）；《中国古代文学作品选》；《商务实用汉语》等
06	加尔各答大学	中央公立大学	加尔各答	文凭、证书	《基础汉语课本》（华语教学出版社）

续表

编号	学校名称	类型	所在地	学位	使用教材或开设课程
07	古吉拉特邦中央大学	中央公立大学	甘地纳加尔	本科、硕士	本科：《基础汉语课本》（华语教学出版社）；《初级汉语阅读与写作》；《商务汉语》；《中级汉语课程》；《高级汉语课程》；《话说中国》（华语教学出版社）；《中国俗语和短语鉴赏》；《国语文学概论》 硕士：《中国现代文学》；《翻译理论与实践》；《高级汉语口语》；《中文小说精选》；《新闻汉语导读》（北京语言大学出版社）
08	恰尔肯德邦中央大学	中央公立大学	兰齐	文凭、证书、本科、硕士	《基础汉语课本》（华语教学出版社）；《漫谈中国》；《中国概况》
09	贾米亚·米利亚·伊斯兰大学	中央公立大学	新德里	文凭、证书	《新版实用视听华语》（正中书局）；《远东生活华语》（远东出版社）；《基础汉语课本》（华语教学出版社）
10	锡金中央大学	中央公立大学	甘托克	本科、硕士	本科：《基础汉语课本》（华语教学出版社）；《初级汉语课本》（北京语言大学出版社）；《新实用汉语课本》（北京语言大学出版社）；《汉语会话 301 句》（北京语言大学出版社）；《博雅汉语准中级加速篇》（北京大学出版社）；《桥梁使用汉语中级 教程》（北京语言大学出版社）等 硕士：《中国古代文学史长编》（北京师范大学出版社）；《中国文学史》（印度 GBD 出版社）；《新闻汉语导读》（北京语言大学出版社）；《汉语高级听力教程》（北京大学出版社）；中国经典小说等
11	孟买大学（孔子学院）	中央公立大学	孟买	文凭、证书	《基础汉语课本》（华语教学出版社）；《HSK 标准教程》（北京语言大学出版社）

续表

编号	学校名称	类型	所在地	学位	使用教材或开设课程
12	提斯浦尔大学	中央公立大学	提斯浦尔	证书	《基础汉语课本》（华语教学出版社）等
13	英语和外语大学	中央公立大学	海得拉巴	文凭、证书	《发展汉语》（北京语言大学出版社）；《基础汉语课本》（华语教学出版社）等
14	班加罗尔中央大学	中央公立大学	班加罗尔	文凭、证书	《基础汉语课本》（华语教学出版社）等
15	英迪拉•甘地国立开放大学	中央公立大学	新德里	文凭、证书	《基础汉语课本》（华语教学出版社）等
16	印度理工学院马德拉斯分校中国学研究中心	公立大学	金奈	文凭、证书	介绍中文、当代全球政治中的中国、中国的政治与外交政策等
17	印度理工学院比莱分校汉语培训中心	公立大学	比莱	选修课	初级汉语；中华文化；中文写作；中国书法
18	印度理工学院孟买分校	公立大学	孟买	选修课	汉语交际课程；高级汉语课程
19	印度管理学院班加罗尔分校	中央公立大学	班加罗尔	选修课	商务汉语
20	新那烂陀佛教大学	名誉大学	那烂陀	文凭、证书	《基础汉语课本》（华语教学出版社）等
21	曼尼普尔大学	中央公立大学	英帕尔	证书	《基础汉语课本》（华语教学出版社）等
22	圣雄甘地国际印地语大学	中央公立大学	沃尔塔	高级文凭、文凭、证书	《基础汉语课本》（华语教学出版社）等
23	都安大学	邦立大学	德拉敦	本科、硕士	本科《基础汉语课本》（华语教学出版社）；中国文化概论；《读报纸学中文》硕士：中国地理概论；古典汉语概论；中国现代文学史；中国古代文学史

续表

编号	学校名称	类型	所在地	学位	使用教材或开设课程
24	旁遮普大学	邦立大学	昌迪加尔	文凭、证书	《基础汉语课本》（华语教学出版社）等
25	迈索尔大学	邦立大学	迈索尔	文凭、证书	《基础汉语课本》（华语教学出版社）；《初级汉语课本》（北京语言大学出版社）等
26	桑吉佛教印度研究大学	邦立大学	桑吉	硕士、文凭、证书	《基础汉语课本》（华语教学出版社）等
27	本地治里大学	邦立大学	本地治里	文凭、证书	《基础汉语课本》（华语教学出版社）等
28	阿姆倍伽尔博士马拉特瓦达大学	邦立大学	奥兰加巴德	高级文凭、文凭、证书	《基础汉语课本》（华语教学出版社）等
29	贾达普尔大学	邦立大学	加尔各答	证书	《基础汉语课本》（华语教学出版社）等
30	摩揭陀大学	邦立大学	菩提伽耶	文凭、证书	《基础汉语课本》（华语教学出版社）等
31	马哈西•达雅南德大学	邦立大学	罗塔克	文凭、证书	《基础汉语课本》（华语教学出版社）等
32	因德尔•库马尔•古杰拉尔旁遮普科技大学	邦立大学	卡普塔拉	证书	《基础汉语课本》（华语教学出版社）等
33	迦梨耶尼大学	邦立大学	迦梨耶尼	文凭、证书	《基础汉语课本》（华语教学出版社）等
34	国防部外语学院	政府机构	新德里	文凭、证书	《基础汉语课本》（华语教学出版社）等
35	印度国防学院	政府机构	浦那	文凭、证书	《基础汉语课本》（华语教学出版社）等
36	印度智慧中心	教育基金会	新德里	文凭、证书	《基础汉语课本》（华语教学出版社）等

续表

编号	学校名称	类型	所在地	学位	使用教材或开设课程
37	基督教青年联合会－职业研究所	教育基金会	新德里	文凭	《基础汉语课本》（华语教学出版社）等
38	曼格拉姆大学	私立大学	古尔冈	本科	《基础汉语课本》（华语教学出版社）等
39	金德尔全球大学	私立大学	索尼巴	文凭、证书	/
40	拉夫里科技大学汉语教学中心	私立大学	帕格瓦拉	选修课、证书	《HSK 1标准课程》（北京语言大学出版社）
41	阿米提大学	私立大学	诺伊达	文凭、证书	《基础汉语课本》（华语教学出版社）等
42	韦洛尔科技大学（孔子学院）	私立大学	韦洛尔	文凭、证书	《HSK 1标准课程》（北京语言大学出版社）
43	阿育王大学	私立大学	索尼巴	证书	普通话教学项目
44	SRM科学技术学院	私立大学	金奈	证书	/

*以上信息来自各学校官方网站。

6 结语：印度汉语教学的前景展望及对策建议

印度的汉语教学经历了100多年的曲折起伏，目前已经取得了相当大的成就，成为热门课程。随着中印两国经贸关系和文化交流的日益密切，加上印度中文培训学校的大量出现，在印度学中文的人也越来越多。根据中国驻印度大使馆教育处统计，目前印度学习中文的学生已超过20 000人，其中在校生中学习汉语专业的学生约2000人。如前所述，位于新德里的尼赫鲁大学和德里大学以及位于西孟加拉邦的国际大学历来是印度汉语教学研究的核心机构，由于中文教学师资强，跟中国名校的合作和交流多，这三所大学是汉语言文学专业的学生的首选。虽然在过去一段时间由于上述原因，印度汉语教学以新德里和西孟加拉邦为中心的现象有所改变，可是汉语在印度各地，特别是在二、三线城市的普及率不高。最近两年中印在边境上的摩擦影响了双边关系的平稳。2018 年和 2019 年两国间的两次非正式首脑会晤也表示双方都希望通过对话的渠道来解决彼此的误解和边界问题。中印贸易额的逐步增加也说明求同存异是两国的共同诉求。2020 年新冠疫情的蔓延对全世界的高等教育产生了较大的影响，印度的汉语教学也受到了边境对峙和疫情的双重压力。在这种世界秩序下，印度的汉语教学也面临新的挑战和机遇。

6.1 提高印度汉语教学的研究水平

在印度大学里学汉语的学生来自印度各地，家庭背景和学习语言的目的各异。有的学生来自企业家庭，考虑到跟中国做生意的便利和未来的优势，家长让他们学习中文。大多数学生来自普通家庭，他们认为学中文容易找到工作。到印度发展的中资企业大多数会选择新德里和周边的开发区：古尔冈和诺伊达。近几年来中国大企业如华为、中兴、小米、OPPO、VIVO、联想、字节跳动、中国航空公司等在新德里首都区设立了办公室，汉语言专业的毕业生在这些公司可以拿到四五万卢比的月薪。赴印度的商务团也会找精通汉语和印地语的兼职翻译，有的学生选择做自由口译和笔译。汉语毫无疑问是印度兼职翻译的外语当中最吃香的语言，当兼职翻译可以每天赚 100 美元。另外，过去十年中来印度的中国游客和旅游团也越来越多。根据相关数据，每年来印度的中国游客大概有 35 万人，很多学习中文的学生在课余时间兼职当导游。

由于上述原因，在当前的印度汉语教学里“钱”成为学生的最大激励因素，经常会出现学生半途而废的现象。印度汉语教学的核心学校尼赫鲁大学目前本科学生有 110 人，硕士及硕士以上的学生只有 66 人。在其他大学中文系里读硕士及硕士以上的学生更是屈指可数。在印度的很多中国问题专家都根本看不懂中文，也没法使用第一手材料来研究中国。因此无论是合作或对抗，深入学习和研究汉语应该成为印度对华政策必不可少的一部分。

6.2　培养当地汉语教师，教材本土化

在上述44所拥有汉语教学的印度大学中从事汉语教学的老师有60余名。其中尼赫鲁大学中国与东南亚研究系（11名）、国际大学中国学院（6名）和新建的古吉拉特邦中央大学（4名）的师资力量最强，其他学校的师资力量薄弱。印度大学拨款委员会（UGC）每年召开的全国教师资格证考试（NET），汉语教学专业基本上只有6～8人考上。实际上其中继续研究汉语或从事汉语教学的人更少。另外，印度大学的汉语教学基本上没有“汉语教师培训”这门课程，学生毕业之后虽然具备当老师的基本条件可是经常缺少教学技巧，对专业的整体认识不清晰，导致教学手段单一而枯燥。这方面印度的大学可以向中国学习。中国很早就开始培养对外汉语教学师资，设立了“对外汉语教学课程”，特别是中国各地的师范大学在这方面起了极大作用。因为在印度是印度人教印度人汉语，所以“对外汉语课程”或许无法完全复制中国的做法，但是可以从中吸取经验教训。

印度大多数大学里的汉语教材陈旧，书里描写的词汇和情况基本上为20世纪八九十年代的中国社会，有关研究资料和数据库也严重缺乏。另外，印度的语言种类繁多，很多学生入大学之后才正式开始使用英语，而无论是大学里的汉语教材或老师的教法都是以汉语和英语的双语方式来进行的。由于语言水平参差，有时候学生无法深入了解课上的内容，学得不扎实。这种差距可以通过教材来弥补，学校及出版社可以考虑用印度各地主流语言如印地语、孟加拉语、泰米尔语、马拉地语、坎那达语等来编写教材，教材课文的内容在介绍中国的情况的同时也可以用汉语介绍印度的情况。这样不仅会提高学生对学习汉语的兴趣，也会助于学生了解中印文化的相似之处。

6.3 跟中国的大学和汉语培训机构开展在线教育合作

新型冠状病毒的蔓延给全世界的高等教育带来了前所未有的挑战。虽然印度各地的学校启动了在线课堂，可仍然面临种种问题。印度的汉语教学也面临学生缺乏

基础设施、缺乏兴趣和在线课堂效果欠佳等问题。教汉语跟教其他传统课程不一样，特别是教刚开始学习汉语的学生的时候老师需要不断纠正学生的发音、辨音和声调等问题，而印度目前最流行的远程会议软件如 Zoom 和 Google Meet 无法有效地满足这个需求。根据相关数据，印度目前有 5.6 亿网络使用者。随着印度二、三线城市智能手机和网络的普及，印度在线教育的需求也会不断增加。印度开办汉语教育的大学和学校可以设计汉语教学 App 和在线课程，也可以跟中国学校合作，这样不仅节省时间、金钱成本，又能突破地域、场地的限制。

6.4 回归到中印交流的文化本质

俗话说“树高千丈，叶落归根”，印度和中国之间的“根”就是两国几千年以来的文化和民间交流。这两个文明古国之间“天下大同”“互学互鉴”“和而不同”的哲学概念是相同的。语言和文化关系密切，充分了解一种语言的文化背景才能真正学好一种语言。学习汉语的学生在学习商务、翻译、经济、政治等课程的同时，也需要掌握中国的饮食习俗、问候礼仪、说话技巧等方面的知识。

在中印文化和民间交流中翻译的作用不可或缺。古代法显、玄奘、鸠摩罗什、义净等的翻译工作不仅促进了两国人民彼此的了解和信任，对后人了解当时的历史颇具参考价值。在当代中印文化交流中这样的翻译工作非常罕见，除了季羡林翻译的印度史诗《罗摩衍那》《摩诃婆罗多》和《五卷书》等书，金克木的印度文学译著、姜景奎翻译的《苏尔诗海》等译著、墨普德翻译的《鲁迅诗集》《中国当代诗歌集》《艾青诗歌、寓言》等书和狄伯杰的《论语》《四书》《诗经》的翻译以外，其他直接用汉语和印地语或印度其他语言进行翻译的作者和译著寥寥无几。2013 年中印两国政府签署了“中印经典和当代作品互译出版项目”，在此框架协议下，25 种中国经典和当代作品将被译为印地语，同样中方负责把印方的 25 部著作翻译成中文。[14]68 中印之间翻译工作的进一步发展不仅有助于吸引印度读者对中国文化的兴趣，也会促进学习汉语的学生更好地理解和研究中国文化、历史和文学。

（陈冰睿 / 校对）

参考文献

[1] GEOFF W. The polity of yelang and the origins of the name "China" [J]. Sino-platonic papers, 2009, 188:1-26.

[2] MUKHERJI P. The overland and maritime silk routes in the perspective of Imperial China's geopolitical strategy and its role as a catalyst for a Sino-Indian cultural amalgamation [C] // SELVAM A G, DESAI A K. Seminar compendium on "India and South-East Asia: maritime trade, expeditions and civilizational linkages". Ezhimala: Indian Naval Academy, 2017.

[3] CUTTS E H. Chinese studies in Bengal [J]. Journal of the American oriental society, 1942, 62(3):171-174.

[4] 狄伯杰. 当代印度的中国文学译介——问题与挑战 [J]. 郝岚，王宏健，译 . 东方丛刊 , 2018（2）：59-70.

[5] KITSON P J. Forging romantic China: Sino-British cultural exchange 1760-1840 [M]. New York: Cambridge University Press, 2013.

[6] 郁龙余. 中国学在印度 [J]. 学术研究 , 2000（1）：120-123.

[7] MANJAPRA K.Age of entanglement: German and Indian intellectuals across Empire [M]. Cambridge, MA: Harvard University Press, 2014.

[8] 章立明，周东亮. 印度汉语教学的百年流变及前景展望（1918—2018）[J]. 国外社会科学，2019（4）：71-78.

[9] 林立. 泰戈尔与印度国际大学中国学院的建立 [J]. 史学月刊，1994（5）：73-79.

[10] 谭云山. 印度之汉学 [J]. 赵波，译 . 图书月刊，1941，1（7-8）：54-81.

[11] 郁龙余，刘朝华. 中外文学交流史：中国—印度卷 [M]. 济南：山东教育出版社，2015.

[12] 雷易. 印度的中国学研究概览 [J]. 蔡晶，译 . 深圳大学学报，2010，27（6）：10-14.

[13] 郁龙余，刘朝华. 湘贤翘楚：谭云山、谭中父子 [J]. 书屋，2019（10）：4-9.

[14] 狄伯杰. 印度对中国经典著作的翻译 [J]. 文化软实力，2013（3）：66-68.

Analysis of the Historical Discourse of Chinese Language Studies in India

Aditya Kumar Pandey[1]

Abstract China and India are both two ancient civilizations with a history of several thousand years. The history of exchanges between these two Asian giants is also more than two thousand years old. Buddhism which emerged in India, reached China during the Eastern Han Dynasty and gradually merged and rooted itself within the traditional Chinese culture. The spread of Buddhism from India to China laid a strong foundation for literary and lingual exchanges between the two civilizations. Since ancient times, scholars and monks from the two countries actively studied each other's languages, and they undertook the tedious task of translating religious literature. In the 21st century, China and India are two emerging economies. The combined population of the two countries accounts for one third of the global population. China is also India's largest trading partner. Under such circumstances, learning Chinese language not only serves as a tool to understand China, but also the best way to foster trust, reduce misunderstandings and make trade more convenient. This paper will analyze the historical discourse of Chinese language education in India, from its inception to the present day. Based on the historical experiences, it tries to predict the future development trends of Chinese language education in India and offer suggestions for amelioration of the discipline.

Key Words India; China; Buddhism; Language; Chinese; Chinese language education

1 PhD Candidate, SRF Scholar, Young Sinologist 2018, Centre for Chinese and Southeast Asian Studies, Jawaharlal Nehru University.

1 ANCIENT SINO-INDIAN LITERARY EXCHANGES: FRIENDLY EXCHANGES BASED ON BUDDHISM

As two neighboring countries, the history of exchanges between China and India often exceeds that of exchanges between any other two countries in the world. Much before Buddhism entered China, the two nations already had mutual exchanges. One can easily find references to China in the two Indian epics, *Ramayana* and *Mahabharata*. Some scholars also believe that China's English name "China" which is used in the world is also derived from ancient India's word "Cīna" which was used to address the country and its various products.[1] Buddhism entered China through the ancient Silk Route during the Eastern Han Dynasty and gradually localized after a period of tussle with China's existing local schools of thoughts such as Taoism and Confucianism. Many Buddhist scholars and monks of the two countries had exchanged visits. For example, the Chinese monk Fa Xian walked to India in the fourth century AD. During 399–412 AD, he visited various kingdoms in the Indian subcontinent and collected a large number of Buddhist scriptures. After returning to China, he devoted himself to the translation of Buddhist scriptures and wrote the book *Record of Buddhist Kingdoms* with the help of the Indian monk Buddhabhadra who was living in China. In the fifth century AD, a prince from South India named Bodhidharma, travelled to the Shaolin Monastery located near Luoyang city of Henan province in China. He not only translated many Sanskrit Buddhist scriptures into Chinese but also created Zen Buddhism. During the Tang Dynasty, Buddhism became a mainstream religion in China and cultural exchanges became more frequent. Reverend Chinese monk Xuanzang visited various kingdoms in India from 629 to 645 AD. At that time, India already had a relatively complete education system. Nalanda University in Bihar had thousands of students studying multifarious courses like Buddhism, astronomy, mathematics, medicine, and fine arts. Xuanzang spent two years at Nalanda University, and under the guidance of the famous abbot Shilabhadra, he mastered the knowledge of Buddhism, Indian logic and ancient Sanskrit. According to local records, Xuanzang was also invited to teach while studying at Nalanda University and offered ancient Chinese courses to other students. After returning to China, he compiled his experience in India into *The Great Tang Dynasty Record of the Western Regions*, which later influenced the creation of Wu Cheng'en's *Journey to the West*. After the 11th century AD, due to the invasion of foreign powers, Indian Buddhist scriptures and records were destroyed and lost, thus Xuanzang's records naturally became important historical resources for studying ancient India. In the Ming Dynasty, during 1405–1433 AD, Zheng He made seven voyages to the Western oceans, he also visited some cities in eastern and southern India, like Tamralipti (present day Tamluk, West Bengal), Chittagong (now in Bangladesh), Cochin and Calicut.[2]40 He not only paid visits to the local kings but also traded Chinese products like fishing nets and cooking ware with the local people. One can still find the traces of his voyage in the south Indian city of Kochi.

The translation work and records of these monks and scholars further propelled the cultural exchanges between China and India and proved to be a valuable source of inspiration for future generations. It is worth mentioning that long-term literary exchanges and bilateral trade also had a certain impact on the language systems of the two countries. Many Sanskrit words were transliterated and directly incorporated in Chinese language. For example: "刹那" (chànà) is derived from the ancient Sanskrit word क्षण (kshan); "比丘" (bǐqiū) is derived from भिक्षु (bhikshu) and so on. We can also find Chinese-related words in dialects across India which indicate that the product originated from China. For example, in northern India, peanuts are called Chiniya Badam; the Sanskrit word Cīnapatta means thin tough silk or silk linen from China; in South Indian language Malayalam, fishing nets are called Chinavala, and frying pan is called Chinachatti, indicating that these products came to India from China.[2]45-46 In that era of borderless world, such exchanges between China and India, to a certain extent, showcase the spirit of respect and mutual learning between the two civilizations.

2 CHINESE LANGUAGE EDUCATION IN INDIA DURING THE COLONIAL PERIOD: THE BUDDING PHASE OF CHINESE LANGUAGE EDUCATION IN INDIA

The seventeenth century saw a remarkable shift in the political and social conditions in both China and India. After the establishment of the Qing Dynasty in 1636 AD, China started a closed-door policy. In 1600 AD, the British East India Company came to India for the purpose of trading, but soon started colonizing it through their down-and-dirty methods. In 1772, the British colonial government established its capital in Calcutta (present day Kolkata), which was the largest port city in India at that time. The city soon became India's key industrial and commercial hub. The earliest Chinese teaching in India also started in Calcutta. Many missionaries and scholars from Britain and other Western countries came to Calcutta to carry out various education and cultural transformation works. Amongst them a missionary named Johannes Lassar started teaching Chinese language at the College of Fort William established by the British colonial government in Kolkata around 1805. This could be called as the first Chinese language class of documented history in modern India. [3]173 Mr. Lassar was of Armenian origin. He was educated in Macau and was involved in the translation of the Bible. There are different opinions on why the British colonial government commissioned Chinese classes in Kolkata. Some scholars believe that because many countries in Southeast Asia such as Myanmar, Vietnam, Laos, and the Philippines used Chinese characters at that time, understanding Chinese characters would enable the British colonial government to better consolidate its influence in such countries and spread Christianity more easily. Another argument is that because the Macartney Mission, the first British diplomatic mission that arrived in China in 1792 failed in the negotiations, the British government was more cautious, and aimed at understanding China's customs by learning Chinese.[3]172

While Mr. Lassar was engaged in Chinese language education in Kolkata, another missionary named Joshua Marshman also began to engage in Chinese language education. Marshman came to Serampore near Kolkata in 1799 with his wife and two children. Commissioned by the British colonial government, Marshman carried out a lot of translation work, such as the translation of the *Bible* into Bengali and Sanskrit, and the translation of *Ramayana* into English. In 1806, Marshman met Lassar who was already engaged in Chinese language teaching and requested him to teach Chinese. In the same year, Marshman along with his two sons, John Clark Marshman and Benjamin Wickes Marshman, and other missionaries' children started studying Chinese from Lassar. Three years later, in 1809, Marshman published an English translation of *The Analects* under the guidance of Lassar and his two native Chinese assistants. In the next few years, Marshman and Lassar jointly published many works, such as *Dissertation on the Chinese Language* (1810), *Elements of Chinese Grammar* (1814), *Clavis Sinica* and *Dissertation on Chinese Characters* (1814), etc.[4]61 Marshman published a Chinese translation of the Bible in 1822 AD, which is considered as the first complete Chinese translation of the Bible.[5]62 The efforts of these missionaries and their willingness to endure hardships proved to be milestones in Chinese language studies in India in the early British colonial period.

Picture 1 John Clark Marshman

3 CHINESE LANGUAGE EDUCATION IN INDIA IN THE FIRST HALF OF THE 20TH CENTURY: THE ESTABLISHMENT AND DEVELOPMENT OF THE DISCIPLINE

Since the end of the nineteenth century, the trade exchanges between Kolkata,

India's largest port city, and East Asia became more frequent. Many Chinese businessmen, especially those from the southern regions of China, came and settled in Calcutta. The first Chinatown in Indian history was also established on the outskirts of Calcutta. In 1918, the University of Calcutta established the Department for Oriental Studies, which started conducting research on Chinese, Japanese languages and etc. [6]121 In order to create an excellent teaching and research environment, the university invited scholars from all over the world. In 1922, two Japanese professors named Prof. Masuda and Prof. Kimura were invited to offer courses in Japanese and Chinese.[7]52 One of the most outstanding among the first batch of students they trained was Prabodh Chandra Bagchi (1898–1956). In the same year, he was commissioned by University of Calcutta to carry-out research at Visva-Bharati University established by Noble laureate Rabindranath Tagore in Shantiniketan, near Kolkata. At that time Tagore had also invited Professor Sylvain Lévi, a well-known expert in India and Oriental studies at the University of Paris, to teach at the Visva-Bharati University.[8]72 Under the guidance of Prof. Lévi, Mr. Bagchi conducted research on Tibetan Buddhism, Chinese, Pali and Sanskrit. He once accompanied Professor Lévi and his wife

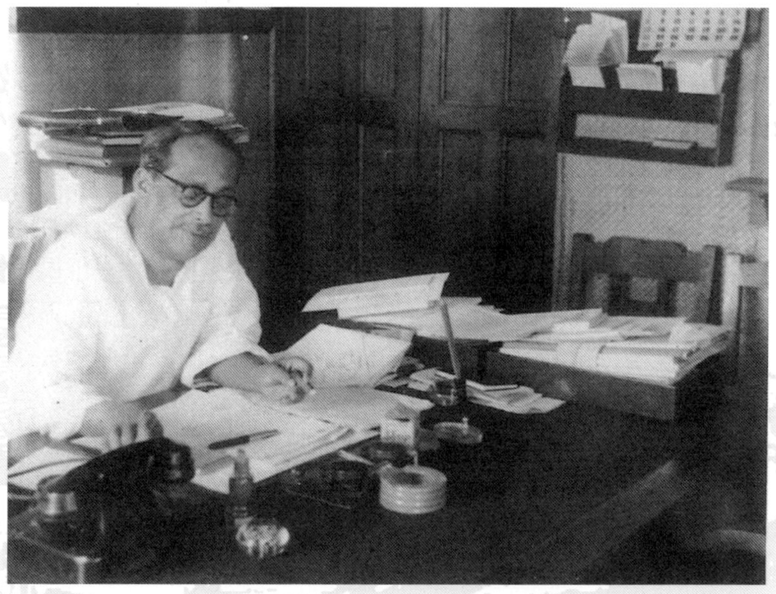

Picture 2 Prabodh Chandra Bagchi

to a study tour in Nepal. During 1923–1926, Mr. Bagchi received a government scholarship. He went to France to conduct research and obtained a doctorate degree. His masterpiece *India and China: A Thousand Years of Cultural Relations* is considered to be a comprehensive reference book on India-China relations even till date.

Although Chinese language education had gained popularity in India in the 1920s and 1930s, there were some limiting factors which hindered its growth. The first limiting factor was that Chinese language education in India during this period was centered on Buddhism and used Chinese as a tool for understanding Buddhist scriptures and religious texts. The second limiting factor was the lack of teachers, most of the teachers involved in Chinese language education during this period were Oriental researchers from Western countries. Tagore's first visit to China in 1924 brought a breakthrough development to Sino-Indian literary exchanges, and the Chinese literary circle seemed to have set off a "Tagore wave". Many Chinese literati such as Xu Zhimo, Chen Duxiu, Guo Moruo, Hu Shi, Bing Xin and so on, were influenced by Tagore. Gradually, many Chinese scholars such as Zeng Shengti, Xu Beihong, Wei Fengjiang and Jin Kemu came to Visva-Bharati University to study. Tan Yunshan, who was studying in Hunan at that time, read Tagore's speech and articles on Indian culture in the newspapers, and thus developed a great interest in India.[9]74

During his visit to China, Tagore went to Shanghai, Beijing, Hangzhou, Nanjing, Jinan, Taiyuan, Wuhan and other cities. He was deeply influenced by the local customs and profound culture of China, and even remembered his first trip to China in a poem he wrote just before his demise. In order to promote the cultural exchanges between the two ancient civilizations, Tagore always had the dream of establishing a Chinese language school at Visva-Bharati University, but it was only in 1937 that his dream was finally realized. Tagore visited Singapore in 1927, and Tan Yunshan, who was involved in Chinese teaching in Singapore, met him for the first time. Tagore invited him to teach at Visva-Bharati University to which Tan Yunshan agreed without any hesitation. In 1928, Tan Yunshan moved to Shantiniketan, and started Chinese language classes. Out of the five students in his first batch, two were professors at Visva-Bharati University, and three were research scholars.[10]55 They were Sri Probhat Kumar Mukherji, Prof. F. Benot, Sri Sujit Mukherjee, Dr. Chowdhury, and Sri Pate. Among them, Sri Probhat Kumar Mukherji was a well-known Bengali writer and the head librarian of the Visva-Bharati University library at the time. He was later assigned the task of writing the autobiography of Tagore.

Picture 3 Cheena Bhavana, Visva-Bharati University

The establishment of Sino-Indian Cultural Society in Nanjing in 1935 played an important role in promoting Chinese language education in India. For the next ten years or so, Mr. Tan Yunshan devoted himself to collecting books and raising funds. Owing to his efforts and aid from many Sino-Indian friendship envoys, the Cheena Bhavana and the Chinese Library were established in Visva-Bharati University in 1937. Cheena Bhavana trained many Chinese language talents in India, including Vasant V. Paranjpe, K. Vankataramanan, Amitendranath Tagore etc. Among them, Mr. Paranjpe served as the Indian Ambassador to China from 1955–1957.[9]73 Thanks to the efforts of Tan Yunshan, the Chinese and Indian governments agreed to establish scholarships for foreign students in 1943. In

November of the same year, ten Indian students went to study in China.[11]380 The exchange of foreign students further promoted the development of Chinese language studies in India.

In the 1930s and 1940s, Chinese language education in other universities in India, except for the Cheena Bhavana of Visva-Bharati University, progressed at a snail's pace. In the 1940's, Fergusson College located in Pune established a small center for Chinese studies. Dr. P.V. Bapat and Dr. V.V. Gokhale of the center started a comparative study of Buddhist texts in Pali, Sanskrit and Chinese.[12]10 In addition, famous Indian scholar Raghu Vira (1902–1963), was also devoted to the establishment of China-India friendly relations based on Buddhist studies. In 1932, he founded the International Academy of Indian Culture with an aim of studying the history of India-China relations. In the article "Ramayana in China" published in 1938, he studied the influence of the Indian epic *Ramayana* on Chinese culture. During 1955–1956, he also visited the Mogao Grottoes in Dunhuang, which was highly valued by Chinese and Indian academic circles and senior leaders. His son, Prof. Lokesh Chandra, later became his successor and continued to conduct research on the Dunhuang Mogao Grottoes and Sino-India relations. Today, Prof. Chandra, who is currently over 90 years old, is acknowledged as a living legend in the field of Sinology throughout the world. Also, the Indian School of International Studies established also opened the East Asian Studies Department in 1943. The director of the Department, V. P. Dutt, who had earlier pursued research on Chinese history at Stanford University and Peking University and was proficient in the Chinese language, attached great importance to the study of Chinese language in international research. The college also organized the "Asian Relations Conference" in New Delhi from March to April 1947, where many lectures in China were delivered by renowned scholars.

Although Chinese language education in India gained initial development and success before independence, it still lacked completeness and structure. India and China, colonies and semi-colonies of foreign powers respectively, carried out very little exchanges, and most scholars studying Chinese language largely focused on the Buddhist element of Sino-Indian relations. The inadequacy of teachers and study materials and the constricted academic scope constituted the restrictive factors to the development of Chinese language education in India in the first half of the 20th century. India gained independence on August 15, 1947 and the People's Republic of China was established on October 1, 1949. The two countries formally established diplomatic relations on April 1, 1950. At that time, India became the first non-socialist country to establish diplomatic relations with China. After the establishment of diplomatic relations, the relationship between the two countries has greown by leaps and bounds, and Chinese language education in India entered into a new era.

4 CHINESE LANGUAGE EDUCATION IN INDIA IN THE SECOND HALF OF THE 20TH CENTURY: GAINING FOOTHOLD AMIDST POLITICAL TENSIONS AND TURBULENCES

After the establishment of China-India Friendship Association in 1952 in Beijing and the signing of Five Principles of Peaceful Coexistence (Panchsheel Treaty) in 1954, departments of Chinese language and China studies sprang up in universities all over the country. In 1948, the School of Foreign Languages (SFL) established by the Ministry of Defense (MoD) rolled out courses in various foreign languages with Chinese language being an important part of the curriculum. In the early 1950's the National Defense Academy (NDA) located in Pune also started to offer Chinese language courses for defense and government personnel. In 1956, the Department of Buddhist Studies was established at the University of Delhi to commemorate the "2500th anniversary of the birth of Buddha". Professor P.V. Bapat served as the founding chairperson of the department.[1] This department could be considered as a predecessor to Center for Chinese Studies (later renamed as the Department of Chinese and Japanese Studies in 1969) which was established in 1964. In 1961, Banaras Hindu University in Varanasi, the ancient city of Uttar Pradesh, established the

1 Cited in: http://du.ac.in/du/index.php?page=buddhist-studies.

Department of Foreign Languages. Chinese language was among the first seven foreign language courses offered by the department. Since the late 1950s, due the border disputes with China which India had inherited from the British colonial rule, many contradictions and confrontations between the two countries erupted, which finally led 1962 India-China border war. The bilateral ties hit an all-time low and the Chinese language education in India was also deeply impacted.

After the border war in 1962, the development of Chinese language education in India got steered in a completely new direction. Due to political and strategic reasons, this discipline which traditionally focused on the history of China-India relations, Buddhism, and culture, now diversified into research around China's politics, economy, diplomacy, and military. Prof. Tan Chung, who came to India to study in 1955, inherited his father's legacy. Like his father Prof. Tan Yunshan, he also became an important figure in the field of Chinese language education in India. After obtaining a bachelor's and master's degree in India, Tan Chung began to teach Chinese at the National Defense Academy (NDA) in Pune. After being dismissed in 1963–1964, he joined Delhi University as an associate professor in the newly opened Center for Chinese Studies.[13]8 This center later added Japanese and Korean language curriculum, and is currently known as the "Department of East Asian Studies". Although the relationship between India and China faced an unprecedented low in the 1960s and 1980s, the Indian government's attention to higher education and the establishment of many prestigious universities drove the growth of Chinese language education in India during this period.

5 CHINESE LANGUAGE EDUCATION IN CONTEMPORARY INDIA: THE SYSTEMATIZATION OF THE DISCIPLINE AND INDIA'S "MANDARIN WAVE"

In order to realize India's dream of becoming a remarkable world power, the Indian government attached great importance to national higher education since the 1960s. The establishment of Jawaharlal Nehru University in 1969 gave a great impetus to higher education in India. This university was established to inculcate noble ideas in mind and provide accessibility to education to students from weaker sections of society. Since its emancipation, the majors of international relations and language and literature have been the flagship majors of the university. One of the earliest established schools of the university, the School of International Studies (SIS) had started the Centre for East Asian Studies (CEAS), which focuses on the political, economic and diplomatic fields of China and other East Asian countries. In addition to this, the School of Language, Literature and Culture Studies (SLL & CS) started the Chinese language programme under the Centre for Afro-Asian Languages in 1973.[1] Subsequently with the increase in demand for the East Asian languages, the Centre for East Asian Languages (CEAL) was established in the 1980s, and finally the Centre for Chinese and South East Asian Studies (CCSEAS) in 1996. Mr. Haraprasad Ray was one of the teachers of Chinese language in Jawaharlal Nehru University during the early days. In 1978, Prof. Tan Chung came to Jawaharlal Nehru University from Delhi University and began to train the Chinese language talents at the university.

In 1978, the then Foreign Minister of India, Sri Atal Bihari Vajpayee visited China which paved way for the normalization of India-China relations. Since the beginning of the 1980s, the two countries have resumed academic exchanges. During this period, the first batch of Chinese language talents started to appear in Jawaharlal Nehru University, amongst which Prof. Priyadarsi Mukherji, Prof. Bali Ram Deepak, Prof. Sabaree Mitra and Prof. Manik Bhattacharya have become living legends in the field of Chinese teaching in India. Prof. Deepak and Prof. Mukherji also won the prestigious Special Book Award of China in 2011 and 2014 respectively. Prof. Priyadarsi Mukherji is the grandson of Sri Probhat Kumar Mukherji, one of Prof. Tan Yunshan's first students at the Cheena Bhavana of Visva-Bharati University. He began to learn Chinese and read Chinese literature from a very young age. After Indian Prime Minister Rajiv Gandhi visited China in 1988, India-China relations developed by leaps and bounds. The two countries began a large number of student exchange programs, focusing on learning each other's language and culture. The establishment of the Institute of

1 Cited in: https://www.jnu.ac.in/sllcs/cc%26seas.

Chinese Studies (ICS) in New Delhi in 1990 expanded the field of Chinese studies in India. In a sense, the institute is the first think tank in India that specializes in Chinese issues. Its publication *China Report* is already an authoritative journal in the field of social sciences and international relations.

The period 1991–1992 was equally important to the economic development of China and India. The opening of the Indian economy and Deng Xiaoping's southern tour became the main driving forces of the economic development of the two countries. Chinese language education in India which then focused on diplomacy, strategy and military affairs, found a new direction of development. Chinese teaching in universities across India also evolved with the times. Apart from Jawaharlal Nehru University, Chinese teaching and research of Prof. A. Nayak, Prof. Reena Ganguli and Prof. Avijit Banerjee from Cheena Bhavana of Visva-Bharati University, Prof. Anita Sharma from the Department of East Asian Studies of University of Delhi, and Professor Kamal Sheel from the Banaras Hindu University in Varanasi also achieved accords and success.

China's growing economic strength, the increase of bilateral trade, and the increasing number of Chinese tourists to India led to the first "Mandarin wave" in India in the late 1990s. After China joined the World Trade Organization in 2001, leading Chinese companies such as Huawei, Haier, and ZTE successively entered the Indian market and started recruiting Chinese language talents. In 2005, Premier Wen Jiabao visited India and the two countries announced the establishment of "Strategic and Cooperative Partnership for Peace and Prosperity".[1] In 2006, President Hu Jintao visited India. In a series of memorandums signed between the two countries, education and cultural exchanges and cooperation became important parts. In the same year, India and China started an annual "Youth Representative Exchange Program". In 2009, the Vellore Institute of Technology in southern India signed an agreement with Zhengzhou University of China and established India's first Confucius Institute. Over the past few years, the institute has contributed to the development of

1 Cited in: https://www.indiatoday.in/magazine/diplomacy/story/20050425-chinese-premier-wen-jiabao-visit-paves-way-for-sino-indian-strategic-partnership-787893-2005-04-25.

Chinese language teaching in South India and has also organized HSK (Hanyu Shuiping Kaoshi) exams for Chinese language students. In the same year, India's higher education policy underwent fundamental reforms. Through the Central University Act of 2009, the central government established 20 new central universities across India, out of which at least three universities have opened Chinese language departments. Among the newly built universities, the Central University of Gujrat (CUG) and the Central University of Jharkhand (CUJ) are located in second- and third-tier cities, respectively. In 2010, Doon University in Uttarakhand, also started degree courses in Chinese language. The opening of Chinese language teaching in these universities has largely broken the phenomenon of Chinese teaching being centered in large cities in India and provided poor students from underdeveloped areas with an opportunity to learn Chinese language.

In recent years, with the easing of relations between the two countries and the efforts of the governments and relevant departments, Chinese language education in India has become a household name. In 2011, the Central Board of Secondary Education (CBSE) in India included Chinese as a foreign language in secondary school curriculum, and the two countries jointly announced that 2011 will be the year of China-India Friendly Exchanges. The establishment of India's second Confucius Institute in Mumbai, the economic center of India in 2013, further promoted the spread of Chinese language and culture in western India. Taking advantage of the "Mandarin wave" in India, many private universities have also started offering Chinese language courses. Among them, the achievements of K.R. Mangalam University, O. P. Jindal Global University and Lovely Professional University in the field of Chinese language education have been recognized and accorded by the academia. In recent years, the number of private institutions providing Chinese language training in big cities in India has also increased, and many of them are run by native Chinese people.

The current situation of Chinese language education in India is slown as Table 1.

Table 1 Universities in India which set up Chinese courses*

Serial No.	Name of University/ Institution	Category	Location	Degree/ Course Offered	Study Materials
01	Jawaharlal Nehru University	Central University	New Delhi	B.A., M.A., M.Phil., PhD	B.A.: *Elementary Chinese Reader* (1–4) (Sinolingua Press); *Chinese Bridge* (Vol.1,2) (BLCU Press); *Spoken Chinese Course* (BLCU Press); *Modern Advanced Chinese Course* (BLCU Press); *Speaking Chinese-About China* (Sinolingua Press); *A Guide To Chinese Essay Writing* (Peking University Press); *Developing Chinese* (BLCU Press); *Talking About China* M.A.: *History of Chinese Literature* (GBD Publications); Chinese newspapers/news clips; Chinese classic novels; introduction to Chinese; Overview of Chinese politics
02	University of Delhi	Central University	New Delhi	Diploma; Certificate	*Elementary Chinese Reader* (1–4) (Sinolingua Press); *Speaking Chinese—About* China (Sinolingua Press)
03	Visva-Bharati University	Central University	Santiniketan	B.A., M.A., PhD	B.A.: *Practical Chinese Reader Elementary* (BLCU Press); *Chinese Grammar for Foreigners* (Sinolingua Press); *Guided Reading in Journalistic Chinese* (BLCU Press); *Dictionary of Tang Poetry Appreciation* (Chongwen Publishing House); *Overview of China* (Peking University Press) M.A.: *Selected Works of Modern China* (Foreign Languages Press); *Literature and Art* (Foreign Language Press); *History of the People's Republic of China* (Beijing Institute of Technology Press)

To be continued

Continued

Serial No.	Name of University/ Institution	Category	Location	Degree/ Course Offered	Study Materials
04	Banaras Hindu University	Central University	Varanasi	Diploma; M.A., PhD	Diploma: *Elementary Chinese Reader* (Sinolingua Press); M.A.: *Advanced Chinese Course* (BLCU Press); *Selected Works of Modern China 1919—1949* (Foreign Languages Press); *Selected New Works of Chinese Literature* (BLCU Press); *The Complete Works of Lu Xun* (People's Literature Publishing House)
05	Aligarh Muslim University	Central University	Aligarh	B.A., M.A.	B.A.: *Elementary Chinese Reader* (1-4) (Sinolingua Press); *Speaking Chinese—About China* (Sinolingua Press); *Modern Advanced Chinese Course* (Vol. 1, 2) (BLCU Press); *A Guide To Chinese Essay Writing* (Peking University Press) M.A.: *History of Modern Chinese Literature*; *Advanced Interpretation Course*; *The Complete Works of Ji Xianlin*; *History of Chinese Literature* (GBD Publications); *Selected Works of Ancient Chinese Literature*; *Business Practical Chinese*
06	University of Calcutta	Central University	Kolkata	Diploma; Certificate	*Elementary Chinese Reader* (1-4) (Sinolingua Press)

To be continued

Continued

Serial No.	Name of University/ Institution	Category	Location	Degree/ Course Offered	Study Materials
07	Central University of Gujarat	Central University	Gandhinagar	B.A., M.A.	B.A.: *Elementary Chinese Reader* (1–4) (Sinolingua Press); *Elementary Chinese Reading and Writing*; *Business Chinese*; *Read About China*; *Appreciation of Chinese Idioms and Phrases*; *Introduction to Chinese Literature* M.A.: *Modern Chinese Literature*; *Theories and Practice of Translation*; *Advanced Conversational Chinese*; *Selected Chinese Novels*; *Guided Reading in Journalistic Chinese* (BLCU Press)
08	Central University of Jharkhand	Central University	Ranchi	Diploma; Certificate; B.A., M.A.	*Elementary Chinese Reader* (1–4) (Sinolingua Press); *Speaking Chinese—About China* (Sinolingua Press); *Overview of China*
09	Jamia Millia Islamia	Central University	New Delhi	Diploma; Certificate	*Practical Audio-Visual Chinese* (Cheng Chung Book); *Far East Everyday Chinese* (The Far East Book Co. Ltd.); *Elementary Chinese Reader* (1–4) (Sinolingua Press)
10	Sikkim University	Central University	Gangtok	B.A., M.A.	B.A.: *Elementary Chinese Reader* (1–4) (Sinolingua Press); *Chinese For Beginners* (BLCU Press); *New Practical Chinese Reader* (BLCU Press); *Conversational Chinese 301* (BLCU Press); *Boya Chinese* (Peking University Press); *Bridge: A Practical Intermediate Chinese Course* (BLCU Press)

To be continued

Continued

Serial No.	Name of University/ Institution	Category	Location	Degree/ Course Offered	Study Materials
					M.A.: *The History of Ancient Chinese Literature* (BNU Press); *History of Chinese Literature* (GBD Publications); *Guided Reading in Journalistic Chinese* (BLCU Press); *Advanced Chinese Listening Course* (Peking University Press); Classic Chinese Novels
11	University of Mumbai (Confucius Institute)	Central University	Mumbai	Diploma; Certificate	*Elementary Chinese Reader* (1–4) (Sinolingua Press); *HSK Standard Course* (BLCU Press)
12	Tezpur University	Central University	Tezpur	Certificate	*Elementary Chinese Reader* (1–4) (Sinolingua Press)
13	English and Foreign Languages University	Central University	Hyderabad	Diploma; Certificate	*Developing Chinese* (BLCU Press); *Elementary Chinese Reader* (1–4) (Sinolingua Press)
14	Bengaluru Central University	Central University	Bengaluru	Diploma; Certificate	*Elementary Chinese Reader* (1–4) (Sinolingua Press)
15	Indira Gandhi National Open University	Central University	New Delhi	Diploma; Certificate	*Elementary Chinese Reader* (1–4) (Sinolingua Press)
16	IIT Madras China Studies Centre	Public University	Chennai	Diploma; Certificate	China in Contemporary Global Politics; State, Politics and Foreign Policy in China; Introduction to Chinese Language; etc.

To be continued

Continued

Serial No.	Name of University/ Institution	Category	Location	Degree/ Course Offered	Study Materials
17	IIT Bhilai Chinese Language Training Centre	Public University	Bhilai	Elective Course	Chinese for Beginners; Chinese Culture; Chinese Writing; Chinese Calligraphy
18	IIT Bombay	Public University	Mumbai	Elective Course	Chinese Communication Course; Chinese Advance Course
19	IIM Bangalore	Public University	Bangalore	Elective Course	Business Chinese
20	Nava Nalanda Mahavihara	Deemed University	Nalanada	Diploma	*Elementary Chinese Reader* (1–4) (Sinolingua Press)
21	Manipur University	Central University	Imphal	Certificate	*Elementary Chinese Reader* (1–4) (Sinolingua Press)
22	Mahatma Gandhi Antarra-shtriya Hindi Vishwavi-dyalaya	Central University	Wardha	Advanced Diploma; Diploma; Certificate	*Elementary Chinese Reader* (1–4) (Sinolingua Press)
23	Doon University	State University	Dehradun	B.A., M.A.	B.A.: *Elementary Chinese Reader* (1–4) (Sinolingua Press); *Introduction to Chinese Culture*; *Newspaper Chinese* M.A.: Introduction to Geography of China; Introduction to Classical Chinese; History of Modern Chinese Literature; History of Ancient Chinese Literature
24	Panjab University	State University	Chandigarh	Diploma; Certificate	*Elementary Chinese Reader* (1–4) (Sinolingua Press)

To be continued

Continued

Serial No.	Name of University/ Institution	Category	Location	Degree/ Course Offered	Study Materials
25	University of Mysore	State University	Mysore	Diploma; Certificate	*Elementary Chinese Reader* (1–4) (Sinolingua Press); *Elementary Chinese Textbook* (BLCU Press)
26	Sanchi University of Buddhist-Indic Studies	State University	Sanchi	M.A.; Diploma; Certificate	*Elementary Chinese Reader* (1–4) (Sinolingua Press)
27	Pondicherry University	State University	Pondicherry	Certificate	*Elementary Chinese Reader* (1–4) (Sinolingua Press)
28	Dr. Babasaheb Ambedkar Marathwada University	State University	Aurangabad	Advanced Diploma; Diploma; Certificate	*Elementary Chinese Reader* (1–4) (Sinolingua Press)
29	Jadavpur University	State University	Kolkata	Certificate	*Elementary Chinese Reader* (1–4) (Sinolingua Press)
30	Magadh University	State University	Bodh Gaya	Diploma; Certificate	*Elementary Chinese Reader* (1–4) (Sinolingua Press)
31	Maharshi Dayanand University	State University	Rohtak	Diploma; Certificate	*Elementary Chinese Reader* (1–4) (Sinolingua Press)
32	I. K. Gujral Punjab Technical University	State University	Kapurthala	Certificate	*Elementary Chinese Reader* (1–4) (Sinolingua Press)
33	University of Kalyani	State University	Kalyani	Diploma; Certificate	*Elementary Chinese Reader* (1–4) (Sinolingua Press)
34	School of Foreign Languages	Government Institute	New Delhi	Diploma; Certificate	*Elementary Chinese Reader* (1–4) (Sinolingua Press)

To be continued

Continued

Serial No.	Name of University/ Institution	Category	Location	Degree/ Course Offered	Study Materials
35	National Defence Academy	Government Institute	Pune	Diploma; Certificate	*Elementary Chinese Reader* (1–4) (Sinolingua Press)
36	Bhartiya Vidya Bhavan	Educational Trust	New Delhi	Diploma; Certificate	*Elementary Chinese Reader* (1–4) (Sinolingua Press)
37	YMCA-Institute for Career Studies	Educational Trust	New Delhi	Diploma; Certificate	*Elementary Chinese Reader* (1–4) (Sinolingua Press)
38	K. R. Mangalam University	Private University	Gurugram	B.A.	*Elementary Chinese Reader* (1–4) (Sinolingua Press)
39	O.P. Jindal Global University	Private University	Sonipat	Diploma; Certificate	/
40	Lovely Professional University	Private University	Phagwara	Open Minor; Certificate	*Standard HSK 1 Course* (BLCU Press)
41	Amity University	Private University	Noida	Diploma; Certificate	*Elementary Chinese Reader* (1–4) (Sinolingua Press)
42	Vellore Institute of Technology (Confucius Institute)	Private University	Vellore	Diploma; Certificate	*Standard HSK/Course* (BLCU Press)
43	Ashoka University	Private University	Sonipat	Certificate	Mandarin Language Teaching Program
44	SRM Institute of Science and Technology	Private University	Chennai	Certificate	/

* The above information was collected through the official websites of the institutions.

6 CONCLUSION: THE PROSPECTS AND SUGGESTIONS FOR CHINESE LANGUAGE EDUCATION IN INDIA

Chinese language education in India has experienced a hundred years of ups and downs. So far, it has achieved considerable achievements and development and has become a popular discipline. With the increasingly close economic and trade relations and cultural exchanges between China and India, and the emergence of Chinese language course in educational institutions in India, the number of students studying the language has also gradually soared up. According to the statistics of the Educational Section of the Chinese Embassy in India, there are currently more than 20,000 students majoring in Chinese in India, and about 2,000 of them are studying Chinese in universities. As mentioned earlier, Jawaharlal Nehru University, University of Delhi and the Visva-Bharati University have always been the core of Chinese language education and research in India. Since these universities have ample faculties and frequent cooperation and exchanges with famous Chinese universities, hence these three universities have always been the first preference for students majoring in Chinese language and literature. Although in the past few years, the phenomenon of Chinese language education in India being centered in New Delhi and West Bengal has changed, the popularity of Chinese language in various parts of India, especially in second and third tier cities, is still not high. The friction between China and India on the border in the past two years has affected the stability of bilateral relations. The two informal summits between the two countries in 2018 and 2019 have also expressed that both sides hope to resolve their misunderstandings and border issues through dialogue channels. The gradual increase in trade volume between China and India also shows that seeking common ground while reserving differences is a characteristic of the relationship between the two countries. The spread of the novel coronavirus in 2020 has had a greater impact on higher education all over the world, and Chinese language education in India has suffered a double-hit of border disputes and the pandemic. Under this world order, Chinese language education in India faces new challenges and opportunities.

6.1 IMPROVING THE RESEARCH STANDARDS OF CHINESE LANGUAGE EDUCATION IN INDIA

The students studying Chinese language in Indian universities come from all parts of India, their family backgrounds and the purpose of language learning are also different. Some students belong to corporate families, for the convenience of doing business with China and the future advantages, their parents make them learn Chinese. Most students come from humble family backgrounds; they consider that it is easy to find a job after learning Chinese. Many Chinese enterprises in India have set up their base at New Delhi and surrounding development zones like Gurgaon and Noida. In recent years, large Chinese companies such as Huawei, ZTE, Xiaomi, OPPO, VIVO, Lenovo, Byte dance, China Airlines and others have set up offices in the New Delhi Capital Region, and the graduates of Chinese language majors can easily get a monthly salary of 40,000 to 50,000 rupees working in these firms. Business delegations from China visiting India also hire part-time translators fluent in Chinese, English and Hindi. Hence, many students also choose careers like freelance interpretation and translation. Chinese is undoubtedly the most popular language among the foreign languages of freelance translators/interpreters in India, and a freelance translator/interpreter can easily earn up to one hundred dollars a day. In addition, the number of Chinese tourists and tourist groups visiting India has rapidly increased in the past decade. According to relevant data, there are about 350,000 Chinese tourists visiting India every year. Many students studying Chinese also work as tour guides.

For the above reasons, in the current Chinese language education in India, 'money' has become the biggest motivation factor for students, and students lured by quick money often tend give up on the courses halfway. The pillar of Chinese language education in India, Jawaharlal Nehru University currently has 110 students enrolled in undergraduate courses, while only 66 students are enrolled in masters or higher degrees. The number of students pursuing masters or higher degree in the Chinese departments of other universities is even fewer. Many experts on China issues in India cannot understand Chinese at all, nor can they use first-hand materials to study China. Therefore, whether it is cooperation or confrontation, in-depth study and research of Chinese language should become an indispensable part of India's China policy.

6.2 TRAINING INDIAN CHINESE LANGUAGE TEACHERS AND LOCALIZING TEACHING MATERIALS

There are more than 60 permanent teachers engaged in Chinese teaching in the 44 Indian universities listed above. Among them, Centre for Chinese and South East Asian Studies of Jawaharlal Nehru University (11 faculties), Cheena Bhavana of Visva-Bharati University (6 faculties) and the newly built Gujarat Central University (4 faculties) have the highest number of faculties, and other universities and institutions generally have meagre faculty strength. In the National Eligibility Test (NET) organized by the University Grants Commission (UGC) of India every year, merely 6-8 candidates pass the Chinese teaching major. Among those who pass this exam, even fewer students undertake research in Chinese language or engage in Chinese language teaching. In addition, there is basically no "teacher training" course in Chinese language departments in Indian universities. Although students fulfill the basic academic requirements, they often lack teaching skills and have an unclear overall understanding of the profession, so sometimes teaching becomes monotonous and boring. In this regard, Indian universities can learn from China. Chinese universities train native teachers for teaching Chinese language through a course called "Teaching Chinese as a Foreign Language" (TCFL), which is specially taught in normal (teacher training) universities across China. Since it would be Indian nationals teaching Chinese language TCFL an not be exactly replicated in India but lessons can be drawn from it.

The Chinese language textbooks in most universities in India are outdated, and the vocabulary and details described in these books are basically from the Chinese society in the 1980s and 1990s. Relevant research materials and databases are also severely outdated and scanty. In addition, India has a wide variety of languages. Many students officially start to use English only after entering the university. Usually, the Chinese textbooks and the teaching in the universities are bilingually conducted in Chinese and English. Due to the language barrier, students are some times unable to comprehend the content of the class and their learning base is not solid. This gap can be filled by restructuring the textbooks. Universities and publishers can consider using Indic languages such as Hindi, Bengali, Tamil, Marathi, Kannada etc., to design textbooks and contents. Such bilingual textbooks would be able to not only impart knowledge about China to the students, but also compare China with India using Chinese. This will not only enhance student's interest in learning Chinese, but also help students to understand the similarities between Chinese and Indian cultures.

6.3 DEVELOPING ONLINE EDUCATION COOPERATION WITH CHINESE UNIVERSITIES AND CHINESE LANGUAGE TRAINING INSTITUTIONS

The spread of the novel coronavirus has brought unprecedented challenges to higher education worldwide. Although universities and educational institutions across India have launched online classrooms, most of them are encountering various problems. Chinese language education in India also faces problems such as lack of infrastructure, lack of interest among students, and ineptness of online classrooms. Teaching Chinese is different from teaching other traditional courses, especially while teaching students who are just starting to learn Chinese language. Teachers need to constantly correct the students' pronunciation, intonations and tones. The most popular meeting software in India such as Zoom and Google Meet cannot effectively meet this requirement. According to relevant data, India currently has 560 million Internet users. With the growth of smartphones and Internet usage in the second and third tier cities in India, the demand for online education in India is bound to increase. Universities and institutions offering Chinese language programs in India can try to design apps and online courses to teach Chinese. In this regard, they can also consider cooperating with Chinese universities and institutions with relevant experience. This will not only save time and capital, but also overcome physical and infrastructural hindrances.

6.4 RETURNING TO THE CULTURAL ESSENCE OF CHINA-INDIA EXCHANGES

Just as the Chinese saying goes "a tree may grow a thousand meters high, but its leaves always return back to its roots", the "root" between India and China is the cultural and people-to-people exchanges between the two countries that have been taking place for thousands of years. These two ancient civilizations share the same philosophical concepts of "world as one big family", "mutual learning", and "harmony without difference". There is a close relationship between language and culture. Only by fully understanding the culture related to a language can one truly learn a language. While studying business, translation, economics, politics and other such courses, students who learn Chinese language also need to master Chinese food customs, greeting etiquette, and speaking skills.

Translation has played an important role in Sino-Indian cultural and people-to-people exchanges. The translation work of great figures such as Faxian, Xuanzang, Kumarajiva, and Yijing not only promoted mutual understanding and trust between the two peoples, but also became the main reference material for understanding the history of the time. Such translation work is very rare in contemporary Sino-Indian cultural exchanges. Apart from the translation of Indian epics *Ramayana*, *Mahabharata* and *Panchatantra by* Prof. Ji Xianlin, the Indian literary works by Prof. Jin Kemu, *Sur Sagar* by Prof. Jiang Jingkui, *Poems of Lu Xun*, *Contemporary Chinese Poems*, *Poems and Fables of Ai Qing* and other books by Prof. Priyadarsi Mukherji and *Analects*, *Four Books*, *Book of Songs* and other books by Prof. B.R. Deepak, there are very few other authors and translations directly translating in Chinese and Hindi or other Indic languages. In 2013, China and India's national authorities signed an MOU of China-India Translation Project. Under this project, each country will translate 25 titles of the other's ancient classics and contemporary literature.[14]68 The progress of translation work between China and India will not only help attract Indian readers' interest in Chinese culture, but also enable students who are

Studying Chinese to better understand and study Chinese culture, history and literature.

（Proof read by Chen Bingrui）

REFERENCES

[1] GEOFF W. The polity of yelang and the origins of the name "China" [J]. Sino-platonic papers, 2009, 188:1-26.

[2] MUKHERJI P. The overland and maritime silk routes in the perspective of Imperial China's geopolitical strategy and its role as a catalyst for a Sino-Indian cultural amalgamation [C] // SELVAM A G, DESAI A K. Seminar compendium on "India and South-East Asia: maritime trade, expeditions and civilizational linkages". Ezhimala: Indian Naval Academy, 2017.

[3] CUTTS E H. Chinese studies in Bengal [J]. Journal of the American oriental society, 1942, 62(3):171-174.

[4] 狄伯杰. 当代印度的中国文学译介——问题与挑战 [J]. 郝岚，王宏健，译 . 东方丛刊 , 2018（2）：59-70.

[5] KITSON P J. Forging romantic China: Sino-British cultural exchange 1760—1840 [M]. New York: Cambridge University Press, 2013.

[6] 郁龙余. 中国学在印度 [J]. 学术研究 , 2000（1）：120-123.

[7] MANJAPRA K.Age of entanglement: German and Indian intellectuals across Empire [M]. Cambridge, MA: Harvard University Press, 2014.

[8] 章立明，周东亮. 印度汉语教学的百年流变及前景展望（1918—2018）[J]. 国外社会科学，2019（4）：71-78.

[9] 林立. 泰戈尔与印度国际大学中国学院的建立 [J]. 史学月刊，1994（5）：73-79.

[10] 谭云山. 印度之汉学 [J]. 赵波，译 . 图书月刊，1941，1（7-8）：54-81.

[11] 郁龙余，刘朝华. 中外文学交流史：中国—印度卷 [M]. 济南：山东教育出版社，2015.

[12] 雷易. 印度的中国学研究概览 [J]. 蔡晶，译 . 深圳大学学报，2010，27（6）：10-14.

[13] 郁龙余，刘朝华. 湘贤翘楚：谭云山、谭中父子 [J]. 书屋，2019（10）：4-9.

[14] 狄伯杰. 印度对中国经典著作的翻译 [J]. 文化软实力，2013（3）：66-68.

The Story of Chinese Language and Its Phases of Development in India in Past One Decade

Usha Sahoo[1] *Rasika Prabhakar Pavaskar*[2]

Abstract We live in a highly globalized world today, where people and enterprises are constantly seeking to diversify their business and skill sets. Being multi-lingual is considered a major asset in such matters. And with China becoming a place of keen interest, both from a business and tourism point of view, learning Mandarin is a natural choice for a lot of Indians. And with growing business ties between India and China Education, professionals and youth seem to be keen to learn the language. To the backdrop of such a dynamic market condition operates Yeh China, India's first and largest private language institute that imparts Chinese language training to Indians. Each year, the organization enrolls hundreds of Mandarin language learners from toddlers to corporate head honchos. Begun in 2010, Yeh China Education always focused for creating awareness about rich culture of China and its language. The institute has its goals to reach more and more students through good customized curriculum, digital learning and HSK and YCT certification. The major challenge is to cater people from different parts of India with different mother tongue. This research which is mostly collected the data and interviews of teachers teaching Chinese and simplifying the language to Indian people by integrating the curriculum with our local languages.

1 Director of Yeh China Education.
2 Postgoaduate student for BTCSOL degree of Zhengzhou University, China.

Key Words Chinese language; Indian languages; Hindi; Phonetic system

After the industrial revolution, trade between countries all over the world started increasing gradually. As the international trade and exchanges of goods went on increasing, companies from outside the countries started bringing their business into the countries they were importing and exporting goods from. As foreign companies started increasing their business in the country, the need for local employees and foreign employees to work together started increasing. As these employees started working together the problem of understanding each other's language started occurring gradually. To overcome this problem, people came up with the idea to learn the foreign languages for better communication. And that's how Chinese language was introduced in India. In the beginning, people were scared to select Chinese language as third language because of its script. Chinese language is a pictorial language that makes it difficult to read and write whereas Indic languages as compared to Chinese language are their easy to read and write. But slowly and gradually people started to show more and more interest in Chinese language and the number of people studying and learning Chinese language increased day by day. Some Indians only studied till basics just to be able to understand the language, while a few did not stop when they were able to understand the Chinese people speaking. They went even further to study the language to such a depth to be able to teach the language to other Indians who are interested in learning the language but are not able to do so either because they are not able to speak and understand the teacher speaking English or they are not able to find a teacher at all. At the very first, teachers who appeared and passed the HSK exams took upon themselves to teach the interested students. Then slowly and gradually coaching classes started introducing Chinese language as one of the languages being taught in their institutes. Soon after coaching classes teaching only Chinese language were established. As the time went by more and more coaching institutes and colleges started introducing Chinese language as a part of their curriculum. Slowly Chinese language was also introduced in schools as a third language option in their curriculum. Teachers with HSK level 3 and higher were given the chance to teach level one of Chinese language and higher according to the level of the teacher. For the teachers teaching in private coaching classes, clearing HSK level 3 and above was the bar set to be able to teach Chinese language, whereas for teachers wanting to teach in universities or school, the degree in teaching was necessary to be able to teach in schools and colleges. Slowly and gradually, the demand to learn Chinese language went on increasing and more and more teachers were born. Soon after, interested students and teachers started applying for scholarships to go to China to study the language in more depth. Some who couldn't spend much time out of the country selected the one-year language course, while some went for the one semester language course. Similarly, there were some who selected the degree courses in teaching Chinese language to students of other language. Soon after Confucius Institute (now renamed as Center for Language Education and Cooperation) started collaborating with different colleges and institutes in India, thus giving out more scholarship opportunities to the aspiring Chinese teachers of India. Later on, the teachers who came back from China with a degree in teaching Chinese language were also appointed as teachers to teach in schools and colleges. After coming back to India, these trained teachers used all their knowledge gained during their training, to teach language to students here in India thus creating more Chinese language experts in the country.

Teachers use comparisons between Chinese language and Indian languages while teaching Chinese language; to make the understanding of the language easier; especially with Hindi and Marathi languages. The comparison with Indian languages while teaching the initials and finals allows students be able to understand the pronunciation of initials and finals more clearly as the pronunciations of initials and finals in the *pinyin* system of Chinese language are similar to the pronunciations of alphabets in Indian languages Hindi and Marathi. Using the similarities in the pronunciations of Chinese language and Indian languages, the initials and finals in Chinese language can be associated with the alphabets in Indian languages having the same pronunciations as the initials and the finals in Chinese language. This can be used to produce a chart containing the initials and finals in *pinyin* of Chinese language along with their pronunciations in Indian language; thus making the pronunciations of initials and finals easier to understand and remember. Similarly, taking the advantage of the same, while teaching kids, the pronunciation of words being thought to the kids can be written in Indian languages, allowing the parents of the kids to be able to read the words and thus help their kids in practicing and revising the words at home even without learning the language. For example, the word " 妈妈 " is written as "मामा" for the parents to be able to read the word and help their kids practice the same at home. Along with the similarity in pronunciation of the initials and finals, the similarity of using different tones while speaking is also seen in Indian languages and Chinese language. Chinese language has four major tones and one neutral tone, whereas Indian language has only two. The tones in Chinese language are shown while writing the *pinyin* but are not there while writing the Chinese script, whereas in Indian languages the tones are included while writing the Indian script. Besides the tones, there are also similar words in both Chinese language and Indian languages, that are pronounced the same with the same meaning. For example: " 茶 " in Chinese language and in Indian language have the same pronounciation and meaning.

As there as similarities in the language, dissimilarities in them also exist. The grammatical structure of sentences in Chinese language and Indian languages is different. The grammatical structure of sentences in Chinese language is similar to that of English; that is, subject-verb-object. For example, in Chinese language, " 他吃饭了 ", " 他 " is the subject which means "he", " 吃 " is verb which means "to eat", " 饭 " is object which means "food". Similarly, in the sentence " 她买面包 ", " 她 " is the subject, " 买 " is the verb and " 面包 " is the object. However, the grammatical structure for sentences in Indian languages is subject-object-verb. For example, in Indian language, "उसने खाना खाया", "उसने" is the subject which means "he", "खाना" is the object which means "food" and "खाया" is the verb which means "ate". Similarly, in the sentence "वो बाजार गयी" ; "वो" is the subject, "बाजार" is the object and "गयी" is the verb. Not only this, there are many other dissimilarities between Chinese language and Indian languages. For instance, in Chinese language, while writing the sentence; the structure of the words in the sentence does not change. The action, the tense, the doer or the gender of the doer do not have any effect on the words in the sentence. For example, in Chinese language, consider the sentences " 他吃饭了 " and " 她吃饭 " , the first sentence tells us that "he ate food"; the sentence is in the past tense which means the action is already done. In the second sentence, " 她吃饭 " is in simple present tense which tells us "she eats". In both sentences the action remains the same, i.e., to eat; however, the tense of the action and the gender of the doer in both the sentences is different. But this does not affect the verb form in the sentence. In both the sentences, despite of the tense and the gender being different, the action being done shows no changes in its form, it remains the same in both the sentences, i.e., " 吃 ". However, in Indian languages, the form of the word changes according to the tense and the gender of the subject. For instance, in Indian languages, consider the sentences above "वो बाहर गयी थी " and "वो बाहर जाएगा". The first sentence is in past tense which tells us "she went out"; whereas the second sentence is in future tense which tells us that "he will go out". In both sentences, the action being done is same, i.e., "जाना"; however, the verb form in both the sentences changes according to the gender and tense. Moreover, in Chinese language while using the third person pronoun, the pronunciation and the *pinyin* of the third person pronoun is same for "he", "she" and "it"; however, the characters for all three are different. In addition, the third person pronoun does not show any changes in itself in accordance to the difference of tenses and other things in the sentence. On the other hand, in Indian languages, the third person pronouns "he", "she" and "it" are pronounced and written the same. However, the gender of the subject can be identified based on the changes in the verb. In addition to this, the pronoun for the third gender changes its form along with the verb according to the changes in the tense. The same is applied to most of the other Indian languages.

India is a large multilingual country. Each and every state of India has its own different state language. With so many different languages in India, not every person is able to speak and understand English. For many people the medium

Yeh China | Easy Pinyin-alphabet chart | Skill Live

A	B	C	CH	D	E	F	G
आ Aa	प pa	त्स ts	छ chha	त ta	अ a	फ pha	क Ka
H	I	J	K	L	M	N	O
ह Ha	इ e	ची chi	ख kha	ल la	म ma	न na	ओ o
P	Q	R	S	SH	T	U	Ü
फ pha	छी chhi	र ra	स sa	श sha	थ tha	उ yu	इउ yuh
W	X	Y	Z	ZH			
व va	षी shi	य ya	च ch	च् chh			

Picture 1 Consists of the finals and initials of *pinyin* in Hindi

of the speaking and understanding things is Hindi, Marathi, Gujrati, Punjabi and other different languages spoken in India. The challenge is to simplify the Chinese language and make people understand it easily to attract more and more students. With the general fear of Chinese being one of the most difficult language in the world, students generally choose European languages over Chinese. Therefore, the need to find a way to connect with them while teaching Chinese language arose. The biggest challenge came over when the businessmen, people of different fields, and students of different categories started learning the Chinese language. Not all of the people wanting to study Chinese language was comfortable with the usage of the English language as a medium of studying the Chinese language. That is why the usage Indian languages as a reference while teaching Chinese language became an important part of teaching methods that teachers use while teaching the Chinese language. Hence, the development of Chinese language curriculum for Indians included the comparisons and the references with the Indian languages in the part of teaching the Chinese language. Around more than fifty freelancing teachers teaching Chinese language and the owners and heads of different institutes teaching Chinese language were interviewed. The question asked to them during the interview was, "whether they use references to Hindi or other Indian local languages used while teaching the Chinese language?" The responses of the teachers and the institute owners and heads put a new light on the usage of references to Indian local languages while teaching Chinese language. After the interviews, it was found that more than 99 percent of the teachers and the institute owners and heads use references to the local Indian languages while teaching the Chinese language. The director of the Oriental Dialogue, Aditi Wadnerkar said, "I use Devanagari script while teaching Chinese." Prajakta Sharma, the Director of the Adroit Institute, Pune said, "I use Hindi and Marathi while teaching." Yashodhara Gadgil, the Proprietor of the Yin Yang Centre for Chinese language in her interview said, "The grammar part or you can say language 'का लहेजा' (the tone of the language) is very close to Hindi or Marathi except subject-verb-object format. So sometimes I use Marathi or Hindi."

Picture 2　Illustration of "奶奶" and "妈妈" in Hindi and English with Picture

In addition to the interviews of the teachers and the owners and heads of the different institutes, students studying Chinese language were also interviewed. They were questioned about their views on the usage of references to the Indian local languages while learning the Chinese language. Amongst the students that were interviewed, most of the students found it extremely comfortable and easy to understand the language if the local Indian languages were used as a reference while teaching the Chinese language. Many students found that the Chinese language and the grammar was easy to understand and remember if correlated with the local Indian languages. Miss Sumedha Adhalrao, a third-year student, studying the bachelor's degree in Chinese language from Mumbai University when asked the question replied, "I found that the usage of local Indian languages proved to be very useful while learning Chinese language. Local Indian languages like Hindi, Marathi makes it easier for us to understand the difficult vowels and pronunciations of Chinese *pinyin* system like z, c, s, zh, ch, sh, etc. Also, the comparisons between the Chinese language and the Indian language grammar patterns makes it easier to understand and remember the Chinese grammar patterns."

The conclusion of this research is to simplify the language to help more learners in India increase the spead of the language acquisition in India. The hope is to develop more content as per the learning speed of Indian people with collaboration with Chinese and Indian expert teachers.

过去十年印度的汉语教学史及其发展历程

伍　莎[1]　潘雅茜[2]

摘要　如今，我们的生活高度全球化，人们和企业都在不断寻求贸易和技能的多样化。在这种情况下，成为一名多语学习者是个不错的选择。从商业和旅游的角度来看，中国的潜力巨大，学习汉语自然也成了大多数印度人的选择。随着印度和中国贸易往来的增多，专业人士和青年学者也热衷于汉语学习。就是在这样一个充满活力的市场背景下，印华中文学校应运而生。它目前是印度最大的一家专门教印度人学习汉语的私立培训机构。每年，这所机构招收数百名汉语学习者，从小学生到企业家，各行各业、各年龄段的学生都有。自 2010 年开始，印华中文学校就以学习汉语和了解中华文化为理念培养学生。学校的目标是通过精心定制的课程、数字化的学习、HSK 和 YCT 的认证来吸引越来越多的学生。其中遇到最大的挑战是这些印度学生来自不同地区，讲不同的语言。本文主要收集了汉语教师的反馈和访谈资料，他们在教学过程中将本土语言和课程相结合，帮助学生更好地理解和掌握汉语。

关键词　汉语；印度的语言；在印汉语教学；语音系统

工业革命之后，世界各国间的贸易往来逐渐增多。随着国际进出口贸易的不断增加，国外的公司也开始在与自己有货物进出口交易的国家设立公司。越来越多的

1　Yeh China 汉语教育机构主管。
2　郑州大学汉语国际教育专业在读研究生。

外资企业开始增加本土贸易活动，这就需要本土员工和国外员工在一起工作，语言差异问题也就随之出现了。为了解决这个问题，人们开始学习外语以方便交流。所以汉语也就自然而然传播到了印度。由于汉字是意音文字，兼有表意和表音两种功能，相较于印度文字而言，汉语难以读写，所以刚开始人们不敢选择汉语作为第三语言。但是渐渐地，越来越多的人对汉语萌生了兴趣、改变了看法，学习汉语的人数也日渐增多。他们当中的一些人只学到基本能听懂的程度，而有一些人不满足于只是简单地掌握这门语言，他们努力对它进行深入研究，想成为汉语老师，为那些听不懂英语或根本找不到老师的学生授课。刚开始，那些已通过汉语水平考试的老师给喜欢学汉语的学生上课；随后，有些培训机构开始设立汉语培训课程；到后来，专门培训汉语的机构纷纷建立。随着时代的发展，越来越多的培训机构和学校开始设立汉语课程。汉语也逐渐成为学校课程中第三语言的选择之一。汉语水平三级或以上的老师才能给汉语水平一级或二级的学生们授课。私人培训机构的老师汉语水平达到三级就能授课，但对于那些想要在大学或学校里任教的老师来说汉语水平要求会更高，他们必须具备在学院讲课的能力。学汉语的学生越来越多，印度开始涌现大量从事汉语教学的老师。再后来，对汉语感兴趣的学生和老师可以申请奖学金去中国深造。有些人不想花太长时间，就在中国选择一学期或一年的课程就读。同样地，也会有人选择在中国学习汉语教学的课程。孔子学院（现更名为“教育部中外语言交流合作中心”）开始和印度不同的教育机构和学校合作，给学生们提供丰厚的奖学金来鼓励他们学习汉语。那些在中国读完国际汉语教育课程的毕业生回到印度后，在高校或教学机构担任汉语教学工作，这些经过专业培训的老师会运用他们在中国学到的全部知识来教印度学生学汉语，以培养更多精通汉语的人。

为了让学生们更好地理解，汉语教师在教汉语的过程中会将印度语言和汉语放在一起比较，特别是印地语和马拉提语。这样做是为了让学生们更清楚声母和韵母的发音，因为汉语中声母和韵母的发音和印地语、马拉提语的有些字母的发音比较相似。教师可以制作一张声母韵母表，写出汉语的声母韵母，并在下面标上印度语言中发音相似的字母，学生们阅读和记忆就会容易许多。我们可以利用这种方法教小孩子学习汉语，汉语的读音可以先用印度语言标注出来，即使孩子们的父母没有学过汉语教学也能用印度语言帮助孩子在家复习汉语词汇。例如，“妈妈”可以用印地语字母写成“मामा”。印度语言中的字母和汉语中的声母、韵母发音有相似之处，但两种语言声调不同。汉语有四种声调和轻声，印度语言只有两种声调。汉语的声调标在拼音上，汉字通常不标音，但印度语言的声调在书写时都会标记出来。除了有不同的声调，汉语中某些词的发音和含义在印度语言中几乎毫无差别。例如，“茶”在汉语和印度语言中的发音和意思都是一样的。

语言有相似也会有不同。汉语的句子结构和印度语言的句子结构不同。汉语的句子结构和英语较为相似，一般是主语—谓语—宾语。例如，汉语中说“他吃饭了”，在这句话中“他”是主语，“吃”是谓语，“饭”是宾语；再如，“她买面包”，在这句话中“她”是主语，“买”是谓语，“面包”是宾语。但是在印度语言中，句子结构却是主语—宾语—谓语。例如，印地语中“उसने खाना खाया”（他吃饭了），“उसने”是主语“他”，“खाना”是宾语“食物”，“खाया”是动词“吃”。再如，“वो बाजार गयी”（他们去集市了），“वो”是主语，“बाजार”是宾语，“गयी”是谓语。除此之外，汉语和印度语言还有很多差异。在不同时态的汉语句子中汉字的字形不会发生任何改变，句子中动词形式没有变化，主语也无阴阳性之分。例如，在汉语中“他吃饭了”和“她吃饭”，前者的意思是是他吃过饭了，是过去完成时，说明“吃饭”这个动作已经做过了。而后者“她吃饭”只是一个简单的一般现在时的句子，只是在陈述“她吃饭”这件事。在这两个句子中，动词都是“吃”，时态和主语的阴阳性却有不同，但这些都没对句子中的动词形式造成影响。但在印度语言中，单词的形式要根据时态和主语的阴阳性发生变化。例如，在印地语句子“वो बाहर गयी थी”和“वो बाहर जाएगा”中，第一个句子使用过去时态，表示他已经到外面了。第二个句子用将来时态，表示他马上要出去。在这两个句子中，使用的是同一个动词“जाना”，但是根据主语的阴阳性和句子中的时态，动词的形式发生了改变。另外，汉语中的第三人称单数代词“他、她、它”，这几个字的发音和拼音相同，写法不同。而在印地语中，第三人称代词的“他、她、它”在读音和写法上完全一致，但当第三人称代词作主语时，会根据句子的时态和动词的形式发生改变，主语要和动词的性数保持一致。这一规则适用于印度的大多数语言。

图 1　印地语拼音的韵母和声母构成

印度是个多语种大国，每个邦都有自己的地方语言，并不是每个人都会讲英语。大多数人讲印地语、马拉提语、古吉拉特语、旁遮普语或其他语言。汉语教学的难点是如何简化汉语这门语言，让人们更容易理解，从而吸引更多的学生学习汉语。汉语是世界上最难学的语言之一，因此很多学生更愿意学习欧洲语言。所以，在教印度学生汉语时就需要我们找到一种可以和他们沟通的方式。教学中面临的最大的挑战是这些学生来自各行各业，汉语水平参差不齐。不是所有学生都喜欢将英语当作学习汉语的媒介，这也是在汉语教学过程中用印度语言授课越来越重要的原因。因此，针对印度学生的汉语课程设置，我们加入了一些汉语与印度本土语言的比较作为参考。我们对 50 多位从事汉语教学的老师和培训机构的校长进行了采访，向他们询问是否在汉语教学中将印地语或印度其他本土语言当作教学媒介，他们的回答让我有了新的认识，几乎 99% 的老师承认在汉语教学中使用了印度本土语言。《东方对话》栏目组的主任阿迪提 • 瓦德纳卡在接受采访时回答说："在汉语教学中我会使用梵语。”沃德普纳学校的主任也说：“我在教学中使用印地语或马拉提语。”印度汉语阴阳学习中心的雅诗达·加吉尔在采访中也承认：“汉语语法和声调非常接近于印地语和马拉提语，只是在句子结构上有些许差别。所以有时候我会使用印地语或马拉提语教学。”

图 2　用印地语和英语图解“奶奶”和“妈妈”

除了这些学校的老师和校长，我们也对一些学习汉语的学生进行了采访。我们就汉语教学过程中是否应该使用印度本土语言的这个问题向他们进行询问，大部分学生觉得在这个过程中使用印度本土语言更有利学生理解，学习过程也会更愉快，而且他们还发现将汉语的语法结构和一些印度本土语言结合起来学习更容易理解和记忆。苏美达·阿达乐是孟买大学的一名本科三年级的学生，她在采访中回答说：“我发现在汉语教学过程中使用印度本土语言是非常有用的。像印地语、马拉提语可以帮助我们更好地理解汉语拼音中一些比较难发音的字母，如‘z，c，s，zh，ch，sh’等。而且将印度语言和汉语的句子结构放在一起比较，更有利于我们理解和记忆这些语法。”

本研究的目的是简化汉语教学语言，帮助在印汉语学习者加快他们学习汉语的进度。希望在不久的将来，中印专家能通力合作，打造适合不同水平的印度学生的汉语教材。

（蔡育靓 / 翻译，白万丽 / 校对）

Part 2

第二部分
在印汉语教育的挑战与机遇

The Challenges and Opportunities of Indian Chinese Language Education

Chinese Language Craze Among the Youth of Bihar: Challenges and Opportunities

Bhavana Kumari[1]

Abstract Learning a foreign language is always considered a way to improve not only one's social and cultural understanding towards a foreign land but it is also said that the more foreign languages one can speak, the smarter and more creative with immense analytical skill, the learner is. Chinese language is known as one of the world's most spoken and interesting language. With the opening of the Chinese economy and its successful growth for more than four decades, the number of Chinese language learners has increased manifold. Chinese language learners get a competitive edge over the others in terms of career choices.

India and China are two ancient civilizations of the world and they both play a key role in the Asian economy, culture and influence around the world. Thus, both countries need to understand each other closely and learning the language of each other will make the process smoother and trusty. The number of Indian students learning the Chinese language has also increased substantially over the past two decades.

This research is about the Chinese language craze among the youth of Bihar, an eastern state of India. Bihar was the state where Xuanzang (玄奘), the great Chinese Buddhist monk and scholar who travelled in early

1 Research Scholar, Jawaharlal Nehru University, New Delhi, India.

Tang dynasty (618 to 906) and established the cultural, educational and religious foundations between the two ancient civilizations. This paper will explore the challenges and opportunities that students of Bihar have when they try to learn Chinese language. Despite the fact that every year a large number of Chinese tourists visit Buddhist monasteries in Bihar and learn about the ancient interactions between India and China, not much pro-active work has been done at educational levels to increase the charm of learning Chinese language in the state. The paper will dig deep and try to find out the reasons behind the lack of good Mandarin learning programmes and institutions in Bihar and also look for some solutions to the issue. This paper is both qualitative and quantitative in nature.

Key Words Chinese language; Language learning; Youth of Bihar; People-to-people exchange; Cultural interaction

1 BACKGROUND

China has become the leading global power that has a substantial position in the world. Since its reform and opening up year (1978), China started interacting and integrating more closely with the world and one thing that has taken a skyrocketing path of popularity is the craze for studying the Chinese language. It is rare to find a country where the Chinese language is not being studied. Sometimes it is also not just because of the economic or job purpose but the language is studied by school kids, undergraduates, and postgraduate students or even freelance professionals as they are fascinated with the unique writing style of Chinese characters and interesting stories of history attached to it.

An Indian grammarian Patañjali (4 century BCE–2 century BCE), who wrote a famous ancient text *Mahabhashya* (*Great Commentary*), says that “when a word is pronounced, an artha ‘object’ is understood”. Artha is a Sanskrit word that can be translated as "meaning" and also as "object". Understanding of both contexts is immensely important for language learners. Linguists also believe that every learner must have a proper understanding of words and word combinations, also known as collocations, so that he/she can master the art of word formation, its combinations and also its contextual sense. The possibilities for developing such level of understanding increase and further yield best results only when the learner has the opportunity to be in the region/country where the target language originated or is spoken. China has provided such opportunities by providing several scholarships to foreign learners of Chinese language. The role of governments from both the host country and the recipient one is crucial to hold such collaborative initiatives.

A famous American poet, polymath and physician of the nineteenth century, Oliver Wendell Holmes Jr., said, "Every language is a temple, in which the soul of those who speak it is enshrined." [1] All the earlier mentioned authors and philosophers have emphasized on the importance of language learning and following the path of wisdom that comes as a fruit of learning any language and in this case a foreign language. According to Modern Language Association (MLA) language enrolment data, there have been 11,366 enrolments for the Chinese language in 1980 fall semester in United States of America. The enrolment numbers gradually went up from 19,427 to 34,153 and 59,876 in 1990, 2002 and 2009 respectively. In 2016 fall, the enrolment numbers slowed down a little. These data are of the fall semester of the respective years.

The popularity of any language shoots up with its economic value and the development of the society where it is spoken, be it Sanskrit, Arabic, Spanish, German, English, Japanese, etc. The native speakers of these languages and their power whether in terms of knowledge, science, art & culture, or innovation, have changed human civilization in unprecedented ways. Table 1 shows a list of ten most popular languages in today's times according to their Power Language Index (PLI). Mandarin ranks second on the list. Hindi ranks tenth and English remains

1 https://libquotes.com/oliver-wendell-holmes-sr/quote/lbn0l3h, accessed: 2020-09-23.

the topmost powerful language in the world.

Table 1 Ten most popular languages

RANK	SCORE	LANGUAGE	NATIVE (MM)	GEOGRAPHY	ECONOMY	COMMUNICATION	KNOWLEDGE & MEDIA	DIPLOMACY
1	0.889	English	446.0	1	1	1	1	1
2	0.411	Mandarin*	960.0	6	2	2	3	6
3	0.337	French	80.0	2	6	5	5	1
4	0.329	Spanish	470.0	3	5	3	7	3
5	0.273	Arabic	295.0	4	9	6	18	4
6	0.244	Russian	150.0	5	12	10	9	5
7	0.191	German	92.5	8	3	7	4	8
8	0.133	Japanese	125.0	27	4	22	6	7
9	0.119	Portuguese	215.0	7	19	13	12	9
10	0.117	Hindi*	310.0	13	16	8	2	10

* Source: World Economic Forum (2016)

If all Chinese dialects/languages (Mandarin being the largest) are considered as one it would not change the rank ordering. However, if Urdu and Hindi—and all the Hindi dialects—are taken as one it would vault it past Portuguese and Japanese.

In India, the history of the modern Chinese language learning started somewhere in the late 1930s. Rabindranath Tagore (1861–1941), sobriquets Gurudev, a great Indian philosopher and poet in collaboration with Professor Tan Yunshan, a famous Indologist, established pioneer institution named Cheena-Bhavana at Vishwa Bharti University in West Bengal, for teaching Chinese language, literature and art to the Indian students and strengthen India-China friendship. Professor Tan Yunshan is known as the Xuanzang of modern China who lived in India for over thirty years, and even took his last breath in Bodhgaya, Bihar.[1] After Cheena-Bhavana, Chinese language Studies was started at Delhi University in 1964.[2] Jawaharlal Nehru University started Chinese language programme under Centre for Afro-Asian Languages (CAAL) in 1973, but as more students started learning the language the Centre for East Asian Languages (CEAL) was established in the 1980s, and then the present Centre for Chinese and South East

1 Nair, V G. "A mosaic life of ordinary uniqueness", 1958-10-10, http://ignca.gov.in/divisionss/kalakosa/kalasamalocana/in-the-footsteps-of-xuanzang-tanyun-shan-the-man-and-his-mission/, accessed: 2020-09-22.

2 https://www.studyfrenchspanish.com/language-courses-delhi university/#:~:text=After%20starting%20with%20the%20Chinese,the%20Korean%20language%20in%202001, accessed: 2020-09-23.

Asian Studies (CCSEAS) was established in 1996.[1] Dr. Babasaheb Ambedkar Marathwada University (then Marathwada University) started Chinese language diploma course in 1986. Since then several departments were set up from eastern to western and northern to southern states of India, but one state, Bihar that should have been the hub of Chinese studies was left with not much progressive work done. This paper will make an attempt to re-visit the reasons that could have led to the decline of Chinese language study programme in Bihar. Though the ancient interaction between the state and China was mainly based on the lines of studying the Buddhist's sutras and exploring its significance to the society, today in the modern times those ancient relations can rejuvenate and further expand to read and understand the modern art, literature and science of both India and China. According to a data of 2018–2019, Bihari students constitute more than 30 percent of the total number of students' enrolment in Bachelor and Master degree programmes at Jawaharlal Nehru University.[1] Even in the universities like Banaras Hindu University in Uttar Pradesh, Vishwa-Bharti University in West Bengal, Sikkim University in Sikkim, Central University of Jharkhand that are located close by Bihar, a significant number of students who study Chinese language come from Bihar. But the enrolment of students in Mandarin programmes in their native state is exceptionally low. This question needs a sincere and serious attention. The subsequent sections of the paper will talk about the progress of Chinese language studies in Bihar, the opportunities the learners have there and the challenges they face which ultimately push them to migrate to others states and continue their determination to study foreign language.

2 DEVELOPMENT OF CHINESE LANGUAGE EDUCATION IN BIHAR

By turning through the pages of history one can analyse that the people of Bihar have always accepted new ideas, faiths, philosophies, religions, art & culture, political theories and what not. Almost all the religions that flourished in the

1 CCSEAS, JNU official website.

Indian subcontinent have their deep connections with Bihar. Some religions and philosophies either originated from Bihar or were well accepted among the people of the region. The name Bihar is derived from the Pali and Sanskrit word "vihāra" (Devanagari: विहार) meaning "abode" or "monastries". Ideas that originated, debated and discussed in Bihar were also passed on to the neighbouring regions and countries including China. So, even in present times, students of Bihar have the craze for learning foreign languages particularly the Mandarin. They take huge interests in learning the language and make a career in it. However, it is disappointing that the mechanism of establishing any good national level Chinese language learning institution could not develop and students have to leave their families to pursue their dreams. But still, efforts have been made by the central and state government and some individual institutions that are worth mentioning.

On February 12, 2007, Xuanzang Memorial Hall, in the presence of dignitaries from India and China including Chinese Foreign Minister Mr. Li Zhaoxing and the Bihar Chief Minister Mr. Nitish Kumar was inaugurated.[1] This event gave impetus to the revival of goodwill relation between India and China particularly from the perspective of the development of Bihar. In 2009, an Academy of Foreign Languages and Cultural Cooperation (AFLCC) was established in Magadh University that offers one-year certificate courses in several foreign languages including Chinese.[2] Magadh University VC Rajendra Prasad visited China in November 2019 to study the prospect of educational collaborations between the university and Chinese institutions of higher learning.[3] According to Hari Mohan Prasad, director of AFLCC, around 20 Chinese tourists became members of the cooperation along with several Japanese, Germans and French and offered to provide service as a teaching consultant. Nava Nalanda Mahavihara University started the one-year certificate and two-year undergraduate diploma course of

---

1 https://artsandculture.google.com/exhibit/xuanzang-memorial-n%C4%81land%C4%81-xuanzang-memorial-nava-nalanda-mahavihara/-gLy1Bey76EHJA?hl=en, accessed: 2020-09-25.

2 Verma, Kumod. "MU academy offers courses in foreign languages", 2009-4-12. http://timesofindia.indiatimes.com/articleshow/4390185.cms?utm_source=contentofinterest&utm_medium=text&utm_campaign=cppst/, accessed: 2020-09-26.

3 Qadir, Abdul. "No plan to shelve Chinese course: Magadh University VC", 2020-6-29. https://timesofindia.indiatimes.com/city/patna/mu-vc-no-plan-to-shelve-chinese-course/articleshow/76678388.cms, accessed: 2020-09-25.

Chinese language. As per the official website of the university since 2010, more than fifty students from the department managed to get a secured job in various sectors.[1] The university also has a PhD programme for Chinese language and literature discipline.

In June 2011, Bihar Chief Minister Nitish Kumar visited China on a weeklong trip. His trip's agenda included research and collaboration between the state and China in various sectors including education, culture and promotion of tourism. As Dr. Yukteshwar Kumar, a sinologist and columnist on China, also a senior lecturer at University of Bath, writes in his assessment of Mr. Kumar's trips to China, "these are all right step at right time in the right direction."[2] Mr. Nitish Kumar's trip to China did strengthen the ties between the state and China and yielded positive results. According to the official website of Nalanda University, it started the one-year diploma course in Chinese language, but the recent update could not be made available.[3] Patna University has been offering six-month certificate courses in Chinese, German and French since 2017 with thirty students enrolled in 2018.[4] Lalit Narayan Mithila University, Darbhanga established Institute of Foreign Language with an aim to provide the Certificate and Diploma course in Chinese, German, Spanish, Korean, French, Japanese and Arabic languages. However, due to the unavailability of teachers, the institute only offers certificate courses in French language currently with the first batch started in 2016.[5]

Apart from the university and government institutions level, there are private Chinese language learning centres in Bihar majorly in the capital city Patna, such as Be Polyglot Chinese Language Institute, Chinese Language class, Brit American, etc.[6] Though the standard of language teaching in these institutes are

1 Official website of Nava Nalanda Mahavihara, https://www.nnm.ac.in/department/chinese-and-japanese/about-chinese-and-japanese/, accessed: 2020-09-25.

2 Kumar, Yukteshwar. "An assessment of Nitish Kumar visit to China", Chennai Centre for China Studies, 2011-6-27. https://www.c3sindia.org/archives/an-assessment-of-nitish-kumars-visit-to-china/, accessed: 2020-09-26.

3 Official website of Nalanda University, https://nalandauniv.edu.in/academics/sll/, accessed: 2020-09-26.

4 http://timesofindia.indiatimes.com/articleshow/69847516.cms?utm_source=contentofinterest&utm_medium=text&utm_campaign=cppst. 19 June 2019, accessed: 2020-09-26.

5 https://resultfor.in/mithila-university-foreign-language-certificate-diploma-course/#:~:text=Hence%20for%20getting%20an%20easy,%2C%20Chinese%20%26%20Japanese%20and%20Arabic, accessed: 2020-09-26.

6 https://www.justdial.com/Patna/Language-Classes-For-Chinese/nct-10294790, accessed: 2020-09-26.

not up to the level of institutes in big metro cities like Delhi and Mumbai but the scope of progress can definitely be seen.

3 CHALLENGES AND OPPORTUNITIES

A famous Chinese saying about language learning is, "a new language learned is like a new life lived".[1] The life of language learners is also the same. They think everything from two different perspectives, one that they have inherited and another that they have acquired after learning the language and through it the cultural, social and political thoughts of the people of the target language. So, the life of any language learner is full of different, sometimes unexplored opportunities and challenges. If the target language that the learner has opted to study is not well known and the people around them are not completely aware of the future results, then the pressure on the learner increases. This section will highlight and mention the various challenges that students from Bihar encounter when they think of making a career in Chinese studies and the Chinese language per se. Later, what opportunities learners think they have after getting a degree with their hard work are also discussed in this section.

For this section of paper, the author has interviewed thirteen people who belong to different parts of Bihar and how they assess their journey of learning the language and how that made a positive and successful development in their life. Some interviews are conducted through telephonic conversations and some through questionnaires. As per their responses, six factors are identified in this section that at some point proved to be a hindrance in their journey of learning the Chinese language. The participants have also identified the changes from the time they started studying the language till today and also suggested some ideas and points that can be beneficial for the development of Chinese language study programs in Bihar.

1 https://www.chineseclass101.com/chinese-vocabulary-lists/top-10-quotes-about-language-learning/, accessed: 2020-09-24.

3.1 SOCIAL AND CULTURAL

Mrs. Arpana Raj, Assistant Professor of Chinese language at Central University of Jharkhand, started studying Chinese language in 2003. She shares that since in Bihar there was a trend set of pursuing Engineering and Medical courses, only those students who selected these options were considered wise and on the right career track. Courses in foreign languages were not easily accepted by relatives and well-wishers. Mr. Nishit Kumar, a PhD scholar from Jawaharlal Nehru University, New Delhi, expresses that none of his family members or relatives knew about learning foreign languages during the time he started learning the Chinese language. Mr. Abhimanyu Kumar, currently working as a sales assistant at Air China, New Delhi office, did not face many social constraints, as for him and his family, the university's brand name was more important than the course he was studying. Family members of another participant in the survey, Mr. Vivek Kumar, feel that there is no social status related to this skill. His relatives think that people should first get some good and high-profile degrees and secure a good government job or some profession that is well appreciated and bring high social status to the family like becoming a civil service officer. Ms. Anupam Kishan, a 23-year-old girl, explains the mindset of the people in the society around her and says that people question how anyone can make a career in language; one should have a technical degree for "secured" job. As she belongs to Bihar, the people there are more passionate for government jobs like jobs in the banking sector, railways and public service commission. She also stresses that such attitudes are not only seen in students but their parents also feel the same. Mr. Ajay Krishna, a foreign expert of Indic Studies at Xi'an International Studies University shares his experience and recalled back some discussion with his family members, relatives and friends at the time he wanted to study foreign language. He explains that Bihar was and is still largely an agriculture-based society. Then with the span of time when the agriculture sector did not expand and show many good results people started vouching for secured government jobs that will give them a fixed salary and would have less risks. Pursuing something new seems to be risky for the people of Bihar, and thus youth wanted to become doctors, engineer, probationary officers in banks, etc. This social and cultural thinking has developed not in one or two decades but in span of several decades or even since the last century. It will again take time to change.

3.2 FINANCIAL

Bihar's Net/Gross State Domestic Product (NSDP/GSDP) is lowest among all the States and Union Territories of India.[1] Net State Domestic Product is the state equivalent to the country Net Domestic Product (NDP). As per Reserve Bank of India's report, Bihar has performed worst with US $640 NSDP per capita and US $2,395 NDP per capita on Purchasing Power Parity (PPP) Index in 2018–2019.[2] Though Bihar has performed better with its past decades' growth it is lagging far behind the other regions of India. So, the people there expend their money on things that can give them quick, regular, and long-term benefits. That is why even if parents have to take loans and spend a huge amount of money on their child's education to make them a doctor or engineer, they don't hesitate much as they are sure of the return revenue. They refrain from spending time and money in fields where they feel that the future is not secured and well explored. The author of this paper herself went through such experience when she had to choose between either becoming an architect or pursue an unknown career in the field of Chinese studies. Although the cost and total fees for the architecture courses were much higher compared to the Chinese language course, her parents preferred to make their daughter an architect, which would ultimately be a well-recognized and respected profession and will also bring a good income. But it was the passion of learning something new that finally convinced her parents to let her pursue her own career of interest. Mr. Ajay Krishna believes, as per the current situation, learning Chinese language is a stream with "low investment, high gain"characteristics. But he got to know this only after spending some good amount of time in this field.

1 "MOSPI net state domestic product, Ministry of Statistics and Programme Implementation, Government of India", accessed: 2020-09-28.

2 "MOSPI net state domestic product, Ministry of Statistics and Programme Implementation, Government of India", accessed: 2020-09-28.

3.3 LACK OF ACADEMIC ENVIRONMENT

Mrs. Arpana Raj believes that there is no good Chinese language learning program in Bihar. There was a lack of materials particularly at the time she started learning the Chinese language in 2003. Another participant of the survey, Mr. Kant Kumar, PhD scholar at JNU, has to practice his listening sessions (Kouyu) using audio tapes. Though the development of ICT has surely helped in those aspects, he believes students studying in Bihar are still not well equipped with updated and advanced technologies of Chinese language learning. He believes that the Chinese language programs running at Nalanda University and Magadh University are of good standard. Mr. Nishit Kumar also feels that there is no good Chinese language program in Bihar. Mr. Alok Singh, MBA graduated from Nankai University, Tianjin, says there are couple of institutes in Bihar that teaches Chinese language, but those are not up to the mark. As per him, Chinese learning/scholar communities need to put in extra effort to work on it and fill the gap. Ms. Anupam says all universities in Bihar should start bachelor's degree in the Chinese language and treat this as any other subject. She also identifies that the monotonous and conventional way of teaching the language should go away and the institutions should upgrade to the levels to Chinese language teaching standard of China.

3.4 LACK OF EXPOSURE AND INFORMATION

It is indeed strange that the part of country from where large chunk of students come to learn Chinese language is still lacking any good Chinese language institution. Mr. Nishit Kumar had no access to learning Chinese language at his native place when he started learning the language. He knew no one from his state who studied the language before he thought of pursuing his career in this field. He found no changes in the language learning process of students from his state and also from other places except the use of technological devices and a few Apps on mobile. He feels the burden of English treated as a superior language to communicate has an under-current impact on people for not choosing Chinese. Chinese language has a different script and tones. This makes it a difficult language to learn. This is also a reason for students to not choose to study this language. Mr. Nishit adds that people of Bihar should be made aware of the ancient interactions between India (Bihar in particular) and China. Young minds should dig out Chinese source materials to know more about it. Buddhist scripture were written in Pali and Prakrit and then translated into Chinese (mainly by Xuanzang). Mr. Nishit is optimistic that, in future, given the opportunity and space, people of Bihar will learn this language just like any other language.

Ms. Anupam's dream is to study abroad and be a learned assistant professor at a very young age. Pursuing her passion for Chinese might make her dream come true but the only hurdles she faces is the lack of information and she feels much time is wasted on just hunting for reliable sources of information. Mr. Abhimanyu Kumar says that when he started pursing bachelor in Chinese language from Jawaharlal Nehru University, he was happy that he could make it to the premier university of India. He did not know anyone who could have learned the Chinese language and make career out of it. But, with time he realised the importance of the language and particularly when he got opportunity to study in China on Confucius scholarship. He also acknowledges that there is very little information regarding studying foreign language for career at his native place. By the time another participant of the survey, Devvrat, started learning Chinese language in 2017, people were becoming aware of the prosperous prospect of studying the language and as he said he was blessed to have a brother who told him about Chinese language and also said there would be great opportunities in future.

3.5 SENSE OF INSECURITY FOR EMPLOYMENT

Mrs. Arpana Raj says that no good job opportunities in Bihar are available after learning the Chinese language. Nishit Kumar said he is unsure about future, and learning any foreign language was alien for his family members. Mr. Abhimanyu feels that currently there are very few opportunities available for Chinese learners in Bihar. Mr. Vivek Kumar tells in his interview that there was a huge insecurity in his family regarding getting good jobs in the field of language. His family members were more in favour of asking him to get some technical degree that will eventually help him land up with good jobs after graduation. He further adds that he does not believe that few Buddhist tourist sites in Bihar can generate the required amount of employment for Chinese language learners in Bihar. Besides this there are now many students who are studying in the other nearby universities like BHU and Vishwa Bharti that can easily fulfil the limited demands of tourist guide for the Buddhist tourism in Bihar. After completing his post-graduate program in India, Mr. Vivek studied at Beijing Language and Culture University (BLCU) for two years and is currently working in Guangzhou. Though he is satisfied with his work, very often he feels homesick and wishes he could have a good job offer in his home state. For Mr. Kant Kumar, the job opportunities available in Bihar are satisfactory and he is optimistic about the future prospects of this stream.

3.6 LACK OF GOVERNMENT PRO-ACTIVE PARTICIPATION, INCENTIVES AND ENCOURAGEMENT

Mr. Kant says that the government must actively participate in promoting Chinese studies programs in Bihar both in terms of language & literature and IR studies. He suggested that the central and state government should arrange funding to support the Chinese studies. Mrs. Arpana thinks, if the Central and State universities come up with a department of Chinese language and degree courses in Chinese, it will cater to the need of people and society. Mr. Abhimanyu adds further to the discussion that Bihar state government needs to take initiative to promote Chinese language learning program, only then it can survive for longer period of time. It can take examples from other states like Jharkhand, Gujarat, Maharashtra, etc., as they have started such programs a few years back and now universities from those states are doing great in terms of Chinese language learning. Mr. Vivek Kumar emphasizes that while the state government is not taking any firm and sincere steps in the promotion of Chinese language by introducing regular courses at the university level and also by establishing ties with the Chinese universities, the development of Chinese language in the state is not possible. Mr. Ajay suggests that Bihar can become the "language learning hub" if the government comes up and supports the promotion of the language in the state. It will also bring investment, industries and infrastructure that will help in the overall development of Bihar.

4 CONCLUSION

The economic development and decisive role of China on regional and global platform increases the need for learning Chinese language. The pre-existing linkages between Bihar and China will not only boost the developing process of Bihar but will also cater to the healthy relation between India and China. Even without any advanced infrastructure, the students from Bihar have come out, learned the language and worked in various sectors and strengthened the India-China friendship. The people of Bihar, though they lean more towards government jobs and professions that they feel with give them a secured future, in the time span their thinking have changed and now even more people are ready to choose careers that are adventurous and not well-explored. It is there in their ancient culture to embrace new thoughts and paths. Good government administration and support is required because no plan can succeed without the sufficient funding and supportive policies. A joint India-China educational institute can be set up with considering the mutual respect and requirement of both sides. Like Delhi–Beijing, Bengaluru–Chengdu, Kolkata–Kunming, Ahmedabad–Guangzhou, and Nalanda–Xi'an can become sister cities between India and China, Bihar and Shaanxi can be cultural sister states between the two great Asian civilizations. The two ancient Indian empires, "Maurya" and "Gupta" Empire had their capital in Patliputra (now Patna, the capital city of Bihar). China also has its two most significant dynasties, Han and Tang dynasties centred in Shaanxi province. But all this required efficient experts who were good in policy making and well-versed in the language that both nations speak. Nelson Rolihlahla Mandela, the former president of South Africa said, "If you talk to a man in a language he understands, that goes to his head. If you talk to him in his language that goes to his heart." For better understanding, speaking with people in the language that they understand should always be the first step to lay a trusty foundation of friendship between the two nations.

REFERENCES

[1] KUMAR R. Institutionalization of Chinese language teaching in India: issues, challenges and the way forward[M]//NAYAK S, RAKESH R. Understanding China in the 21st Century. Phoenix: Heritage Publishers, 2020.

比哈尔邦青年的汉语热：挑战与机遇

白婉娜[1]

摘要　学习外语是深入理解国外社会和文化的有效方法，可以说，一个人掌握的外语越多，就越有创造力。汉语是世界上使用人数最多、最有趣的语言之一。中国改革开放40多年来，随着经济的高速发展，汉语学习者的数量不断增长。在职业选择方面，汉语学习者比其他学习者更有竞争优势。

印度和中国是世界两大文明古国，它们在亚洲经济、文化乃至全球事务中都发挥着重要作用。因此，两国需要加深对彼此的了解，增强互信，学习对方的语言将使这一进程更顺利。过去20年来，印度学习汉语的学生人数也大幅增加。

本文采用了定性分析与定量分析法相结合的方法，对印度东部比哈尔邦青年的汉语热进行分析。比哈尔邦是唐初（公元618至906年）中国伟大的佛僧和学者玄奘游学之地，为两个古代文明之间的文化、教育和宗教交流的典型。本文旨在探讨比哈尔邦学生在学习汉语时所面临的挑战与机遇。尽管每年有大量中国游客参观比哈尔邦的佛教寺院，了解印度和中国之间古老文明的互动，但在教育层面未有太多积极主动的推动。本文旨在深入探讨比哈尔邦缺乏良好的汉语学习项目和培训机构的原因，并提出解决办法。

关键词　汉语言；语言学习；比哈尔邦青年；人文交流；文化互动

1　印度新德里贾瓦哈拉尔·尼赫鲁大学研究员。

1 背景

中国自1978年改革开放以来，逐渐成为世界上具有实质性影响力的强国，中国开始与全球进行更密切的互动与合作，其中一方面体现是汉语学习热，这是一条飞速发展的流行之路，很难找到一个没有研究汉语的国家。这不仅是出于经济或工作的目的，很多中小学生、大学生、研究生以及自由职业者也在学习汉语，这是因为他们对中国汉字独特的书写风格及其中蕴含的有趣的历史故事而着迷。

公元前4世纪至公元前2世纪，印度语法学家帕坦伽利写了一本著名的古代注疏《大疏》，提到“当一个词被读出来时，一个‘物体’的意思（阿尔塔）就可以被理解”。阿尔塔（Artha）是一个梵语词，可译为“意思”，也可翻译为“物体”。这两种语境的理解对语言学习者来说是非常重要的。语言学家还认为，每个学习者都必须对单词和单词组合或搭配有恰当的理解，这样才能掌握单词形成的艺术、组合以及语境意义。只有当学习者到目的语国家，才能提高理解水平，并取得最佳学习效果。中国为外国汉语学习者提供了获得奖学金的机会，东道国和接收国政府的作用对于采取这种合作举措至关重要。

19世纪美国著名诗人、内科医生奥利弗·温德尔·霍姆斯说：“每一种语言都是一座庙宇，在这座庙里，讲这种语言的人的灵魂都被铭刻在里面。”[1]前面提到的所有作者和哲学家都强调了语言学习的重要性，强调学习语言是智慧之路。根据现代语言协会（MLA）语言培训的报名数据，1980年秋季学期，美国的汉语专业学生入学人数为11 366人，1990年、2002年和2009年的入学人数分别上升到19 427人、34 153人和59 876人，2016年秋季入学人数略有减少。这些数据是当年秋季学期的数据。

任何语言的普及都伴随着它的经济价值和社会变化而迅速发展。梵语、阿拉伯语、西班牙语、德语、英语、日语等，这些语言的母语者及其力量，无论在知识、科学、艺术和文化、创新方面，都以前所未有的方式改变了人类文明。表1列出了当今使用人口最多的10种语言。根据它们的语言索引（PLI），汉语排名第二，印地语排

1 https://libquotes.com/oliver-wendell-holmes-sr/quote/lbn0l3h, 检索日期：2020年9月23日。

名第十，英语仍然是世界上使用人口最多的语言。

表 1　当今使用人口最多的 10 种语言

排名	分数	语言	母语	地理	经济	交流	知识与媒体	外交
1	0. 889	英语	446. 0	1	1	1	1	1
2	0. 411	普通话	960. 0	6	2	2	3	6
3	0. 337	法语	80. 0	2	6	5	5	1
4	0. 329	西班牙语	470. 0	3	5	3	7	3
5	0. 273	阿拉伯语	295. 0	4	9	6	18	4
6	0. 244	俄语	150. 0	5	12	10	9	5
7	0. 191	德语	92. 5	8	3	7	4	8
8	0. 133	日语	125. 0	27	4	22	6	7
9	0. 119	葡萄牙语	215. 0	7	19	13	12	9
10	0. 117	印地语	310. 0	13	16	8	2	10

⋆ 资料来源：世界经济论坛（2016 年）

⋆ 如果将所有的汉语方言（普通话使用者是最大的群体）作为一个对象考虑，本表的排序不会发生变化。然而，如果将乌尔都语、印地语及其他印度方言算作一个对象，那它的分数将超过葡萄牙语和日语。

在印度，现代汉语学习的历史始于 20 世纪 30 年代末。印度哲学家、诗人泰戈尔（1861—1941）与印度学家谭云山合作，在西孟加拉邦印度国际大学率先创建了中国学院，为印度学生教授汉语、文学和艺术，加强印中友谊。谭云山被称为“现代中国的玄奘”，他在印度生活了 30 多年，最后在比哈尔邦的菩提迦耶辞世。[1] 在中国学院之后，1964 年德里大学开始进行汉语研究。[2] 贾瓦哈拉尔 • 尼赫鲁大学于 1973 年在亚非语言中心（CAAL）开设了汉语课程，但随着学习汉语学生的增多，20 世纪 80 年代成立了东亚语言中心（CEAL），1996 年成立了目前的中国和东南亚研究中心（CCSEAS）[3]。巴巴萨赫卜 • 安贝德卡尔 • 马拉特瓦达大学，当时名为马拉特瓦达大学，于 1986 年开设中文文凭课程。从那时起，印度全国有几所大学都设立了中文系，但比哈尔邦这个本应成为中国研究中心的大邦，在汉语课程推广方面却没取得多少进展。比哈尔邦与中国在古代的互动主要是基于学习佛经和对社

1　Nair, V G. “A mosaic life of ordinary uniqueness”, 1958-10-10, http://ignca.gov.in/divisionss/kalakosa/kalasamalocana/in-the-footsteps-of-xuanzang-tanyun-shan-the-man-and-his-mission/, 检索日期：2020 年 9 月 22 日。

2　https://www.studyfrenchspanish.com/language-courses-delhi university/#:~:text=After%20starting%20with%20the%20Chinese,the%20Korean%20language%20in%202001, 检索日期：2020 年 9 月 23 日。

3　CCSEAS, JNU official website.

会意义的探索，如今可将古代的友好关系进一步振兴和扩展，读懂和理解印中两国的现代艺术、文学和科技发展。根据 2018 年至 2019 年的数据，来自比哈尔邦的学生人数占贾瓦哈拉尔·尼赫鲁大学学士和硕士学位课程学生总数的 30% 以上。[1] 即使在北方邦的贝拿勒斯印度教大学、西孟加拉邦的印度国际大学、锡金的锡金大学、比邦附近的贾坎德中央大学等大学中，学习汉语的学生也有相当多来自比哈尔邦。但是就比哈尔邦内大学而言，汉语课程的学生入学率非常低。这个问题值得关注。

2　比哈尔邦汉语教育的发展

回顾历史，可以看出比哈尔邦人民乐于接受新的思想、信仰、哲学、宗教、艺术和文化、政治理论等。几乎所有在印度次大陆活跃的宗教都与比哈尔邦有着深厚的联系，有些宗教和哲学要么起源于比哈尔邦，要么在该地区有很多的受众。比哈尔邦的名字来源于巴利语和梵语中的“维哈尔”（天城体：विहार），意思是“住所”或“修道院”。在比哈尔邦产生、辩论和讨论的思想也传递给包括中国在内的邻国和其他国家。因此，即使在现在，比哈尔邦的学生也有学习外语的热情，特别是汉语。他们对学习这门语言有极大的兴趣，并以此为职业。然而，令人失望的是，比哈尔邦并无国家级汉语学习机构的建立机制及发展规划，学生不得不离开家乡去追求自己的梦想。不过中央和邦政府及其他机构仍在努力。

2007 年 2 月 12 日，中国外交部前部长李肇星先生和比哈尔邦首席部长尼蒂什·库马尔先生及中印政要共同出席玄奘纪念馆落成典礼。[1] 这一事件推动了印中两国友好关系的恢复，特别是从比哈尔邦的发展来看。2009 年，玛加德大学成立了外语和文化合作学院（AFLCC），提供包括中文在内的几种外语的一年制证书课程。[2] 玛加德大学校长拉金德尔·普拉萨德于 2019 年 11 月访问中国，研究该大学

1　https://artsandculture.google.com/exhibit/xuanzang-memorial-n%C4%81land%C4%81-xuanzang-memorial-nava-nalanda-mahavihara/-gLy1Bey76EHJA?hl=en, 检索日期：2020 年 9 月 25 日。

2　Verma, Kumod. “MU academy offers courses in foreign languages”, 2009-4-12. http://timesofindia.indiatimes.com/articleshow/4390185.cms?utm_source=contentofinterest&utm_medium=text&utm_campaign=cppst/, 检索日期：2020 年 9 月 26 日。

与中国高等院校之间的教育合作前景。[1] AFLCC 主任哈利・莫汉・普拉萨德说，邀请了大约 20 名中国游客与几名日本、德国和法国游客一起担任教学顾问。新那烂陀佛教大学开设了一年制的汉语言证书课程和两年制的中文本科文凭课程。该大学的官方网站显示，自 2010 年以来，该部门有 50 多名学生获得了有保障的工作。[2] 该大学还设有中文和文学学科博士课程。

2011 年 6 月，比哈尔邦首席部长尼蒂什・库马尔开启了为期一周的中国行，此行的目的是推动和促进印度比哈尔邦和中国在教育、文化和旅游等领域的研究与合作。巴斯大学（University of Bath）高级讲师、研究中国问题的汉学家和专栏作家余克德什瓦尔・库马尔博士对库马尔部长中国之行评价道："这些都是正确的步伐，在正确的时间朝着正确的方向前进。"[3] 尼蒂什・库马尔的中国之行确实加强了两国的联系，并取得了积极的成果。根据那烂陀大学的官方网站，该校虽已开设一年制的中文文凭课程，但最近并无更新。[4] 帕特纳大学自 2017 年以来一直提供半年制的中文、德语和法语证书课程，2018 年有 30 名学生注册。[5] 达尔班加的拉利特・纳拉扬・米提拉大学设立了外语学院，目的是提供中文、德文、西班牙文、韩文、法文、日文和阿拉伯文的证书和文凭课程。然而，由于没有教师，该研究所只提供了法语证书课程，目前第一批课程于 2016 年开始。[6]

除了大学和政府机构，主要在比哈尔邦的首府帕特纳有部分私人汉语学习中心，如多语种汉语学院、汉语班、英国裔美国人等。[7] 虽然这些学校的语言教学水平不能达到德里和孟买等大城市的水平，但取得的成果是值得肯定的。

1　Qadir, Abdul. "No plan to shelve Chinese course: Magadh University VC", 2020-6-29. https://timesofindia.indiatimes.com/city/patna/mu-vc-no-plan-to-shelve-chinese-course/articleshow/76678388.cms, 检索日期：2020 年 9 月 25 日。

2　Official Website of Nava Nalanda Mahavihara, https://www.nnm.ac.in/department/chinese-and-japanese/about-chinese-and-japanese/, 检索日期：2020 年 9 月 25 日。

3　Kumar, Yukteshwar. "An Assessment of Nitish Kumar visit to China", Chennai Centre for China Studies.27 June 2011.https://www.c3sindia.org/archives/an-assessment-of-nitish-kumars-visit-to-china/, 检索日期：2020 年 9 月 26 日。

4　那烂陀大学网站，https://nalandauniv.edu.in/academics/sll/, 检索日期：2020 年 9 月 26 日。

5　http://timesofindia.indiatimes.com/articleshow/69847516.cms?utm_source=contentofinterest&utm_medium=text&utm_campaign=cppst. 19 June 2019, 检索日期：2020 年 9 月 26 日。

6　https://resultfor.in/mithila-university-foreign-language-certificate-diploma-course/#:~:text=Hence%20for%20getting%20an%20easy,%2C%20Chinese%20%26%20Japanese%20and%20Arabic, 检索日期：2020 年 9 月 26 日。

7　https://www.justdial.com/Patna/Language-Classes-For-Chinese/nct-10294790, 检索日期：2020 年 9 月 26 日。

3 挑战与机遇

有一句关于语言学习的中国名言：“一种新的语言就像一种新的生活。”[1] 语言学习者的生活也是一样的。他们从两个角度来思考一切，一个是他们继承的，一个是他们在学习另一种语言之后获得的，通过它来思考和理解所学语言国家的文化、社会和政治思想。因此，语言学习者的生活充满了不同的，有时是未经探索的机遇和挑战。如果学习者的目标语言是小众的，而且周围的人也未完全意识到学习这门语言未来会带来什么好处，在这样的情况下学习者的压力也会增加。本节旨在强调来自比哈尔邦的学生想从事汉语学习和汉语类相关工作时遇到的各种挑战，还讨论了学习者获得学位后他们认为能获得的工作机会。

这一部分，作者采访了 13 名来自比哈尔邦不同地区的人，以及他们对自己学习汉语历程的评估，及其在生活中取得的成功的进展。有些访谈是通过电话交谈，有些是通过问卷调查。根据他们的回答，本节确定了 6 个因素，这些因素在某种程度上被证明是他们学习汉语的障碍。参与者还阐释了从开始学习语言到现在的变化，并提出了一些有利于比哈尔邦汉语教学计划发展的想法和观点。

3.1 社会和文化

贾坎德中央大学汉语专业助理教授阿尔贝娜·拉杰于 2003 年开始学习汉语。她认为，比哈尔邦的人热衷于工程和医学专业，认为只有选择这些专业的学生才是选择了明智的和正确的职业生涯，外语专业不容易被家人和亲戚接受。来自新德里尼赫鲁大学的博士学者尼希特·库马尔表示，在他开始学习汉语时，他的家人或亲戚未曾学习任何外语。阿皮曼俞·库马尔目前在中国航空公司新德里办事处担任销售助理，他表示并没有面临太多的社会限制，以至于他和他的家人认为，大学的排名和名气比所学习的课程更重要。另一名受调查者维韦克·库马尔称，仅掌握语言技能的人没有社会地位。他的亲戚认为，要首先从高等学府获得学位，之后在政府机构任职，成为一名公务员，才会受人尊敬，提高社会地位。23 岁的阿努潘·基山解

1 https://www.chineseclass101.com/chinese-vocabulary-lists/top-10-quotes-about-language-learning/, 检索日期：2020 年 9 月 24 日。

释了她周围社会中人们的心态，并说人们质疑通过学习语言就能获得就业机会，人们认为掌握一门技术，获得有保障的工作最重要。据她讲，比哈尔邦的人更热衷于在政府工作，比如银行业、铁路和公共服务委员会。她还强调，这种态度不仅学生有，他们的父母也有。西安外国语大学从事印度研究的外国专家阿杰·克里希那分享了他的经验，并回顾了他想学习外语时与家人、亲戚和朋友的一些讨论。他解释说，从过去到现在比哈尔邦基本上还是一个以农业为主的社会，农业部门没有扩大，取得的成果有限。人们热衷于有保障的政府工作，因为有固定的收入，而且风险小。追求新事物对比哈尔邦的人民来说是有风险的，因此年轻人想选择医生、工程师、银行职员等职业。这种社会和文化思想不是在一二十年内发展起来的，而是在几十年甚至自 20 世纪以来发展起来的，需要时间来改变。

3.2　金融

比哈尔邦的国内生产净值 / 总值在印度所有邦中最低。[1] 据印度储备银行的报告，从 2018 年至 2019 年购买力评价指数来看，比哈尔邦人均购买力为 640 美元，而印度国民人均为 2 395 美元。[2] 尽管比哈尔邦的经济在过去几十年一直持续增长，但仍远远落后于印度其他地区。因此，那里的人们愿意把钱花在可以给他们带来快速、定期和长期利益的事情上。这就是为什么即使父母要贷款花大量的钱在孩子的教育上，让他们成为医生或工程师，他们也不会犹豫，因为他们确信投入就有所回报。他们不会把时间和金钱花在他们认为未来没有保障和未充分探索的领域。笔者也有过这样的经历，被要求必须在建筑师或在汉语教学领域从事未知职业中做出选择。虽然学习建筑课程的成本和总费用比学习汉语课程高得多，但父母更愿意让女儿成为建筑师。这最终将是一个被大家认可和受尊重的职业，也将带来丰厚的收入。但正是我学习新事物的热情最终说服了父母，让我追求自己感兴趣的事业。阿杰·克里希那认为，根据目前的情况，学习汉语具有“低投资、高收益”特征，但他在这

1　“MOSPI net state domestic product, Ministry of Statistics and Programme Implementation, Government of India”, 检索日期：2020 年 9 月 28 日。

2　“MOSPI net state domestic product, Ministry of Statistics and Programme Implementation, Government of India”, 检索日期：2020 年 9 月 28 日。

个领域花了很多时间才知道这一点。

3.3　缺乏学术环境

阿尔贝娜·拉杰认为比哈尔邦没有良好的汉语学习项目。另一位问卷参与者，尼赫鲁大学博士学者康特·库马尔表示在做听力口语练习时必须使用录音带。虽然信息和通信技术的发展确实在学习方式上有所帮助，但他认为，比哈尔邦的学生仍然没有很好地掌握更加先进的汉语学习技术。他认为，那烂陀大学和玛加德大学的汉语课程水平高。尼希特·库马尔也觉得比哈尔邦没有好的汉语学习项目。天津南开大学工商管理硕士阿洛克·辛格表示，比哈尔邦有几所教授汉语的学院，但这些学院都没有达到较高的水平。根据他的说法，汉语学习者／学者专家社区需要付出更多努力来填补这一空白。阿努潘说，比哈尔邦的所有大学都应该开设汉语学士学位，并将其放在与其他学科同等重要的位置。她还认为，语言教学的单调和传统的方式应该被取缔，教学机构应该对标中国的对外汉语教学标准。

3.4　缺乏接触和信息

奇怪的是，印度拥有大量汉语学生的城市仍然缺乏好的汉语培训机构。尼希特·库马尔开始学习汉语时，他家乡没有学习资源。甚至在他想从事这一行业之前，他家乡并没有人学习过汉语。他发现，除了使用移动设备和较少的应用程序外，并无其他学习途径。他认为，英语在交流中的优势，限制了人们学习汉语。汉语有不同的笔画和音调，这使它成为一门很难学习的语言，也是学生不选择汉语的原因。尼希特补充说，应该让比哈尔邦的人们意识到古代印度（特别是比哈尔邦）和中国之间的互动，年轻人应该多挖掘中国的资料，更多地了解中国。库马尔乐观地认为，在未来，如果有机会和渠道，比哈尔邦的人将像学习其他语言一样学习汉语。

阿努潘儿时的梦想是出国留学，成为一名博学的助理教授，汉语可能会助她梦想成真。但缺乏足够信息是她奔赴梦想的障碍，她觉得很多时间浪费在了寻找可靠的信息来源上。阿皮曼俞说，当他在贾瓦哈拉尔·尼赫鲁大学攻读汉语学士学位时，他很高兴能进入印度一流大学学习。他并未结识过那些通过学习汉语而找到工作的人，但是，随着时间的推移，他意识到学习汉语的重要性，特别是当他有机会申请中国孔子学院奖学金赴华学习时。他还坦陈，在他的家乡学习外语的信息非常少。当另一位调查参与者德夫拉特于2017年开始学习汉语时，人们开始意识到学习汉语的光明前景，正如他所说，他很幸运有一个哥哥鼓励他学习汉语，并告诉将来会因此获得很多机会。

3.5　就业不安全感

阿尔贝娜·拉杰认为，汉语并不能帮助学习者在比哈尔邦获得良好的工作机会。尼希特·库马尔说，自己对未来不确定，学习外语对他的家人来说是陌生的。阿皮曼俞认为，目前在比哈尔邦，学习汉语后能获得的就业机会很少。维韦克·库马尔在接受采访时说，他的家人在通过学习语言而获得好工作这一问题上存疑。他的家人更倾向于让他去获得技术性学位，这将最终帮助他在毕业后找到好工作。他进一步补充说，他不相信比哈尔邦的佛教旅游景点能为比哈尔邦的汉语学习者创造必要的就业机会。此外，现在还有许多学生在比哈尔邦临近的大学学习汉语，如贝拿勒斯印度教大学和印度国际大学，能够轻松满足比哈尔邦佛教旅游导游数量的有限要求。在完成了印度的研究生学业之后，维韦克又在北京语言大学学习了两年，目前在广州工作。虽然他对他的工作很满意，但他经常要承受思乡之苦，并希望能在自己的家乡找到好工作。康特·库马尔认为，比哈尔邦的就业机会令人满意，对未来乐观。

3.6　缺乏政府的积极参与、激励和鼓励

库马尔说，政府必须积极参与并促进比哈尔邦的汉语学习计划的实施，无论是在语言和文学方面，还是在国际关系研究方面。他建议中央和邦政府安排资金支持汉语学习。阿尔贝娜认为，如果中央和邦属大学开设中文系和学位课程，就能满足人们和社会的需要。阿皮曼俞在讨论中进一步补充道，比哈尔邦政府需要主动推广汉语学习计划，只有这样才能维持汉语教育的长远发展。可从其他邦的大学借鉴汉语教学的成功案例，如贾坎德邦、古吉拉特邦、马哈拉施特拉邦，这些邦的邦属大

学几年前就开设汉语课程，在汉语学习方面做得很好。维韦克强调，政府需采取坚定有效的措施，给予政策支持，在高校开设正规课程，与中国的大学建立联系，否则汉语教学是不可能在该邦得到发展的。阿杰认为，如果政府出台并支持在该邦推广汉语，比哈尔邦可以成为“语言学习中心”，此举将带动投资、工业和基础设施建设，有助于比哈尔邦的全面发展。

4 结论

中国在区域和全球平台上的经济发展和决定性作用，增加了学习汉语的需要。比哈尔邦与中国之间原有的联系不仅将推动比哈尔邦的发展进程，而且将促进印度与中国之间的友好关系。即使没有任何先进的基础设施，来自比哈尔邦的学生学习了汉语，走出比哈尔邦，在各个部门工作，可加强印中友谊。比哈尔邦的人民虽然更倾向于政府的工作和职业，认为这给了他们一个有保障的未来，但随着时代的进步和时间的推移，他们的想法已经改变。现在更多的人准备选择冒险和充满不确定性的职业，在他们古老的文化中孕育着新思想和新道路。这一切还需要政策的保障和支持，没有足够的资金和政策支持，任何计划都不可能成功。结合印中要求，可以建立印中联合教育机构。像德里—北京、班加罗尔—成都、加尔各答—昆明、广州—艾哈迈达巴德和那烂陀—西安一样，比哈尔邦和陕西省可以结为印度和中国两大亚洲文明古国之间的文化交流伙伴。“孔雀王朝”和“古普塔王朝”这两个古老的印度王国，曾将首都设在巴特利普特拉（现在的巴特纳，比哈尔邦首府）；汉、唐是中国两个重要的朝代，它们都将首都设在陕西省。但是，所有计划都需要专业的决策者了解两国情况，精通两国语言。南非前总统纳尔逊•罗利拉拉•曼德拉说：“如果你用他明白的语言交谈，会让他记在脑子里。若用他的母语交谈，他会铭记于心。”为更好地了解对方，用彼此的语言交谈应永远是奠定两国友谊与互信基础的第一步。

（孙美幸／翻译，甘露婷／校对）

参考文献

[1] KUMAR R. Institutionalization of Chinese language teaching in India: issues, challenges and the way forward[M]//NAYAK S, RAKESH R. Understanding China in the 21st Century. Phoenix: Heritage Publishers,2020.

The Chinese Experience at Doon University: Challenges and Opportunities

Tanvi Negi[1]

Abstract China and India as the Trans-Himalayan neighbours share a long history of civilizational dialogue. The transmission of knowledge across the porous borders and the process of mutual learning created what can be considered the most glorious part of their history. With China's rapid economic development and its rising political importance and influence in the international arena, the study of Chinese as a foreign language has also gained prominence in the world. In India many universities, colleges and schools are establishing or strengthening and developing their Chinese language programs. Doon University, a public state university situated in the hill state of Uttarakhand in North India established its Chinese language program in the year 2010.

Chinese being a tonal and pictographic/ideographic language is very difficult for a L2 learner coming from a non-alphabetical and non-tonal language background to learn. The challenges we face as teachers of a foreign language cannot be separated from challenges the students face while learning a foreign language. This paper is an attempt to present a comprehensive study of the Chinese language program in

1 Ms. Tanvi Negi has been teaching in the Department of Chinese Studies at Doon University as an Assistant Professor since 2010. She completed her Bachelors and Masters from Jawaharlal Nehru University. In 2008, she was awarded with one-year scholarship by the Ministry of Human Resource Development to study at South East Normal University in Guangzhou, PRC. Her research interests include Teaching of Chinese as a Foreign Language, Modern and Contemporary Chinese Literature and Translation Studies.

Doon University and will discuss the objectives behind the program, the challenges faced by the students and the current scenario and future of Chinese studies in India. The attempt is to define the challenges and opportunities a regional university in its nascent stage faces and its role in the overall development of Chinese Studies in India.

Key Words Doon University; Chinese studies in India; Challenges in L2 learning; TCFL

China and India are two of the greatest civilizations in the world who have emerged as powerful economies in the post-modern globalized world after going through a tumultuous period of foreign invasion, and social transformations in the modern era. These "Trans-Himalayan" neighbors share not only a common border but also a history and cultural connections. We are what Prof. Tan Chung has very affectionately called "cultural cousins". The history of civilizational dialogues between these two great nations is centuries old. The transmission of knowledge across the porous borders and the process of mutual learning created what can be considered the most glorious part of their history. India had a spiritual influence on China through Buddhism that travelled from India to China where it was not only welcomed but also adapted to the local cultural needs. Buddhist monks travelled between these two countries learning and propagating the Buddhist teachings. The profound influence of India on China is not only visible in the spiritual realm but in the language as well. The Chinese language bears the marks of this influence in its vocabulary very evidently. Therefore, it is safe to infer that the teaching and learning of each other's language is but an ancient phenomenon in these two countries.

With China's rapid economic development and its rising political importance and influence in the international arena, the study of Chinese as a foreign language has also gained prominence in the world with over 40 million people around the world learning it as a second language. The sudden increased interest in learning

Chinese is what was termed the "Mandarin Wave". Universities all over the world have departments devoted exclusively to studying China, Chinese language and Chinese culture. India also witnessed a gained interest in the teaching and learning of Chinese language in the new millennium with the deepening of trade relations between the two countries. Chinese language programs were established in many public and private universities and colleges and the existing programs were developed. Despite the fact that teaching of Chinese language did enjoy the attention that it deserved, there still is a long way to go.

Students from Doon University celebrating Chinese New Year

1 CHINESE LANGUAGE PROGRAM IN DOON UNIVERSITY: OBJECTIVE AND STRUCTURE

Doon University, a public state university situated in the hill state of Uttarakhand in North India established its Chinese language program in the year 2010. Chinese was among the first three languages to be introduced under the School of Languages, the other two being Spanish and German. By introducing degree programs in foreign languages, Doon University became the first and the only university in the northern Himalayan belt to do so. The Chinese language program was an important part of the larger vision to enhance the employability of the students by making them skilled professionals who would cater to the demands of the market by gaining proficiency in foreign languages. Apart from the need to make the courses skill-oriented, it was also seen as equally important to nurture talent that can carry out academic research in the field of foreign language education, area studies, culture studies, translation and interpretation studies. Therefore, a multidisciplinary approach to foreign language education was seen as inherent to the development the of School of Languages. The objective behind launching the School of Languages with Chinese as one of the three languages may be seen as multifold. The most apparent one was the increased demand of professionals proficient in Chinese language, which we can call the economic factor. The increased and improved trade relations between the two countries witnessed an unbelievably large number of Chinese companies being started in India which increased the demand exponentially more than the supply. The second reason could be political and cultural that is, the need to learn and understand our neighbours so as to foster better relations. Uttarakhand situated in Himalayas shares a border with China and therefore becomes important. There is evidence of trade activities carried out between China and Uttrakhand in ancient times, as noted by Subhani, "regular and steady trade floated through the entire Himalayan range. ...traders across the hump met periodically to barter the products of their countries"[1]224.

As the only university in the state and northern Himalayan belt to offer degree courses in Chinese language, Doon University became a sought-after destination for the students from the region. The structure of the course was designed to be both job-oriented and research-oriented, with courses in the Bachelor program focusing on developing language skills and Master's focusing on enhancing students' analytical abilities and research aptitude. Keeping in view the above, the courses offered in Bachelor's range from reading, writing, comprehension, newspaper Chinese, and composition writing to Chinese culture. The aim is not only to equip students with conversational Chinese but also ensure that they have the required repository of vocabulary to discuss about Chinese society, culture, and history, as well as read a Chinese newspaper. The Master program offers courses mainly on ancient, modern and contemporary Chinese literature, translation studies and interpretation. Students are required to write a Master's dissertation of 10,000 Chinese characters, the Chinese Department in Doon University is perhaps the only department in India to do so.

The Chinese language program in Doon University started in 2010 with 25 seats, and only 9 were filled that year. In 2011, 13 students enrolled, 18 in 2012, 16 in 2013, 26 in 2014, 25 in 2015, and since then the Department has run at full capacity of 25 to 27 students. As can be seen from this data, Chinese was not the most popular language in Uttarakhand in the beginning, but it slowly and steadily picked up the pace. The reason for less enthusiasm for Chinese language is the common understanding that Chinese is a very difficult language. The gradual increase in the number of students enrolling in the program is due to the popularity and success of the course. The first student from the Department who won a scholarship to study in China was in 2014, which greatly enhanced the popularity of the course. When asked why you chose to study Chinese language, the answers are following, with the most common being "because my parents/elder siblings told me to", closely followed by "it will yield better job opportunities". There are some who are motivated to learn Chinese because it is becoming a global superpower and some want to learn about the culture and find the language challenging. As can be seen, the main driving force behind the decision to learn Chinese for the students is mainly economic, as they want to get a well-paying job after completing their Bachelor's. Since many students come from economically weaker households, this is well understood. However, what has been observed is that the students who are motivated to learn Chinese to further their knowledge of Chinese and are passionately in love with everything Chinese, do infinitely better than the students who are in it only to get a good job.

2 TEACHING CHINESE AS A FOREIGN LANGUAGE IN DOON UNIVERSITY: DIFFICULTIES AND CHALLENGES

The academic field of Teaching Chinese as Foreign Language (TCFL) in China began in the 1950s when the first batch of foreigner students were received in China. "In this era, there is a record for teaching of Chinese as second language in China; in 1947, Professor Wang Minyuan who was holding a post of Professor in the Department of Western Languages in Peking University, 'took on the concurrent responsibility to train eleven students sent by the Indian Government to China in Chinese language'. This is the earlier records in China pertaining to the teaching of Chinese as a foreign language, in fact Professor Wang Minyuan is the pioneer of Chinese language teaching in China."[2]244 Since then, the field has received wide attention within and outside China with the establishment of Confucius Institutes all over the world. The research and practice of teaching Chinese as a foreign language is now a vibrant field with universities and departments in the universities dedicated to it. The emergence and development of TCFL in China corresponded to the development in the field of Foreign Language Acquisition in the West. The western theories of Structural Linguistics, Psycho-linguistics, Communicative Approach, etc. had a lasting impact on Chinese scholars involved in researching the field of TCFL.

"Teaching of Chinese language in India began back in 1918 in Calcutta University, West Bengal. Due to shortage of students, the course had to be abandoned. Later in 1937 with the setting up of Cheena Bhavana（中国学院）in Viswa Bharti University also located in West Bengal, Chinese language teaching was formally institutionalized."[3]16 In the later decades Chinese language programs were set up all over the country; however, the number remained abysmal. It is in recent decades that the teaching of Chinese language, literature and culture has gained some momentum. Prof. Tan Chung opines, "The greatest obstacle in popularizing Chinese language in India is a psychological problem, that it is too risky to commit one's limited life span to learning it."[4]164 The point he stresses on is the popular view that Chinese is arguably the most difficult language in the world and since Chinese does not belong to the same language family as English or Hindi, acquiring it will amount to an impossible task, is essentially a faulty one. India is a multicultural, multi-ethnic and multilingual country, and the majority of the Indian population is multilingual, therefore, it is safe to say that Indians have the capacity to acquire more than one language. So what makes Chinese challenging or difficult? Prof. Tan Chung answers this question by laying down the challenge that every teacher of Chinese confronts. What a "Chinese language teacher deals with is not merely a language. The Chinese script for instance, is an ancient phenomenon, with two thousand years of history. We are dealing with a subject which is embodiment of one of the longest and richest cultures and civilizations of the world."[4]175 Therefore, teaching Chinese does not only means teaching a student to speak Chinese but also to be able to speak with correct sounds, tones, and intonation, to be able to write Chinese characters with correct stroke order and to be able to read and translate literary and non-literary texts.

Chinese being a tonal and pictographic/ideographic language is very difficult for an L2 learner coming from a non-alphabetical and non-tonal language background to learn. The students in Doon University mainly hail from the State and in recent years, students from other States have also started to enroll in the Chinese language program here, making the classroom an interesting mix of influence of different mother tongues and cultures. The medium of instruction in the schools in North India and specifically Uttarakhand is English, and the popular language spoken is Hindi. The other regional languages spoken in the Uttarakhand State are Garhwali, Kumaoni, Jaunsari, Jaunpuri, etc.

The linguistic challenges that learning Chinese poses are mainly in the areas of pronunciation, reading, grammar, comprehension and characters. The following study and observations are based on the writer's experience of teaching in Doon University and mainly focuses on the difficult areas as observed in the said select sample (students learning Chinese in Doon University).

2.1 PRONUNCIATION: SOUNDS / TONES

The sound chart is the first thing that is taught to the students when they begin learning Chinese. What we have observed with students here is that the sounds students find most difficult are "z, c", and "nü, lü", which are mainly the sounds that are not present in their Hindi or English. Some students cannot differentiate between "s" and "sh" probably because in Kuamaoni (a regional language of the State) "s" sound does not exist. It has been found that the students get confused with similar sounding sounds like "duo/dou, guo/gou, nü/niu". Another problem area noticed is pronouncing the Chinese sounds as English words like "liang" is pronounced as "l-i-y-a-n-g" or "tuan" as "th-w-a-i-n". The interference of English pronunciation is very evident. To solve these problems dictations are given to students, and repetitions of similar sounding sounds is done in the class.

Probably one of the most difficult part of spoken Chinese is mastering the tones. Many researchers have time and again focused on the importance of it. According to McGinnis, "There is nothing secondary about tone in Chinese, yet to most learners of Chinese as a second language, the supra-segmental feature of lexical tone is so far removed from their native language experience as to render the mastery of tones problematic, neglected or both"[5]228. Chiang suggests that producing correct tones is not easy. "It requires correctly perceiving the tones（听调）, distinguishing the tones（辨调）, memorizing the tones（记调）, producing the tones in isolation（发音）, and finally, producing the correct tones for every word in natural speech."[6]219 Prof. Tan Chung even goes so far as to say that, "Reading the sound alone is incomplete reading, therefore, no reading at all."[4]177

Therefore, it is safe to say that speaking in correct tones is but a necessity for mastering Chinese language. However, this is one area that the students here have been seen lacking. Even students in advanced levels and with otherwise a good command over spoken and written Chinese have been observed making mistakes in tones while reading or speaking. The most often seen problem is distinguishing between the first and second tone. For example "bù"（不）in "bùmáng"（不忙）will have fourth tone and second tone in "búduì"（不对）. There is a tendency among students to end a sentence with either third or fourth tone irrespective of whatever the tone is on the last character. The reason for bad tones can be attributed to a lack of Chinese language atmosphere in the classroom and to less time devoted to teaching and learning tones. Researchers have recommended memorization to play a key role in Chinese language learning, as Chiang states that learning Chinese requires "a unique memorizing effort: remembering masses of new words, along with their tones and characters"[6]220. Therefore one strategy to master tones is memorizing the tones which is doable when the vocabulary is less but as the number of words to learn increase exponentially it becomes more and more difficult. Therefore, a rigorous practice of reading needs to be developed in the students.

2.2 READING

Reading a Chinese text differs from reading a text in any other language as Chinese is a non-alphabetic and a tonal language. While reading there is a strong tendency among students to Indianize the intonation of foreign language. A case in point is Indian English. Reading Chinese as researchers have pointed out involves "the basic awareness of the basic units of spoken language, the basic units of writing system and the mapping between the two"[6]187. Therefore the successful reading of a Chinese text involves two processes of "character recognition" and "character production". The importance of reading has received a lot of attention in Foreign/Second Language Acquisition. Scholars argue that reading fluency should be an important goal in a Chinese language curriculum where, "Reading fluency refers to a level of reading accuracy and rate where decoding is relatively effortless; where oral reading is smooth and accurate with correct prosody; and where attention can be allocated to comprehension"[6]195. Therefore a student of advanced level should be able to read a Chinese text fluently, accurately, with correct tone and intonation and should be able to comprehend what he/she is reading. In Doon University, reading is another area where the students lag far behind, for reading for them translates into just reading the sounds that are also sometimes wrong. The most glaring problem witnessed is the coupling of wrong characters together, stressing on the wrong word and not pausing at the right places. The students have a tendency of reading every two words together whether they belong together or not. For example., “于是，在这 类家 长的 潜意 识中 就深 深地 烙上 了一 种不 容易 解得 开的 情结”. As can be seen in this example this way of reading can never lead to comprehension, therefore the students never know what they are reading and what it means. For them reading becomes a meaningless exercise.

The only method to improve reading ability is to read more and listen to more Chinese audio texts. Therefore, the text books need to have more scope for reading practice and extensive reading is required in the classrooms.

2.3 CHARACTERS

The Chinese script has often been cited as one of the biggest obstacles in Chinese language learning. The Chinese language competence is more often than not equated with successful memorization and command over Chinese characters. It is said that advanced reading proficiency requires the mastery of some 3,500 characters. Many researches have focused on the learning of Chinese characters where learners have been noticed to use methods like rote repetition, using mnemonic devices, learning characters through etymology-oriented approach, etc. The most often posed query to us in the first few months of learning Chinese is, “how to learn characters? Is there a quick way to learn them?” The traditional mode of teaching has always stressed a lot of importance on mastering the Chinese characters. However, with the proliferation of digital writing in the 21st century many course designers and language teachers and researchers have begun to question the importance of it. For those text book designers whose aim is at the acquisition of conversational skills, they have done away with characters altogether. Some have suggested a partial and restricted use of characters to focus on enhancing communicative competence. However, in Doon University the Chinese language program aims at nurturing a talent that will not only cater to the market demands but also help in furthering understanding of Chinese society and culture, therefore focus on character learning is urgent. Since Chinese characters are culturally loaded, it is all the more important to teach them to students to enhance their understanding of Chinese culture.

2.4 GRAMMAR

Chinese grammar is fundamentally different from English and Hindi grammar. A majority of the text books focus on extensive explanation of grammar points（语法点）, which goes to show the importance given to grammar. The traditional method of language teaching, i.e. Grammar Translation method, was replaced by the communicative approach in language learning laying emphasis on enhancing learners communicative/linguistic competence. Structural linguistics gave a new approach to understanding the mysterious phenomenon of acquiring a foreign language. "Chomskyan linguists made the convincing case for a Universalist model, one which established that at a deep level all languages shared the same properties."[7]16 Therefore teaching or learning a second or foreign language is done through L1 or L2. However, some unique features in Chinese grammar makes it difficult for an Indian learner who comes from a multilingual background. The main areas where the students have been found to struggle are as follows:

a. Verb Complements, complement of duration, single and compound direction complement, potential complement, resultative complement, etc. Since neither English or Hindi has an equivalent of Verb Complements it poses a challenge for the students.
b. *Ba* constructions: The disposal *ba*（把） is one of the most important and commonly used constructions in Chinese. It is a unique sentence structure in Chinese, which can hardly find any equivalent in European languages such as English. Even though it can be used in most of the sentences students still very rarely form sentences using *ba*（把）.
c. Classifiers: Chinese has a unique feature of Classifiers that is non-existent in English or Hindi. The students are able to learn and use the nominal classifiers, however since they associate it with quantity and not with an object, their understanding of them is limited. It has also been noted that for objects that the students do not know the classifier they use *ge*（个）.

d. In Chinese sentences the reason or cause for an action is mentioned first and the result or consequence later which is not same in English or Hindi.

e.g.: 为了学习汉语，她去中国留学。

The most often mistakes made by the students are due to the interference of their mother tongue or English. Interference applies to bilinguals or multilinguals who manifest confusion and overlap between their languages. Extensive research has been done on the phenomenon of L1 and L2 interference. Dr. Geeta Kochhar in her study posits that since Indians are multilinguals and they learn Chinese through another foreign language (L2) which is English, it is more difficult for them to master Chinese language. It has been observed not only in students at the intermediate level but also in advanced level students, a tendency to think in English and then translate the idea into Chinese. Therefore, the interference of English can be seen in the sentences they construct.

Basic and Intermediate level:
a. 我学习汉语在杜恩大学。
I learn Chinese at Doon University.
b. 我让他跟我一起来有空的时候在。
I asked him to come with me when he is free.
c. 下雨来了。
The rain has come. (This is literal translation of how it is said in Hindi.)
Advanced level:
a. 你可以找到这些句子在很多文学中。
You can find these sentences in many literatures.
b. 因为我的父母总是教我帮助人民在他们困难的时候。
Because my parents have always taught me to help people when they are in trouble.
c. 他买了一件礼物为了给她。
He bought a gift to give her.
d. 我将捐一些钱给穷人，并为穷人的孩子学习。
I will donate some money to poor people and for their children to study.

As can be seen from the above examples, a wrong methodology is applied by students while writing in Chinese. The same mistakes are made even when they reach an advanced level. Because Indians are multilinguals or bilinguals at the very least, they have a habit of shifting between languages when thinking or talking. Therefore, for them it makes sense and is easier to form a sentence first in English or Hindi and then translate into Chinese. The reason why they are unable to form correct sentences while doing so is that they do not have a firm grasp on Chinese grammar. Most of the students depend very early on in their language studies on the use of digital tools like digital dictionaries. Their phones have apps (Pleco, etc.) that provide them with a Chinese equivalent for every English word and therefore they very quickly forget what little grammar they had learnt. The method to tackle this problem is using the grammar to make as many sentences as possible and to read as many Chinese texts as possible. The urgent need for a strong grammatical foundation is required.

Apart from the above-mentioned difficulties faced by students as observed while teaching Chinese language in Doon University, there are other challenges that hamper an effective teaching/learning environment, especially in the case of a regional University like Doon University. The lack of infrastructure is the first challenge. The lack of native faculty means lack of authentic Chinese language environment which directly influences students' motivation. The lack of scholarships has also been noticed to dampen the students' enthusiasm. The number of scholarships given to study in China is way less than the number of students applying for them. It has been observed that one year of study in China greatly improves the listening and spoken ability of the students.

3 FUTURE OF CHINESE STUDIES IN INDIA: CHALLENGES AND OPPORTUNITIES

The National Education Policy 2020 lays focus on the multidisciplinary approach to education and highlights the value of language teaching and translation. It states in its point 22.14, "India will also urgently expand its translation and interpretation efforts in order to make high quality learning materials and other important written and spoken material available to the public in various Indian and foreign languages. For this, an Indian Institute of Translation and Interpretation (IITI) will be established. Such an institute would provide a truly important service for the country, as well as employ numerous multilingual language and subject experts, and experts in translation and interpretation, which will help to promote all Indian languages". The importance given to language teaching and translation can be seen as a welcome recognition for the field. This also means that there is now a greater responsibility that all the foreign language departments will have to take on, to create language professionals who are experts in translation studies.

The future of Chinese studies is therefore bright; however, there are many challenges to its holistic growth. The field of Chinese language teaching is over eighty years old in India and still there are no text books that cater to the Indian students. The research of Chinese language acquisition is still a field that enjoys way less attention than other fields like China Studies, International Relations, Chinese Literature, etc. The growth of the Chinese studies field is not possible without the financial and strategic support of the Government, private foundations, institutions, publishers and individuals. The changing dynamics of China-India relations also pose a challenge for the growth of Chinese Studies in India. In Doon University the applications for admission in the current academic year saw a marked decrease in Chinese language as compared to other languages. As on 12th September 2020, applications for the Chinese language program stood at 17, in stark contrast with all other foreign languages with more than 100 applications.

China and India have a long history of mutual learning and cultural exchanges, the two neighbouring countries have much to learn and gain from each other. As Prof. Tan Chung states, "Indian civilization is a huge container that can accommodate virtually everything, while Chinese civilization is a huge melting pot that transforms all different materials in it into a new compound. India is the 'Unity in Diversity' that projects more Diversity than Unity, China is the 'Unity in Diversity' that tends to replace Diversity with Unity." [8]124 The importance of learning Chinese is undisputed, and Doon University as an effective player in the field of Chinese Studies in India has an important role to play in the development of the field.

REFERENCES

[1] PATTANAYAK D P. Languages for the masses and Chinese languages in India [J]. Anthropological linguistics, 1985, 27 (2).

[2] 赵金铭 . 对外汉语教学法回视与再认识 [J]. 世界汉语教学，2010，2（24）.

[3] KOCHHAR G.Teaching Chinese to Indian students: an understanding[J]. Journal of technology and Chinese language teaching, 2013, 4(1).

[4] TAN C.Teaching Chinese language in India [J]. China report, 1986, 22(2).

[5] SCOTT M.Tonal spelling versus diacritics for teaching pronunciation of Mandarin Chinese [J]. Modern language journal, 1997, 81 (2).

[6] KE C, LI Y A. Chinese as a foreign language in the US [J]. Journal of Chinese linguistics, 2011, 39(1).

[7] BLOCK D.A short history of second language acquisition [J]. The social turn in second language acquisition. Edinburgh: Edinburgh University Press.

[8] TAN C. Sino-Indian cultural synergy: twenty centuries of civilizational dialogue [J]. China report, 2006, 42(2).

杜恩大学的汉语教学：挑战与机遇

丹　妮[1]

摘要　中国和印度以喜马拉雅山脉为界，拥有悠久的文明对话史。尽管中印边境问题犹存，但两国人民跨越边界传播知识、相互学习，创造了辉煌的历史。随着中国经济的快速发展，以及中国在国际舞台上政治重要性和影响力的不断提升，对外汉语研究也在世界范围内得到了重视。在印度，许多大学、学院和学校正在设立或发展各自的汉语项目。位于印度北部山区北阿肯德邦（Uttarakhand）的公立杜恩大学2010年起设立了汉语项目。中文是一种有声调的象形语言（表意语言），对于一个没有拼音和声调语言背景的第二语言学习者来说，学习中文非常困难。作为外语教师，我们面临的挑战与学生学习外语时面临的挑战息息相关。本文将对杜恩大学的汉语项目进行全面研究，并将讨论该项目背后的目标、学生们面临的挑战，以及印度汉语研究的现状和未来，从而分析一所地方性大学在初创阶段所面临的挑战和机遇及其在印度汉语研究整体发展中的作用。

关键词　杜恩大学；印度汉语研究；第二语言学习的挑战；对外汉语教学

1　丹妮教授2010年至今在杜恩大学中国学系任教，担任助理教授。获印度尼赫鲁大学学士和硕士学位。2008年参加印度人力资源发展部（现更名教育部）奖学金项目，赴中国东南师范大学学习一年。丹妮教授的研究方向是对外汉语教学、中国现当代文学和翻译研究。

中国和印度是世界上最大的两个文明体，它们在经历了近代外国入侵和社会变革的动荡时期后，在全球化的世界中成为强大的经济体。这两个“跨越喜马拉雅”的邻国不仅边界毗邻，而且有历史和文化联系，谭中教授亲切地称中印人民为“文化表亲”。这两个伟大国家之间的文明对话史长达几个世纪。两国人民跨越边界的“鸿沟”传播知识、相互学习，创造了两国最辉煌的历史。佛教从印度传到中国，不仅受到当地人民欢迎，而且适应了当地的文化需求，对中国人产生了影响。佛教僧侣游走于中印两国，学习并传播佛教教义。印度对中国产生的影响在汉语词汇中有明显体现。因此可以肯定地推断，在这两个国家，教授和学习彼此的语言已是自古就有的一种现象。

随着中国经济的快速发展及其在国际舞台上重要性和影响力的不断上升，对外汉语研究也在世界范围内受到重视，全世界有4 000多万人将汉语作为第二语言学习。学习汉语的兴趣突增也被称为“汉语热”。世界各地的大学都有专门研究中国、中文和中国文化的院系。随着中印两国贸易关系不断加深，进入新千年后，印度对汉语的教学也越来越感兴趣。许多公立、私立大学和学院都设立了汉语项目，并开发

杜恩大学的学生们庆祝中国新年——春节

了现有课程。尽管近几十年来，汉语教学受到了应有的关注，但仍然任重而道远。

1　杜恩大学的汉语项目：目标与结构

杜恩大学位于印度北部山区北阿肯德邦，是一所公立大学，2010年设立汉语项目。中文是该大学语言学院最先引进的三种外语之一，另外两种是西班牙语和德语。杜恩大学是喜马拉雅北部第一所也是唯一一所设立外语学位项目的大学。汉语技能是提高学生们就业能力很重要的一部分，通过熟练掌握外语，学生们将成为满足市场需求的专业人员。课程以技能培养为导向，除此之外，也重视培养能在外语教育、区域研究、文化研究、翻译和口笔译研究领域开展学术研究的人才。因此，跨学科的外语教育方式是语言学院发展的内在要求。杜恩大学创办以汉语为三大语言之一的语言学院是基于多重背景的。最明显的一个原因是对精通汉语的人员的需求增加，我们可以称之为经济因素。两国之间日益密切的贸易关系促使大量中国公司在印度兴办，本地汉语专业人员供不应求。第二个原因是政治和文化因素，即需要学习和了解我们的邻国，以促进双方友好关系。位于喜马拉雅山区的北阿肯德邦与中国接壤，其地理位置十分重要。据史料记载，在古代，中国与北阿肯德邦有贸易往来。正如苏帕尼所说："长期稳定的贸易活动遍及整个喜马拉雅山脉……商人们也会越过山峰，定期在这里会面，以交换本国产品。"[1]224

作为印度和喜马拉雅北部唯一一所开设汉语学位课程的大学，杜恩大学是该地区众多学生的求学之地。汉语学位课程既面向求职又面向研究，学士课程侧重于培养语言技能，硕士课程侧重于提高学生的分析能力和研究能力。综上所述，本科课程阅读、写作、理解和中国文化，其目的是让学生掌握中文会话，确保他们积累一定的词汇量，能用中文讨论中国社会、中国文化、中国历史，能阅读中文报纸。硕士课程主要包括古代、现代和当代中国文学，翻译研究和口译课程。学生们必须写一篇一万字的中文论文才能取得硕士学位，全印度可能只有杜恩大学中文系才有这个要求。

杜恩大学的汉语项目始于2010年，当年准备招25名学生，最终却只招到了9名。

2011年该校中文系招收了13名学生，2012年招收18名，2013年招收16名，2014年招收26名，2015年招收25名。之后，该系每年招生人数维持在25至27人。从这些数据可以看出，中文最初并不是北阿肯德邦最受欢迎的语言，但它渐渐发展起来。之所以大家一开始对中文不那么感兴趣，是因为大家普遍认为中文是一门非常难学的语言。由于该课程的成功普及，汉语项目招生人数逐年增加。2014年，中文系第一次有学生获得奖学金去中国学习，大大提高了该课程的知名度。当有学生被问及为什么选择学习中文时，答案往往是“因为我的父母/哥哥姐姐告诉我，这会带来更好的工作机会”。那些被打动去学习中文的人中，有的是因为觉得中国正在成为一个全球超级大国，有的则是想了解中国文化，认为中文具有挑战性。显而易见，学生们学习中文的动力主要是经济因素，因为他们想在获得学士学位后找到一份高薪的工作。这一点很好理解，因为许多学生来自收入较低的家庭。然而，据观察，那些以进一步增长中文知识为学习目的并热爱中文的学生，比那些只为找到一份好工作的学生学得更好。

2 杜恩大学对外汉语教学：困难与挑战

在中国，对外汉语教学（TCFL）学术研究始于20世纪50年代，当时中国接收了第一批外国留学生。“这一时期，国内的汉语作为第二语言教学也有记载。1947年，时任北京大学西方语文系教授的王岷源就‘兼任训练印度政府派来北大的十一个学生的华语学习事’。这是在国内有关对外汉语教学较早的记载。其实，王岷源先生也是汉语教学的先驱。”[2]244 此后，随着孔子学院在世界各地建立，汉语教学这一领域受到了国内外的广泛关注。如今，对外汉语教学的研究和实践是一个充满活力的领域，各个大学、院系都致力于此。对外汉语教学在中国的出现和发展与西方外语学习领域的发展是相对应的。西方结构语言学、心理语言学、交际法等理论对研究对外汉语教学领域的中国学者产生了深远的影响。

“1918年，印度西孟加拉邦的加尔各答大学开设汉语教学课程。但由于生源不足，该课程不得不取消。之后，在1937年，同样位于西孟加拉邦的国际大学成立中国学院，汉语教学正式迈入正轨。”[3]16 在之后的几十年里，印度各地都设立了汉语项目，但是数量仍然很少。近几十年来，中文、中国文学和文化教学取得了一些进展。谭中教授认为：“在印度推广汉语的最大障碍是心理障碍，人们认为把自己有限的生命投入汉语学习中风险太大。”[4]164 他强调，人们普遍认为汉语是世界上最难学的语言，而且由于汉语和英语或印地语属于不同的语系，掌握汉语是一项不可能的任务。这个观点在本质上是错误的。印度是一个多文化、多民族和多语言的国家，大多数印度人掌握多种语言，可以说印度人都能够掌握一种以上的语言。那么是什么让他们觉得学习汉语具有挑战性或有难度呢？谭中教授通过列举每位中文教师遇到的挑战回答了这个问题：“中文教师教的不仅仅是语言。例如，汉字是一种古老的文字，具有两千年的历史。我们所教的科目代表着世界上最悠久和最丰富的文化和文明。”[4]175 所以，教授中文不仅是教学生说中文，更要让学生用正确的音调、语调说话，用正确的笔画顺序书写汉字，阅读和翻译文学及非文学文本。

汉字是一种表音表意文字，对于一个没有拼音和声调语言背景的第二语言学习者来说，学习汉语非常困难。杜恩大学的学生主要来自本邦，近年来，来自其他邦的学生也开始报名加入这里的汉语项目，教室成了不同母语和文化交织的趣味混合空间。印度北部特别是北阿肯德邦学校的教学语言是英语，通用语言是印地语。北阿肯德邦其他地区会说加尔瓦尔语、库蒙语、詹萨里语、江浦里语等。

中文学习的挑战主要在发音、阅读、语法、理解和汉字等方面。以下研究和观察是基于作者在杜恩大学的中文教学经验，重点讨论在所选样本（杜恩大学学习中文的学生）中注意到的困难。

2.1　发音：语音、声调

学生们开始学习中文时，首先要学的是拼音。我们注意到，学生们认为最难发的音是“z”“c”和“nü”“lü”，主要是因为印地语或英语中不存在这些发音。一些学生无法区分“s”和“sh”，可能是因为库蒙语（印度的一种地方性语言）中不存在“s”音。学生们也会把类似的发音弄混，比如“duo/dou”“guo/

gou”“nü/niu”。另一个问题是，把汉语拼音读成英语单词，如将“liang”读成“l-i-y-a-n-g”，或将“tuan”读成“th-w-a-i-n”，英语发音的干扰非常明显。为了解决这些问题，老师们会给学生做听写，并在课堂上重复类似的发音。

或许，中文口语学习中最难的一个部分就是掌握声调了。许多研究人员多次强调声调的重要性。麦金尼斯认为：“汉语中的声调没有次要的，然而对于大多数把汉语作为第二语言的学习者来说，由于词汇声调的超音段特征与他们的母语相去甚远，以至于他们对声调的掌握存在问题或被忽视，或是二者兼有。”[5]228 蒋提出，发出正确的声调并不容易，“它需要正确听调、辨调、记调、发音，然后才能自然地发出每个单词的正确声调”[6]219。谭中教授甚至说：“单单发音是不完整的阅读，这相当于根本没有阅读。”[4]177

因此，可以肯定地说，用正确的声调说话只是掌握中文的必要条件。然而，这只是学生们欠缺的诸多领域之一。即使是水平较高的学生，或者是对中文口语和书面语掌握较好的学生，在阅读或说话时也会发错调。最常见的问题是区分变声字，例如“不”（bù）在“不忙”（bùmáng）中是四声，而在“不对”（búduì）中要读成二声。学生们倾向于用三声或四声来结束一个句子，而不管最后一个字的声调是什么。声调学不好的原因可能是课堂上缺乏中文学习氛围，以及在声调教学的时间上付出较少。研究者建议发挥记忆在中文学习中的重要作用，正如蒋所说，学习汉语需要“一种独特的记忆力：即记住大量的新单词，以及它们的声调和书写方式”[6]220。因此，掌握声调的一个策略就是记忆声调，这在词汇量较少时还可行，随着要学习的单词数量呈指数增长，记忆将变得越来越困难。因此，学生需要进行严格的阅读练习。

2.2 阅读

阅读中文文本不同于阅读其他语言的文本，因为中文是非字母的声调语言。在阅读时，学生们常将外语的语调印度化，就像印度英语一样。研究人员指出，阅读中文包括“对口语和写作系统基本单位以及两者之间映射的基本认识”[6]187。因此，阅读中文文本需经历“汉字识别”和“汉字输出”两个过程。阅读在外语/第二语言习得过程中的重要性受到了广泛关注。学者们认为，阅读流畅性应该视为中文课程教学的一个重要目标。“阅读流畅性是指阅读的准确性和速度，即阅读起来不费力，阅读口语流畅准确，韵律正确，注意文章的理解。”[6]195 因此，高水平的学生应该能够流利、准确、语调正确地阅读中文文本，并且能够理解他/她正在阅读的内容。在杜恩大学，阅读方面学生们远远落后，因为他们认为阅读只是去练习有时会出错的发音。他们在阅读时最大的问题就是把错误的汉字连在一起，强调错误的字，而不强调在正确的地方停顿。学生们倾向于两个字一起读，不管这两个字能不能放在一起。例如：“于是，在这 类家 长的 潜意 识中 就深 深地 烙上 了一 种不 容易 解得 开的 情结”。这个例子说明，这种阅读方式永远不会让人理解，因此学生们永远不知道自己在读什么及其意思。对他们来说，阅读成了一项毫无意义的练习。

提高阅读能力的唯一方法就是多阅读，多听中文音频文本。因此，教科书需要包含更多的阅读练习，学生们在课堂上需要进行大量阅读。

2.3 汉字

汉字经常被认为是中文学习的一大障碍。中文能力往往与记忆和掌握汉字的数量成正比。要想提高阅读能力，一个人需要掌握大约 3500 个汉字。许多研究学者非常重视汉字学习。他们注意到很多学习者死记硬背，或用记忆工具、词源学等方法学习汉字。在学习中文的最初几个月里，我们最常遇到的问题就是如何学习汉字书写，有没有快速学习汉字的方法。传统的教学模式一直强调掌握汉字的书写，然而随着 21 世纪电子式书写的普及，许多课程设计者、语言教师和研究者们开始质疑汉字书写的重要性。重在传授交流技巧的教科书设计者甚至完全抛弃了汉字书写。一些人认为限制使用汉字能够提高交际能力。然而，杜恩大学的汉语项目旨在培养满足市场需求且有助于加深对中国社会和文化理解的人才，因此汉字书写的学习是当务之急。由于汉字具有文化内涵，所以教学生们写汉字可增强他们对中国文化的理解。

2.4 语法

中文的语法和英语、印地语的语法是完全不同的。大部分汉语教材都侧重于讲解语法点，这表明了语法的重要性。在强调提高学习者交际、语言能力的语言学习中，传统的语言教学方法——语法翻译法——被交际法取代。结构语言学为理解外语学习的神秘现象提供了一种全新的方法。“美国语言学家乔姆斯基为普遍主义模式提出了令人信服的理由，这种模式认为，从深层次来看，所有语言都具有相同的属性。”[7]16 因此，教授或学习第二语言或外语需要通过第一或第二语言来完成。然而，中文语法的一些独特之处让多语言背景的印度学习者很难理解。以下是几大难点：

（1）动词补语、时量补语、简单趋向补语、复合趋向补语、可能补语、结果补语等。英语和印地语没有动词补语，这对学生来说是一个挑战。

（2）把字句：把字句是中文中最重要、最常用的结构之一，是一种独特的中文句式结构，在英语等欧洲语言中几乎找不到对等句式。尽管“把”可以用在大多数句子中，但学生们仍然很少用“把”来造句。

（3）量词：中文中有量词，而英语或印地语中是没有量词的。学生们可使用名词性量词，但是由于他们把名词性量词和数量联系起来，而不是和宾语联系起来，所以他们对名词性量词的理解是有局限的。还有一点，当学生们不认识宾语指代的物体时，就会用“个”来代替。

（4）中文句子先提到动作产生的原因，再提到结果或后果，这与英语或印地语是不一样的。例如：为了学习汉语，她去中国留学。

学生们的错误往往是母语或英语的干扰造成的。尤其是双语或多语背景的学生，他们会混淆所掌握的语言。针对第一语言和第二语言的干扰现象，学界已有大量研究。吉塔·科恰尔博士在其研究中提到，因为印度人会多种语言，他们通过另一种外语（第二语言）即英语来学习中文，这使得他们掌握中文更难。中级水平和高级水平的学生都倾向于用英语思考，然后再翻译成中文。从他们所造的句子中就可以看出英语干扰的痕迹。

初级和中级水平：

（1）我学习汉语在杜恩大学。

I learn Chinese at Doon University.

（2）我让他跟我一起来有空的时候在。

I asked him to come with me when he is free.

（3）下雨来了。

The rain has come.（这是印地语式的直译。）

高级水平：

（1）你可以找到这些句子在很多文学中。

You can find these sentences in many literatures.

（2）因为我的父母总是教我帮助人民在他们困难的时候。

Because my parents have always taught me to help people when they are in trouble.

（3）他买了一件礼物为了给她。

He bought a gift to give her.

（4）我将捐一些钱给穷人，并为穷人的孩子学习。

I will donate some money to poor people and for their children to study.

从上面的例子可以看出，学生们在用中文写作时使用了错误的方法。即使达到了高级水平，他们也会犯同样的错误。因为印度人一般都掌握至少两种语言，所以他们在思考或说话时会在不同的语言间切换。因此，对于他们来说，要造一个汉语句子，首先要用英语或印地语造句，然后将它翻译成汉语，这样更容易。但是这样并不能造出正确的句子，因为他们对中文语法掌握不牢固。大多数学生在语言学习过程中较早地依赖于数字工具，如电子词典。他们手机里下载了 Pleco 等应用程序，这些程序能够提供英语单词的中文对等词，但他们很快就忘记了所学的一点点语法。

要想解决这个问题，学生们需要多造句来练习语法，多阅读中文文本。夯实语法基础刻不容缓。

以上就是笔者在杜恩大学教授中文时所观察到的学生们面临的问题，除此之外，在杜恩大学这样的地区性大学中还有一些影响有效教学、学习环境的问题。第一，基础设施短缺。第二，本地师资力量不足意味着缺乏真正的中文学习环境，这直接影响到学生的学习动力。第三，奖学金的缺乏也抑制了学生学习中文的积极性。获得去中国学习奖学金的学生的数量远远少于申请奖学金的学生的数量。据观察，在中国学习一年汉语能够大大提高学生的听力和口语水平。

3 印度汉语研究的未来：挑战与机遇

《2020年国家教育政策》强调跨学科的教育方法，以及语言教学和翻译的价值。该政策第22.14条指出："为让公众获得印度的语言和其他语言的高质量学习材料及重要书面和口语学习材料，印度亟需在口笔译方面加强努力。为此，印度将成立口笔译研究所，这个机构将为该国提供极其重要的服务，并聘用众多多语种语言和学科专家以及口笔译专家，从而促进印度所有语言的发展。"印度政府重视语言的教学和翻译可以看作是对该领域的一种认可，这也意味着现在所有的外语系都必须承担起更大的责任，培养翻译研究方面的语言专家。

因此，尽管汉语研究整体发展面临诸多挑战，但其前景还是光明的。在印度，汉语教学已有80多年的历史了，但仍然没有适合印度学生的教科书。与中国研究、国际关系、中国文学等其他领域相比，汉语习得研究仍然较少受到关注。没有政府、私人基金会、机构、出版商和个人的财政和战略支持，汉语研究就不可能得到发展。中印关系的动态变化对印度汉语研究的发展也是一个挑战。与申请其他语言项目的人数相比，杜恩大学本学年申请汉语项目的人数明显减少。截至2020年9月12日，申请汉语项目的人数为17人，与此形成鲜明对比的是，其他外语项目的申请人数在100人以上。

中国和印度有着悠久的相互学习和文化交流的历史，这两个邻国有很多相互学习和借鉴的方面。正如谭中教授所说，“印度文明是一个巨大的容器，几乎可以容纳所有东西，而中国文明是一个巨大的熔炉，可以将所有不同的材料转化为一种新的合成物。印度这个‘多样性中的统一体’强调多样性多于统一性，而中国这个‘多样性中的统一体’倾向于用统一取代多样性”[8]124。学习中文的重要性是毋庸置疑的，杜恩大学作为印度汉语研究领域的重要参与者，在该领域的发展中发挥着关键作用。

（孙美幸 / 翻译，陈冰睿 / 校对）

参考文献

[1] PATTANAYAK D P. Languages for the masses and Chinese languages in India [J]. Anthropological linguistics, 1985, 27 (2).

[2] 赵金铭 . 对外汉语教学法回视与再认识 [J]. 世界汉语教学，2010，2（24）.

[3] KOCHHAR G. Teaching Chinese to Indian students: an understanding [J]. Journal of technology and Chinese language teaching, 2013, 4(1).

[4] TAN C. Teaching Chinese language in India [J]. China report, 1986,22(2).

[5] SCOTT M. Tonal spelling versus diacritics for teaching pronunciation of Mandarin Chinese [J]. Modern language journal, 1997, 81 (2).

[6] KE C, LI Y A. Chinese as a foreign language in the US [J]. Journal of Chinese linguistics, 2011, 39(1).

[7] BLOCK D. A short history of second language acquisition [J]. The social turn in second language acquisition. Edinburgh: Edinburgh University Press.

[8] TAN C. Sino-Indian cultural synergy: twenty centuries of civilizational dialogue [J]. China report, 2006, 42(2).

汉语教学在印度的发展趋势：新机会与挑战

司雷和[1]

摘要 2020年是中印建交70周年，但这两大文明的交流早就超出这70年的时间，两个文明之间的交流源远流长，关系古老悠久。印度的汉语教学虽然是个新现象，但印度自古就有不少汉语专家。到了21世纪，中国进一步向世界开放，不同行业对会中文人才的需求大大增加。21世纪印度同世界及中国的关系日渐密切，很多印度年轻人选择就读汉语专业。同时，汉语教学的过程中也出现了诸多挑战。本文旨在探索汉语教学在印度的发展趋势及其重要性。

关键词 汉语；教学；印度；发展趋势

近年来，中国的世界地位愈发重要，在诸多领域都达到了领先水平。到了21世纪，中国进一步向世界开放，吸引了全世界的目光，了解中国人民和中国文化成为一种新的潮流。学习汉语，加强与中国的交流越来越重要，因此，学习汉语的年轻人也越来越多。2000年以来，印度学习汉语的人数显著增多，他们有的想从商，有的想从事翻译工作，有的想成为导游，有的想做学术研究，汉语学习者的就业选择越来越丰富。但是，汉语教学在印度的蓬勃发展其实并非一个新现象。

1950年4月1日，印度共和国与中华人民共和国建交，印度成为同中国建交的第一个非社会主义国家。2020年是中印建交第70周年，但中印两大文明的交流历史远超70年。中印之间的交往源远流长，两国的关系古老而悠久。印度的汉语教

1 锡金大学语言与文学学院中文系助理教授。

学虽然是个新现象，但印度自古就有不少汉语专家。

在本文中，笔者探索了汉语教学在印度的发展趋势及其重要性。笔者将汉语在古代印度的传播、近代印度汉语教研的重启与当下印度汉语教学发展趋势相联系，讨论了当下印度汉语教学所面临的挑战、解决措施及必要性。

1　古代中印交流中汉语的传播

在古代，中印人文交往频繁，从公元1世纪到6世纪，印度佛教传到中国，这个时期两国之间有关佛教的交往十分密切。据6世纪《高僧传》记载，很多印度僧人在中国从事梵文佛经的汉译工作。另据记载，早在1世纪印度僧人迦叶摩腾（Kashyapamatanga）就被认为是佛教在中国传播的先驱。[1]4 这就说明一些古代印度学者，尤其是僧人精通汉语，这可以算是汉语在印度发展的最早证明。

公元8世纪，印度有三个家族在唐朝的宫廷任职，即迦叶佛（Kashyapa）、鸠摩罗（Kumara）和乔达摩（Gautama）。这三个家族主要从事有关天文学文献翻译的工作。公元718年，乔达摩家族的第三代族人——乔达摩・悉达（Gautama Siddha）把印度的《九曜》年历翻译成中文。这些例子都证明印度不少学者通晓汉语。[1]8 在印度，虽然没有某所学校教授汉语的历史记录，但是印度与中国佛教的交往促使很多印度僧人和学者学习汉语。

2　近代印度的汉语传播

由于各种历史原因，唐代以后印度和中国之间学术、宗教和文化方面的交流锐减，但到了20世纪，两国之间的学术和文化交流又逐渐复苏。1924年4月泰戈尔访华，促进了中印之间交流的发展。从中国回印度后，泰戈尔急切地希望在和平乡国际大学设立一所中国学院。1927年，他在新加坡遇到了年轻的中国学者谭云山，并邀请他访问国际大学。谭云山来到国际大学后便开始教授汉语，最初他只有5个学生。谭云山是泰戈尔的主要合作伙伴，也是他设立中国研究中心的重要帮手。1937年4月10日，这所中国研究中心在和平乡建立，这是近代印度设立的第一所研究中国及中国文化的中心。[1]14

20 世纪 30 年代，拉古 • 维拉开始从事中国文化和中印关系史相关研究，他促进了印度与中国的学术交流。他在新德里设立的国际印度文化学院是一所积极研究中国相关课题的学院。1938 年，拉古 • 维拉还编写和出版了《罗摩衍那在中国》这部重要的学术著作。20 世纪 30 年代后期，浦那的弗格森学院开设了中国研究中心。在这里巴帕特（Bapat）和戈克（Gokro）等学者对梵文、巴利文、中文和藏文佛经进行了比较研究。在此期间，印度著名的中国研究学者师觉月（Prabodh Chandra Bagchi）于 1923 年前往法国，在法国汉学家西尔万 • 列维（Sylvain Lévy）的指导下学习中文。从 1945 年到 1956 年，他在国际大学任教并从事研究工作，在中印文化交流的各个领域都获得了很多重要研究成果。[1]14

3 当前印度汉语教学

在当代印度，和平乡国际大学在促进汉语教学和研究上所做的贡献首屈一指。国际大学的中国学院在一开始主要进行有关中国的研究，后来开始进行汉语教学。初期，蒋介石和周恩来曾向该学院捐赠了大量古代汉语书籍，这些书籍吸引了不少学者前来进行中国古代文化传统方面的研究。

20 世纪 60 至 80 年代，印度一些大学开始设立汉语专业课程，比如新德里的尼赫鲁大学、瓦拉纳西的贝拿勒斯印度教大学、昌迪加尔的旁遮普大学和奥朗加巴德的安贝德卡尔大学。虽然这些大学开设了汉语专业的本科、硕士及短期课程，但当时鲜有人问津。此外，由于汉语老师较少，学习汉语的学生也少。总体来说，当时汉语教学在印度并不如现在普及。

21 世纪，展翅高飞的中国引起了世界各国的注意。21 世纪的印度同样也与全世界紧密相连，与中国的关系也越发密切。但是，中印两国之间的交流、人民之间的交往却存在沟通方面的障碍与挑战。此外，在印度需要中文人才的领域越来越多。学术、经贸商务、机械、信息技术、政治、外交事务谈判、翻译、医疗、旅游、新闻媒体、艺术等领域对中文人才的需求与日俱增，但人才却寥寥无几。这些都促使越来越多的印度高校开设汉语课程，如锡金中央大学、古吉拉特中央大学、台拉登大学、贾坎德中央大学等。很多私立院校也开设了汉语教程，如金德尔大学、阿育王大学、阿米提大学等。21世纪初，印度出现了“汉语热”现象，过去几百年间发展缓慢的汉语教学蓬勃发展，汉语在印度的发展进入了新的阶段，也有了新的机遇。

4 汉语教学在印度面临的挑战

虽然印度的汉语教学有了新的开端和发展，但依然存在不少困难，学生在学习汉语的过程中面临很多问题。最初，汉语学生较少，当时他们面临的问题在于教学条件落后，如几个学生共用一本词典、一本书。此外，学生目前还面临教材有限的问题，这使学习汉语难上加难。

首先是汉语课程和教材问题。在初级阶段，学生主要学习汉语的发音、声调、单词、句子和语法结构。初级阶段持续一年，在这一年内，学生需要充分掌握汉语的基本原则、汉字、发音、声调和语法。尼赫鲁大学选用的教材主要是北京语言大学出版的四册《基础汉语课本》，同时学生在课堂上还进行听力训练；在学习中文的第二和第三年，大学使用中级中文教材，涉及口语、听力、阅读和写作训练。印度西孟加拉邦的国际大学采用的教材是两册《桥梁》，给学生讲解复杂的语法和其他内容。国际大学开设了四年制本科课程，到大学四年级，学生不仅需要掌握中国文学、历史、地理、政治等相关知识，还要学习古代汉语和诗歌、报刊翻译和商务汉语等。[1] 印度尼赫鲁大学的硕士课程有报刊翻译、文学翻译、小说、同声传译、政治思想、文学史、中国经济等。[2] 大学里的课外活动也丰富多彩，学生积极参加各种各样的互动，如文化交流活动、汉语比赛、中国文化比赛、戏剧表演、歌舞活动等。春节期间，使馆和学校共同组织春节联欢会，老师会鼓励学生演出中国家喻户晓的小品或者课堂上学过的小故事。这些都大大提高了学生的自信。

1 CCSEAS BA Courses, Jawaharlal Nehru University, https://www.jnu.ac.in/sllcs/cseas_ba, Also see Cheena Bhavana B.A. Courses,Visva Bharati University, http://docs.wixstatic.com/ugd/05676d_fa7cdec1de9a493b9f4ca7935595e6f9.pdf.
2 CCSEAS MA Courses, Jawaharlal Nehru University, https://www.jnu.ac.in/sllcs/cseas_ma. Also See Cheena Bhavana M.A. Courses,Visva Bharati University, http://docs.wixstatic.com/ugd/05676d_c7a32c4ca8ae4154ab37f1febe48b4e1.pdf

但是到了本科三年级，本应将汉语作为教学语言，然而，全印度都没有这样用汉语全面开展教学的课程。印度的很多大学也没有听力课所需要的设备，如语音室或多媒体教室。大学教程和教材陈旧，无法满足学生的需求，也是学生学习汉语过程中的一大障碍。学习汉语不仅是学习单词和语法，还要掌握好标准发音、声调和口音等。学习一门语言，需要了解当地文化、传统习俗、风俗习惯。尼赫鲁大学位于印度首都新德里，学生同来自中国的留学生，中国旅行团，出差人士，驻印度使、领馆外交官的交流机会多，国际大学也很早就同中国学者有学术交往。可是，其他大学在这方面机会就相对较少。另外，有的设立了本科和硕士学位点的印度高校在课程设置中缺少富有弹性的汉语课程架构。很多学生进入大学学习汉语时并没有长期学习的计划，但是他们至少要上三年大学才能毕业。此外，其他中文机构虽然提供短期课程，但教学质量欠佳，所以大部分学生慢慢地对汉语失去了兴趣。印度高校的汉语学生赴华交流机会有限，不是每个学生在大学学习期间都能获得奖学金去中国学习汉语。另外，新入职的中文老师很少接受教学相关的训练，他们只能依靠自己所掌握的汉语和学习汉语的经验来教学，这就造成了教学过程中的不足。来自中国的老师能更有效地帮助学生学好语言，但是大部分印度高校却没有来自中国的汉语教师。

目前，很多学生学习汉语仅仅一年后就开始从事有关中国政治、经济、国际关系等方面的研究，而研究中国语言、文学、文化、历史、传统习俗等方面的学生却很少。同中国的文化交流也因此受到很大影响，有关中国文化、语言、文学、历史的论坛和会议很少，而关于国际关系、经济等议题的研讨会、交流会却越来越多。

为了解决这些问题，印度高校同中国高校需要加强沟通与交流，我们需要每学期让每个班的一些学生去中国进行一到两个学期的汉语学习；需要促进学生进行多方面、多领域的研究，除国际关系、经济、政治的研究外，还需要促进语言、文学、文化、历史、哲学思想等方面的研究；高校之间也需要教师交流项目，让印度新入职的教师去中国进行汉语教学的训练，请中国的汉语教师到印度教授汉语。汉语教材是汉语教学中最重要的部分，中印高校需要合作在印度出版“印度化”的教材。

此外，印度每所大学和学院都应该配备语音室及多媒体室，以便学生观看中文电影和节目，提高他们的听力水平和表达能力。学生现在使用网上词典非常便捷，可是这些词典却不能教授学生汉语词汇的用法，所以需要优秀的教师通过科学的教学方法给学生正确的引导。解决上述所有问题，汉语在印度的发展才能得以实现。

5　结论

总的来说，中印两国高校需要更广泛的相互交流，印度的汉语教学是实现这一点的重要手段。正确引导汉语在印度的发展非常重要。在古代，中印两国在佛教、哲学思想、传统习俗等方面的交流广泛，梵文和汉语是该时期交流中的主要桥梁。在 21 世纪，为了重新达到曾经的交流水平，我们不能忽视汉语教学的重要性。

参考文献

[1] MITRA S, XUE K, THAMPI M, et al. Encyclopedia of India-China cultural contacts, Volume I[M].New Delhi: MaXposure Media Group (I) Pvt. Ltd., 2014.

The Trend of Chinese Language Learning in India: New Opportunities and Challenges

Snehal Ajit Ulman[1]

Abstract 2020 marks the 70th anniversary of establishment of diplomatic relations between India and China, but the two ancient civilizations' contacts are not limited to the past 70 years. They have had an ancient age-old history dating back a long time. In a layman's eyes, Chinese teaching in India is a new phenomenon, however, they are unaware that India had Chinese language experts since ancient times. In the 21st century, China was more accessible to the world and the need for Chinese knowing talent grew manifold. India also was intimately connected to the world as well as China in the 21st century. This attracted many young minds to pursue their career as a Chinese language expert. However, there also emerged many challenges. In this essay, the author explores the development, orientation and importance of Chinese teaching in India.

Key Words Chinese; Teaching; India

Recently, China has risen to an important position in the international arena and has come out on the top in many different areas. In the 21st century, as China increasingly opens up to the world, it has attracted the attention of the whole

1 Assistant Professor, Department of Chinese, School of Language and Literature, Sikkim University.

world. Understanding Chinese people and Chinese culture has attracted new momentum. Learning Chinese and enhancing exchanges with China has never been more significant. This has led to a strong urge among youngsters to learn Chinese language. In India, many students started learning Chinese language since the year 2000, some for business, some to work as translators, some to work as tour guides and many others inclined towards research. Thus, the prospects of learning Chinese in India have expanded greatly. However, this trend of Chinese language development in India is not at all a new phenomenon.

The Republic of India and People's Republic of China established diplomatic relations on 1st April 1950. India became the first non-socialist country to establish diplomatic ties with China. This year (2020) is the 70th anniversary of the establishment of diplomatic ties between the two nations. However, the civilizational dialogue between the two countries is not limited to this short span of 70 years. The civilizational exchanges between the two countries date back to ancient times, and the relations are ancient and age-old. Chinese learning in India may be a new phenomenon through a layman's perspective, but what they are unaware of is that India has had Chinese language scholars from the very beginning. This essay explores the development of Chinese learning in India, its trend and importance, connects the trend of Chinese learning in recent times to the propagation of Chinese language in ancient India as well as the resurrection of Chinese learning and research in the modern era in India, and talks about various challenges of teaching and learning Chinese in India in the present times and suggests some necessary measures to overcome them.

1 THE PROPAGATION OF CHINESE THROUGH ANCIENT INDIA CHINA EXCHANGES

Both India and China had frequent cultural and people-to-people interactions in ancient times. Between 1st century CE and 6th century CE, there was considerable material and spiritual interaction happening between India and China. During this period Indian Buddhism spread to China. According to the

6th century book *Eminent Monks*, many Indian Buddhist monks went to China and were involved in the translation of Sanskrit Buddhist texts into Chinese. It is said that the Indian monk Kashyapamatanga was the pioneer of propagation of Buddhism to China.[1]4 These examples indicate that ancient Indian scholars, especially the Buddhist monks, were well-versed in Chinese and can be considered as the earliest proof of development of Chinese language in India.

In 8th century CE, three families from India served in the court of the Tang Dynasty Emperor. They were Kashyapa, Kumara and Gautama. These three families were involved in the translation of Astronomical texts. In 718 CE, the third generation of the Gautama family, Gautam Siddha, translated the Navagraha Calendar in Chinese.[1]8 All these examples stand to prove that many Indian scholars knew Chinese. Although, there is no mention of a school or university teaching Chinese in India in ancient times, but Buddhist interactions had urged many monks and scholars to learn Chinese language in India.

2 CHINESE LANGUAGE IN MODERN INDIA

Due to many historical reasons, there had been a considerable decrease in scholarly, religious and cultural interactions between India and China after the Tang Dynasty. However, in the 20th century, there was a resurgence of academic and cultural interaction between the two countries. After the visit of Rabindranath Tagore to China in April 1924, the interaction received a new stimulus. After he returned from China, Tagore was very keen to set up a centre for the study of China and Chinese civilization in his Visva-Bharati University at Santiniketan in Bengal. He met a young Chinese scholar Tan Yunshan while in Singapore in 1927 and invited him to visit Visva-Bharati. Tan Yunshan came and stayed on in Visva-Bharati to start teaching Chinese language, initially with just five students. Tan Yunshan became Tagore's main collaborator and assistant in setting up what became the first centre for Chinese studies in modern India, which was eventually inaugurated on April 10, 1937.[1]14

In the 1930s, the International Academy of Indian Culture located in New Delhi, another institution that engaged in China studies, was founded by Raghu Vira who began to study Chinese culture and the history of the India-China relationship and developed academic links with China. In 1938, he wrote his work *Ramayana in China* which is an important research work. In the late 1930s, Fergusson College in Pune opened a centre for China studies. Scholars Bapat and Gokro began to make a comparative study of Sanskrit, Pali, Chinese and Tibetan Buddhist texts. However, most prominent among Indian scholars of China studies in this period, Prabodh Chandra Bagchi went to France in 1923. He studied Chinese under the guidance of the French sinologist Sylvain Levy. From 1945 to 1956, he taught and did research at Visva-Bharati University. He produced many important works on various aspects of the cultural interaction between India and China through history.[1]14

3 CHINESE LANGUAGE TEACHING AND LEARNING IN PRESENT TIMES

Visva-Bharati University in Santiniketan became India's first University to promote Chinese language teaching, learning and research. In the beginning Cheena Bhavana mostly promoted China studies or research on China, however gradually Chinese language teaching was started. In the initial period, both Chiang Kai-shek and Zhou Enlai donated numerous ancient Chinese books. These books attracted many scholars to Cheena Bhavana to carry out research on ancient Chinese culture and traditions.

In the 1960s, 1970s and 1980s, some Indian universities started offering Chinese language courses, like Jawaharlal Nehru University in New Delhi, Banaras Hindu University in Varanasi, Panjab University in Chandigarh and Dr. Babasaheb Ambedkar Marathwada University in Aurangabad. Although these universities offered Bachelor, Master and Diploma courses, only a few students showed interest in learning Chinese language and research. Moreover, due to a smaller number of Chinese teachers, students were also fewer. Chinese learning during that time had not become as popular as it is now.

In the 21st century, the Chinese economic growth reflected China's rise. Such a flight caught the eye of the entire world. India, too, came to be connected closely with the world as well as China in the new century. However, there were many communication obstacles and challenges in interactions between the two countries and its people. The demand for Chinese language talent in the fields of academics, trade and business, machinery, information technology, political and diplomatic work and dialogues, translation, medicine, tourism, news and media, art, etc. had increased manifold. However, the cultivation of new talent had remained low. This urged many new universities to offer Chinese language courses. Some examples of new universities offering Chinese courses are Sikkim University, Central University of Gujarat, Doon University, Central University of Jharkhand, etc. Some private universities like Jindal Global University, Ashoka University, Amity University, etc. started Chinese programmes. India was experiencing Mandarin Wave at the start of 21st century. Chinese language learning, which had been stagnant for the past few centuries, suddenly received a stimulus. A new stage of development of Chinese language in India has now been initialized, and a new opportunity has opened up.

4 THE CHALLENGES FACED BY CHINESE LANGUAGE TEACHING AND LEARNING IN INDIA

Although Chinese language teaching and learning say a huge new start and promotion in India, learning the language in India still faces many challenges. Students face many problems in the course of learning the language. In the initial years, the students joining the course were few. Their problems were mostly related to the inadequate facilities of learning Chinese, like a group of students using a single dictionary or sharing of the textbook. The study material was also very limited. Currently students still face the problem of non-availability of textbooks, thus increasing the challenges of studying Chinese.

The Chinese language course and materials in the universities in India are discussed first. At the elementary level, students learn pronunciation and the tones. They study new words as well as sentence and grammar patterns. The elementary stage lasts for a year. During this time frame, students are required to grasp the basic principles, characters, pronunciation, tones and grammar of the Chinese language. The study material or textbooks used in Jawaharlal Nehru University include the four volumes of *Elementary Chinese Reader* published by Sinolingua. Students also listen to recordings in the classroom to practice their listening ability. The second-year and third-year courses include intermediate level speaking, listening, reading and writing textbooks. Visva-Bharati University in Santiniketan uses the two volumes of *Bridge* to teach students complex grammar and language components. Visva-Bharati University has 4 years of B.A. course duration. In the 4th year, students have to study not only Chinese literature, history, geography, politics, etc., but also ancient Chinese analects and poems. Besides this, students also learn translation of newspapers and business Chinese.[1] At the Master's level in Jawaharlal Nehru University and Visva-Bharati University, the courses include newspaper translation, literary translation, novels, consecutive and simultaneous interpretation, political thought, history of literature, economics of China, etc.[2] There are many extracurricular activities where students willingly participate. There are cultural exchange events, Chinese competitions, Chinese cultural competitions, dramas and skits, dancing and singing programmes. During the Spring Festival, almost all students participate in the Spring Festival event jointly organized by the University and Chinese Embassy. Teachers encourage students to perform some famous Chinese drama or stories learnt in the classroom, which boosts the students' self-confidence.

So far so good, but it is a must for the university to use Chinese as the medium of instruction right from the third year of student's curriculum. However, it is

1 CCSEAS BA Courses, Jawaharlal Nehru University. https://www.jnu.ac.in/sllcs/cseas_ba. Also see Cheena Bhavana B.A. Courses, Visva Bharati University, http://docs.wixstatic.com/ugd/05676d_fa7cdec1de9a493b9f4ca7935595e6f9.pdf.

2 CCSEAS MA Courses, Jawaharlal Nehru University. https://www.jnu.ac.in/sllcs/cseas_ma. Also See Cheena Bhavana M.A. Courses, Visva Bharati University, http://docs.wixstatic.com/ugd/05676d_c7a32c4ca8ae4154ab37f1febe48b4e1.pdf.

unfortunate to see that this is not the case. Many universities lack the multimedia equipment required for the listening ability class. The course is old and outdated and many times does not fulfil the requirements of the Indian students. All these turn out to be impediments in the course of learning Chinese. Learning Chinese does not mean learning only the grammar and new words, but correct pronunciation, tone of speech and the way of speaking are equally important to grasp. The local culture, traditions and conventions, customs and habits, etc. need to be thoroughly understood while learning a language. Jawaharlal Nehru University is located in the capital city of New Delhi, and thus the students have lot of opportunities to interact with Chinese students, different tourist groups coming from China, businessmen, as well as the embassy personnel. Visva Bharati University has had interactions with scholars from China since early times. However, other universities seldom get such opportunities. Moreover, some universities lack a flexible framework of Chinese for the Bachelor's and Master's level. Currently, many students that join the Chinese course at the university do not have a long-term plan to study Chinese. But they have to study Chinese for a minimum of three years to graduate. Besides this, there are other institutions that provide short term courses, but lack quality teaching. This causes many students to gradually loose interest in learning the language. The opportunities to go to China to study Chinese are very limited for Indian university students. Not all students get scholarships to go to China to study Chinese during their time at the university. Besides this, newly recruited teachers seldom receive teacher training. These teachers mostly rely on their experiences of learning the language to teach the students. This creates a gap in the course of Chinese teaching. Most of the Indian universities do not have Chinese language teachers coming from China, who can teach the students more effectively.

Students from many different fields have started learning Chinese. They start their research on Chinese politics, economy, international relations, etc., just after learning the language for a year or so. Very few students study and do research on Chinese language, literature, culture, history, traditions and customs. This has also affected the cultural interactions with China. Conferences and dialogue forums on Chinese culture, language, literature, history, etc., have decreased in number, while seminars and conferences on subjects like international relations, economics, etc. are increasing day by day.

In order to solve these problems, communication and interaction between Indian and Chinese universities needs to be increased. There is a need to send at least one batch of students learning Chinese in Indian universities to China to study the language for a period of one or two semesters. There is a need to promote the students to carry out multidimensional and multidisciplinary research. Besides international relations, economics and politics, students need to be urged to do research and study Chinese language, literature, culture, history, philosophical thought, etc. Universities also need to have a teacher exchange programme, whereby newly recruited Chinese teachers from India can go to China for training and Chinese language teachers from China can come to India to teach Chinese. Chinese study material is an important component of Chinese learning. Chinese and Indian Universities need to cooperate and publish Indianized material in India itself. Besides this, Indian universities need to have basic amenities like audio rooms and multimedia rooms, which will help the students to watch Chinese movies and Chinese programmes and thereby improve their listening ability. Students nowadays have started using online dictionaries, which has made learning Chinese convenient. However, these dictionaries fail to teach students the usages of words in Chinese. Therefore, it is required for a good teacher to correctly guide the students and teach Chinese with outstanding Chinese pedagogy. The development of Chinese in India can only be achieved when these challenges are solved.

5 CONCLUSION

In short, Indian and Chinese universities need to have extensive interactions and increase contact. Chinese teaching and learning in India are important components to achieve this. It is important to correctly steer the trend of development of Chinese language in India. Interactions related to Buddhism, philosophical thought, traditions and customs, etc., between India and China during ancient times were very extensive. Sanskrit and Chinese were the major link for that interaction. In order to revive a similar level of interaction in this 21st century, Chinese language teaching and learning cannot be ignored.

(Proofread by Wang Meicen)

REFERENCES

[1] MITRA S, XUE K, THAMPI M, et al. Encyclopedia of India-China cultural contacts, Volume I[M]. New Delhi: MaXposure Media Group (I) Pvt. Ltd., 2014.

印度未成年学生中文学习的路径与展望

张文娟[1]

摘要　印度中小学鼓励多语种学习，但中文却一直未能进入印度官方推荐的语言名单。从2010年开始，通过两国政策和项目方面的努力，部分印度学校开始开展中文教学实验。但因为各种原因，中文教学的实验并没有得到更大范围的推广。两国关系的起伏也影响着印度政府对中文教学的官方态度，最近的《印度国家教育政策2020》将中文从推荐语言名单中删除就是例证。不过在印度教育系统之外，还有商业平台、华人学校等在努力推广中文教学。比较而言，由市场驱动的中文教学更有生命力，笔者也因此建议华人中文教学可适当参考市场模式。

关键词　印度；未成年人；中文教学；学校教育；商业平台

笔者长期在印度大学工作，子女便入印度学校读书，因此对印度未成年人学习中文的路径特别关注，从而对印度中小学开展中文教学的政策，以及商业培训机构针对未成年人开展的中文教学有了比较直观的认识，在这里谈谈笔者的个人感受。

1　印度学校教育中语言的设定及开展中文教学的政策现状

印度学校的课程设计由邦和联邦的教育理事会设定，在这里我们主要关注联邦层级中等教育委员会（Central Board of Secondary Education，简称CBSE）的语言学习政策。CBSE提供的语言范围包括30种，要求其会员学校必须从其中选出两种作为必修的语言，而且其会员学校的学生到八年级时，必须掌握其中三

1　金德尔全球法学院副教授，金德尔全球大学印中研究中心执行主任。

种语言。[1] 从 CBSE 的外国语言学习名单中，我们看到，中文不在其中。

不过，随着中印交流的加深，两国都意识到，在中小学课堂加入彼此的语言对双边人文交流是有好处的。2010 年 9 月，人力资源发展部（现更名教育部）部长卡尔皮·西巴尔（Kapil Sibal）到天津参加世界经济论坛时表示："中国是我们强大的邻居，也是世界资源的巨大消费者，我们不能无视这一点。把中国介绍给印度最好的方式，是将汉语列入我们的基础教育，让我们的孩子对中国感兴趣，增进了解。"[2] 西巴尔部长还在北京对印度记者说："来，让足够多的印度人学习中文吧！让大量的中国老师到印度教授我们的孩子吧！这就是我们激发印度孩子对中国感兴趣的最好方式。"[3] 当时西巴尔部长还告诉时任中国教育部部长袁贵仁："要让印度孩子学习中文，就必须有标准和考试，这肯定需要您的支持。"[4]

经过两国教育部门近两年的谈判，到 2012 年 8 月，时任印度驻华大使、现任印度外交部部长苏杰生代表印度政府与时任国家汉办（现更名为中国中外语言交流与合作中心）主任许琳签订了《国家汉办与印度中等教育委员会谅解备忘录》[5]，中国将在语言类大学中帮助印度培训 300 名中文教师，以支持印度的中小学开展中文教学[6]。苏杰生对记者说："这一备忘录为在印度中小学开设中文奠定了基础，这将会促进学术研究人员、老师、专家、培训者和学生的相互交流，也包括课程设计、教学材料及辅助教学资源的交流，这的确是两个邻居增进关系的重要一步。"[7]

1 CBSE policy, https://cbse.nic.in/curric~1/studies02.pdf.（涉及语言包括印地语、英语、阿萨姆语、孟加拉语、古吉拉特语、坎纳达语、克什米尔语、马拉地语、马拉雅拉姆语、曼尼普尔语、信德语、泰米尔语、泰卢固语、乌尔都语、雷布查语、林布语、不丹语、梵文、阿拉伯语、波斯语、法语、德语、葡萄牙语、俄语、西班牙语、尼泊尔语和米佐语。）

2 K. J. M. Varma, "Chinese language to be part of CBSE curriculum: Sibal", *Outlook*, 2010-09-15, https://www.outlookindia.com/newswire/story/chinese-language-to-be-part-of-cbse-curriculum-sibal/693552.

3 K. J. M. Varma, "Chinese language to be part of CBSE curriculum: Sibal", *Outlook*, 2010-09-15, https://www.outlookindia.com/newswire/story/chinese-language-to-be-part-of-cbse-curriculum-sibal/693552.

4 K. J. M. Varma, "Chinese language to be part of CBSE curriculum: Sibal", *Outlook*, 2010-09-15, https://www.outlookindia.com/newswire/story/chinese-language-to-be-part-of-cbse-curriculum-sibal/693552.

5 中国驻印度大使馆，《国家汉办与印度驻华使馆签署汉语教学谅解备忘录》，2012 年 8 月 24 日，http://in.china-embassy.org/chn/zygx/zyjy/zyjyxw/t964318.htm.

6 Sutirtho Patranobis, "Mandarin now an option for CBSE students", *Hindustan Times*, 2012-08-24, https://www.hindustantimes.com/world/mandarin-now-an-option-for-cbse-students/story-UhrLi8mJXaHnXEc5NTzsTN.html.

7 Sutirtho Patranobis, "Mandarin now an option for CBSE students", *Hindustan Times*, 2012-08-24, https://www.hindustantimes.com/world/mandarin-now-an-option-for-cbse-students/story-UhrLi8mJXaHnXEc5NTzsTN.html.

印度CBSE从2011年4月开始，将中文列入会员学校可选择外语范围。[1] 2013至2014年，CBSE在印度6座城市[2]的22所学校中，选择六年级到八年级的学生参与试点课程，将中文作为第三种语言学习。[3] 2014年2月，CBSE甚至想推动更多学校开设中文课程。[4]但遗憾的是，2016年协议到期后，印度政府没有再续签协议，在试点学校教书的22名教师被要求当年学期结束后立刻离开印度。[5] CBSE也向印度外交部申请续签备忘录，但没有得到回应。据一些学校反映，很多家长从经济视角看学习中文的潜力，学习中文的需求很大，尤其像孟买这样的商业中心。[6]但因为师资短缺，大多数试点学校陆续从课程设置上放弃了中文，学生只好转向印地语或法语的学习。[7]实际上，中国汉语教师赴印度教学，一段时间内很难拿到签证，这也是在备忘录期间项目没有被大范围实施的重要原因。[8]

值得关注的是，印度政府2020年7月29日发布的《国家教育政策2020》对此有所调整。虽然调查中发现印度中小学中使用的教学语言有31种，但不容忽视的是，英语作为教学语言的学校越来越多。[9]倾向印度教民族主义的莫迪政府更关注印度本土语言的学习，对于越来越多学校重视用英语教学表达了担忧。因此，其政府主导的《国家教育政策2020》对此做了应对，虽然还坚持“三种语言”的做法，却调整了部分内容。在基础教育和准备教育阶段（即六年级之前），新国家教育政策强

1 https://www.icbse.com/news/mandarin-chinese-class-vi-cbse-schools-rl74.
2 这6所学校位于德里、孟买、加尔各答、班加罗尔、斋普尔和拉普尔。
3 Puja Pednekar, “Mandarin classes for CBSE students halted as China contract ends”, *Hindustan Times*, 2016-03-21, https://www.hindustantimes.com/mumbai/no-mandarin-classes-for-cbse-students/story-ibB8wCMbTrYyDNELEI24IK.html.
4 http://cbseacademic.nic.in/web_material/Notifications/2014/8_Chinese_2014.pdf.
5 Puja Pednekar, “Mandarin classes for CBSE students halted as China contract ends”, *Hindustan Times*, 2016-03-21, https://www.hindustantimes.com/mumbai/no-mandarin-classes-for-cbse-students/story-ibB8wCMbTrYyDNELEI24IK.html.
6 Puja Pednekar, “Mandarin classes for CBSE students halted as China contract ends”, *Hindustan Times*, 2016-03-21, https://www.hindustantimes.com/mumbai/no-mandarin-classes-for-cbse-students/story-ibB8wCMbTrYyDNELEI24IK.html.
7 Puja Pednekar, “Mandarin classes for CBSE students halted as China contract ends”, *Hindustan Times*, 2016-03-21, https://www.hindustantimes.com/mumbai/no-mandarin-classes-for-cbse-students/story-ibB8wCMbTrYyDNELEI24IK.html.
8 Puja Pednekar, “Mandarin classes for CBSE students halted as China contract ends”, *Hindustan Times*, 2016-03-21, https://www.hindustantimes.com/mumbai/no-mandarin-classes-for-cbse-students/story-ibB8wCMbTrYyDNELEI24IK.html.
9 British Council, “India school education system: an overview”, 2019-07, https://www.britishcouncil.in/sites/default/files/school_education_system_in_india_report_2019_final_web.pdf.

调三语教育，即英语、印地语和另一种印度本土语言的学习。但对教学语言有了更具体的建议，在以印地语为母语的邦，学校尽量用印地语开展教学，同时开展英语和南印度的一种语言学习；而在非印地语为母语的邦，则可以用本邦法定语言开展教学，同时开展英语和印地语的课程教学。总之，在六年级之前，所有学校至少要开展两种印度本土语言的学习。政策还建议在八年级之前，学校都要坚持母语教学。梵文可在所有阶段的学校教育中作为选修课开展教学。

新政策建议，外国语言（英语除外）的学习从六年级开始，并采用列举式推荐了外国语言的名单，但名单中没有中文。不过值得留意的是，2019 年 5 月的草案中，中文还位列其中，草案的原文是："外国语言，如法语、德语、西班牙语、中文、日语可以提供给感兴趣的中学生作为选修课。"[1] 但是，印度有关部门出于安全考虑，把中文从推荐名单上去掉了，加入了泰语、韩语等语言。[2] 印度教育部试图淡化这种变化，表示名单列举不可穷尽，中小学对开展的外语学习有自由选择权。[3]

据笔者了解，目前首都新德里附近的公立和私立学校中将中文作为可选择外语课程的，只有泰戈尔国际学校，该校从 2001 年开始开设中文选修课。其学校网站显示，该校六到十年级的学生，必修英文和印地语，可以在梵文、法语和中文中选一门作为第三语言。[4] 中国多位国家领导人访印时，也顺访了这所学校。某会上，笔者曾见过泰戈尔国际学校的校长，她表示，自己经常为聘用不到合适的中文老师而苦恼。由此可见，师资短缺是在印度开设中文课程的主要困难之一。

经了解，首都新德里还有一所学校开设中文课，那就是美国驻印度大使馆所设立的美国学校。中文是他们的课程之一。美国学校会通过富有竞争力的全球招聘程序，长期为美国学校的孩子们配备两位母语为中文的全职教师，一位为低年级组授

1 "A choice of foreign language(s) (e.g. French, German, Spanish, Chinese, Japanese) would be offered and available to interested students to choose as elective(s) during secondary school."

2 Priscilla Jebaraj, Suhasini Haidar, "National Education Policy 2020 | Mandarin dropped from language list", *Hindu*, 2020-08-01, https://www.thehindu.com/education/national-education-policy-2020-mandarin-dropped-from-language-list/article32249227.ece.

3 Priscilla Jebaraj, Suhasini Haidar, "National Education Policy 2020 | Mandarin dropped from language list", *Hindu*, 2020-08-01, https://www.thehindu.com/education/national-education-policy-2020-mandarin-dropped-from-language-list/article32249227.ece.

4 Tagore International School, https://tagoreint.com/vv/V2.0/about-us/academics.

课，另一位专门为高中学生授课。这两位教师不仅母语为中文，而且有丰富的教学经验和教育学专业背景。当然，美国学校主要针对美国公民的孩子，虽然有少数名额给国际学生或印度学生，但鉴于学费昂贵和入学竞争性极强，受益的学生非常有限。

2　印度本土中小学教育系统之外的可能路径与展望

中文学习，除了被纳入教育系统，通常还有商业化的中文培训平台及华人华侨创立的中文学校，笔者对此也做了调研，并就未来发展做了展望。

因为众多原因，印度的华人学校已经变成了历史。据全印华人华侨协会名誉会长丘开勇先生介绍，他的中文就是在德里的华文学校学习的，后来学校的学生越来越少，1962 年之后，学校就关闭了。位于加尔各答的培梅中学是 1962 年之后还坚持开设的华文学校，但因为学生锐减和房地租赁争议等原因，也于 2010 年关闭。[1]

华人学校的关闭及中小学中文学习的不活跃，造成了一种结果——印度二代或三代华人几乎不会说中文。个别能说中文的，主要是早期在华人学校学习的。而对于新华侨，考虑到回国教育对接的难度，也大都将孩子留在中国国内学习。

另一个重要的中文学习路径是商业培训机构。商业模式在满足和开发兴趣方面往往比政策模式更有活力。对于印度商业机构开展中文培训的现状，笔者原本不太关注，但为做研究，便专门进行了搜索，出乎意料，印度从事中文培训的商业机构数量不少，也小有规模。商业机构的存在，说明市场需求的存在。也就是说，虽然近几年印度政府对中文学习的政策支持较少，但是，民间学习中文的热度或许有增无减。

就商业中文培训机构的现状，本文简单归纳了以下几个特点。其一，这些中文培训机构主要分布在孟买、德里、班加罗尔、金奈等商业发达的城市，这说明中文学习与商业需求有很大关系。其二，中文培训对象很多元，有针对参加汉语水平考

1　“Kolkata’s last surviving Chinese school set for 2nd innings”, *Time of India*, 2017-07-09, https://timesofindia.indiatimes.com/city/kolkata/last-surviving-city-chinese-school-set-for-2nd-innings/articleshow/59507413.cms.

试（HSK）人员的应试课程，针对商务人士、职业人士开展的应用中文课程，还有针对未成年人或幼儿的少儿中文。有少数机构也开展翻译人员的培训。除了少数机构只针对成年人教学，大多数机构都有针对未成年人的培训项目。其三，培训模式也很多元，有一对一家教模式，有培训班模式，还有一年或两年的全职学习模式，甚至有的培训机构跟托幼机构或学校合作，让中文成为对方教学或课后辅导班的常规项目。其四，培训机构创立者基本上都学过中文，出于对中文的热爱或者有中文教师资源而创业。也有个别嫁入印度的中国人开展在线中文培训。其五，大多数培训机构的规模较小，也有少数机构通过在线平台、设立分支机构和与学校合作开设常规培训项目等扩大培训范围。

中文培训的商业模式，主要取决于市场。如果中印之间的商业交流不中断甚至增加，中文培训的市场就会存在。虽然现在印度还没有像新东方这样的综合培训机构，但是，新东方模式对印度中文培训的商业化运作启发不小。期待创业者能够引入风险投资，建立集幼儿培训、未成年课外辅导、HSK 考试培训、商务中文培训、翻译培训、中国留学辅导于一体的中文培训品牌，并在孟买、德里、班加罗尔和金奈几个大城市设分支机构或加盟点。

另外，此商业模式也可以用于华人学校。近两三年，加尔各答老一代华人也呼吁让培梅中学复课。笔者认为，培梅中学的基础很好，能复课是最好的。如果政策允许，复课后的培梅中学最好变成中文国际学校，不仅招收华人子弟，还要面向印度和国际学生，这就不会出现生源问题。另外，最好采取商业化运作模式，建立连锁品牌，这样也可以在需求更大的城市设立分校或加盟学校。

印度是一个以尊重多元化为傲的国家，中国又是印度最大的邻居，而且两国在历史上交流很多，对彼此语言的学习是两国深度交流的基础。虽然近几十年来，中印关系不够稳定，但商业交流、人文交流等都没有中断过，也是无法中断的。因此，中文的学习也不会中断。政策模式可能会有起伏，但是，商业模式会因为市场需求的存在而充满活力，帮助那些真正想学习中文的人随时得到提升。

Options and Prospects for Children in India to Learn Chinese

Zhang Wenjuan[1]

Abstract Indian school education encourages multi-language learning. However, Chinese has not been one of the languages on the official list. From 2010, through joint efforts in policy and programmers, Chinese teaching has been experimented in some Indian schools. The experiment was not able to be scaled up due to many reasons. It is evident that the ups and downs of India-China relationship have a big impact on the Chinese teaching in India such as the removal of Chinese from the recommendation list of National Education Policy 2020. It is worthy of notice that in addition to school education there are also various of commercial platforms and Indian Chinese initiatives for Chinese learning. Comparatively, market-driven Chinese teaching is more dynamic which also drives the author to recommend it as a reference for Indian Chinese initiative.

Key Words India; Children; Chinese learning; School education; Commercial platform

I have been working in an Indian university for a long time, amd my children also go to Indian schools, so I pay special attention to the ways through which Indian minors learn Chinese. Therefore, I have an intuitive understanding of the policy

1 Associate Professor of Jindal Global Law School, Executive Director of India-China Research Center of Jindal Global University.

of Chinese teaching in primary and secondary schools in India and the Chinese teaching for minors that are conducted by business training institutions. Here, I would like to talk about my personal feelings.

1 LANGUAGE LEARNING IN INDIAN SCHOOLS AND THE CURRENT POLICIES ON OFFERING CHINESE AS A FOREIGN LANGUAGE SUBJECT

In India, the school syllabus is decided by education boards including various boards at the state level and the Central Board of Secondary Education (hereafter referred to as CBSE). Here I mainly refer to CBSE policy. According to CBSE policy on language studies, its member schools should choose two languages from the 30 languages listed by the board. [1] By eighth grade, their member schools' students should master three languages from the list. The list does not included Chinese language.

However, with increasing interactions between China and India, both countries realized that introduction of each other's language in their school education system will be beneficial for cultural and educational exchange. In September 2010, Mr. Kapil Sibal, Minister of Human Resources Development (changed into Ministry of Education in July 2020) participated in the World Economic Forum in Tianjin. He said, "China is our powerful neighbour and emerging as a biggest consumer of global resources. We cannot ignore this fact. The best way to introduce China in India is to introduce its language at primary level so that our kids develop interest and knowledge about China." [2] He told Indian journalists there, "Let us get enough Indians to learn Chinese. Let us have a lot of Chinese trainers in India who will teach the young students in schools. That is how we evoke interest in our kids about China. There is no other way to do it."[3] Mr. Sibal

1 CBSE policy, https://cbse.nic.in/curric~1/studies02.pdf. (The language includes Hindi, English, Assamese, Bengali, Gujarati, Kannada, Kashmiri, Marathi, Malayalam, Manipuri, Oriya, Punjabi, Sindhi, Tamil, Telugu, Urdu, Lepcha, Limbu, Bhutia, Sanskrit, Arabic, Persian, French, German. Portuguese, Russian, Spanish, Nepali and Mizo.)

2 K.J.M. Varma, "Chinese language to be part of CBSE curriculum: Sibal", *Outlook*, 2010-09-15, https://www.outlookindia.com/newswire/story/chinese-language-to-be-part-of-cbse-curriculum-sibal/693552 .

3 K.J.M. Varma, "Chinese language to be part of CBSE curriculum: Sibal", *Outlook*, 2010-09-15, https://www.outlookindia.com/newswire/story/chinese-language-to-be-part-of-cbse-curriculum-sibal/693552 .

also told the Chinese Education Minister Mr. Yuan Guiren that if he introduced Chinese in the CBSE system as a course, he needs to collaborate with Yuan for standards and tests.[1]

After nearly two years of negotiations by responsible agencies of the two countries, in August 2012, a memorandum of understanding to introduce Chinese as an option for foreign language in schools run by CBSE was signed by Indian Ambassador S. Jaishankar and Xu Lin, Director General of Hanban. (It is now renamed Chinese Foreign Language Exchange and Cooperation Center)[2] China will help train 300 teachers in its language universities for enabling the MOU implementation.[3] After the MOU signing, Ambassador Jaishankar told journalists, "The MOU that has just been concluded lays the basis for cooperation between India and China on the teaching of Mandarin Chinese as a foreign language in Indian schools. It envisages the exchanges of academic staffs, teachers, trainees, experts, and students. It provides for development of curriculum and exchange of educational material and aids. This is indeed an important step forward in the growing relationship between the two neighbours."[4]

CBSE was set to launch Chinese in class Ⅵ from April 2011.[5] In 2013–2014, "CBSE chose 22 schools among six cities[6] in Delhi, offered Mandarin as the third language for 6th–8th grade on a pilot basis in 2013–2014." [7] In Feb. 2014, CBSE had even thought to expand the program to more schools.[8] It is a regret that when the MOU between Hanban and Indian Embassy expired in 2016, the Indian government decided not to renew the MOU. The Chinese language instructors

---

1 K.J.M. Varma, "Chinese language to be part of CBSE curriculum: Sibal", *Outlook*, 2010-09-15, https://www.outlookindia.com/newswire/story/chinese-language-to-be-part-of-cbse-curriculum-sibal/693552 .

2 Chinese Embassy in India, "Memorandum of Understanding between Hanban and India Embassy in China", 2012-08-24, http://in.china-embassy.org/chn/zygx/zyjy/zyjyxw/t964318.htm.

3 Sutirtho Patranobis, "Mandarin now an option for CBSE students", *Hindustan Times*, 2012-08-24, https://www.hindustantimes.com/world/mandarin-now-an-option-for-cbse-students/story-UhrLi8mJXaHnXEc5NTzsTN.html.

4 Sutirtho Patranobis, "Mandarin now an option for CBSE students", *Hindustan Times*, 2012-08-24, https://www.hindustantimes.com/world/mandarin-now-an-option-for-cbse-students/story-UhrLi8mJXaHnXEc5NTzsTN.html.

5 https://www.icbse.com/news/mandarin-chinese-class-vi-cbse-schools-rl74.

6 The six schools are located in Delhi, Mumbai, Kolkata, Bangalore, Jaipur and Lapur.

7 Puja Pednekar, "Mandarin classes for CBSE students halted as China contract ends", *Hindustan Times*, 2016-03-21, https://www.hindustantimes.com/mumbai/no-mandarin-classes-for-cbse-students/story-ibB8wCMbTrYyDNELEI24IK.html.

8 http://cbseacademic.nic.in/web_material/Notifications/2014/8_Chinese_2014.pdf.

of the pilot schools were asked to leave India once the semester was finished that year. [1] CBSE has requested the Ministry of Foreign Affairs to extend the MOU, however, no reply was given. Some schools mention that there is a huge demand for Mandarin from a business point of view, especially for the ones in business-centric cities such as Mumbai. [2] Due to a lack of qualified teachers, pilot schools dropped Chinese from their syllabus. For students, they had to shift to other languages such as Hindi or French. [3] Even if the MOU were valid, teachers from China could not easily get visas in a certain period which is one of the reasons that the program cannot be scaled up. [4]

About language studies, the newly passed *National Education Policy* (hereafter as NEP) in July 2020 made some adjustments which are worthy of attention. Even though a survey showed that there are 31 languages as the medium of instruction in schools across the country, schools using English medium instruction are expanding, which upsets the Modi Government with tremendous efforts for Hindu nationalism.[5] The newly published NEP puts more efforts on the study of Indian native languages. NEP continues to emphasize that at the foundational stage and preparatory stage that is before 6th graded students should learn English, Hindi and another native language. But it has a more detailed recommendation of using the native language as medium of instruction. It recommends that in states with Hindi as the mother tongue, schools shall try to use Hindi as the medium of instruction, meanwhile, schools can start teaching English language and a South Indian language. In non-Hindi states, schools could use their state language as the medium of education while teaching students

1 Puja Pednekar, "Mandarin classes for CBSE students halted as China contract ends", *Hindustan Times*, 2016-03-21, https://www.hindustantimes.com/mumbai/no-mandarin-classes-for-cbse-students/story-ibB8wCMbTrYyDNELEI24IK.html.

2 Puja Pednekar, "Mandarin classes for CBSE students halted as China contract ends", *Hindustan Times*, 2016-03-21, https://www.hindustantimes.com/mumbai/no-mandarin-classes-for-cbse-students/story-ibB8wCMbTrYyDNELEI24IK.html.

3 Puja Pednekar, "Mandarin classes for CBSE students halted as China contract ends", *Hindustan Times*, 2016-03-21, https://www.hindustantimes.com/mumbai/no-mandarin-classes-for-cbse-students/story-ibB8wCMbTrYyDNELEI24IK.html.

4 Puja Pednekar, "Mandarin classes for CBSE students halted as China contract ends", *Hindustan Times*, 2016-03-21, https://www.hindustantimes.com/mumbai/no-mandarin-classes-for-cbse-students/story-ibB8wCMbTrYyDNELEI24IK.html.

5 British Council, "India school education system: an overview", July 2019, https://www.britishcouncil.in/sites/default/files/school_education_system_in_india_report_2019_final_web.pdf.

English and Hindi. In summary, for kids before 6th grade, schools should offer at least two Indian native languages for them to learn. NEP also recommends that wherever possible, the medium of instruction should be in the native language until at least Grade 5, but preferably till Grade 8 and beyond. It also recommends that Sanskrit would be available as an elective course across all grades.

NEP recommends that foreign language study (except English) begins from the 6th grade with a list as examples. Chinese is not mentioned in the list. But in the draft of May 2019, Chinese was mentioned as an example. Here is what the draft says, "A choice of foreign language(s) (e.g. French, German, Spanish, Chinese, Japanese) would be offered and available to interested students to choose as elective(s) during secondary school." The involved ministries later raised security concerns regarding Mandarin teaching to Indian students. [1] So on the final list, Chinese was removed while Korean, Thai and other Asian languages were added in. The Ministry of Education downplayed the change and pointed that "it is not an exhaustive list of allowed languages. Schools are free to offer other languages." [2]

According to my personal knowledge, there is only one school in the national capital region which offers Chinese as a foreign language. It is the Tagore International School which offers Chinese as a third language from 2001. On their school website, it shows that for students from 6th grade to 10th grade, while English and Hindi are compulsory courses, they also offer Sanskrit, French and Chinese as electives for the third language learning. [3] Several Chinese leaders visited this school while they visited India. In a conference I happened to meet the principal of Tagore International School. She mentioned that one of her challenges is to finding qualified Chinese teachers to work with her school. It is evident that one of the difficulties for schools to open Chinese courses is the shortage of qualified teachers.

1 Priscilla Jebaraj, Suhasini Haidar, "National Education Policy 2020 | Mandarin dropped from language list", Hindu, 2020-08-01, https://www.thehindu.com/education/national-education-policy-2020-mandarin-dropped-from-language-list/article32249227.ece.

2 Priscilla Jebaraj, Suhasini Haidar, "National Education Policy 2020 | Mandarin dropped from language list", Hindu, 2020-08-01, https://www.thehindu.com/education/national-education-policy-2020-mandarin-dropped-from-language-list/article32249227.ece.

3 Tagore International School, https://tagoreint.com/vv/V2.0/about-us/academics.

It is interesting to learn that the American Embassy School in Delhi also offers Chinese regularly. They hire two Chinese teachers through global competitive procedure with one for junior students and one for senior students. The two teachers should be Chinese native speakers, with rich teaching experiences and studies of education background. American Embassy School is mainly for American kids in India. Only a small number of seats are open for Indians and other internationals. Due to the high tuition fee and the limited seats, few kids are able to get access to Chinese through this school.

2 OTHER OPTIONS FOR CHINESE LEARNING EXCEPT SCHOOL EDUCATION AND THE PROSPECTS FOR THEM

In addition to school education, for Chinese learning, there are also commercial training platforms and schools established by Indian Chinese. For writing this paper, I conducted research and raise some expectations for the future.

Due to various reasons, schools established by Indian Chinese were closed. Mr. Qiu Kaiyong, Honorary President of Indian Association of Chinese told me that his Chinese was taught by a Chinese school in Delhi, which was closed after 1962. Another school, Pei May Chinese School in Kolkata has continued to exist after 1962. However, due to the reasons of student shortage and lease control disputes the school was also closed in 2010. [1]

The closure of Chinese schools and the scarcity of Chinese options in Indian school education caused that the second or third generation of Indian Chinese cannot speak Chinese. The very few who can speak Chinese were trained by the old Chinese schools. For Chinese who are working in India, they usually leave their kids in China for avoiding the loss of mother tongue learning and also for ensuring the education connection back home.

Another important platform for Chinese learning in India is through market-

1 "Kolkata's last surviving Chinese school set for 2nd innings", *Time of India*, 2017-07-09, https://timesofindia.indiatimes.com/city/kolkata/last-surviving-city-chinese-school-set-for-2nd-innings/articleshow/59507413.cms.

oriented training institutions. Compared to policy model, commercial model is more energetic. It meets and also develops learning interests. I had little attention to this model till I started writing this essay. With a quick search on google, I found so many Chinese language learning institutes. It surprised me. This shows there is a market for Chinese learning. That is, even if the school education policy is not very active the individual interest in Chinese learning doesn't drop, instead it has increased.

Based on my search, here are the summary of my findings about the commercial training platforms. First, these training institutions are mainly in cities such as Mumbai, Delhi, Bangalore and Chennai. It seems that the distribution has positive correlation with economic prosperity. Second, it has a variety of training programs targeting at different population such as people for preparing HSK, for professional Chinese learning, and for kids' Chinese learning. Also, some is for training for translation skills. Most of the training institutions have programs for children. Third, various training models have been developed. Such as one-to-one tutorship, short-term training sessions and one to two years of full-time trainings. Some even collaborate with schools or crèches for regular training programs. Fourth, the founders of the institutions have learned Chinese. Their resources on Chinese training or their passion toward Chinese learning help them with the building of institutions. There are also few founded by Chinese who get married with Indians. Fifth, in terms of scale it is still small. But there are some efforts to reach more potential learners through online platforms, establishing branches or to collaborate with schools for platform extension.

The commercial model is based on market demand. If the commercial exchange exists or increases, the training market will be there. Though comprehensive training models such as New Oriental School in China are successful models, the New Oriental model can be introduced in India as well. It is expected that some entrepreneurs could bring venture capital to develop a Chinese training brand with various programs in it such as Chinese for kids, after-school curriculum, HSK training, business Chinese, translation and guidance for study in China. It can establish branches or get a franchise in big cities such as Mumbai, Delhi,

Bangalore and Chennai.

The commercial model can also be used in Chinese schools. In the last two to three years, the old generation of Indian Chinese in Kolkata called upon the re-opening of Pei May Chinese School. I personally believe it will be amazing if Pei May can be resumed since it had a very good foundation. If policies allow, it is better for Pei May Chinese School to become an internationalized Chinese school which would prevent the shortage of students. The brand strategy would also help set up branches in other big cities with higher demand of Chinese learning.

India is proud of respecting diversity. Furthermore, China is a big neighbour of India with a long history of cultural exchange. Language learning of each other is the basis for the two countries to build deep understanding. It is true that the bilateral relationship encountered ups and downs over the past few decades. However, economic exchange, across-culture marriage, culture and education exchanges have never stopped. In fact, these cannot be stopped. Therefore, the demand of Chinese learning will exist for long. Whereas policy model is vulnerable to the bilateral relationship, market model would be more energetic for helping the learners to improve themselves in a timely manner.

(Proofread by Bhavana Kumari)

Part 3

第三部分 在印汉语教学教法研究

The Research of Chinese Language Teaching Pedagogy in India

印度初级汉语学习者正音教学对策研究

孙　鹏[1]

摘要　随着“汉语热”在印度兴起，大批印度学龄前儿童、中小学生和大学生，以及从事商业贸易、语言教育培训等行业的专业人士，甚至部分家庭妇女和退休人士都开始学习汉语，并将其作为职业选择，推动了在印汉语教育的发展。但受本土汉语师资和学习条件的限制，这些初学者大都有汉语发音方面的问题。因此，在印汉语教育的首要任务就是在初级汉语学习者中推广汉语正音教学。为此，需要加强对印度初级汉语学习者语音偏误的研究，编撰实用性正音教材，组织开展本土教师培训，创新语音教学方法，充分利用网络多媒体教学手段等，以助提高初学者的汉语水平。

关键词　印度；初级汉语；语音偏误；正音教学

印度是一个多民族、多语言的国家，单是宪法规定的官方语言就有印地语、孟加拉语、泰卢固语、泰米尔语等22种之多，英语也是全国性通用语言。在这种多语言的环境下，印度人从小就养成了学习多种语言的习惯。印度政府的教育政策也规定学生在学习母语印地语和英语以外，还要学习一种外语。因此，他们常学习法语、西班牙语、德语等西方语言，也会学习汉语、日语、韩语等东方语言。进入21世纪，更是出现了“汉语热”。除尼赫鲁大学、德里大学和国际大学这些原来的汉语重镇外，还有将近40所高校和科研院所新开设了汉语课程。[1]25 此外，大批商业语言培训机构也将汉语纳入培训课程，吸引了很多汉语学习者。教授汉语成为很多语言教师和退休人员的职业选择。随着汉语学习者人数增多，如何快速提高汉语学习者汉语水

1　郑州大学南亚研究所研究员。

平，特别是口语表达水平成为在印汉语教育面临的十分急迫的问题。为有效解决这一问题，必须重视开展汉语正音教学。笔者结合在印度长期从事初级汉语教学积累的经验，谈谈在印度开展汉语正音教学的一些行之有效的做法，以就教于各位专家。

1　印度汉语初学者的构成和语音偏误程度

为了更好地了解印度汉语初学者的语音偏误，进而提出有针对性的解决方案，我们有必要先了解一下印度汉语初学者的构成及其语音偏误程度。按照汉语学习者的年龄和职业，我们可以将印度初级汉语学习者划分为学龄前儿童、中小学生、大学生和社会大众。一般来说，未成年学习者的汉语语音偏误普遍较轻，成年的语音偏误较重。按照学习条件和专业性，我们可以将汉语初学者分为以下四个部分。

首先是高校中文专业的学生。各高校中文专业的学生是印度汉语初学者中学习条件最好、能够接受专业汉语教学培养的群体，也是将中文作为职业选择最坚定的群体。这一群体规模小，但是学习时限长，经过系统的汉语教育，汉语水平也是最高的。他们一般来自传统的汉语教育重镇尼赫鲁大学、德里大学和国际大学等。20世纪30年代，泰戈尔创办的国际大学建立中国学院，谭云山致力传播中国语言与文化，带来了大量中国的图书，学院也一直有中国教师从事汉语教学，成为印度汉语教育的领头羊。[2]10 后来，随着政治形势的变化，德里大学和尼赫鲁大学的中国学研究相继崛起，发展迅速，汇聚了许多印度顶尖的汉学家，成为中国学研究的新高地，汉语教学水平一直位居一流地位。[1]25 这些高校一般都是由印度研究中国学的专家学者讲授汉语阅读和翻译，口语课多由一些来自中国、新加坡和马来西亚的华侨华人教师讲授。受教材和学习条件的限制，这些高校汉语学习者的规模都非常小，属于精英教育，往往阅读能力比较好，口语交际能力相对不高，有些学习者语音偏误严重。

其次是设有孔子学院等专业汉语教学机构的学生。2009年以来，随着孔子学院和孔子课堂等专业汉语教学机构在印度高校出现，印度汉语教育由精英教育转变为大众教育。汉语成为很多学生的选修课或必修课。这些学生跟从来自中国的汉语教师和志愿者学习汉语，他们的启蒙教育是所有印度初级汉语学习者中条件最为优越的。孔子学院和中文教学中心的到来，不仅给高校带来了丰富的图书资料，也带来了最为先进的教学理念和教学方法，它们针对汉语学习者的发音问题进行专业的正音训练，所以这些学习者的语音偏误也相对较低。

图 1　2016 年 9 月孙鹏博士在韦洛尔科技大学进行汉语教学

第三是商业语言培训机构的学生。孔子学院带来的“汉语热”不仅扩大了高校汉语学习者的规模，也催生了众多汉语培训机构，进一步在学前班、中小学和社会大众中扩展汉语教学，形成了在印汉语教育发展的新高潮。正如尼赫鲁大学狄伯杰教授所说的，孔子学院在印度的出现有力提升了人们学习汉语的兴趣，尼赫鲁大学中国和东南亚研究中心的学生录取规模由过去的十几人发展到现在一两百人，这也从侧面反映出“汉语热”在印度兴起的不争事实。[1][3]

在这些培训机构中比较知名的有孟买印华中文学校、班加罗尔普通话学校、黄河学院等。它们大多是由在华生活过或者在孔子学院接受过正规汉语培训的教师教授汉语，或者雇佣退休专业汉语教师从事汉语教学。由于商业语言培训机构非常注重培训效果，侧重汉语口语交际能力的培养，所以他们也会学习孔子学院的汉语发音和正音教学方法，甚至出版教材，开发相关的学习词语的应用程序，举办各种学

图 2　2015 年 5 月孙鹏博士在第二届全印度中文比赛上

图 3　2013 年 12 月在班加罗尔普通话学校举办汉语水平考试

习比赛，巩固汉语教学的效果，学生汉语水平提升较快。

在这一群体中发音偏误最小的是学龄前儿童和中小学生。由于这个年龄段的学生学习兴趣浓厚，受母语负迁移影响较小，最容易接受正音教学，成效也是最为显著的。

最后是自学汉语者。这些汉语初学者往往通过网络或者书籍自学汉语，受学习时间和学习条件限制，他们的发音偏误较重，纠正起来也最为吃力。

当然，除了以上几类，汉语初学者还包括华侨华人的子女、在华生活多年的印度人子女等。他们在初学汉语时因为有汉语环境，发音偏误也相对较小。

2 印度汉语初学者的语音偏误分析

受印度多语言文化的影响，印度汉语初学者普遍受母语负迁移影响较大。因此，学习和了解初学者母语与汉语的发音差异，进而组织开展正规的汉语发音教学和正音教学显得非常重要。

印度汉语初学者的语音偏误主要体现在声母、韵母、声调、轻声、音变、连调和儿化等方面。中声母、韵母是重点，声调是难点，而轻声、音变、连调和儿化这些问题则不是非常突出，学习者只要接受过正规的汉语语音教学，基本都能掌握发音规则，从而消除语音偏误。我们在这里就声母、韵母和声调语音偏误做一分析。

在声母发音问题上，印度汉语初学者普遍学习较快，发音也较好。主要问题集中在送气音（p，t，k，h）、舌面音（j，q，x）、舌尖后音（zh，ch，sh，r）和舌尖前音（z，c，s）上。具体来说，主要表现在以下三个方面：

第一是不送气音与送气音的混淆，导致送气音“p，t，k”错发成不送气音“b，d，g”。由于印地语中缺少送气音，“p”和“b，t”和“d，k”和“g”发音相近，所以学生在学习“p，t，k”声母时，经常错误发为“b，d，g”。受印地语母语负迁移的影响，导致部分学生“k ，h”不分，或者“h”发音困难，也存在“p，f”不分的情况。[4]18

第二是舌面音“j，q，x”发音困难。对于声母“j”的发音，学生掌握起来比较容易，但容易受英语负迁移的影响而错发成 [dʒ] 而不是 [tɕ]。声母“q”的发音也会错发成“k”。对印度学生来说，声母“x”的发音是非常困难的，因为这个 [ɕ] 音在当地语音没有对应音，而经常会发为“xerox”中的 [zi] 音。还有学生无法区分“x”与“sh”，而经常混淆二者的发音。

第三是舌尖后音与舌尖前音的混淆。对印度学生来说，舌尖后音“zh，ch，sh，r”相对来说较为容易掌握，舌尖前音“z，c，s”中的“z”和“c”发音容易产生偏误，

“z”常发音成“zoo”的［z］，“c”常发成［k］。有的初学者会将“z，c，s”与“zh，ch，sh”混淆。有的初学者常把“zh，ch，sh”念成近似“ j，q，x”的舌面音。

在韵母发音问题上，受英语负迁移的影响，“a，o，e”常被发为［ʌ］，［əʊ］，［ɜː］；“i，u，ü”的发音中，“ü”是印度汉语初学者最难掌握的，主要是由于印度当地语言中没有近似的“ü”发音，所以经常会发近似［iu］的音。在复韵母中，受英语负迁移的影响，“ai，ao，ui，un”常会产生偏误；受印地语负迁移的影响，部分学生“an”和“ang”“en”和“eng”不分。[4]20 另外部分学生在发“ang”和“eng”的时候会在结尾处多一个［k］音。

声调是印度汉语初学者感受学习起来最困难的部分。其主要问题表现为，阴平声调值不足，为 3–3 调值，而不是正常的 5–5 调值，且发音短促，类似汉语的去声。阳平声调是印度汉语初学者非常难以掌握的声调，普遍存在语音偏误，特别是在语句朗读过程中，形成独特的印度语调，一旦固化，纠正起来非常困难。上声声调是印度初学者产生语音偏误较多的声调，表现为开始调值高而无法完成上声 2–1–4 的声调发音。在去声的发音上，印度汉语初学者常受英语发音负迁移的影响形成拖音，尾音上常带有颤音，而不是短而快的降调。

3　印度汉语初学者正音教学的策略

汉语语音教学是汉语教学的基础，而汉语正音教学是“以纠正学生语音偏误为重点，以提高学生汉语发音水平为目标”[5]18，是语音教学的重要组成部分。针对印度汉语初学者所存在的语音偏误，笔者在多年的在印汉语教学过程中，采取了一些针对性的解决方法，效果显著。

3.1　科学运用《汉语拼音方案》，坚持由易而难的教学原则

我们在实际课堂教学中，应充分利用《汉语拼音方案》的声母表、韵母表和声调表挂图，采用声母与韵母分别分段讲授，配合《HSK 标准教程》的课文练习，注重语言交际的方法，快速而又高效地教授声母、韵母和声调。首先讲授“b，p，m，f”，同时学习韵母“o”；接着学习“d，t，n，l，g，k，h”，同时学习韵母“e”；

接着使用气息感应法，就“b”和“p，d”和“t，g”和“k”的送气音与不送气音做正音讲述，即用一条软纸条置于口前，在发送气音“p，t，k”时，故意加大气流和延长送气时间，让学生通过观察纸条飘动来认识送气音与不送气音的区别，然后让学生自己动手练习，效果非常明显。针对个别同学“p，t，k”清音浊化的问题，可以让其用手放在咽喉处，感知声带的动作，要求清音声带不振动。使用这两个方法，学生很快就能掌握送气音的发音方法。

图4　2016年9月，韦洛尔孔子学院学生在使用气息感应法正音

有意识地讲授声调时，可以引入韵母“a”的讲解，进而学习声调，从第一声开始，接着讲述第四声，然后是第三声，最后是第二声，这是遵循先易后难的原则。然后将韵母“a”与刚刚学过的声母进行拼读，特别选择“mama”“baba”这些亲属称谓，引起学生的学习兴趣，进而学习和掌握四个基本声调和轻声。

3.2　坚持有针对性和实用性原则，因材施教

在“g，k，h”的语音教学中，除了注意纠正学生的清音浊化和送气音不送气的问题，还要注意“h”的发音问题。有些同学“h”发音困难，或者容易与“k”混淆，教师可以先讲述“h”的发音位置，使用夸张法强调口腔打开，然后用学生熟悉的印度姓氏“Mohan”作为参考纠音，学生很快就能掌握发音要领。在集中学

习韵母“a，o，e”时，要使用夸张法，要求学生发“a”音时，口腔张大；发“o”音时，口唇成圆形；而发“e”音时，则是口腔半开。学习“i，u，ü”时，由于学生通常发“i”和“u”音时不存在问题，重点讲授“ü”的发音方法。强调由“i”带“u”的发音方法。即保持“i”的发音不变，嘴唇逐渐向前变成“u”的发音口型的方法。对仍然将“ü”发［iu］的学生，告知其只需要在发“i”音时嘴唇向前突出使肌肉变得紧张，而口腔内空间不发生变化，注意只是变为“u”的口型，而不发“u”音，始终保持发“i”音，即可实现。

3.3 坚持“精讲多练”“以一带多”的原则

对于“j，q，x”的发音，我们强调“j”的发音类似于英语中“jeep”中的“j”而非“juice”中“j”的音。一般可以让学生观看这三个音的发音位置示意图，让其了解这三个音的发音位置是相同的。然后让其先发“jeep”的“jee”音，保持发音位置，给予更大的气流，从而发出“q”的音，最后将嘴唇拉长到最大值，发“x”的音，这样学生很容易掌握发音位置。对印度学生来说，“zh，ch，sh”的发音相对容易。教授“zh”的发音，我们采取的是用“orange”和“bridge”中的“ge”和“dge”的发音［dʒ］，要求发音保持长一些；“ch”则用“chicken”中“ch”的音；“sh”则为“fish”中“sh”的音，保持长值；“r”则与“rose”中“r”的发音相似。这些发音都强调音值较长，舌尖要接触上颚。“r”的发音在英语中是圆唇，而在汉语里是扁唇。而“z，c，s”则先强调舌尖要接触齿背，而不是上颚和齿龈，与“birds，tests，silk”中的“ds，ts，s”类似，要求学生牙齿不得打开，防止发出类似英语“see”的音。

对于这些发音位置相同，而存在实际发音困难的声母，适合采用“精讲多练”[5]18和“以一带多”的原则，结合初学者熟悉的发音习惯，从而在不断机械模仿记忆中固化。

3.4 坚持利用规则，简化记忆的原则

在学习复韵母时，强调要牢固记忆“ai，ei，ao，ou，an，en，ang，eng，ong”，然后再学习和认读与介母拼读的情况。进而将零声母和隔音符号“ ’ ”和

“i，u”写成“y，w”，以及“ü”与“j，q，x”拼读写作“u”，与“n”和“l”拼读仍写为“ü”的规则，等等。老师要将这些细小却又十分重要的拼读规则讲清楚，学生掌握后很快就能熟记汉语拼音方案，达到事半功倍的效果。

3.5　坚持夸张和有趣的原则

对于印度汉语初学者来说，很多韵母和声调的学习都是比较困难的，这时候就需要教师在教授语音的时候，采取夸张的方法，发音时口唇变化要明显，提高音高，适当延长音值，甚至加上夸张的肢体动作，以便于给学习者留下深刻的印象。

图5　奇卡拉大学学生在学习汉语声调

教师在讲授声调时，建议采用先阴平，后去声，再上声，最后阳平的顺序，即坚持从易到难的顺序，让学生逐渐体会声调的不同。由于印度学生中普遍存在阴平声调音高不够的问题，我们让学生们站起来双手打开平举，大声发音，尽量保持声音平稳，并保持一定音长。在发阳平声调时，可以先向学生说明其发音类似英语的升调，要让学生发音要达到最高点。也可以用去声带阳平的方式，即让学生朗读去声加阳平的词组，如“斗牛”（dòuniú）等，学生就会很容易发出正确的音来。在发上声声调时，采用“2-1-1”的半三声的发音方式，可以让学生边发音边点头，这样就可以让学生体会到发音效果。最后的去声强调降调需要短而快，不能拖音。发音时，可以让学生快速坐下，以加强对声调的感受。在朗诵四声时，可以让学生用手在空中比画声调的走向，以加深对声调的印象。

3.6 充分利用现代化教学手段的原则

在训练方法上，坚持利用多媒体等教学手段，借助音频、视频等多媒体教学资源， 直观地展现教学内容， 创造学习语境，让学生不断重复与模仿，听音辨音，听音固音，通过大声朗读，锻炼听音辨音能力，强化记忆训练。在此基础上不断温故知新，从而巩固正音效果。

图 6　2014 年 9 月孙鹏博士在孔子学院日活动中教授汉语

总之，为了更有效地帮助印度汉语初学者解决语音偏误问题，需要我们这些从事对印汉语教学的工作者们不断了解学习者的语音特点，在正确掌握《汉语拼音方案》的规则基础上，努力学习印度地方语言，与印度本土汉语教师多做交流，共同寻找印度地方语言与汉语的异同之处，不断完善和总结经验，将之应用于在印汉语教学之中。同时，要有针对性地编撰具有实用性的正音教材，不断加大对汉语学习者的语音训练。今后要更加注重发挥印度本土汉语教师的主体作用，支持他们开展汉语教学和研究，组织开展本土汉语教师教材和教法培训，帮助他们掌握最新的汉语语音教学方法，提高汉语发音水平，进而有效提高印度汉语初学者的汉语发音水平。在当前新冠疫情依旧严竣的情况下，汉语正音教学要充分利用网络多媒体教学手段，用云课堂云教学、在线直播等方式，让高质量的汉语教学走进印度汉语初学者的生活，从而营造真实的汉语听说环境，以助提高印度初学者的汉语学习的整体水平。

参考文献

[1] 李哲凯. 印度汉语教学历史与现状研究 [D]. 西安：陕西师范大学，2018.

[2] 木克土. 印度汉语教学的问题及对策研究——以 Doon 大学为例 [D]. 济南：山东师范大学，2012.

[3] 苑基荣."汉语热"在印度持续升温 [N]. 人民日报，2018-04-26（03）.

[4] KOCHHAR G. Teaching Chinese to Indian students: an understanding[J]. Journal of technology and Chinese language teaching, 2013, 4（1）：16-36.

[5] 赵立博. 论汉语正音课的教学原则 [J]. 现代语文，2014（3）：18-20.

The Strategies of Pronunciation Teaching for Primary Chinese Learners in India

Sun Peng[1]

Abstract With the rise of "Mandarin Wave" in India, a large number of Indian pre-school children, primary and secondary school students and college students, as well as businessmen, language trainers, and even some housewives and retirees began to learn Chinese as a career choice, which promoted the development of Chinese education in India. However, due to the lack of local Chinese teachers and learning conditions, most of these beginners have problems in Chinese pronunciation. Therefore, Chinese education in India needs to promote Chinese pronunciation teaching among primary Chinese learners. Therefore, it is necessary to strengthen the research on the phonetic errors of Indian primary Chinese learners, compile practical orthographic textbooks, organize the training of local teachers, innovate phonetic teaching methods, and make full use of network multimedia teaching means, so as to improve the Chinese level of beginners

Key Words India; Primary Chinese; Phonetic error; Phonetic teaching

India is a multi-ethnic and multilingual country. There are 22 official languages in the Indian constitution, such as Hindi, Bengali, Telugu, Tamil, etc. English is also a national language. In this multilingual environment, Indians have

1 Researcher of Institute of South Asian Studies, Zhengzhou University, China.

developed the habit of learning many languages since childhood. The Indian government's education policy also requires students to learn a foreign language in addition to their mother tongues, Hindi and English. Therefore, they often opt to learn French, Spanish, German or other Western languages, and also opt to learn Japanese, Korean or other Oriental languages. Since the new century, Chinese has also become a foreign language for Indian students to learn, and there has been a "Mandarin Wave". In addition to the Jawaharlal Nehru University, Delhi University and Visva-Bharati University, nearly 40 universities and institutes offer Chinese language courses.[1]25 In addition, a large number of commercial language training institutions have also included Chinese training programs, attracting a lot of learners. Teaching Chinese has become a career choice for many language teachers and retirees. With the expansion of the source of Chinese learners and the increase in the number of Chinese learners, how to quickly improve the Chinese level of learners, especially the level of oral expression, has become a very urgent problem for Chinese education in India. In order to effectively solve this problem, we must pay attention to the development of Chinese Orthographic teaching. Based on the experience accumulated in primary Chinese teaching in India for a long time, I will report some effective methods of carrying out Chinese pronunciation teaching in India.

1 COMPOSITION AND PHONETIC ERRORS OF CHINESE LANGUAGE BEGINNERS IN INDIA

In order to better understand the pronunciation errors of Chinese language beginners in India, and then propose targeted solutions, we need to first understand the composition of Chinese language beginners and their degree of phonetic errors. According to the age and occupation of Chinese learners, we can divide the beginners into pre-school children, primary and secondary students, college students and the public. Generally speaking, the Chinese phonetic errors of juveniles are generally light, while those of adults are more serious. According to the learning conditions and degree of professionalism, we can divide Chinese beginners into the following four groups.

The first group is the students majoring in Chinese in colleges and universities. They are the group with the best learning conditions among Indian Chinese beginners, who can receive professional Chinese teaching and training, and also the group with the firmest choice of Chinese as their career. This group is small in scale, but has a long learning time. After systematic Chinese training, the Chinese level is also the highest. They generally come from Jawaharlal Nehru University, Delhi University and Visva-Bharati University, which are the traditional Chinese language education centers. In the 1930s, Visva-Bharati University founded by Rabindranath Tagore was established as Cheena Bhavana. Mr. Tan Yunshan devoted himself to spreading Chinese language and culture and brought a large number of Chinese books. Chinese teachers have been engaged in Chinese teaching in the college. So he became the leader of Chinese language education in India.[2]10 Later, with the change of political situation, the study of Sinology in Delhi University and Jawaharlal Nehru University rose one after another and developed rapidly. Many top Sinologists from India gathered together and became the highest institution of Chinese studies. Their level of Chinese teaching has always been in the first-class position.[1]25 These universities are generally taught and read by Chinese experts and scholars in India. Oral Chinese classes are taught by Chinese teachers from China mainland, Taiwan and Hongkong, and some overseas Chinese teachers from Singapore and Malaysia. Restricted by teaching materials and learning conditions, the scale of Chinese learners in these universities is very small and belongs to elite education. Usually their reading ability are good, but their oral communication abilities are relatively low, and some of them have serious phonetic errors.

The second group is the students who have set up Confucius Institute and other professional Chinese teaching institutions. Since 2009, with the emergence of Confucius Institute, Confucius Classroom and other professional Chinese teaching institutions in Indian universities, Indian Chinese education has been transformed from elite education to mass education. Chinese has become an elective or compulsory course for many students. These students followed Chinese teachers and volunteers from China mainland to learn Chinese. Their enlightening education is the most advantageous condition for all junior Chinese learners in India. With the arrival of the Confucius Institute and Chinese language teaching center, it not only brought a wealth of books and materials to colleges and universities, but also brought the most advanced teaching ideas and teaching methods. Chinese learners have received professional training on pronunciation teaching, so their pronunciation errors are relatively low.

Picture 1 Dr. Sun Peng teaching Chinese at Vellore Institute of Technology in September 2016

Again, the third group is the students from commercial language training institutions. The "Mandarin Wave" brought by the Confucius Institute has not only expanded the scale of Chinese learners in colleges and universities, but also spawned many Chinese training institutions, further expanding Chinese to preschool classes, primary and secondary schools and the public, forming a new climax of the development of Chinese education in India. As Professor B. R. Deepak of Jawaharlal Nehru University said, the emergence of Confucius Institutes in India has greatly promoted people's interest in learning Chinese. The enrollment scale of students studying in the Centre for Chinese and South East Asian Studies at Jawaharlal Nehru University has grown from a dozen in the past to one or two hundred now, which reflects the indisputable fact that the "Mandarin Wave" is rising in India.[3]

Among these training institutions, the more well-known are Mumbai Yeh China, Bangalore Mandarin School and Yellow River Academy. Most of their directors have lived in China or received formal Chinese training in Confucius Institutes. They teach Chinese by themselves or employ retired professional Chinese teachers to teach Chinese. As commercial language training institutions attach great importance to the training and the cultivation of oral Chinese communicative competence, they also learn the teaching methods of Chinese pronunciation and orthography of Confucius Institute. They even publish teaching materials, develop applications and programs for learning Chinese words, hold various learning competitions, strengthen the effectiveness of Chinese teaching, and improve students' Chinese level rapidly.

In this group, pre-school children and primary and secondary school students have the smallest pronunciation errors. Because of their strong interest in learning and they are less affected by the negative transfer of their mother tongue, they are most likely to accept the pronunciation teaching, and the effect is the most significant.

Picture 2　Dr. Sun Peng at the 2nd All India Chinese Competition in May 2015

Finally, the fourth group is those who study Chinese by themselves. These Chinese language beginners often learn Chinese by themselves through the Internet or books. Due to the limitation of learning time and conditions, their pronunciation errors are more serious, and it is most difficult to correct them.

Of course, in addition to the above classification, Chinese language beginners also include the children of overseas Chinese and Indian children who have lived in China for many years. When they first learn Chinese, because of the Chinese environment, their pronunciation errors are relatively light.

Picture 3 Hanyu Shuiping Test being held at the Bangalore Mandarin School in December 2013

2 ANALYSIS OF PHONETIC ERRORS OF CHINESE LANGUAGE BEGINNERS IN INDIA

Influenced by Indian multilingual culture, Indian Chinese language beginners are generally affected by negative transfer of mother tongue. Therefore, it is very important to learn and understand the differences between beginners' mother tongue and Chinese pronunciation, and then organize and carry out regular Chinese pronunciation teaching and correction teaching.

The phonetic errors of Indian Chinese language beginners are mainly reflected in initials, finals, tones, neutral tones, tone changes, tone sandhi and Retroflex suffixation. Among them, the initials and finals are the key points, the tone is the difficult point, while the problems of neutral tone, tone change, tone sandhi, and even Retroflex suffixation are not very prominent. As long as the learners have received the regular Chinese phonetic teaching, they can master the pronunciation rules and eliminate the phonetic errors. Therefore, we will analyze the initials, finals and tone errors.

On the issue of initials pronunciation, Indian Chinese beginners generally learn faster and pronounce better. The main problems focus on aspirated (p, t, k, h), glossal (j, q, x), retroglossal (zh, ch, sh, r) and fore (z, c, s). Specifically, there are three main aspects:

The first is the confusion of unaspirated and aspirated sounds, which leads to the wrong sending of aspirated "p, t, k" into unaspirated "b, d, ɡ". Due to the lack of aspirated sounds in Hindi, the pronunciation of "b" and "p", "d" and "t", "ɡ" and "k" are similar, so students often mistakenly pronounce "b, d, ɡ" when learning initials "p, t, k". Influenced by the negative transfer of Hindi mother tongue, some students do not distinguish between "k" and "h", or have difficulty in pronouncing "h", and there is no distinction between "p" and "f".[4]18

The second is that the glossal sounds "j", "q" and "x" are difficult to pronounce. It is easy for students to master the pronunciation of the initial "j", but it is easy to be mispronounced as [dʒ] rather than "j" [tɕ] due to the negative transfer of English. The pronunciation of the initial "q" can also be mispronounced as "k". It is very difficult for Indian students to pronounce the initial "x", because there is no corresponding sound for the [ɕ] sound in the local pronunciation, but it is often pronounced as the [zi] in Xerox. Some students can't distinguish "x" from "sh", and often confuse their pronunciation.

The third is the confusion between retroglossal and forward. For Indian students, the retroglossal sounds "zh, ch, sh, r" are relatively easy to master, and the pronunciations of "z" and "c" in "z, c, s" are prone to errors. "z" is often pronounced as Zoos [z] and "c" is often pronounced as [k]. Some beginners will confuse "z, c, s" with "zh, ch, sh". Some beginners often pronounce "zh, ch, sh" as the glossal sounds similar to "j, q, x".

As for vowel pronunciation, influenced by the negative transfer of English, "a, o, e" are often pronounced as [ʌ], [əʊ], [ɜː]; among the pronunciation of "i, u, ü", "ü" is the most difficult for beginners to master, mainly because there is no similar "ü" pronunciation in Indian local language, so they often pronounce the sound similar to "iu". In compound vowels, "ai, ao, ui, un" often have errors due to the negative transfer of English, while "an" is not distinguished from "ang", and "en" from "eng", due to the negative transfer of Hindi.[4]20 Some students will have an extra [k] at the end when they pronounce "ang" and "eng".

Tone is the most difficult part for beginners. The main problem is that the *yinping* tone value is insufficient, which is 3-3 tone value instead of the normal 5-5 tone value, and the pronunciation is short, which is similar to the Chinese falling tone. *Yangping* tone is very difficult for Indian Chinese beginners to master, and there are common phonetic errors, especially in the process of sentence reading, forming a unique Indian tone; once solidified, it is very difficult to correct. The falling-rising tone is the tone that Indian beginners produce a lot of pronunciation errors, which shows that the initial tone value is high and cannot complete the tone pronunciation of falling-rising tone 2-1-4. In terms of the pronunciation of the falling tone, beginners are often influenced by the negative transfer of English pronunciation to form a drag, and the final sound often has a trill rather than a short and fast falling tone.

3 STRATEGIES OF PRONUNCIATION TEACHING FOR CHINESE LANGUAGE BEGINNERS IN INDIA

Chinese phonetic teaching is the basis of Chinese teaching, and Chinese pronunciation teaching is an important part of phonetic teaching, "which focuses on correcting students' phonetic errors and aims at improving students' Chinese pronunciation level." [5]18 In view of the phonetic errors of Chinese language beginners in India, the author has taken some targeted solutions in the process of teaching Chinese in India for many years, and the effect is remarkable.

3.1 SCIENTIFIC USE OF "SCHEME FOR THE CHINESE PHONETIC ALPHABET", ADHERE TO THE TEACHING PRINCIPLE OF EASY TO DIFFICULT

As we have analyzed the main phonetic errors of beginners, we have made full use of the initial consonant table, vowel table and tone table wall chart of "Scheme for the Chinese Phonetic Alphabet" in the actual classroom teaching. In this way, the initial consonants and vowels are taught separately, combined with the text practice of *HSK Standard Course*, and more attention is paid to the method of language communication, so as to quickly and efficiently teach the initials, finals and tones. First, teach "b, p, m, f", and learn the vowel "o" at the same time; then learn "d, t, n, l, g, k, h", and at the same time learn the vowel "e"; then do the correct pronunciation of the aspirated and unaspirated sounds of "b-p", "d-t", "g-k", using the breath induction method. That is, a piece of soft paper is placed in front of the mouth. When the teacher pronouncs the aspirated sounds "p, t, k", he/she deliberately uses large airflow and extended the air delivery time. This helps the students understand the difference between aspirated and unaspirated sounds by observing the paper floating. Then let the students practice by themselves. The effect is very obvious. In view of the problem of voiced "p, t, k" by individual students, we can let them put their hands on their throats to sense the movement of vocal cords and require the voiceless vocal cords not to vibrate. Using these two

Picture 4　The students of the Confucius Institute in Vellore Institute of Technology using the breath induction method to correct pronunciation in September 2016

methods, students can quickly master the pronunciation of aspirated sounds.

In order to teach the tones consciously, we can introduce the explanation of the vowel "a", and then learn the tones. Starting from the first tone, then the fourth tone, then the third tone, and finally the second tone, this is because we adhere to the principle of "easy first, then difficult". Then the vowel "a" is spelled with the consonants that have just been learned, and the kinship terms such as "mama", "baba" and "gege" are specially selected to arouse students' interest in learning, and then learn and master the four basic tones and neutral tone.

3.2 ADHERE TO THE PRINCIPLE OF PERTINENCE AND PRACTICALITY AND TEACH STUDENTS ACCORDING TO THEIR APTITUDE.

In "g, k, h" phonetic teaching, in addition to paying attention to correct students' voiced and aspirated, also pay attention to the problem of the "h" pronunciation. Some students have difficulty in pronouncing "h", or easily confuse it with "k". The teacher can first tell the pronunciation position of "h", use exaggerate actions to emphasize the opening of the mouth, and then correct the pronunciation with the Indian surname "Mohan", which is familiar to the students. Students can quickly master the pronunciation essentials. When learning "a, o, e", because we have learned it before, we use the exaggeration method in concentrated learning. When we pronounce the "a" sound, our mouth will be enlarged; while pronouncing "o", the lips will be round, and "e" is half open mouth. When learning "i, u, ü", because the students do not have any problems in pronunciation of "i" and "u", we focus on the pronunciation of "ü" with the pronunciation of "i" with "u". That is, to keep the pronunciation of "i" unchanged, the lips gradually move forward into the mouth shape of "u". For the students who still pronounce "iu", they are told that they only need to protrude their lips forward for muscular tension, while the space in the oral cavity does not change. They should only change the mouth shape into "u", but not make "u" sound, and always make "i" sound.

3.3 ADHERE TO THE PRINCIPLE OF "INTENSIVE SPEAKING AND MORE PRACTICE" AND "TRY TO BE CONCISE"

For the pronunciation of "j, q, x", we emphasize that the pronunciation of "j" is similar to "j" in "jeep" rather than "j" in "judge". Generally, students can look at the schematic diagram of the pronunciation position of these three sounds, so that they can understand that the pronunciation positions of these three sounds are the same. Then let the students pronounce "jeep" first part "jee", and keep the pronunciation position, give more airflow, so as to make the "q" sound. Finally, lengthen the lips to the maximum value and pronounce the "x" sound. In this way, students can easily master the pronunciation position. For Indian students, the pronunciation of "zh, ch, sh" is relatively easy. We adopt the pronunciation of "ge" and "dge" in "orange" and "bridge" as [dʒ], which requires the pronunciation to be longer, "ch" from "ch" in "chicken", "sh" from "sh" in "fish", and "r" is similar to "r" in "rose". These pronunciations emphasize that the sound value is long and the tip of the tongue should touch the upper jaw. "r" is a round lip sound in English and a flat lip sound in Chinese. However, "z, c, s" emphasize that the tip of the tongue should contact the back of the teeth rather than the upper jaw and gingiva. It is similar to "ds", "ts", "s" in "birds, tests, silk". It requires students not to open their lips to prevent them from making English "see" sounds.

For these initials that have the same pronunciation position but are difficult to pronounce in practice, it is suitable to adopt the principles of "intensive speaking and more practice"[5]18 and "Try to be concise", combined with the familiar pronunciation habits of beginners, so as to solidify in the continuous mechanical imitation memory.

3.4 ADHERE TO THE PRINCIPLE OF USING RULES AND SIMPLIFYING MEMORY

When learning compound vowels, it is emphasized to memorize "ai, ei, ao, ou, an, en, ang, eng, ong", and then learn and recognize the situation of the spelling of preposition. Then the zero initials and sound insulation symbols " ' " and

Picture 5 The students from Chitkara University are learning Chinese tones

"i", "u" are written as "y", "w", and when "ü" follows with "j, q, x", it should be spelled as "u", but when it follows with "n" and "l", it should be still spelled as "ü". After these small but important spelling rules are explained clearly, students can quickly memorize the "Scheme for the Chinese Phonetic Alphabet" and achieve the effect of twice the result with half the effort.

3.5 STICK TO THE PRINCIPLE OF EXAGGERATION AND FUN

For beginners, it is difficult to learn many finals and tones. At this time, it is necessary for teachers to adopt the exaggeration method when teaching pronunciation. The change of lips should be obvious, the pitch should be increased, the value of pitch should be extended appropriately, and the exaggerated body movements should be added to make a deep impression on the learners.

When we teach the tone, we use the order of *yinping* tone first, then falling tone, then falling-rising tone, and finally *yangping* tone. That is to insist on the order from easy to difficult, so that students gradually realize the difference of tones. Due to the problem that Indian students are not high enough in intonation, we asked the students to stand up, open their hands, and speak aloud. They are required to keep the voice steady and maintain a certain length. In the pronunciation of *yangping* tone, we can explain to the students that its pronunciation is similar to the rising tone of English sentences, so that the students' pronunciation should reach the highest point. You can also use the way to remove the *yangping* tone of the vocal cords, that is, let the students read the phrases of "falling tone + *yangping* tone", such as "dòuniú" (bullfight), and so on. Students can also easily pronounce the correct sound. In the pronunciation of the falling-rising tone, the use of 2-1-1 half three tone pronunciation method, students can pronounce while nodding, so that students can experience the pronunciation effect. The last falling tone emphasizes that the falling tone needs to be short and fast, and can't drag. When pronouncing the falling tone, students can sit down quickly to strengthen the feeling of the tone. When reciting four tones, let the students use their hands to compare the direction of the tone in the air, so as to deepen the impression of the tone.

3.6 THE PRINCIPLE OF MAKING FULL USE OF MODERN TEACHING METHODS

In terms of training methods, adhere to the use of multimedia teaching means, such as CD-ROM, video and other multimedia teaching resources, intuitively show the teaching content, create learning context, let students constantly repeat and imitate, listen to sound discrimination, listen to sound fixation, exercise the ability of listening and distinguishing sound through reading aloud, and strengthen memory training. On this basis, constantly review the old and learn the new, so as to consolidate the sound effect.

In a word, in order to help Chinese language beginners in India solve the problem of phonetic errors more effectively, we need those workers who are engaged in

Picture 6 Dr. Sun Peng teaching Chinese at the Confucius Institute Day in September 2014

teaching Chinese to India to accumulate the phonetic errors of the learners. On the basis of correctly mastering the rules of the "Scheme for the Chinese Phonetic Alphabet", we should make efforts to learn the local languages of India, communicate more with Indian local Chinese teachers, and jointly look for the similarities and differences between Indian local languages and Chinese, and constantly improve and sum up experiences and apply them to Chinese teaching in India. At the same time, it is necessary to compile practical teaching materials of correct pronunciation, and constantly increase the phonetic training for Chinese learners. In the future, we should pay more attention to the teaching of Chinese pronunciation in India and help them to improve their pronunciation and teaching methods. In the current situation of the COVID-19 pandemic, Chinese orthography teaching should make full use of network multimedia teaching means, cloud classroom, cloud teaching, online live broadcast and other ways, so as to make high-quality Chinese teaching into the life of Indian Chinese beginners, so as to create a real Chinese listening and speaking environment, and help to improve the overall level of Indian beginners' Chinese learning.

(Proofread by Snehal Ajit Ulman)

REFERENCES

[1] 李哲凯. 印度汉语教学历史与现状研究 [D]. 西安：陕西师范大学，2018.

[2] 木克土. 印度汉语教学的问题及对策研究——以 Doon 大学为例 [D]. 济南：山东师范大学，2012.

[3] 苑基荣. “汉语热”在印度持续升温 [N]. 人民日报，2018-04-26（03）.

[4] KOCHHAR G. Teaching Chinese to Indian students: an understanding[J]. Journal of technology and Chinese language teaching, 2013, 4（1）：16-36.

[5] 赵立博. 论汉语正音课的教学原则 [J]. 现代语文，2014（3）：18-20.

印度初级汉语教学之数字教学刍议

韩雨薇[1]

摘要 数字教学是初级汉语教学的重点和难点内容，由于数字与学生生活息息相关，无论是数字表达、量词、序数词、时间、价格和数学计算等都离不开最为基础的数字。因此尽早让学生接触数字，巩固记忆，对初级汉语学习时间、价格表达、量词使用、简单数学计算等都至关重要。数字教学需要让学生了解汉语数字表达规律，以方便学生快速记忆数字。同时，还需要在数字教学中渗透文化内容，如数字禁忌和一些特殊数字表达习惯等，帮助学生理解文化差异。

关键词 印度；初级汉语；数字教学；教学设计

数字教学一直以来都是初级汉语教学中的重点和难点，数字与序数词、量词、时间、价格等知识点有着千丝万缕的联系，因此教会学生学好数字，意义重大。

然而，在很多教材的编写过程中，为了减轻学生学习压力，编者一般都将数字教学内容安排在教材的后半部分，内容安排也较为分散。笔者在印度教授初级汉语时，就打破教材编写顺序，结合学生生活实际需要，在学生学会简单的日常会话后，便引入了数字教学，教学效果良好。在这里，就简单介绍一下我们的做法。

1 数字教学越难，越要让学生早接触

虽然各种版本的初级汉语教材都将数字教学作为重点内容[1]59，但其出现在教材里的位置均不相同，笔者在孔子学院经常使用的汉语教材为《长城汉语》和《HSK

1 石家庄市第九中学教师。

标准教程》。前者第四单元出现数量词，而后者第五课才出现数量词；前者第四、五、七单元里出现数量词，第五单元集中讲授数词规则，后者第五、七、十一、十四课中有关于数字的教学内容，第五课集中介绍数词规则。《HSK 标准教程》中关于数字教学内容分类比较细，分别为表示年龄、日期、时间、价格的数量词学习。如何让学生们顺利掌握中文数字的听说读写，熟练运用到生活之中，成为汉语教师必须思考的问题。

由于数字与学生们的生活息息相关，所以我们可以打破教材编写的顺序，在学习汉字笔画时，就以“一、二、三、四、五”这五个笔画简单的数字导入，介绍写法的同时，教授发音和意义，并用肢体语言表达法让学生学习记忆。[2]18 在此基础上，用同样的方法介绍“六、七、八、九、十”的写法和读音，加上肢体语言，让学生牢固记忆这些数字表达。这种在一开始就引进数字教学的方式，使学生学会了简单数字的书写，并学会了肢体语言记忆。加上在语音教学过程中教师不断重复这些数字的读音，学生慢慢形成了机械记忆，为以后学习使用这些数字打下了基础。

图 1　2014 年 9 月，韩雨薇在 VIT 孔子学院日活动上教授汉语数字

2　用文化带数字，由浅入深，让学生了解数字在中国文化中的意义

为了更好地让学生了解数字的文化含义，我们引入了数字的文化教学方法，由文化带数字，激发学生学习数字的兴趣。[3]60 我们在数字教学中添加了很多数字文化元素，既简单易懂，又实用而生动有趣，将各个知识点相互勾连起来，帮助学生形成牢固记忆。

在学习了一到十的数字写法与肢体语言表达方法后，要不断地复习和考核。因为这些汉字简单易写，学生会很有成就感。然后在复习中要求学生去跟读"一、二、三、四、五"，务必让学生形成快速读出五个数字的习惯。这种整体练习识读，可以帮助学生获得整体语感。对于"六、七、八、九、十"这几个数字，在复习时，加入肢体语言，教会学生熟练运用肢体语言表达中国数字，这种方法激发学生学习兴趣，学习主动性高，学得也很快。[4]271 接下来，要巩固已学的知识，加入一个小活动，让学生学唱《我的朋友在哪里》，通过在黑板上板书改动过的歌词，让学生跟唱歌曲的旋律，在快乐的歌声里学习数字。[5]13 改编后的歌词如下："一二三四五六七，我的朋友在哪里？在这里，在这里，我的朋友在这里。"这时候教师要一边唱，一边走到学生中间去，活跃课堂气氛。印度学生非常热爱歌唱，所以这时候的课堂氛围一定会非常轻松活跃，学习效果显著。

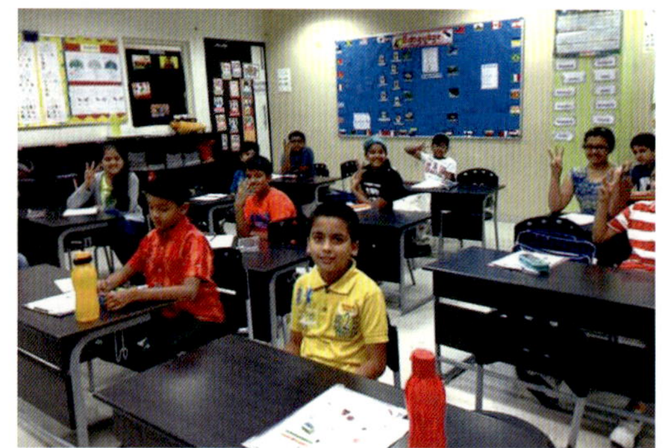

图 2　2015 年 4 月，印华中文学校的学生跟随韩雨薇学习数字

接着为学生讲述中国人喜欢的数字"六""八""九"，它们象征着顺利、财富和长久，最讨厌的数字"三"（散）、"四"（死）等；中国人出行喜欢选择"三、六、九"的日子，中国古代皇帝自称"九五之尊"等。对这些文化小常识的讲解，学生们非常欢迎，教师此时也可以询问学生喜欢什么数字，喜欢哪个日期等，既能活跃课堂气氛，也能巩固数字知识。

3　注意启发式教学，适当引进新的知识点

数字教学中时间教学是难点中的难点，在讲授中国人喜欢的数字日期时，顺势

引出一个语法点，即星期的教学。先教会学生识读“星期几”，然后介绍将“几”替换成数字，表达非常容易。教授学生只用记住一个词语“星期”，然后再加上一到六的数字就可以表示星期一到星期六的日子。但是也要注意提醒学生注意有一个特例，我们通常不说“星期七”，而是称作“星期日”或“星期天”。为了巩固课堂所学的星期几的表达方式，可以进行一轮快问快答，把星期一到星期天的顺序打乱，随意抽取，随机点名，请他们用汉语做出反应。测试一下学生的掌握情况。确保每个学生都被抽检到，且都能掌握。

图 3　2015 年 7 月，韩雨薇与韦洛尔科技大学孔子学院学生在一起

在此基础上，用表格的形式展示 1 至 99 的数字。引导学生学习数字 11 至 19 的表达方式，然后让学生自己猜测 21 至 99 的表达方法。随后举一反三，随机抽取数字让学生回答，测试学生的反应能力，出现错误及时纠正，直到所有学生都能熟练表达这些数字。

然后介绍第二个语法点，即“月份”的表达。先在板书上书写一到十二的数字，然后让学生学会识读“月”这个生词，学生们马上就能领会其中规律。但是，还是要再做练习，直到学生们都能够熟练掌握月份的表达方式。在这一过程中，注意抽检与依次回答相结合，通过这种随机抽取月份让学生回答的方式，来巩固所学内容。

4　以一带多，掌握全部数字表达方式

在教会学生 1 至 100 的内容后，集中学习“零、百、千、万”。在掌握这些生字后，学习 100 至 10 000 的表达方法。通过学习“零”，学习 101 至 109 的表达方法，进而让学生掌握 101 至 999 的表达方式。然后再接着学习 1 000 至 10 000 的表

达方法，掌握 1 001 至 99 999 的表达方法。继续随机抽取数字，抽查学生的学习反馈。此时，会有学生开始翻看前面 1 至 10 的拼音记录，试图组合读出比较大的数字。对这一内容教师应该反复练习，根据课堂的反应，确定练习的数量和课后作业量。

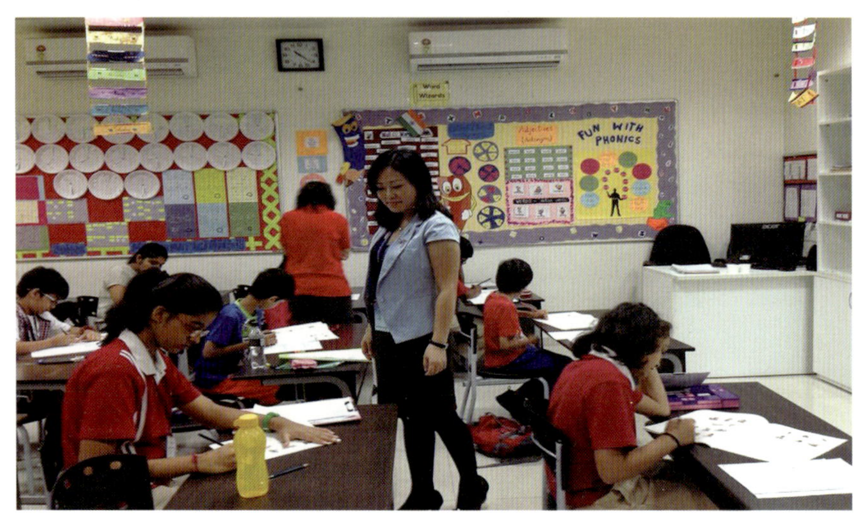

图 4　2015 年 4 月，韩雨薇在孟买印华中文学校组织 YCT 考试

在大多数同学都掌握了大数字的表达方法后，再接着教授一个语法点，也是中国人的表达习惯，即关于数字“1”的表达。在电话号码和房间号码里它的读音要发生变化。这时教师可以多举几个例子，在黑板上板书一组电话号码，再给出一组房间号码，教学生准确读出，特别注意“1”的变音。等学生熟练了之后，教师可以组织一个小活动，三人一组，请两位学生到黑板前，请另外一位学生用中文说出自己的电话号码和房间号码，让学生在黑板上写下来。写完后三人核对一下看看是否正确。这种活动既考核了学生的数字识读能力，也考察了学生的听音辨音能力，还考察了学生的书写记忆能力，一举多得，是一种非常有效的考察方式。我们的实验结果表明，在这种活动中，学生参与性和主动性都比较强，但是测试结果却有很大的差异。有的学生已经充分掌握了数字的表达方法，也能注意到“1”在电话号码中的变音问题，但也有同学只能写出几个数字，无法很好地完成记录，仍需要课下多加努力才能跟上。最后的十分钟，教师可以引入本单元的教学重点——问年龄。

重点句型“你多大了？”“我××岁了。”。由于学生已经掌握了数字的表达方法，此时只需要强调数字加上“岁”就是正确回答年龄的方法，特别注意学生经常受英语负迁移的影响，漏掉“岁”而直接回答数字，针对这一问题一定要注意纠正。在讲授完这一内容后，教师可以组织两人互相问答活动，要求学生根据自己的实际情况作答。有错必纠，务必要求学生当堂掌握所学知识，为下一节课的教学内容做好铺垫。

通过以上内容的介绍，我们了解了初级汉语教学的难点——数字教学，以及如何在短短的一两节课的时间内，做到各部分内容顺利衔接，各个教学小板块之间顺畅过渡，营造生动的课堂教学氛围。通过良好的师生互动和启发式教学，使学生在轻松的气氛中学习语言，掌握汉语中数字的表达。[6]150 在课堂教学中，通过增加各种文化知识点，以学生活动的形式穿插进行，使整节课保持一个相对活跃的气氛，教师教得轻松，学生学得愉快，记忆深刻。实现了汉语教学向课堂45分钟时间要质量、要成绩的教学目的。

图5　2015年5月，韩雨薇在第二届全印度中文比赛上

综合分析我们在孔子学院进行的数字教学步骤，不难发现，我们在教学过程中实际上打破了原有的教材编排顺序，根据学生的实际情况和接受能力做出安排。通过教材的整合，将各种元素有机地整合在一起，使数字教学内容更独具匠心，使其过渡自然，浑然一体，不再是原来支离破碎的样子。这种教学内容安排更便于教师授课，也更加有利于学生学习，符合学生对汉语数字认识规律。因此，我们认为，教师不应一味盲目地按照教材的顺序进行教学，而应大胆地对内容进行裁剪和整合，

使之更贴近学生的实际。把数字教学与数字文化知识的介绍，以及学生的活动相结合，进行合理的教学设计，充分调动学生的学习积极性，帮助学生克服对数字学习的畏难情绪，使枯燥的数字教学内容活起来。这种课程设计能抓住学生的心，使初级汉语教学中的数字教学难点成为学生乐意学习的“甜点”。

参考文献

[1] 彭凡. 对外汉语教学中的数字教学方法探究 [J]. 新课程研究，2019（9）：59-60.

[2] 琚天娇. 体态语在波黑萨大孔院初级汉语综合课中的应用研究 [D]. 安阳：安阳师范学院，2019.

[3] 李思思. 浅谈中国文化与汉语数字教学 [J]. 语文教学与研究，2013（2）：60-61.

[4] 闫振宇. 肢体语言在对外汉语教学中的应用及策略——以数字教学和词汇教学为例 [J]. 明日风尚，2018（18）：271.

[5] 余佩. 对外汉语数字教学案例分析 [D]. 武汉：湖北工业大学，2018.

[6] 许兰娟. 游戏法在对外汉语中文数字教学中的应用——以美国埃尔克哈特市康科德高中为例 [J]. 长春教育学院学报，2013，29（19）：150-151.

Proposals on Teaching Numerals at Elementary Chinese Language Teaching in India

Han Yuwei[1]

Abstract Teaching of numbers is the key and difficult content of primary Chinese language teaching. Because numbers are closely related to students' life, the expression of numbers, quantifiers, ordinal words, time, price and mathematical calculation are inseparable from the most basic numbers. Therefore, it is very important to let students get familiar with numbers as soon as possible and form an in-depth memory for the number system. It is very important at the time of the elementary Chinese language learning, to be exposed to price expressions, quantifier learning, simple mathematical calculation, etc. Teaching of numbers requires let students to understand the rules of Chinese numeral expressions, in order to facilitate them to quickly memorize the numbers. At the same time, we also need to incorporate cultural contents in the teaching method of the number system, such as taboo and some special expression habits, to further help the learners understand the cultural differences.

Key Words Elementary; Chinese teaching of numbers in India; Teaching design

Number teaching has always been the key and difficult point in elementary Chinese language teaching. Numbers are closely related to ordinal number words,

1 Teacher from Shijiazhuag No.9 Middle School.

quantifiers, time, price and other knowledge points. Therefore, it is of great significance to teach students to learn numbers well.

However, in the process of compiling many textbooks, in order to reduce students' learning pressure, content for teaching of numbers appears late in general textbooks, and the content's arrangement is relatively scattered. When I was teaching elementary Chinese in India, I adopted the method of breaking the compil sequence of teaching materials, combining it with the actual needs of students' lives, and introducing the Chinese number system to students after they learned simple daily conversations which received good teaching results. Here, we will briefly introduce our practice.

1 THE MORE DIFFICULT THE NUMBER TEACHING IS, THE EARLIER STUDENTS SHOULD BE EXPOSED TO IT

Although various editions of elementary Chinese language textbooks take number teaching as the key content,[1]59 their appearance in the textbooks is different. The Chinese textbooks that the author often uses in Confucius Institute are *Great Wall Chinese* and *HSK Standard Course*. The former textbook introduces the number system in unit four, while in the latter, the number system is introduced only in unit five. In the former, there are numeral words in units four, five and seven, focusing on teaching numeral rules in unit five. The latter also has teaching contents about numbers in the fifth, seventh, eleventh and fourteenth units. In the fifth lesson, we focus on the rules of numerals. It can be seen that the classification of number

Picture 1 Ms. Han Yuwei teaching Chinese numbers at the VIT Confucius Institute Day in September 2014

teaching contents in HSK standard course is relatively detailed, and contains expressions about age, date, time and price. Therefore, how to make students master the listening, speaking, reading and writing ability of Chinese numbers, and further skillfully apply them to daily lifestyle, has become a problem that Chinese language teachers must ponder on.

Because numbers are closely related to students' lives, we can break the order of compiling textbooks. When learning Chinese characters, we can introduce the writing method with the five numbers with simple strokes, "1, 2, 3, 4, 5", teach their pronunciation and meaning, and let students learn and remember them along with body language expression.[2]18 On this basis, we can introduce "6, 7, 8, 9,10" in the same way, including their method of writing and pronunciation, together with body language expressions, and let students firmly remember the number expressions. Although students can't use it in verbal communication, as a simple Chinese character, they have learned to write and also learned the body language. In addition, the pronunciation of these numbers is repeated in the process of phonetic teaching, and students gradually form mechanical memory. This lays the foundation for learning and using these numbers in the future.

2 LET STUDENTS UNDERSTAND THE SIGNIFICANCE OF NUMBERS IN CHINESE CULTURE

In order to better help students understand the cultural meaning of numbers, we introduce the cultural teaching method of numbers, which can stimulate students' interest in learning numbers.[3]60 Therefore, we added a lot of culture elements to number teaching methods. It makes the learning not only easy to understand, but also practical, vivid and interesting. It links the various knowledge points to help students form an in-depth memory.

After learning the numeral writing method and body language expression method from one to ten, we should constantly review and assess the results. Because these

Chinese characters are easy to write, students will have a sense of achievement. Then in the review, the students are required to follow up with 1, 2, 3, 4, 5 to make sure that students form the habit of reading out five numbers quickly. This kind of holistic reading practice can help students acquire the overall sense of language. For the numbers 6, 7, 8, 9, 10, teachers instruct students to use body language to express Chinese numbers skillfully while practicing. This method can stimulate students' interest in learning, as there ia a high learning initiative and student can learn quickly.[4]271 Next, the tutor needs to consolidate the numbers within ten. The teacher can organize a small activity like letting the students learn to sing "where is my friend". By writing the changed lyrics on the blackboard, and letting the students sing the melody of the song, they can learn the numbers in the form of a happy song.[5]13 The adapted lyrics are as follows: "1, 2, 3, 4, 5, 6, 7, where is my friend? Here, here, my friend is here." At this time, the teacher should go to the students while singing to energize the classroom's atmosphere. Indian students love singing, so the classroom atmosphere at this time will be very relaxed and active, and the learning outcome is also very significant.

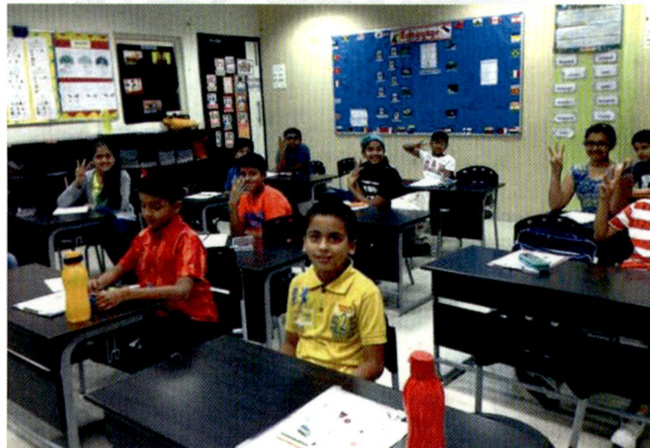

Picture 2 The students of Yinhua Chinese School learning numbers under the guidance of Ms. Han Yuwei in April 2015

Then the teacher should tell the students about the favorite Chinese numbers like "Six", "Eight" and "Nine", which symbolize success, wealth and permanence. The most annoying numbers are "four" (Sounds like "dead" in Chinese) and "three" (Sounds like "scattered" in Chinese). Chinese people like to choose the date with numbers "3, 6, 9" for travel. The emperor called himself with "Jiu Wu Zhi Zun" (the royal prerogative) and so on. Students like these explanations about cultural knowledge very much. Teachers can also ask students what numbers they like and which dates they like. It will not only energize the classroom's atmosphere but also consolidate numeral knowledge.

3 PAY ATTENTION TO HEURISTIC TEACHING AND INTRODUCE NEW KNOWLEDGE POINTS APPROPRIATELY

Time teaching is a difficult aspect of the number teaching system. When teaching Chinese people's favorite date number, a grammar point is introduced which is the teaching of weekday. First, teach students to read *xingqi* ("week" in Chinese), and then introduce how to add the number after *xingqi*. Teach students to remember only one word *xingqi* and add a number from one to six to represent the days from Monday to Saturday. But we should also pay attention to remind students that there is a special case, that is, *xingqi ri* (Sunday) can also be called *xingqi tian*. In order to consolidate the expression of the day of the week learned in class, we can carry out a round of quick questions and answers, shuffle the order from Monday to Sunday, randomly select and call names, and ask them to respond in Chinese. Check the students' mastery. Make sure that every student is reviewed and there are no problems.

Picture 3 Ms. Han Yuwei with students from the Confucius Institute at Vellore Institute of Technology in July 2015

On this basis, the numbers 1 to 99 are shown in the form of table. Guide students to learn the expressions of numbers 11 to 19, and then ask students to guess the expressions of 21 to 99. Then draw inferences from one instance and draw random numbers for students to answer. Test students' reaction ability and correct mistakes in time until all students can express these numbers skillfully. Then introduce the second grammatical point, the expression of "month". First, tutors write the numbers from one to twelve on the blackboard, and then let the students learn to read the new word *yue* (month). The students can immediately understand the rule. However, we still need to do more exercises until the students can master the expression of the month. In this process, attention should be paid to the combination of spot-checking and answering in turns. Randomly select a month and ask students to give the answer. By this way, students can consolidate what they have learned.

4 WITH THE PRINCIPLE OF "TRY TO BE CONCISE", MASTER ALL NUMERICAL EXPRESSIONS

After teaching the content of 1 to 100 for students, they should concentrate on learning *ling* (zero), *bai* (hundred), *qian* (thousand) and *wan* (ten thousand). After mastering these new words, we should teach them to learn how to express the numbers from 100 to 10,000. By learning *ling* (zero), learn the expression of 101 to 109, and then let students master the expression of 101 to 999. Then let them learn the expression method of 1,000 to 10,000 and master the expression

Picture 4 Ms. Han Yuwei organized the YCT test at Yinhua Chinese School in Mumbai in April 2015

method of 1,001 to 99,999. Continue to randomly select the number, and spot check students' learning feedback. At this point, some students will start to look at the Pinyin records of the previous 1 to 10, try to read the larger numbers. For this content, teachers should practice repeatedly, and determine the number of exercises and homework according to the classroom's reaction.

After most students have mastered the expression of large numbers, we should teach them a grammar point, which is also a Chinese expression habit, that is, the expression of the number 1. Its pronunciation changes in phone numbers and room numbers. At this time, the teacher can give several more examples, write a group of telephone numbers on the blackboard, then give a group of room numbers, and teach students to read out accurately, paying special attention to the pronunciation change of 1. After the students become proficient, the teacher can organize a small activity in groups of three. Ask two students to come to the blackboard. And ask the other student to say his telephone number and room number in Chinese. Let the students write down the numbers on the blackboard. After writing, ask three people to check and see if the numbers are correct. This kind of activity tests not only the students' abilities of reading numbers, but also the abilities of listening and distinguishing sounds, as well as the abilities of writing and memorizing. It is a very effective way to investigate. Our experimental results show that in this kind of activity, students' participation and initiative are relatively strong, but the test results are quite different. Some students have fully mastered the expression of numbers, and can also notice the problem of changing the tone of 1 in the telephone number, but other students can only write a few numbers, unable to complete the record well. They still needs to work harder after class to keep the spirit up. In the last ten minutes, the teacher can introduce the teaching focus of this unit—asking age. "How old are you?""I'm ×× years old." Since students have mastered the expression of numbers, they only need to emphasize that the number plus "year" is the correct way to answer the age. Special attention should be paid to the fact that students are often influenced by the negative learning effects of English, where they can answer numbers directly without "year". In view of this problem, we must pay attention to correct it. After teaching this content, the teacher can let two people ask and answer each other, and ask the students to answer according to their own actual situation. If there is a mistake, the teacher must correct it. The teacher should make sure that all students have mastered the contents which they have learned in class, so as to pave the way for the next class.

Through the introduction of the above contents, we have learned the difficulty of teaching numbers at the elementary level, as well how to achieve the smooth connection of the contents of each part and the smooth transition between the small teaching parts in a short period of one or two courses, so as to create a lively classroom teaching atmosphere. Through the good interaction between teachers and students and heuristic teaching, students can learn the language in a relaxed atmosphere and master the Chinese expression of numbers.[6]150 In the classroom teaching, by adding various cultural knowledge points and expressions in the form of student activities, the atmosphere of the whole class is kept at a relatively enthusiastic level. When the teacher teaches easily, the students learn happily, and the memorization is profound. The goal of Chinese language teaching which asks for quality and achievements in the classroom for 45 minutes is realized.

Picture 5　Ms. Han Yuwei at the 2nd All India Chinese Competition in May 2015

Through a comprehensive analysis of the number teaching steps that we have carried out in Confucius Institute, it is not difficult to find that we have actually broken the original arrangement sequence of teaching materials in the teaching process, and have made arrangements close to their acceptance ability according to the actual learning situation of our students. Through the integration of teaching materials, we integrate various elements organically, so that the sequence of number teaching content is more original, natural and integrated, and is no longer the original fragmented appearance. This teaching arrangement is not only more convenient for teachers to teach, but also more conducive to students' learning, in line with the law of students' understanding of Chinese numerals. Therefore, we believe that teachers should not blindly teach in accordance with the arrangement of teaching materials, but should boldly cut and integrate the content to make it close to the students' ability to learn. Combining the number teaching method with the introduction of numeral cultural knowledge and students' activities, we should make a reasonable teaching design, fully mobilize students' learning enthusiasm, help students overcome the fear of difficulties in number learning, and make the boring number teaching content lively. This kind of curriculum design can catch the students' heart and make the difficulty of number teaching in primary Chinese teaching become the "dessert" that students are willing to learn.

(Translated by Sun Peng, Proofread by Bhavana Kumari)

REFERENCES

[1] 彭凡. 对外汉语教学中的数字教学方法探究 [J]. 新课程研究，2019（9）：59-60.

[2] 琚天娇. 体态语在波黑萨大孔院初级汉语综合课中的应用研究 [D]. 安阳：安阳师范学院，2019.

[3] 李思思. 浅谈中国文化与汉语数字教学 [J]. 语文教学与研究，2013（2）：60-61.

[4] 闫振宇. 肢体语言在对外汉语教学中的应用及策略——以数字教学和词汇教学为例 [J]. 明日风尚，2018（18）：271.

[5] 余佩. 对外汉语数字教学案例分析 [D]. 武汉：湖北工业大学，2018.

[6] 许兰娟. 游戏法在对外汉语中文数字教学中的应用——以美国埃尔克哈特市康科德高中为例 [J]. 长春教育学院学报，2013，29（19）：150-151.

后疫情时代印度线上汉语教学模式探究

龙　娜[1]　赵　阳[2]

摘要　本文通过分析新冠肺炎疫情期间印度汉语线上教学现状，以及在疫情期间实施线上汉语教学过程中存在的基础设施薄弱、师生对在线教育认知不够充分、在线教学软件功能不全、线上课程人际交互体验不佳和在线教学效果褒贬不一等困难，提出在后疫情时代应当建设更专业的语言教学平台，使线上教学常态化，将更多线下课程和活动搬到线上，提升师生线上学习能力，结合学生需求采取灵活的授课模式等方法来积极应对，克服困难，创新地做好后疫情时代印度汉语线上教学工作。

关键词　印度；线上汉语教学；后疫情时代

1　疫情期间印度汉语线上教学现状

2020年新冠肺炎疫情肆虐全球，作为世界第二大人口国，印度确诊人数高达700多万人（2020年10月数据）。疫情所带来的综合性影响深远，对高等教育产生的冲击是前所未有的，教育模式出现了颠覆性的创新。美国波士顿学院国际高等教育研究中心创始人阿特巴赫及中心主任汉斯在大学世界新闻网上发表题为《我们所知道的全球高等教育已经永远改变了》[3]的文章，认为我们早些时候预估的全球国际化基本布局可能维持不变，且全球高等教育会大致保持稳定，但是各种影响教学效果的重要因素和混乱局面仍是不可避免的。这场危机对高等教育的影响相当大，而且大多是负面的，从而加大了各个学习者、各个高等院校和各国之间的差距和不

1　宜春学院文学与新闻传播学院教师。
2　印度拉夫里科技大学汉语教学中心中方院长。
3　Simon Marginson: 2020, http://www.education.ox.ac.uk/global-he-as-we-know-it-has-forever-changed/

平等。

2020 年 3 月，印度宣布全国封锁，中下旬各大高校和教育机构按照要求陆续关闭，停止聚集性教学和学术活动。印度高校反应迅速，笔者所在学校通过自研学习软件 LPU Live，结合 Google Meet 和 Zoom 等在线视频会议软件逐步开展了线上教学，高效利用学生的居家时间，降低疫情带来的影响。在印度，有 30 多所高校开设了汉语专业和证书课程，疫情期间，拉夫里科技大学（Lovely Professional University）、孟买大学（Mumbai University）、国际大学（Visva-Bharati University）和中印学院（India China Academy）等高校或机构通过录播模式、直播模式、录播直播并用方式及电话授课等互联网授课模式，根据学生学习时间碎片化、学习主动性不强等特点，加强多媒体互动体验和个性化学习内容订制，从而提升学生学习兴趣，满足学生学习需求，同时也改变了印度以大城市为中心的线下汉语教学现象。

2　疫情期间印度汉语线上教学实践与困难情况

2.1　在线教育基础设施薄弱

从国家硬件层面上来说，印度教育信息技术和数字网络基础设施建设不尽人意，集中表现为网络基础设施发展不平衡不充分、网速不能满足多人同时在线的需要、网络技术不够普及、居家在线学习的客观环境差异较大、学校教学的多媒体数字化设备储备和学校计算机配置及线上学习软件配备薄弱等，这都使得疫情暴发初期印度的线上教学仍以普惠性的 FM 电台、卫星电视和已录制好的视频资源为主。

从学生层面来说，受家庭经济情况以及地区性影响，疫情居家学习期间，大部分学生选择自学教材加访问视频资源的学习方式。封校后，部分学生面临没有笔记本电脑或智能手机等必需设备来完成线上教育的窘境，即使满足居家学习硬件条件，在线上学习时还面临电力供应不足、网络连接不稳定、慕课平台 SWAYAM 由于短期内访问量超载而瘫痪、线上直播学习卡顿或延时等问题，不能达到线上教学预期效果。

2.2 师生对在线教育认知不够充分

在新冠肺炎疫情暴发之前，印度的高等教育还是以传统的线下授课方式为主，以一些线上优质资源为辅。线上学习，无论采用哪种资源或形式，前提都必须是师生同时具备使用多媒体信息技术和数字化设备进行有效线上传递和接收信息的基本条件。对于教师来说，线上教育无疑是一项全新的挑战，主要表现在：（1）教师教学硬件和环境不佳。印度高校很多老师还停留在传统的板书教学模式，当他们居家教学时，电脑配置、多媒体应用能力和电脑运用技术均无法满足线上教学要求，且同样会遇到网络不稳定和电力供应不足等问题。（2）教师对居家教学认知的偏误。受传统文化影响，很多老师还不习惯居家办公模式，认为在家应以陪伴家人和休息为主，需要时间适应替代传统教学的线上教学。（3）教师信息技术整合能力有待提升。具体表现在无法将丰富的网络资源转化为教学资源，只是简单地通过课件将线下教学内容转化为线上，流于形式。（4）相应技术培训和教学法培训较滞后。线上教学对于印度高等教育来说是一个新生事物，无论是高校还是教师本身，都没有经过高质量的专业培训来提升教师信息技术教育教学的能力。同样，新型教学法对传统教学法所带来的冲击很明显。这些在一定程度上综合反映出至少目前印度教师尚未做好高质量在线教学的专业准备。

在线上学习期间，学生有了较灵活的自我掌控空间，这使得大部分学生往往不能有效掌控自己的学习时间。除了基础硬件设施对线上教学的影响，个体在学习方式和认知能力上的差异也是产生学习结果差异的重要因素，学生往往认为线上课程监管不严、干预较少、考核要求不高、学习压力较小而忽视其重要性，消极对待。可见，不论对于学生还是教师而言，在线学习都对他们的学习能力提出了严峻的挑战。

2.3 在线教学软件功能不全

印度固有的在线教育方式主要依赖电视和广播，而在学校层面主要依赖现有的在线学习平台和课程。可以说，可直接使用的技术和资源和如何有效使用技术和资源是目前印度高等教育在开展线上教育过程中遇到的最大挑战。疫情期间，师生选择较多的主要是以下三类学习平台：一是已存在的线上学习平台。这类平台主要以提供已经上传的各类优质课件和视频课程资源为主，师生根据教学计划自主选择适合于本阶段的课程。但这类平台内容大多过于陈旧，不能满足新时期的需求，且受技术原因影响，访问承载力有限。二是在线教学平台，师生通过该平台进行线上教学。笔者所在学校的 LPU Live 就是此类免费在线教学平台。但受技术限制，很多功能未能完全开发，在使用时仅能满足在线音频的正常传输，无法满足深层次人际交互。三是在线视频会议平台。疫情期间，网络视频会议平台承担了大部分的线上课程教学，一般来说这些平台相对在线教学平台而言，无论是技术还是网络都比较成熟和稳定，这为人际交互提供了基础，但视频会议的需求与线上教学的需求并非完全一致，许多基础教学功能的缺失使得教学的即时性大打折扣。

2.4　线上课程人际交互体验不佳

语言的学习，需要优秀的师资、优质的教材、适时的学习资源和充分的人际交互，其中充分的人际交互又显得格外重要。教学过程中的人际交互主要分为学生与学习内容之间的互动、学生与教师之间的互动以及学生与学生之间的互动。对于汉语课来说，学生与教师之间、学生与学生之间的言语交互是必不可少的，甚至可以说汉语课的绝大部分教学过程就是在教师的引导下，在师生间、学生间的人际言语交互中进行的，学生在高效的人际言语交互中理解和练习知识点。[1]300 在疫情期间，根据印度网络情况，线上汉语教学模式主要分四类：一是教师课前录制好教学视频，学生下载进行异步学习，教师通过即时软件进行互动答疑；二是通过网络进行线上直播课程；三是录播直播并用的组合模式；四是通过电话为某些偏远地区学生进行授课。

在线上汉语教学中，我们发现，无论是直播课还是录播课，言语交互频率和效率都无法达到语言类课程的要求。学生不能有效进行及时互动，教师也无法根据学生的反馈了解教学效果、掌握教学进度并调整教学节奏。缺少人际交互的线上汉语教学只是单一地将知识点从教师传递给了学生，而无法进行进一步互动和沟通，无法取得令人满意的效果。

2.5 在线教学效果褒贬不一

学生在线学习的效果主要取决于学生的自主学习能力。学生往往学习动机强烈，但能力水平不高，以及个体间存在较大自主学习能力差距。无论是录播的教学视频还是直播的即时课程，学习的主体都是学生本身，受到网络条件限制，大部分学生在学习线上课程时为了保证网络流畅，不能打开摄像头，虽然平台可以直观展现学生在线学习情况、体现学习时间和进度等，但教师无法监管他们在学习的过程中是否认真。虽然可以通过事后的作业和测试等进行监督，但当发现教学效果不佳时，教师受学习进度和时间的制约，无法做更多的讲解，只能通过在线文本练习和课后强化练习让学生巩固课程内容。同样，学生由于学习效率、学习氛围和学习主动性等因素的影响，对于线上的效果满意度较低。

3 后疫情时代印度汉语线上教学的启示和建议

3.1 建设更专业的语言教学平台

作为教学的载体，成熟、专业的平台对教学效果有非常重要的作用。教学效果与线上教学平台密不可分，目前线上教学工具的功能尚不能很好地满足线上汉语教学需要。后疫情时代，优质、专业的线上教学平台应该同时具有以下特征和功能：低带宽且无障碍的师生音、视频交互；可录制、可回看教学过程的网络存储；即时文本通讯；数据统计、上传资料、发布作业、阅读材料等管理功能；丰富的教学评测功能，对于教师发布的任务如组词、造句、跟读、拼写等进行系统自动评测，提升效率。这样的在线教学工具不仅可以更好地满足线上汉语教学的需要，并且能通过大数据统计和分析，掌握即时学情和教情，为汉语教学的学术研究和教学改革提供支持。

3.2　线上教学常态化，将更多线下课程和活动搬到线上

在后疫情时代，线上汉语教学的常态化发展能有效解决高校合作难、教师赴印难、学习延续性难等问题，有效缓解汉语教师地区发展不平衡，真正做到教与学无国界。同时我们还应当利用好 App、AR 虚拟场景等网络资源，将课堂上难以全面展示的文化融入教学当中，无论生活交际汉语、商务汉语，还是应试汉语课程，通过网络课程、阅读材料、自我检测等功能，从字词、语法、拼音、书写和纠音等多方面对学生进行针对性训练，并将中国文化、地理、历史、经济等多维度展现给学生。

3.3　提升师生线上学习能力

在经历过疫情初期的彷徨后，在后疫情时代，教师和师生对线上教学逐步适应。为了进一步做好线上教学，师生同步提升学习能力显得尤为重要。学校管理者应当为教师进行系统、专业的多媒体技术、网络教学和直播能力培训；教师应当主动适应新时期发展需要，主动参加教学法及信息技术能力培训，提高自身信息素养和应用能力，了解并熟练掌握主流网络教学平台操作，采取多种教育模式，提升驾驭课堂的能力；学生应当端正态度，意识到线上课程与线下课程同等重要，并习惯通过线上教学和自学达到学习目的。

3.4　结合学生需求采取灵活的授课模式

疫情期间线上的汉语教学经验和教训告诉我们，学习方式互联网化、学习时间碎片化、学习内容个性化将是后疫情时代线上汉语教学的新常态。无论是作为一门外语课程、一门选修课程还是一门技能课程，灵活的线上教学是程式化线下教学的良好补充。我们应当正视数字化鸿沟正在加剧教育的不公平，无法切实地关切那些学业兴趣或动机不强、自主学习能力不足的学生，根据学生不同情况去安排灵活的教学时间，在课前、课中和课后选择不同的教学软件和学习评估方法，通过网络、电话等方式建立有效沟通渠道，真正了解学生的学习进度和难点，有针对性地开展下一阶段教学。[2]9

4　结语

在后疫情时代，同样也是5G蓬勃发展的高科技时代，大力发展互联网线上教育是顺势之举，也是大势所趋，线上学习汉语必将成为最重要、最普遍，也是最便捷的方式。长期以来信息技术对学校教育所产生的变革和影响，通过这次疫情，让教师和学生有了全方位的体验和认同，我们应当积极应对，把此次疫情危机看作推动教育教学变革的一次重要机遇，转变思想，克服困难，创新地做好后疫情时代印度汉语线上教学工作。

参考文献

[1] 王瑞烽. 疫情防控期间汉语技能课线上教学模式分析 [J]. 世界汉语教学， 2020，34（3）：300-310.

[2] 罗荣华. “汉语 +” 线上汉语教学的实践与探索 [J]. 现代教育科学，2019（9）：9-13.

Research on the Online Chinese Teaching Model in India in the Post-COVID 19 Pandemic Era

Long Na[1] *Zhao Yang*[2]

Abstract By analyzing the Novel Corona Virus pandemic situation of online Chinese language teaching in India during the pandemic period, and the difficulties existing in the implementation of online Chinese teaching during the period, such as weak infrastructure, insufficient cognition of online education among teachers and students, incomplete functions of online teaching software, poor interpersonal interaction experience of online courses and mixed results of online teaching, etc., this paper puts forward that in the Post-COVID 19 pandemic era, we should build a more professional language teaching platform to regularize online teaching, move more offline courses and activities online, improve teachers' and students' online teaching and learning ability respectively and adopt a flexible teaching mode in combination with students' needs, actively deal with and overcome difficulties, and creatively do a good job in the post-pandemic era of online Chinese teaching in India.

Key Words India; Online Chinese teaching; Post-COVID 19 pandemic era

1 Teacher, School of Literature and Journalism, Yichun University, China.
2 Chinese Dean, Centre of Chinese Language Teaching, Lovely Professional University, India.

1 CURRENT SITUATION OF ONLINE CHINESE LANGUAGE TEACHING IN INDIA DURING THE PANDEMIC

In 2020, the global outbreak of COVID-19 has been affecting the whole world. As the world's second-most populous country, India has confirmed more than 7 million cases (data in Oct., 2020). The comprehensive impact of the epidemic is very far-reaching, especially its unprecedented impact on higher education. There have been subversive innovations in the educational model. The founder of Boston College Center for International Higher Education (CIHE), Philip G. Altbach, and the director of the center Hans de Wit, published an article titled "Global HE As We Know It Has Forever Changed" [1] on the University World News Network. They state in their paper that earlier humans believed that the basic layout of global internationalization may remain unchanged, and the global higher education system will remain basically stable. However, various important short-term, medium-term, and perhaps long-term consequences and chaos are still inevitable. The impact of this crisis on higher education will be considerable, and most of them are negative, which will increase the gap and inequality among learners, universities and countries.

In March, India announced a nationwide lockdown. In late March, colleges, universities and educational institutions were closed, and collective teaching and academic activities were stopped. However, universities in India responded very quickly. My school gradually carried out online teaching through its own learning software LPU Live, and then combined it with online video conferencing software such as Google Meet and Zoom, so as to make efficient use of students' time at home and reduce the impact of the pandemic. During the pandemic period, universities or institutions such as Lovely Professional University, University of Mumbai, Visva-Bharati University and India China Academy have adopted the Internet teaching mode, such as recorded broadcasts, live broadcasts, combined recorded and live broadcasts, and also telephone teaching. According to the characteristics of students' learning time fragmentation and learning

1 Simon Marginson: 2020, http://www.education.ox.ac.uk/global-he-as-we-know-it-has-forever-changed/

initiative, the school strengthened the multimedia interactive experience and individualized learning content customization to promote students' interests in learning and to meet students' learning needs. At the same time, it also changed the phenomenon of offline Chinese language teaching being largely centered in big Indian cities.

2 PRACTICE AND DIFFICULTIES OF ONLINE CHINESE LANGUAGE TEACHING IN INDIA DURING THE PANDEMIC

2.1 WEAK ONLINE EDUCATION INFRASTRUCTURE

From the perspective of national hardware, India's educational information technology and digital network infrastructure construction is not satisfactory, which is mainly reflected in the unbalanced and inadequate development of network infrastructure. The inability of network speed to meet the needs of multiple people online, lack of popularization of Internet technology by Internet users, great differences in the objective environment of online learning at home, storage of multimedia digital equipment for school teaching, weak equipment of school computer configuration and online learning software, etc., have all caused India's online education at the beginning of the outbreak to rely on FM radio, satellite TV and recorded video resources.

From the perspective of students' own software availability, due to the influence of family economic conditions and the region they belong to, most students choose to study at home by self-learning and visiting video learning resources. After the lockdown, some students faced the dilemma of not having laptops or smart phones and other necessary equipments to meet the needs of online education. Even if they meet the hardware requirements for home learning, they still face insufficient power supply, unstable network connection. SWAYAM, an Indian MOOC platform, is paralyzed due to the overload of visits in a short period of time, and there are phenomena such as slow streaming or delay during live learning, so it cannot achieve the expected results of online teaching.

2.2 TEACHERS AND STUDENTS HAVE INSUFFICIENT AWARENESS OF ONLINE EDUCATION

Before the outbreak of COVID-19, higher education in India was mainly based on traditional offline teaching methods, supplemented by some online high-quality resources. No matter what kind of resources or forms are used in online learning, the premise must be that both teachers and students have the basic ability to use multimedia information technology and digital equipment to transmit and receive information online effectively. For teachers, online education is undoubtedly a new challenge, and it is mainly reflected in the following aspects. First, the teaching hardware and environment for teachers are not that good. Many teachers in Indian universities still stay in the traditional blackboard teaching mode. When they teach at home, computer configuration, multimedia application ability and computer application technology cannot meet the requirements of online teaching, and they also face problems such as unstable network and insufficient power supply. Second, the teacher's misunderstanding of home teaching. They believe that they should mainly accompany their families and take rest at home, and it takes time to adapt to online teaching instead of traditional teaching. Third, teachers' ability to integrate information technology needs to be improved. The concrete manifestation is that the rich network resources cannot be transformed into teaching resources, they just simply transform the offline teaching content into the online teaching content through the course, which is just a mere formality. Fourth, the corresponding technical training and teaching method lags behind. Online teaching is a new phenomenon for Indian higher education. Neither universities nor teachers have the ability to improve teachers' information technology and education capabilities through high quality professional training. Similarly, the impact of the new teaching method on the traditional teaching is obvious. This partly reflects the fact that, at least for now, Indian teachers are not professionally prepared for high-quality online teaching.

During online learning, students have more flexibility in their self-control space, which often causes most students to be unable to effectively control their own learning. In addition to the impact of infrastructure hardware on online teaching, individual differences in learning style and cognitive ability are also important factors in the gap of learning results. Students often ignore the importance of online courses because of lack of supervision, less intervention, low assessment requirements and low learning pressure. They treat online courses negatively and fail to properly evaluate themselves. It can be seen that both for students and teachers, the online education model poses a severe challenge in terms of the former's learning and the latter's teaching ability.

2.3 INCOMPLETE FUNCTION OF ONLINE TEACHING SOFTWARE

Normally, India's inherent online education approach relies heavily on television and radio, while at the school level it relies heavily on existing online learning platforms and courses. It can be said that the idea of directly using technologies vis-à-vis the resources available and how to effectively use technologies and resources are the biggest challenges currently faced by India's higher education system in the development of online education. During the pandemic, teachers and students chose the following three types of learning platforms. First, the existing online learning platforms. This type of platform mainly consists of uploading materials and video resources for various superior courses. Teachers and students can independently choose courses suitable for this stage according to the teaching plan. However, the content of these platforms is mostly too old to meet the needs of the new era, and due to technical reasons, it is often restricted by the page views. Second is the online teaching platform. Teachers and students carried out teaching and learning through online platforms. My school's LPU Live is this kind of free online teaching platform. However, limited by technology, many functions cannot be fully developed, so it can only meet the normal transmission of online audio iles, but cannot meet the need of deep interpersonal interactions. Third is the online video conferencing platform. During the pandemic, online video conferencing platforms consisted most of the online mode of teaching. Generally speaking, compared with online teaching platforms, these platforms are relatively mature and stable in both technology and network, which provides the basis for interpersonal interaction. But the demand of video conference is not completely consistent with the demand of online teaching, and the lack of many basic teaching functions makes the immediacy of teaching highly compromised.

2.4 POOR INTERPERSONAL INTERACTION EXPERIENCE IN ONLINE COURSES

Language learning requires excellent teachers, high-quality teaching materials, timely learning resources and adequate interpersonal interaction, among which adequate interpersonal interaction is particularly important. The interpersonal interaction in the teaching process is mainly divided into the interaction between students and learning content, between students and teachers, and also between students and students. For Chinese language classes, speech interaction between students and teachers, and between students and students is very essential. It can even be said that most of the teaching process of Chinese course is carried out under the guidance of teachers and in the interpersonal language interaction between teachers and students, and students and students. Students can understand and practice knowledge points during efficient interpersonal speech interactive sessions.[1]300 During the pandemic, according to the Internet situation in India, online Chinese teaching modes mainly fall into four categories. First, teachers record teaching videos before class, and then students download them for asynchronous learning, after which teachers interactively answer questions through instant software. Second, live online courses are conducted through the Internet. The third is the combined mode of recording broadcasting and live broadcasting. The fourth is teaching students in some remote areas by telephone.

In online Chinese teaching, we find that the frequency and efficiency of speech interaction cannot meet the requirements of language courses, whether in live or in recorded class sessions. Students could not interact effectively on time, and thus teachers could not understand the effects of their teaching according to the feedbacks received from the students, so that they can then master the teaching progress and adjust their teaching styles. Online Chinese language teaching without interpersonal interaction only transfers knowledge points from teachers to students without further interaction and communication, and it fails to achieve satisfactory results.

2.5 DIFFERENT JUDGMENTS ON ONLINE TEACHING EFFECTS

The effect of students' online learning mainly depends on students' autonomous learning ability. Students often have strong learning motivation, but the ability level is not high and there is a large gap between each individual. Whether it's a recorded or a live course, the main individuals of learning is the students themselves. Due to network constraints, most students cannot turn on the camera during online courses in order to ensure the network availability. Although the platform can intuitively show students' online learning situation, learning time and progress, teachers cannot supervise whether they are really watching videos or listening carefully to the lecture. Though it can be supervised by post-work and tests, when it is found that the teaching effect is not good, the teacher is restricted by the progress and time of study. They still cannot carry out detailed explanations, they can only consolidate course contents through online text exercises and after-class intensive exercises. Similarly, students are less satisfied with the online effect due to subjective and objective factors such as learning efficiency, learning atmosphere and learning initiative.

3 REVELATION AND SUGGESTIONS OF INDIA'S CHINESE LANGUAGE ONLINE TEACHING METHODS IN POST-COVID 19 PANDEMIC ERA

3.1 BUILDING A MORE PROFESSIONAL LANGUAGE TEACHING PLATFORM

As a specialist in field of teaching, I believe that a mature and professional platform plays a very important role in good teaching effect. The teaching effect is closely related to the online teaching platform. The function of the current online teaching tools cannot meet the needs of online Chinese teaching. In the post-COVID 19 pandemic era, the high-quality and professional online teaching platform should have the following characteristics and functions at the same time: low bandwidth and barrier-free teacher-student audio and video interaction; recordable, read-back teaching process network storage; instant text communication; data statistics, uploading and downloading function for homework, reading materials and other management functions; rich teaching evaluation functions, which can automatically evaluate the tasks published by teachers, such as word grouping, sentence making, following and spelling, etc., so as to improve efficiency. Such online teaching tools can not only better meet the needs of online Chinese language teaching, but also grasp the real-time learning situation and teaching situation through big data statistics and analysis, and provide support for academic research and teaching reform in the field of Chinese language teaching.

3.2 NORMALIZE ONLINE TEACHING AND BRING MORE OFFLINE COURSES AND ACTIVITIES ONLINE

In the post-COVID 19 pandemic era, the normalized development of online Chinese teaching can effectively solve problems such as difficulties in cooperation between universities, difficulties for teachers to go to India, and difficulties in continuity of learning. It can effectively alleviate the imbalance of the development of Chinese teachers in different regions, and truly realize the borderless teaching and learning. At the same time, we should also make good use of internet resources such as Apps and AR virtual scenes to integrate cultures that are difficult to fully display during teaching in the classroom. Whether in daily communication Chinese, business Chinese or test-oriented Chinese courses, with the help of online courses, reading materials, self-testing and other functions, the tutor should provide students with targeted training in terms of words, grammar, pinyin, writing, phonetic correction, etc., and show Chinese culture, geography, history, economy and other aspects to students.

3.3 IMPROVE ONLINE LEARNING ABILITY OF TEACHERS AND STUDENTS

After experiencing the initial hurdles of the pandemic, teachers and students gradually adapted to online teaching in the post-COVID 19 pandemic era. In order to further improve online teaching, it is particularly important for teachers and students to enhance their learning ability simultaneously. School administrators shall provide teachers with systematic and professional training in multimedia technology, online teaching and live broadcasting ability. Teachers should take the initiative to adapt to the development needs of the new era, participate in teaching method and information technology ability trainings, improve the information literacy and application ability, understand and master the operation of the mainstream network teaching platforms, adopt a variety of educational models, and improve the ability to control the class. Students should correct their attitude, realize that online courses are as important as offline courses, and get used to learning through online teaching and self-study.

3.4 ADOPT FLEXIBLE TEACHING MODE ACCORDING TO STUDENTS' NEEDS

The online Chinese teaching experience and lessons during the pandemic tell us that Internet-based learning methods, fragmented learning time and personalized learning content will be the new normal of online Chinese teaching in the post-pandemic era. Whether as a foreign language course, an elective course or a skill course, flexible online teaching is a good supplement to advanced offline teaching. We should face up to the fact that the digital divide is exacerbating inequalities in education, failing to pay practical attention to students with low academic interest or motivation and insufficient autonomous learning ability. We shoule arrange flexible teaching time according to students' different circumstances, adop different teaching software and learning evaluation methods before, during and after class, establish effective communication channels through the Internet, telephone and other means, truly understanding students' learning progress and difficulties, and carry out the next stage of teaching in a targeted manner.[2]9

4 CONCLUSION

In the post-COVID 19 pandemic era, which is also the high-tech era with 5G booming in development, it is a certain and inevitable trend to vigorously develop online education. Online learning of Chinese language will become the most important, the most common and the most convenient way. Through COVID-19, teachers and students have a comprehensive experience and recognition of the changes and effects of information technology on school education for a long time. We should actively deal with it, and regard this pandemic crisis as an important opportunity to promote the reform of education and teaching mode, we should also change ideas, overcome difficulties, and do a good job of Chinese online teaching in the post-COVID 19 pandemic era.

（Translated by Bai Wanli, Proofread by Bhavana Kumari）

REFERENCES

[1] 王瑞烽. 疫情防控期间汉语技能课线上教学模式分析 [J]. 世界汉语教学，2020，34（3）：300-310.

[2] 罗荣华. “汉语 +” 线上汉语教学的实践与探索 [J]. 现代教育科学，2019（9）：9-13.

Part 4

第四部分 汉语与中印人文交流

Chinese Language and China-India People- to-People and Cultural Exchange

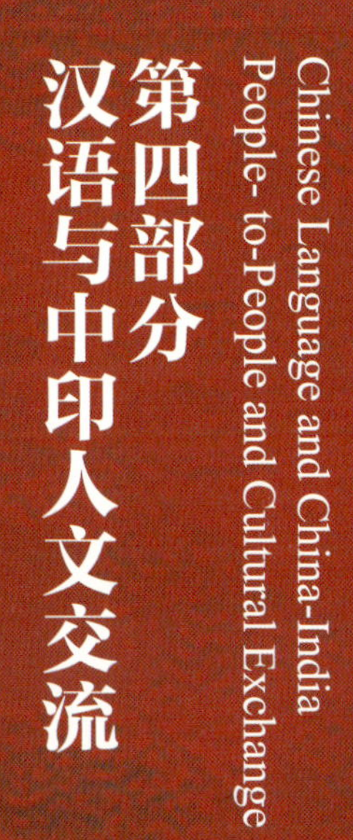

瑜伽－太极交流在中印人文交流中的桥梁作用——以云南民族大学为例

路　芳[1]　马娜娜[2]

摘要　作为世界上最古老的两大文明古国，中国和印度自古就有文化和教育往来。随着“一带一路”倡议的不断推进，云南民族大学利用地缘和政策优势，主动服务和融入此倡议，特别是瑜伽－太极交流在中印人文交流中做出了自己的特色。本文拟从云南民族大学近几年来所进行的瑜伽－太极交流来论述其在中印人文交流中的作用以及在此交流中语言的重要性。

关键词　瑜伽－太极；中印人文交流；云南民族大学

中国和印度同是具有五千年之久文明史的世界古国，都具有深厚的文化积淀和悠久的历史传统，是两大民族宝贵的精神财富，两国有“两千多年的友好交往和文化交流，这已经是人类历史上绝无仅有的现象”[1]1。据《史记》的《大宛列传》和《西南夷列传》所记载可推知，早在张骞通西域之前，中国的西南地区和印度之间就已经有了贸易往来。古代高僧法显、玄奘、义净、鸠摩罗什、菩提达摩、不空金刚等往来于两国之间，增进了两国人民的相互了解，促进了两国政治、经济、科技和文化的交流。近代以来，中印两国人民相互同情、相互支持，共同书写了中印友好交流的新篇章。1857 年，印度爆发了民族大起义，同期，在中国太平天国起义期间，被迫参加英军镇压太平天国的印度官兵调转枪口帮助中国人民抵抗外

1　博士，云南民族大学中印瑜伽学院（国际太极学院）教授，国家健身瑜伽理论研究中心主任，云南民族大学中印瑜伽学院、南亚学院前副院长。
2　云南民族大学中印瑜伽学院（国际太极学院）学生工作办公室主任。

来侵略[2]126；康有为著名的《大同书》也在印度写成，“辛丑、壬寅间，避地印度，乃著为成书”[1]。孙中山、章太炎与印度革命者结下友谊，泰戈尔、辩喜怀着深情访问中国；甘地、泰戈尔、尼赫鲁支援中国的抗日战争，中国学者陶行知、竺可桢、谭云山等访问印度。这些都深深地刻印在历史上，也铭记于两国人民的脑海中。当今世界，随着经济全球化和世界多极化的发展，国际交往的参与主体和参与方式的多元化是一大优势，大量新的公共外交形式不断涌现，丰富了传统意义上政府外交和民间外交的内涵。

1　瑜伽 – 太极成为中印人文交流新方式

进入 21 世纪，瑜伽成为印度总理莫迪着重推行的外交方式、国家名片，风靡全世界。2015 年莫迪访华，与李克强总理共同出席“太极瑜伽相会”中印文化交流活动，共同见证中印两国联合在云南民族大学建立中印瑜伽学院的事件，相关事宜写进了《中华人民共和国和印度共和国联合声明》。2015 年 6 月 13 日，云南民族大学举行中印瑜伽学院揭牌典礼，并于 2017 年和 2018 年分别招收瑜伽专业方向的本科生和硕士研究生。2016 年，被联合国教科文组织誉为“蕴涵的古代哲学影响了印度社会从健康与医学到教育和艺术的方方面面的瑜伽”被列入《人类非物质文化遗产代表作名录》，全世界现已有超过 190 个国家在每年 6 月 21 日举行“国际瑜伽日”活动。印度学者将瑜伽称为软实力；[3] 对于今天的许多印度人来说，瑜伽被理解为印度精神的精髓；在殖民时期，瑜伽甚至是整合了精神、身体和道德层面的文化，曾作为一种符号帮助印度为成为一个独立的民族国家而战。因此，瑜伽被认为是印度对外交流中一种独特而有价值的文化资源。[4]

而中国的太极，经常和瑜伽一起被称为“东方文化的智慧结晶”。2015 年 5 月 15 日，光明日报记者曹元龙发表《从太极和瑜伽看“龙象共舞”》一文，认为太极和瑜伽可以分别作为中国文明和印度文明的文化象征之一。因为瑜伽在于探索身体的奥秘，促进内在精神与外在身体运动的统一，而太极拳是中国民族传统体育运动

1　张翔，《康有为生前为何不出版〈大同书〉全书》，https://www.rujiazg.com/article/18529.

和健身养生项目，有着悠久的历史与文化，是依据中国古典哲学理论、《易经》阴阳之理、道家导引吐纳及古代中医学创造出的符合人体结构、大自然运转规律的综合拳术，注重外修与内修的结合，健身与养性的统一，追求“天人合一”的境界。汪忠长先生认为，“易理”与“道功”，是中华文化的根源，是人类精神与形体的灵粮，人生不但应有高度之智慧学识，也需要锻炼健康之身体，乃能学以致用，神形两全。[5]根据杨黎明等的研究成果，目前太极拳已传播到世界150多个国家和地区，拥有3亿多爱好习练者，太极拳运动已经在国内外广泛开展并具有一定的品牌文化影响力。[6]104概而言之，尽管太极与瑜伽存在动作构成等不同之处，但是都是一种“内省与顿悟的直觉思维方法”，都重视“调身”“调息”和“调心”相结合，都希望通过苦练内功，突破自身极限，寻求更高的精神享受，终极目标在于追求天人合一、梵我合一之“和”。

为了更好地实现瑜伽和太极的对话，加强中印两国人民的进一步了解，2016年4月，在契合国家“一带一路”倡议和云南省面向南亚、东南亚辐射中心的大背景下，云南民族大学在云南省委省政府批准下成立了国际太极学院，并于2017年开始招收太极专业方向的本科生，该学院的成立为探索太极拳专业人才的规范化培养和太极拳的国际化传播途径，为加强文明互鉴和服务大国外交提供了一种新的方式。同时，为进一步扩展和印度的人文交流，云南民族大学多次主办或者承办大型论坛和“国际瑜伽日”，如“第七届中国－南亚国际文化论坛”、现代瑜伽与健康论坛、瑜伽系列学术讲座。应该说，这些措施在促进中印两国民间外交发挥了积极作用。

2 瑜伽－太极文化交流延续了始于两晋南北朝时期的政府间往来

《晋书·苻坚传》有言：“凡六十有二王，皆遣使贡其方物。”这“六十有二王”中包括天竺。研究也表明，晋时西北和西南到印度的交通都不曾断绝，人员往来很多。《晋书·苻坚传》《异物志》《博物志》等著述中都明确提到过政府间关于火浣布的交往。《宋书·蛮夷传》《梁书·诸夷传》保存了来自印度不同时代的国书，还记载了不少天竺诸国遣使贡献以及中国政府派使者去印度的事例。[7]66-71 在季羡林称为中印文化交流活动“鼎盛时代中的鼎盛时代”的唐代，中印两国交通之频繁，交流内容之多，不仅有宗教的交流，还涉及政治（外交）、经济、哲学、科学技术、文学艺术等。而且，中印之间的互相学习从来不是单向的事，而是双向流通的。[2]49 正如《明史》卷三二六中有关“榜葛剌”（孟加拉国）的记载：“官司上下，亦有行移。医卜、阴阳、百工、技艺，悉如中国，盖皆前世所流入也。”[2]148 虽然印度古代缺少真正的史籍，除了四大发明之外，没有确切记载中国文化对印度的影响，但是此记载刚好说明了中国对印度的影响。

瑜伽—太极的交流也延续了这种交流与互动。自云南民族大学的中印瑜伽学院成立以来，多名印度官员，以及部分高校的校长等官员和学者到校访问。云南民族大学代表团 2015 年受印度总理办公室邀请访问印度；2016 年受瑜伽部（AYUSH）邀请访问印度，并参加国际瑜伽大会；2018 年受印度驻华大使馆邀请访问印度，并受到时任印度外交部部长的接见。由于近几年的频繁互动，2019 年 11 月，印度驻华大使唐勇胜到访云南民族大学中印瑜伽学院，称赞学院是“两国之间人类文明联系的光辉典范”；2020 年 10 月，中国驻印度大使馆赠送印度德弗文化大学和辩喜瑜伽大学教学设备以及太极服、太极扇，以鼓励他们对太极开展研究和教学。两所学校表示中印友谊地久天长，两校的合作也会再进一步加深加强。正如被季羡林誉为“中印友好的化身”[8]1 的玄奘西行能让戒日王了解中国的情况，使戒日王对中国留下美好印象，派使节与唐朝通好。瑜伽—太极的交流，也能让中印两国人民不断加深了解，政府间的往来也能够继续加强，达到季羡林曾说过的通过文化交流来促进交流双方文学、艺术、哲学、宗教的发展，增进双方科学技术的昌盛，推动双方社会的前进。[2]150

3 不仅延续了滇缅道的中印文化交流，也促进了语言的相互学习

可以说，云南民族大学中印瑜伽学院和国际太极学院的成立不仅加强了中印交流，还促进了语言的相互学习。学校先后派出多名师生多次赴印度开展人文交流，并先后与印度尼赫鲁大学、印度辩喜瑜伽大学、印度德弗文化大学、印度国际大学

等10余所印度高校建立了合作关系，就师生培养、科学研究、合作办学等方面达成协议。2018年1月，云南民族大学在印度德弗文化大学和印度辩喜瑜伽大学挂牌成立国际太极中心；同年6月，学校和印度尼赫鲁大学达成协议，成立“中印人文交流中心”。2018年12月，云南民族大学太极教师团队到达印度北部北安恰尔邦的德弗文化大学（Dev Sanskriti Vishwavidyalaya），进行了为期一个月的太极教学。此次教学在该校产生了不小的影响，不仅学生来学习太极拳，教师及其子女也被太极拳吸引，授课班级也由两个扩展到四个。教授太极的老师说，授课时感觉语言障碍都不存在了，行动早已超越了语言。这种交流也激发了学生对太极拳内涵的探究，希望和老师探讨瑜伽和太极的相似性和不同点。所以，他们中的一些人不仅喜欢上了太极拳，也喜欢上了汉语。有的学生会在手掌心写上汉字，来请教太极老师字的读音。德弗文化大学的校长助理也表示太极和瑜伽其实有很多可以交流的内容，但是苦于语言的障碍，两国太极和瑜伽爱好者无法进行更深入的交流。回顾2017年，笔者去该校访学期间也受邀为学生开设了汉语课，深受学生的喜爱，也有该校教师专门前来学习。笔者在校园散步时，经常碰到学生过来用汉语“您好！”打招呼。

到印度访学的学生也开始意识到语言对于交流的重要性。2019年2月至8月，中印瑜伽学院25名瑜伽专业学生到印度德弗文化大学进行了半年的学习。其间，一提英语学习就头大的学生们也发现语言对于交流的重要性，也知道了只靠翻译软件还是无法更深入地沟通交流，更体会不到对方文化的精髓。虽然借助翻译软件可以和印度学生一起打球、唱歌、跳舞，建立很好的友谊，但是正如回国学生所表达的：“这次交流让我粗浅地了解到不同国家不同地域的文化差异，也更加系统地认识了瑜伽，虽然语言不通，但是不同语言的表达、不同文化符号之间的交流，能让来自不同国家的人感受到同一种感情。在交流中大家对各自的文化都有自己的坚持与观点，但是也没有说一定要争执对错，这可能就是一种求同存异，尊重、包容与理解。另外，让我感触到的是语言很奇妙，每一种语言的表达都有其不同的寓意，也认识到自己的不足，如果能够和他们在沟通上没有语言障碍，彼此能够更容易地交流，那我们的收获会更多。”[1] 其实，翻开历史，会发现滇印的交流始于2000多年前。云南地处我国与南亚、东南亚的结合部，“古南方丝绸之路”和“茶马古道”造就了历史上开放和鼎盛的云南。瑜伽－太极的交流刚好让这种东方文化的交流进一步加深。习近平主席在2014年访问印度时曾指出，中国太极和印度瑜伽“有惊人的相似之处，两国人民数千年来奉行的生活哲理深度相似”[2]。季羡林认为，东方文化的基本思维方式是综合，表现在哲学上就是“天人合一”。张载的《西铭》说：“乾称父，坤称母，予兹藐焉，乃混然中处。故天地之塞吾其体，天地之帅吾其性。民吾同胞，物吾与也。”这与印度哲学中的“梵我一如”表达了同样的思想。东方文化主张人与大自然是朋友，只有在了解大自然、热爱大自然的条件下，才能伸手向大自然索取人类衣、食、住、行所需要的一切。[9]10 赵启正曾说过“中国立场，国际表达”，用国际上能理解的方式才能收获理想的效果。[10]88 所以，在瑜伽－太极的交流中，更需要语言作为媒介去帮助两国人民寻找东方文化的共同之处，去向世界表达东方的立场、中国的立场。

4 结语：瑜伽－太极文化交流的桥梁作用需要语言的媒介

习近平主席在亚洲文明对话大会开幕式上强调，文明因多样而交流，因交流而互鉴，因互鉴而发展。我们要加强世界上不同国家、不同民族、不同文化的交流互鉴，夯实共建亚洲命运共同体、人类命运共同体的人文基础。[3] 正如季羡林用白糖和钢铁中出现的文化倒流或者回流的例子给我们揭示的一个真理：我们生活在文化交流中，在非常习见的事物背后往往隐藏着一段十分复杂、曲折的文化交流的历史，熟知这样的历史，不仅让我们知道在文化交流的过程中，有枝叶变成树干的文化倒流现象，也能够加强各国各民族之间的相互了解，促进我们之间的友谊，共同维护世

1 来自对云南民族大学中印瑜伽学院（国际太极学院）社会体育指导与管理（瑜伽方向）2017级李姓学生，访谈人：路芳，2020年10月10日。
2 习近平，《携手追寻民族复兴之梦——在印度世界事务委员会的演讲》，2014-09-19, http://www.xinhuanet.com/politics/2014-09/19/c_1112539621.htm.
3 李先发、熊争艳、丁小溪，《习近平出席亚洲文明对话大会开幕式并发表主旨演讲》，2019-05-15, http://www.xinhuanet.com/2019-05/15/c_1124499008.htm.

界和平[2]152–158。两种陌生的文化一旦交流，至少要经过五个阶段，撞击—吸收—改造—融合—同化，特别是在中印文化交流史上[2]3，在这五个阶段的交流中，语言的重要性尤其凸显，就像英国学者奥斯汀所述：以言行事，通过语言，我们可以通过说话来施事，然后取效[11]，文化的交流需要语言的媒介，有语言的助力，就能更好地了解明白文化的意义，文化的符号，进而实现中印文化在新时期的再碰撞、互鉴，共建亚洲命运共同体。

参考文献

[1] 薛克翘. 象步凌空——我看印度 [M]. 北京：世界知识出版社，2010.

[2] 季羡林. 中印文化交流史 [M]. 北京：中国社会科学出版社，2008.

[3] AMIT S, AMIT S. Paraspara, encounters, and confluences: India's soft power objective in Indo-Pacific region[J]. Politics & policy, 2017, 45（5）：733-761.

[4]NEWCOMBE S. The development of modern Yoga: a survey of the field[J]. Religion compass, 2009, 3/6: 986-1002.

[5] 汪忠长. 易与道 [M]. 北京：当代世界出版社，2005.

[6] 杨黎明，杨光. 太极拳的发展与对外传播——以太极拳故里焦作近五年的情况为例 [J]. 辽宁体育科技，2018, 40（3）：104-108.

[7] 薛克翘. 中国印度文化交流史 [M]. 北京：昆仑出版社，2008.

[8] 季羡林. 前言 [M]// 玄奘，辩机，季羡林校注. 大唐西域记校注. 北京：中华书局，2000.

[9] 季羡林.《东方文化集成》总序 [M]// 薛克翘. 中国印度文化交流史. 北京：昆仑出版社，2008.

[10] 赵启正. 公共外交与跨文化交流 [M]. 北京：中国人民大学出版社，2011.

[11] 奥斯汀. 如何以言行事 [M]. 杨玉成，译. 北京：外语教学与研究出版社，2002.

On the Role Played by Yoga-Taichi in India-China Intercultural Exchange: The Case Study of Yunnan Minzu University

Lu Fang[1] *Ma Nana*[2]

Abstract As the two most ancient countries in the world, the cultural and educational exchange between China and India has a long history. With the continuous progress of "the Belt and Road" Initiative, Yunnan Minzu University has used its geographical and political superiorities to actively serve and integrate into the initiative, especially in the Yoga-Taichi exchange which has its own unique characteristics in the Sino-Indian people-to-people exchange. Based on the Yoga-Taichi exchange conducted by Yunnan Minzu University in recent years, This paper discusses the role of Yoga-Taichi in the cultural exchange between China and India and the importance of language in this exchange.

Key Words Yoga-Taichi exchange; India-China people-to-people exchange; Yunnan Minzu University

Both China and India are ancient civilizations of the world with a history of more than 5,000 years. Both have profound cultural heritage and long historical traditions which are the precious spiritual wealth of our two nations. "The more than 2,000 years of friendly exchanges and cultural exchanges between the two

1 PhD, Professor of India-China Yoga College & International Taichi College, Yunnan Minzu University; Director of Research Center on National Health Yoga Theory, the former Vice Dean of India-China Yoga College & School of South Asian Languages and Cultures, Yunnan Minzu University.
2 Director of Student Affairs Office,India-China Yoga College(International Taichi College),Yunnan Minzu University.

countries have been unique in human history".[1]1 According to the records of the *Dawan Commentary Section* and the *Biography of The Ethnic Minority Groups in Southwest China* (Xinanyi Liezhuan) in *The Records of the Grand Historian*, it can be inferred that there had been trade connections between southwest China and India long before Zhang Qian's journey to the Western regions. Ancient monks, Faxian, Xuanzang, Yijing, Kumarajiva, Bodhidharma, Anngha Vajra and other Buddhist monks travelled between the two countries. They enhanced the mutual understanding between people and promoted the political, economic, technological and cultural exchanges between the two countries. Since modern times, the peoples of China and India have sympathized with and supported each other, and jointly wrote a new chapter of China-India friendly exchanges. In 1857, a national uprising broke out in India. At the same time, during the China Taiping Rebellion, Indian officers and soldiers who were forced to participate in the British suppression of the Taiping Rebellion turned their guns to help the Chinese people resist foreign aggression.[2]126 Kang Youwei's famous work, *The Book of Great Harmony* was finished in India. "I completed the book during my stay in India between the year of Xinchou (1901) and Renyin (1902)."[1] The friendship was built between Sun Yat-sen, Zhang Taiyan and the Indian revolutionaries, Tagore and Vivekananda also visited China; Gandhi, Tagore and Nehru supported China's War of Resistance against Japan, Chinese scholars like Tao Xingzhi, Zhu Kezhen, Tan Yunshan and others also visited India. These are all deeply imprinted in history and are remembered by the people of the two countries. In today's world, with the development of economic globalization and world multi-polarization, the diversification of subjects and modes of participation in international exchanges is a significant advantage. A large number of new forms of public diplomacy are continually emerging, enriching the connotation of government diplomacy and folk diplomacy in the traditional sense.

1 张翔，“康有为生前为何不出版《大同书》全书？”，https://www.rujiazg.com/article/18529

1 YOGA-TAICHI HAS BECOME A NEW WAY OF PEOPLE-TO-PEOPLE AND CULTURAL EXCHANGES BETWEEN CHINA AND INDIA

Since the 21st century, Yoga has become the diplomatic method and national name card that Indian Prime Minister Narendra Modi focuses on, and it is popular all over the world. In 2015, Modi visited China and attended the "Taichi and Yoga Meeting" China-India cultural exchange event with Premier Li Keqiang, witnessing the joint establishment of the China-India Yoga College at Yunnan Minzu University. Relevant issues are included in the "Joint Statement between the People's Republic of China and the Republic of India". Yunnan Minzu University held the opening ceremony of the China-India Yoga College on June 13, 2015 and recruited undergraduate and postgraduate students in Yoga in 2017 and 2018 respectively. In 2016, it was praised by UNESCO as "Yoga that contains ancient philosophy that has affected all aspects of Indian society from health and medicine to education and art", and Yoga was then included in the "List of Representatives of Human Intangible Cultural Heritage". More than 190 countries all over the world celebrate "International Yoga Day" on June 21 every year. Indian scholars refer to Yoga as soft power.[3] For many Indians today, Yoga is understood as the essence of the Indian spirit. In colonial times Yoga was even a form of culture that integrated mental, physical and moral dimensions, and was seen as a symbol to help India become an independent nation. Therefore, Yoga is considered as a unique and valuable cultural resource in India's foreign exchanges.[4]

Moreover, the Chinese Taichi, together with yoga, is often called the wisdom crystallization of eastern culture. "On May 15, 2015", reporter Cao Yuanlong Guangming Daily published an article "Looking at the Tango Between Dragon and Elephant from Taichi and Yoga", agreeing that Taichi and Yoga can be regarded as cultural symbols of Chinese civilization and Indian civilization respectively. While Yoga is to explore the mysteries of the body, and promote the inner spirit and the unity of the external body movement, Taijiquan is a traditional Chinese national sport and fitness program with a long history and culture. It is based on the theory of Chinese classical philosophy, the yin-yang theory of *Yijing* (*Book of Changes*), the theory of Taoism, and the ancient Chinese medicine to create Chinese boxing that accords with our body structure and the laws of nature. It focuses on the combination of external and internal training and the unity of fitness and nourishment, and pursues the realm of "harmony between man and nature". Mr. Wang Zhongchang believes that the philosophy of Yi and the practice in Taoism are the roots of Chinese culture and the spiritual food of human spirit and body. One should not only have a high degree of wisdom and knowledge in life, but also exercise a healthy body, so as to be able to apply what he has learned to practice and achieve both the perfection of god and form.[5] According to the research results of Mr. Yang Liming, now Chinese Taichi boxing has been spread to more than 150 countries and regions in the world, with more than 300 million people who are practicing it. Chinese Taichi boxing has been widely carried out in China and abroad and has been a certain influential cultural brand.[6]104 In other words, although there are some differences between Taichi and Yoga, they are both an intuitive thinking method of introspection and enlightenment, both attach great importance to the combination of regulating body, regulating the breath and the mind, and both seek to break through their limits and seek for higher spiritual enjoyment through diligent practice of internal skills. The ultimate goal is to pursue harmony between nature and human.

In order to better initiate the dialogue between Yoga and Taichi, and strengthen the understanding between the peoples of China and India. In April 2016, with the approval of the Yunnan government, Yunnan Minzu University established the International Taichi College under the background of the national "the Belt and Road initiative" and Yunnan Province's geographical advantages in South Asia and Southeast Asia. In 2017, Yunnan Minzu University began to recruit undergraduates in Taichi. The establishment of the college provides a new way to explore the standardized training of Taichi professionals, foster the international spread of Taichi, strengthen mutual learning between civilizations and start a new way of diplomacy. At the same time, in order to further expand cultural exchanges with India, Yunnan Minzu University has hosted large-scale forums and "International Yoga Days" events many times, such as "The 7th China-South Asia International Cultural Forum", Modern Yoga and Health Forum, and Yoga Series Academic Lectures. It can be said that these measures have played a positive role in promoting non-governmental diplomacy between China and India.

2 YOGA-TAICHI CULTURAL EXCHANGES CARRY FORWARD THE INTER-GOVERNMENTAL EXCHANGES THAT BEGAN DURING THE JIN AND SOUTHERN AND NORTHERN DYNASTIES

Book of Jin: Fujian Biography has mentioned: "There are 62 kings, who all send envoys to offer exotic products." Here "the 62 kings" includes those from India. Research has also shows that during the Jin Dynasty, the communication from the northwest and southwest China to India was never cut off, and there were a lot of people-to-people exchanges. *Fujian Biography*, *Record of Foreign Matters* (*Yiwu Zhi*), *Records of Diverse Matters* (*Bowu Zhi*) and other books have clearly mentioned the exchanges between the two governments due to Huohuan fabric. *Book of Song: Biography of the Neighboring Countries* and *Book of Liang: Biography of Foreign Countries* have preserved credential records from different kingdoms in India, and also recorded many cases of envoys sent by India to China and China to India. [7]66-71 In the Tang Dynasty, which Ji Xianlin called the heyday of Sino-Indian cultural exchanges, the frequent communications and exchanges between China and India not only referred to religious exchanges but also involved exchanges in politics (diplomacy), economics, philosophy, science, technology, literature and ar. Moreover, the mutual learning between China and India was never a one-way manner, but a two-way flow.[2]49 The "Bengala"(Bangladesh) recorded in volume 326 of *History of the Ming Dynasty* also mentioned that "during the time of Ming Dynasty, there also exists a system of transferring official documents in Bengala. Medicine, divination, the theory of yin-yang, techniques, crafts and arts are all the same as that in China, which were all presumably introduced from China in the past"[2]148. Although there is no real historical record in ancient India, except for the four great inventions, and there is no detailed record of the influence of Chinese culture on India, this record illustrates the influence of China on India.

The Yoga-Taichi exchange has continued to push forward the communication and interaction between the two countries. Since the establishment of China-India Yoga College of Yunnan Minzu University, many Indian officials, senior officials and scholars of Indian Yoga Department, as well as vice-chancellors of some universities have come to visit. The delegation from Yunnan Minzu University was invited by the Indian Prime Minister's Office to visit India in 2015 and was also invited by the Ministry of Yoga (AYUSH) to visit India and participate in the International Yoga Conference in 2016. It was also invited by the Indian Embassy in China to visit India and welcomed by the Minister of Foreign Affairs in 2018. Due to frequent interactions in recent years, Indian Ambassador to China, Mr. Vikram Misri visited our university in November 2019 and praised it as "a shining example of human civilizational ties between the two countries". In October 2020, the Chinese Embassy in India donated teaching equipment, Taichi clothes, and Taichi fans to Dev Sanskriti Vishwavidyalaya and Vivekananda Yoga Anusandhana Samsthana in India to encourage their research and teaching of Taichi. The two universities said that the friendship between China and India has lasted for a long time, and the cooperation between the two universities and institutes in China will be further strengthened. Xuanzang, who was hailed by Prof. Ji Xianlin as the "incarnation of Sino-Indian friendship"[8]1, helped King Harsha to learn more about China, which greatly impressed King Harsha who later sent envoys to communicate with the Tang Dynasty. Yoga-Taichi exchanges can also deepen the understanding between the peoples of China and India. It helps to promote the development of literature, art, philosophy and religion, the prosperity of science and technology, and pthe progress of both societies through cultural exchanges, just as once stated by Prof. Ji Xianlin.[2]150

3 YOGA-TAICHI CULTURAL EXCHANGES NOT ONLY CARRY-FORWARD THE CULTURAL EXCHANGE BETWEEN CHINA AND INDIA ALONG THE BURMA ROAD, BUT ALSO PROMOTE THE MUTUAL LEARNING OF LANGUAGES

It can be said that the establishment of India-China Yoga College and International Taichi College of Yunnan Minzu University has not only strengthened the exchanges between China and India, but has also promoted the mutual learning of languages. The university has sent many teachers and students to India to carry out cultural exchanges for many times. The university has also established cooperative relations with more than 10 Indian universities, including JNU (Jawaharlal Nehru University), SVYASA (Swami Vivekananda Yoga Anusandhana Samsthana), Dev Sanskriti Vishwavidyalaya, Visva-Bharati University and so on. The agreement was reached on teacher-student training, scientific research, cooperative schooling and other aspects. In January 2018, Yunnan Minzu University established the International Taichi Center at Dev Sanskriti Vishwavidyalaya and SVYASA in India. In June of the same year, the university and JNU in India reached an agreement on establishing the "China-India Humanities Exchange Center". In December 2018, a team of Taichi teachers from Yunnan Minzu University visited Dev Sanskriti Vishwavidyalaya for one month of Taichi teaching. The Taichi teaching teaching has had many positive impacts on the university. Not only did the students come to learn Taichi, but teachers and their children are also attracted by it. The class expanded from two classes to four classes. The teacher who taught the Taichi classes said that the language barrier was gone, and the action transcended the language. Such kind of communication also inspired the students to explore the connotation of Taichi and discuss the similarities and differences between Yoga and Taichi with the teacher. As a result, some of them not only fell in love with Taichi, but also fell in love with Chinese. Some students would write Chinese characters in the palm of their hands to ask the Taichi teacher how to pronounce these characters. "Taichi and Yoga have a lot to communicate about, but the language barrier prevents deeper communication" said the assistant of President of Dev Sanskriti Vishwavidyalaya. During 2017, the two authors were invited to offer Chinese classes for students during their visit to the school, and they were deeply loved by the students. There were also teachers from the school who came to study Chinese specifically. When the two teachers walked on campus, students often came and greeted them in Chinese by saying "*Nin Hao*!"

Students visiting India also began to realize the importance of language for communication. From February to August 2019, 25 yoga students from the China-India Yoga College went to Dev Sanskriti Vishwavidyalaya to study for half a year. When it comes to English learning, students find out the importance of language in communication. They also know that they can't communicate more deeply with translation software. Due to the language barrier, they can't communicate normally and can't understand the essence of each other's culture. Though the students did not understand Hindi, and their English was also not very good, they played games, sang and danced with Indian students Also, with the help of translation software, they established a good friendship with the Indian students. Just as the students who returned to China from India said, "this exchange first gave me a superficial understanding of the cultural differences in different countries and regions, and also a more systematic understanding of Yoga. Although I could not speak their language, the different expressions and cultural communications can make people from different countries feel the same. One can have his/her own stances and views on culture, but there is no need to argue about what is right and wrong. This may be a way of seeking common ground while reserving differences, respect, tolerance and understanding. In additon, what struck me is that language is very wonderful. The expression of each language has its own different meanings and I also realized own shortcomings. If there is no language barrier between us, it will be easier for us to communicate with each other and learn more."[1] Yunnan is located at the junction of China and Southeast Asia. The ancient Southern Silk Road and the Tea-horse Ancient Road have

1 来自对云南民族大学中印瑜伽学院（国际太极学院）社会体育指导与管理（瑜伽方向）2017 级李姓学生，访谈人：路芳，访谈时间：2020 年 10 月 10 日。

contributed to the openness and prosperity of Yunnan in history. The Yoga-Taichi exchange has deepened this kind of oriental cultural exchanges. When President Xi Jinping visited India in 2014, he mentioned that Chinese Taichi and Indian Yoga are surprisingly similar, and the philosophy of life that the peoples of the two countries have pursued for thousands of years is profoundly similar. Prof. Ji Xianlin believed that the fundamental way of thinking of Oriental culture is integration, which is reflected in philosophy as the unity of human and nature. In *Xi Ming (Western Inscription), Zhang Zai wrote*: "Ch'ien [Heaven] is called the father and K'un [Earth] is called the mother. I, this tiny being, am commingled in their midst; therefore what fills up all between Heaven and Earth, that is my body, and that which directs Heaven and Earth is my nature. All people are my brothers and sisters, and all creatures are my companions." It expresses the same meaning as the "The self is Brahman" in Indian philosophy. Eastern culture advocates that people and nature are friends. Only when we understand and love nature, we can ask for everything we need from nature, such as human clothing, food, shelter, and transportation.[9]10. Zhao Qizheng once proposed "a China standpoint" through "an international expression", which can only be realized by using an internationally understandable method.[10]88 Through the exchange of Yoga-Taichi, we can find common ground of Eastern culture, and can express the position of the East and China to the world.

4 CONCLUSION: THE ROLE OF YOGA-TAICHI CULTURAL EXCHANGE REQUIRES LANGUAGE AS A MEDIUM

At the opening ceremony of the Asian Civilization Dialogue Conference, President Xi Jinping advocated that "Civilizations interact due to diversity, mutually learn due to interactions, and develop due to mutual learning. We should strengthen exchanges and mutual learning among different countries, ethnic groups and cultures, and lay a solid cultural foundation for building an Asian community with a shared future for mankind." As Prof. Ji Xianlin showed us the truth with the example of cultural backflow of sugar and steel: we live in cultural exchanges, and behind the very familiar things, ofter lies Knowing this history not only allows us to know there is a phenomenon of cultural backflow in the process of cultural exchanges, but it can also strengthen mutual understanding between countries and ethnic groups, promote friendship between us, and jointly defend world peace.[2]152-158 Once two unfamiliar cultures start to exchange, they must go through at least five stages: impact-absorption-transformation-fusion-assimilation, especially in the history of cultural exchanges between China and India.[2]3 In these five stages of communication, the importance of language is particularly prominent. The British scholar Austin believed that we can act through words and language, and then take effect.[11] Cultural communication requires language as a medium. With the help of language, we can better understand the meaning and symbols of culture, realize the re-collision and mutual learning of Chinese and Indian cultures in the new era, and jointly build an Asian community of shared future.

（Translated by Yu Beibei, Proofread by Aditya Kumar Pandey）

REFERENCES

[1] 薛克翘. 象步凌空——我看印度 [M]. 北京：世界知识出版社，2010.

[2] 季羡林. 中印文化交流史 [M]. 北京：中国社会科学出版社，2008.

[3] AMIT S, AMIT S. Paraspara, encounters, and confluences: India's soft power objective in Indo-Pacific region[J].Politics & policy, 2017,45（5）：733-761.

[4]NEWCOMBE S.The development of modern Yoga: a survey of the field[J]. Religion compass, 2009, 3/6: 986-1002.

[5] 汪忠长. 易与道 [M]. 北京：当代世界出版社，2005.

[6] 杨黎明，杨光. 太极拳的发展与对外传播——以太极拳故里焦作近五年的情况为例 [J]. 辽宁体育科技，2018,40（3）：104-108.

[7] 薛克翘. 中国印度文化交流史 [M]. 北京：昆仑出版社，2008.

[8] 季羡林. 前言 [M]// 玄奘，辩机，季羡林校注. 大唐西域记校注. 北京：中华书局 ,2000.

[9] 季羡林.《东方文化集成》总序 [M]// 薛克翘. 中国印度文化交流史. 北京：昆仑出版社，2008.

[10] 赵启正. 公共外交与跨文化交流 [M]. 北京：中国人民大学出版社，2011.

[11] 奥斯汀. 如何以言行事 [M]. 杨玉成，译. 北京：外语教学与研究出版社，2002.

佛教语境下汉语对理解中印关系的作用

阿润·库马尔[1]

摘要　语言，是人类文明的重要标志之一，是交流的工具、思维的载体。丝绸之路的出现，促进了东西方各国经济贸易和宗教文化等各方面的交流。在丝绸之路上生活的人们，见证了各国之间商品货物的贸易往来，也对外来文化和宗教信仰的传播、传译等起了非常重要的作用，其中影响最大的当属起源于印度但在中国拥有众多信众的佛教。为了使中国的佛教徒真正明白佛教的教义，汉译佛经以及用汉语讲解佛法的现象在中国大量涌现，这又进一步促进了佛教在中国的传播。同时在汉译佛经的影响下，佛教在印度重新兴起，掀起一股新浪潮。因此中印两国对佛教的研究和交流，有助于进一步加深两国的友谊。

关键词　汉语；丝绸之路；佛教

语言是人与人之间思想与情感交流的载体。那么语言是如何产生的呢？语言的产生，又对人类的生活造成了哪些影响呢？世界上有 7 000 多种语言，这些语言的发源地都是哪里？语言是如何演变而来的？语言学家对此众说纷纭。但可以肯定的是，语言的目的在于交流，包括情感的交流和信息的交流。

不管是书面还是口头交流，人与人的交流都需要用语言，同样，国与国的交流也需要用语言。但各国都有各自的语言，不同国家的人们怎样才能相互交流呢？答案就是要学习对方的语言，使自己能理解对方所表达的意思，从而推动两国间文明对话。语言是两个国家沟通交流的重要工具。学习对方的语言，是实现两国沟通交

1　新那烂陀佛教大学巴利语和佛教专业助理教授。

流的第一步。

本文探讨在佛教领域中汉语对理解中印关系的重要性。首先我们来谈谈中印友谊是如何开始的，以及语言在其中所起的作用。

西汉时期，张骞以长安（今西安）为起点，出使西域，开通了中外交流的新纪元。自丝绸之路形成，中国同东西方各国便有了联系，来往者络绎不绝，各国使者、商贾、传教士都在这条路上留下足迹。这里的商业贸易以商品货物交换为主，并伴随着文化宗教等交流。丝绸之路，并非一条“路”，而是一张穿越山川和沙漠且没有标识的道路网，其基本走向定型于两汉时期，包括南道、中道、北道三条路线。货物流通中，以丝绸制品的影响最大，故此得名“丝绸之路”。

丝绸之路同时也是传播各种文化、技术、语言和信仰的平台，连通了世界的东西方，对世界各国产生了深远的影响，不仅仅是在经济方面，在文化方面也是影响巨大。耶鲁大学历史学教授、汉学家芮乐伟·韩森（Valerie Hansen）在《丝绸之路新史》一书中写道：

> 如果只看货物贸易的重量与往来的人数，丝绸之路是历史上人流量较少的道路之一；丝绸之路之所以改变历史，很大程度上是因为丝路上穿行的人们把他们各自的文化传播到世界各地。[1]

在丝绸之路上，曾经出现过很多宗教，有些宗教已经消逝，例如摩尼教；有些则流传至今，例如起源于印度的佛教，它在中国有很多信徒，影响最大。那么在丝绸之路上生活的人们，是否对于宗教信仰的传播、传译、变化起到了至关重要的作用呢？[1]

佛教为何能在中国拥有众多的信众？究其根本，是因为佛教的一些理论和中国本土的儒家、道教的核心思想是相同的，如孝敬长辈、爱护幼小、遵守道德等。

史载：

> 东汉永平十年（公元67年），印度高僧摄摩腾、竺法兰以白马驮载佛经、

佛像抵达洛阳，汉明帝刘庄躬亲迎奉，敕令建造白马寺，供奉经典和佛像于寺内清凉台上，印度二位高僧在此禅居并翻译出第一部汉文佛经——《佛说四十二章经》。[2]

佛陀本人使用巴利语进行佛法的传授，或每到一个地方就用当地的方言为当地人讲解佛法。为了让更多的人明白佛教教义，佛陀还建议他的僧人们使用通用语来传授佛经，并且在传授过程中禁止他们使用晦涩难懂的语言。使用通用语是佛陀一个大胆而明智的决定，这对佛教的传播起到了至关重要的作用。后来的佛经用巴利语或梵语撰写。为了使中国的佛教徒能够真正地理解佛陀所说的法，高僧大德像佛陀一样开始对佛经进行汉语翻译，或直接用汉语书写佛经以及用汉语开坛讲法。佛经的汉译对于佛教在中国的传播起到了非常重要的作用，自摄摩腾、竺法兰两位高僧后，相继出现了鸠摩罗什、不空、真谛、玄奘等译经大师，为后世的佛教研究留下了宝贵的汉译佛经资料。

公元 13 世纪初，由于大量的佛经、佛像、佛塔、佛寺等被焚毁或填埋，以及佛教高僧被迫害，佛教在自己的出生地——印度曾彻底消亡。几个世纪后，佛像、佛经、佛塔、佛寺、佛洞和带有佛陀（Buddha）字样的铭文等跟佛教有关的文物，先后出现在人们的视野里，但是人们却并不知道这些是什么，甚至将佛陀误认为是一个非洲人。因为从佛像上看，佛陀头发卷曲、嘴唇偏厚，长相酷似非洲人。有人还将佛寺误认为是某个皇帝曾经居住的地方，将佛塔误认为是某个皇帝的墓冢。

直到 1858 年后，英国考古学家亚历山大 • 卡宁厄姆（Alexander Cunningham）根据玄奘的《大唐西域记》的描写，发掘并确认了大量的佛教遗迹，辨别了佛陀的真实身份，至此佛教才重现于印度。卡宁厄姆曾经这样评价道："但幸运的是，中国朝圣者旅途的新发现……在迄今为止的黑暗时期里投下了如此多的光芒，以至于我们能清楚地看到印度古代地理上大部分零星散落着的历史梗概。"[3] 由此可见汉译佛经对印度的重要性，印度和中国的友谊也因此而加深。玄奘、法显、义净及其翻译的经书或著作架起了中印友谊的桥梁。由于佛教的频繁交流，中国和印度已经从简单的商品贸易上升到了心灵交流的层面。

在印度佛教曾经一度消亡，因此许多佛教古籍的巴利语或梵语版本已经失传，但幸运的是我们发现了中国的汉语版本以及斯里兰卡和缅甸的巴利语版本的佛教古籍。基本上在印度仅存的佛教古籍都属于小乘佛教（南传佛教），而绝大多数大乘佛教的文献都在中国、韩国和日本。韩国和日本的佛教文献也都是从中国传播而来。在大正藏里面，提到了 1 662 本佛经。[4] 所以想要深入研究佛教，学习汉语是必不可少的。因为如果想要对佛教有更深层次的理解，就需要同时了解大乘佛教和小乘佛教，而研究大乘佛教，汉语就是一项必要技能。当你掌握了汉语，就可以读更多的佛教典籍，也就能对佛教有更深入的认识；作为印度人，就可以越来越了解自己的历史和宗教文化。

由于近年来中国的经济实力和国际地位不断提升，学习汉语的外国人也逐渐增多。大家认识到了学习汉语的重要性，也就有越来越多的印度人愿意学习汉语。不管是出于个人的职业生涯规划，还是对中印两国友谊的考虑，学习汉语都大有益处。

那么如何才能学好汉语呢？以笔者为例，笔者在中国的大学学习了一年汉语。大学里有专业的汉语老师，他们非常认真负责，有丰富的汉语教学经验，让笔者的汉语有了很大的提升。另外，因为笔者身在中国，有一个讲汉语的环境，所以就有很多和中国人对话的机会，这对我口语的提升很有帮助。但对于在印度学习汉语的学生来说，他们可能没有和中国人交流的机会。据我所知，全印度开设中文课程的大学有国际大学、贝拿勒斯印度教大学、尼赫鲁大学和德里大学。国际大学在过去的几十年在中国佛教研究方面颇有建树，但近年来，国际大学也像印度其他大学一样对这方面失去了重视。两国院校合办的孔子学院、汉语学习中心等中文培训机构在印度也并不多。

同时，笔者建议学校也可开设有关印度佛教文化（除佛教历史外）的中文课程来学习汉语课文和语法。例如通过阅读融合儒家、道家和佛家各家思想的道德故事集，以及佛经佛教经典等方式学习中文，而不仅仅是教授经济、政治等方面的课程；编写以印地语或英语为教学语言的汉语学习教材；开发汉语学习的应用程序，还有利用场景学习的方式学习语法等。

当印度学生在读汉语佛经、佛教故事，或者融合儒、道、佛三家思想的故事集的时候，他们就能感受到这是印度和中国所共有的文化宝库，也会懂得语言、文化和国家之间的密切联系，这会让印度学生更加享受学习汉语的过程。我想，通过佛教文化来学习汉语，一定能使中印两国人民的友谊朝着更加坚定稳固的方向发展，中印两国的友谊也将得以加深。

参考文献

[1] 韩森. 丝绸之路新史 [M]. 北京：北京联合出版公司，2015.
[2] 摄摩腾，竺法兰. 佛说四十二章经. 洛阳：白马寺 .
[3] CUNNINGHAM A. Ancient geography of India[M]. London: Trubner and Co., 1871.
[4] NANJIO B. A catalogue of the Chinese translation of Buddhist Tripitaka[M]. London: Clarendon Press，1888.

Role of Chinese Language in Understanding the Sino-Indian Relationship in the Context of Buddhism

Arun Kumar Yadav[1]

Abstract Language is one of the essential needs of human civilization. People often describe it as a tool of communication and a carrier of thinking. The emergence of the Silk Road has promoted the economic and trade cooperation, and religious and cultural exchanges between East and West. People living on the Silk Road have witnessed the trade exchanges of commodities between countries, and also played a significant role in the dissemination and interpretation of different cultures and religious beliefs. The most influential dissemination on this route was the spread of Buddhism, which originated in India but flourished in China with many followers. To make Chinese Buddhists fully understand the teachings of Buddha, the Chinese translation of Buddhist scriptures and the use of Chinese language to explain Buddhism have emerged in China largely, which has further promoted the spread of Buddhism and common values in China. In the meantime, with the influence of the Chinese translation of Buddhist scriptures Buddhism revived in India, setting off a new wave. Therefore, the study of Chinese language and the role of Buddhism between China and India can further strengthen the friendship between both peoples and countries.

Key Words Chinese; The Silk Road; Buddhism

1 Assistant Professor, Department of Pali and Buddhist Studies, Nava Nalanda Mahavihara.

Language is the carrier of thoughts and emotions to communicate with others. So how does language come about? What impact did the production of the language have on human life? There are more than 7,000 languages in the world. Where are the birthplaces of these languages? How does language evolve? Linguists have different opinions on these questions. Nevertheless, we can be sure that the purpose of language is to communicate. The content of communication includes the exchange of emotions and information.

People-to-people communication requires language. Similarly, country-to-country communication also requires language, whether written or oral. However, each country has its own language. How can people from different countries communicate with each other? The answer is to learn the language of the others so that one can fully figure out their meaning in a proper way with right understanding. To promote the civilization dialogue between two countries, language is an essential tool for communication. Learning each other's language is the first step in achieving communication between two countries.

In this article, we will explore the importance of Chinese in understanding Sino-Indian relations in the light of Buddhism. First, let us talk about how the Sino-Indian friendship began and the role of language in it.

During the Western Han Dynasty, Zhang Qian set off from Chang'an (now Xi'an) to the Western Regions, opening a new era of Sino-foreign exchanges. Since the beginning of the Silk Road, China has been in contact with Eastern and Western countries. Envoys, merchants, and missionaries from various countries have left their footprints along the road opened by Zhang Qian. They mainly exchanged commodities, accompanied by religious and cultural exchanges. The Silk Road is not a single trade road but a network of unmarked roads that cross mountains and deserts. The necessary direction of the Silk Road was set in the Han Dynasty, including three routes of South Road, Middle Road and North Road. In the circulation of goods, silk products had the most significant influence, hence got the name of the Silk Road.

The Silk Road is also a platform for spreading various cultures, technologies, languages and beliefs. It connects the East and the West of the world and has a profound impact on countries around the world. In addition to economic aspects, it also affects the culture a lot. Valerie Hansen is a professor of history at Yale University and a well-known sinologist. She wrote in her book *The New History of the Silk Road*:

> If we only observe the weight of the trade in goods and the number of crossing people, the Silk Road is one of the roads with few visitors passing by in history; the reason why the Silk Road changed history is that people walking on the Silk Road spread their unique cultures to the world in a large degree.[1]

There once had many religions and languages on the Silk Road. Some religions such as Manichaeism and languages have disappeared; others have been disseminated so far, such as Buddhism which originated and flourished in India but it has many believers in China and produces the most significant influence on Chinese culture. So did the people living on the Silk Road play a vital role in the spread, interpretation and change of religious beliefs?[1] The answer is "yes".

Why does Buddhism have so many followers and so popular in China? The fundamental reason is that Buddhism has the same connotation as that of Confucianism and Taoism in China, such as honouring the elders, caring for the young and observing morals.

Historical records:

> In the tenth year of Yongping in the Eastern Han Dynasty (67 AD), the Indian monks Kashyap Matanga and Dharmaraksha arrived in Luoyang with white horses carrying Buddhist scriptures and Buddha statues. The emperor Mingdi Liuzhuang personally greeted them and ordered the construction of the White Horse Temple to enshrine Buddha classics and statues on the refreshing terrace in the temple. Two eminent monks from India also lived here and translated the first Chinese Buddhist scriptures–The Sutra In Forty–two Sections said By Buddha.[2]

The Buddha himself used Pali language to teach the Dharma (teachings) whenever he went to stay anywhere. He used the local language to explain his Dharma (teachings) to the local people and suggested his monks to use common language so that his teachings could reach more and more people. He also strictly restricted his monks to learn his teachings in any scholarly language which cannot be understood by common people. Using the common language was a bold and wise decision of Buddha so that it played a great role in spreading Buddhism. Later on the Buddhist scriptures were written down in Pali and Sanskrit. In order to enable Chinese Buddhists to truly understand what the Buddha said, the eminent monk followed the same path of Buddha and began to translate Buddhist scriptures and teach the Buddha Dharma in common language of Chinese people of that time. The Chinese translation of Buddhist scriptures played a leading role in the spread of Buddhism in China. After the two eminent monks of Shemoteng and Zhufalan, other masters of scripture translation appeared successively, such as Kumarajiva, Bukong, Zhenyi, Xuanzang, etc. They left precious Chinese translation of Buddhist scriptures for later generations' Buddhism study.

In the early 13th century, a large number of Buddhist scriptures, Buddha statues, Buddha pagodas and Buddhist temples were burned or buried. Numerous eminent monks were persecuted. As a result, Buddhism once ultimately perished in India where it was born. Several centuries later, Buddha statues, Buddhist scriptures, Buddhist pagodas, Buddhist temples, Buddhist caves, inscriptions with the word Buddha and other things related to Buddhism. reappeared in people's vision Nevertheless, nobody knew them. Someone even mistook Buddha for an African because of his curly hair and thick lips judging from the Buddha statue. There also existed other misunderstangs that the Buddhist temple was a place where an emperor once lived and that the pagodas were a certain emperor's tomb.

It was not until after 1858 that the British archaeologist Alexander Cunningham excavated and confirmed a large number of Buddhist relics based on Xuanzang's *Great Tang Records on the Western Regions* and also discerned the true identity of the Buddha. Therefore, Buddhism reappeared in India. Cunningham once commented: “But the fortunate discovery of the travels of the Chinese pilgrims... has thrown such a flood of light upon this hitherto dark period that we are now able to see our way clearly to the general arrangement of most of the scattered fragments of the ancient geography of India”.[3] It shows the importance of the Chinese translation works of Buddhist scriptures to India. The friendship between India and China has been deepened. Xuanzang, Faxian, Yijing and their translated scriptures or works have bridged the friendship between China and India. Due to the frequent exchanges of Buddhism, China and India have gone from simple commodity trade to the level of spiritual communication.

Buddhism once met extinction in India. Thus, a large amount of ancient Buddhist books cannot be found in Pali or Sanskrit versions for a long time in main land of India but a vast amount of texts were available in Chinese Language in China and in Pali language in Srilanka and Myanmar. We are lucky to find the Chinese versions of ancient Buddhist texts. The remaining Buddhist ancient books in India mostly belong to the Theravada/Hinayana Buddhism (Southern Buddhism), while the vast majority of Mahayana Buddhism classics are in China as well as in Korea and Japan (spread from China). According to Buddhist Tripitaka catalogue, 1662 Buddhist scriptures[4] are mentioned in the Taisho Tripitaka edition, but it is available in very less amount in any Indian language in India. In a word, learning Chinese language is essential for studying Buddhism in depth. Because if you want to have a deep level of understanding in Buddhism, then you should have well-versed in Mahayana Buddhism as well as in Theravada/Hinayana Buddhism at the same time. To study Mahayana Buddhism, Chinese is an essential skill. When a person (especially in the case of Indian) is a master of Chinese, then he/she can read more Buddhist classics and have more feelings and regard for Buddhism and Chinese as an Indian. In this way one can learn more about our Indo-Chinese history, religious culture, relationship and importance of Chinese language.

As China’s economic strength and international status have continued to rise in recent years in academia, the number of foreigners learning Chinese as a language has gradually increased. All of them have noticed the importance of learning Chinese. More and more Indians are willing to learn Chinese now. Whether it is for personal career or the friendship between China and India, learning Chinese is of great benefits.

So how can we learn Chinese well? I studied Chinese at a Chinese university for a year. From my own Chinese learning experience, I feel that there are professional and responsible Chinese teachers in the university with rich Chinese teaching experience. They significantly improved my Mandarin levels. Additionally since I was in China, there were many opportunities to communicate with local people in Chinese, which was very helpful for upgrading my oral Chinese. However, for students studying Chinese in India, they may not have many opportunities to communicate with the Chinese people. As far as I know, many universities offer Chinese courses in all over India such as Vishava Bharati University, Banaras Hindu University, Jawahar Lal Neharu University, Delhi University, etc. In the field of Chinese Buddhist study and research, Vishava Bharati University played a pioneer role in past decades. They have done extraordinary work in the field of Chinese Buddhism, but unfortunately, in recent decades Vishava Bharati University has also ignored this area like other Departments of Chinese of different universities. There are not many Chinese educational institutions such as Chinese learning centers and Confucius Institutes established by the universities/institutes from both countries.

At the same time, I also recommend colleges and Chinese teaching centers to offer some part of Chinese courses on Buddhist culture (especially Buddhist History) to learn Chinese anticles and grammar. For instance, setting courses like Chinese Buddhist scriptures, Buddhist stories or some common ethical values of Confucianism, Taoism and Buddhism, instead of just teaching economic and political contents; develop the compiling Chinese Buddhist-Hindi/English textbooks for Chinese language courses and also develop Chinese learning applications for learning grammar in a playful scenario.

When Indian students read Chinese Buddhist scriptures or Buddhist stories or some common ethical values originated by the influence of Confucianism, Taoism and Buddhism, they will be able to encounter the common stories and cultural heritage of India and China through Buddhism, and then they will feel more connected with the language, culture and country. It will make a more enjoyable process of Chinese learning to the Indian students. I believe that the exchange and learning of Chinese language through Buddhism culture will strengthen the Sino-India friendship and take it in faster and faithful environment.

（Translated by Cai Yu Liang; Proofread by Wang Meicen）

REFERENCES

[1] 韩森. 丝绸之路新史 [M]. 北京：北京联合出版公司，2015.

[2] 摄摩腾， 竺法兰. 佛说四十二章经[M]. 洛阳：白马寺 .

[3]CUNNINGHAM A. Ancient geography of India[M]. London: Trubner and Co., 1871.

[4]NANJIO B. A catalogue of the Chinese translation of Buddhist Tripitaka [M].London: Clarendon Press, 1888.

寓教于艺，相得益彰
——在书画教学中融入汉语学习的教学心得分享

常惟璞[1]

摘要　中国书画和汉字、汉语有着不可分割的联系。教授书画或者汉语，一般都会彼此涉及。本文介绍了笔者在印度教授中国书画文化的过程中，通过艺术讲座、书画交流展、工作坊等形式，穿插进行汉语、汉字教学，从书画艺术角度进行汉语传播的经历和体会。由于印度不少地方也有书法、绘画积淀，学生们对这种教学形式表现出强烈的兴趣，也因而取得了比较好的教学效果。

关键词　汉语学习；书画艺术；教学；中印

笔者是金德尔全球大学商学院的在读博士，也是来自中国的书画爱好者，因此，偶尔会被安排讲授中国书画艺术课程。笔者在课堂上告诉学生，要了解中国书画艺术，汉语学习是必要的。不少初次接触汉语的印度学生常常问汉语难不难、怎样才能学好汉语等。或许因为此前一直生活在汉语环境中，对这个问题没有深入思考。而今身在异国他乡，在课堂上被问的次数多了，也便开始从多个角度思考这个问题。毋庸置疑，汉语被公认为世界上最难学的语言之一，其中汉语难说、汉字难写是最大障碍。但同时，笔者也告诉学生：世上无难事，只要肯登攀。正如中国先贤孔子所说：“知之者不如好之者，好之者不如乐之者。”[1] 学好汉语虽然不容易，但只要有兴趣、有恒心、有方法，就没有过不了的火焰山。

1　印度金德尔全球大学商学院在读博士。

汉语教学研究证明，片面强调结构、功能或文字而使得教学有所偏颇都是不可取的。在世界第二语言教学潮流中，总体上看汉语教学是以结构为中心的综合教学方法。[2]243 而兴趣引导、因材施教、循序渐进适用于大多数语言教学流程。教无定法，贵在得法。笔者尝试在书法、绘画、茶艺等传统才艺教学中引入汉语学习，从眼、耳、口、手、心多感官激发学生的学习兴趣，这在语言教学、艺术交流和文化互动中收到了良好的教学效果，也因此有所心得。愿陈管窥之见，为抛砖之资，期引方家金玉之言。

1 在书画才艺教学中融入汉语教学

书画，是对书法与绘画的统称。书画文化源远流长，是世界文化艺术宝库中的精华，是人类历史上值得品鉴和典藏的艺术珍品。我们常说“书画不分家”，特别是在中国文字初创期，以及传统水墨画之中，“书画同源”表现得尤为典型。同时，以书画为切入点而非仅仅由书法或者绘画切入，也是考虑到其与印度书画文化之间多有包容或重合成分。在方兴未艾的“中文热”中，我们不难发现书画才艺在其中所起的作用。

笔者所在的印度金德尔全球大学，是一所以社会科学为主导的国际化大学，该校非常鼓励跨学科教学和研究，目前已经成立法学、商学、国际关系、公共政策、人文艺术、建筑艺术、金融、环境等 10 个学院，在校学生 65 000 人。在这样一所国际化大学中，跨文化的艺术课程很受欢迎。

学校对在校博士生有授课要求，刚好笔者自己有书画、茶艺方面的爱好，就结合大学现有需求、设施设备及学生现状，偶尔开设介绍中国书画并融入语言教学的中国文化课程。

在文化艺术类课程中开展汉语教学在印度已不鲜见，且已经积累了不少教学成果和经验，但在印度金德尔大学尚属首次，一出现便受到老师和同学们的关注。每次公布课程后都有不少同学报名试听，不少教授也兴趣盎然，咨询可否报名参加。

不少学生在学业繁重的情况下仍然选择报名，有的同学在参加过几期汉语教育或取得证书后，仍坚持报名参加中国书画文化或中国茶文化课程，可见这类课程很受学生欢迎。

2 书画才艺与汉语教学互动的必要性及建议

汉语的基本单元是汉字，书画才艺与对外汉语教学，既有重合部分，又有各自的范畴。如果二者互动良好，将相互促进，相得益彰。

（1）二者互动有利于学习者深化对于汉语、汉字的认识，并从汉字根本功能方面推进汉语教学。书画是与汉语教学联系最为紧密的才艺，相较于剪纸、京剧、音乐、节庆文化等中华才艺，书画，特别是书法，是无时无处不与汉语的发展、汉字的教学息息相关的。对于母语非汉语的学习者而言，可以说，知道了象形文字、六书造字法等汉字发展的历史知识，了解了书法的发展历史，也就清楚了汉字、汉语的发展脉络，相当于找到了开启汉字神秘之门的金钥匙。

图 1 中国驻印度大使馆孙卫东大使在金德尔全球大学参加中国文化周活动书画环节

（2）各种才艺与对外汉语教学结合，有利于促进中印文化互动。印度是中国的重要毗邻大国，在宗教、文化、艺术、经济等诸多方面有共同基因或互补因素，中印关系和走向，影响着两国、亚洲乃至世界的发展方向。当前，反全球化、冷战思维及零和思维模式阻碍了地球村的进一步融合，延缓了各国相互了解和相互信任、合作的进程。孔子学院遇冷、汉语教育中心搁浅、教育合作受阻等，表明语言教学已被猜疑为控制意识形态的工具，被贴上有色标签。而艺术无国界，其交流敏感度、门槛都更低，在山重水复、乱云飞渡的时候，不妨走一步“闲棋”，通过艺术推进国际文化交流，或许会找到更为从容的文化交流途径。

图 2　中印书画艺术家交流掠影

（3）将汉语教学融入书画艺术课程，还有助于提高学生的选修兴趣。与单纯的语言课程相比，书画艺术课程更有专业课特点，对于学生的求职、升学等也有更多好处。从开发学生汉语学习兴趣的角度，在书画课程中融入汉语教学，让学生们在掌握文字前就沉浸在书画的艺术美之中，更有利于培养他们学习和研究中国文化的兴趣。课堂教学中，笔者还会加入一些中印书画比较的内容，实现教学相长。

3　书画才艺教学融入汉语教学引发的思考

（1）不一定所有的汉语学习都要按照语言学的教学方法来设计和推进。课程设计要考虑学生的学习兴趣。如果有的学生只是想从专业角度关注中国文化，或者对中国文化的兴趣是朦胧的，不想付出太多时间，那么在书画、茶艺、陶艺及其他中华才艺的教学中融入汉语教学是比较好的方法。如果强行把这些学生纳入语言学的学习轨道，他们很可能半途而废，对中华文化朦胧的兴趣也会很快在艰难的语言学习中丧失殆尽。若对他们在书画课中融入汉语教学，就有了兴趣和正向激励。课程期间，我们结合“印中研究中心五周年庆典”组织了“星耀东方”中印青年书画展。大家在茗香书韵中引经据典，参加文艺晚会，现场感受中国书画和中国艺术的魅力，收到了良好的效果。这也证明了欣赏书画，不一定非得精通文字，学员们因为想更深入了解中国书画的美，反而会主动学习和解读这种极具魅力的文字——汉字。

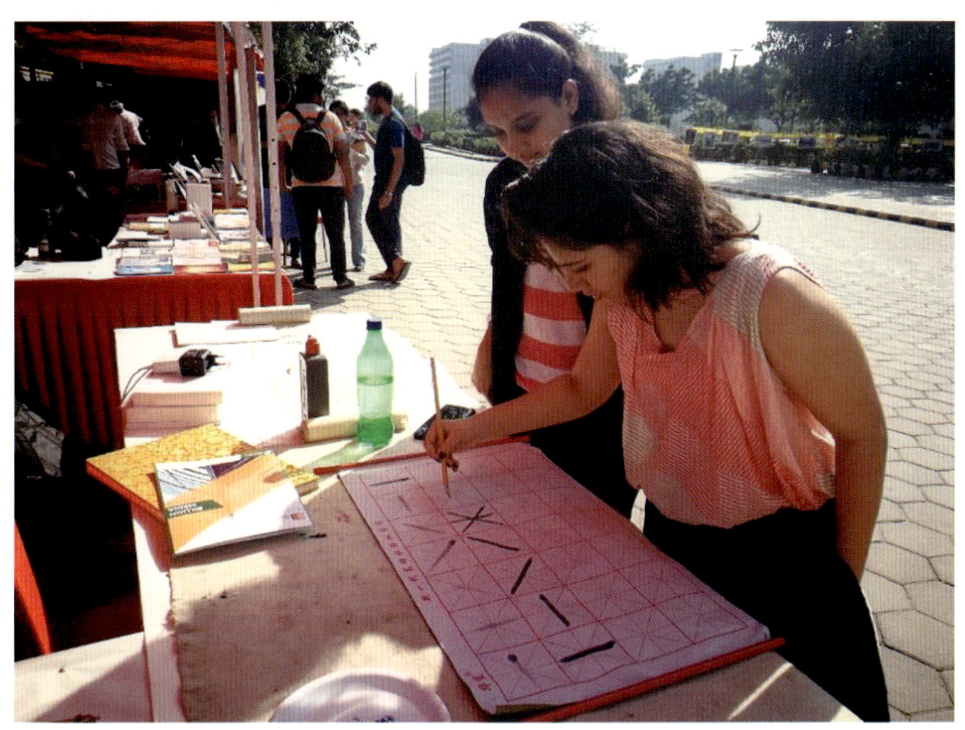

图 3　我也写两笔——体验中国书法活动

（2）汉语教学也好、书画授课也好，不能只是单纯的输出，而要有相互学习和比较欣赏的视角。课程中，要多加入一些比较鉴赏的内容。这对老师的要求也有所提高，有比较文化视角的老师更适合做海外汉语或中国文化的教学。在参观展览、听讲座的过程中，老师也可以有意识地引导学生就感兴趣的话题进行比较研究，这既是对学生学习的检验和考察，也是深化了解印度文化艺术的好机会。没有知己知彼的视角，没有对所在国文化的敬畏和赞赏，就很难把握学生的学习规律，也很难总结出中国文化的魅力和精髓。

由于课堂轻松、课程有趣，学生们纷纷向同学、师友乃至家人推荐书画文艺课程，不少中印知名研究机构，如印中经济文化促进会、印度中国研究中心等机构也向笔者发出邀请，希望能安排中国书画文化讲座。对笔者而言，虽然这种以艺术为先导的语言教学法还在尝试之中，但已引起了学习者的兴趣，有了好的课堂互动，有了好的开始，以及多方的支持，笔者会牢记“路漫漫其修远兮，吾将上下而求索”，不忘初心，在这条路上继续探索。

参考文献

[1] 孔子. 论语·雍也 [M]. 北京：中华书局，2006.

[2] 赵金铭. 对外汉语教学法回视与再认识 [J]. 世界汉语教学，2010（02）：243-254.

附录 1：

课程设计简介

课程名称：中国艺术文化简介——中国书画与汉字

课　　时：30 学时（15 次课程，每周 1 次课，2 小时）

学　　分：2 ～ 4 学分

教学语言：前期以英语为主，中后期逐步加大中文比例。

课程说明：本课程将讲解有关中国书法和绘画的基础知识，并教授相关汉语字、词、短语或句子，加深艺术文化背景下的汉语学习。中国书法和水墨画是密切相关的，因为它们是使用类似的工具和技术完成的。中国艺术（尤其是书画）是一种自我修养和自我表达的艺术，它反映了作家（画家）的心态和心情。比较中国书画与印度书画的相似与相异之处，解析东方书画艺术的独特美。

课业要求：为了从课程中获得最大的收益，学生应该充分参与课堂学习，并有兴趣和热情地学习有关中国书画的基本知识。课程结束后，学生应做到以下几点：

1. 了解中国书画的基本知识；
2. 学会欣赏和体验中国书画之美；
3. 掌握一些书画领域基本的汉字和语言技能。

教学法：该课程将主要以课堂授课的形式进行美术鉴赏和书画实践。学生应提前阅读教材及布置的阅读材料，以使课堂上的讨论更加生动有趣。

主要内容：

第 1、2 周，主要进行课程破冰，简要概述课程内容，并介绍史前及先秦时期的中国艺术；

第 3 至第 9 周，根据中国历史文化时间线，分年代介绍中国汉字及书画发展。包括甲骨文与刻画记事，篆、隶、楷、行、草书体，笔法字法，写实与写意，文人画等；

第 10 周至第 13 周，主要介绍中国近现代文字发展、艺术进程及艺术市场，并与印度书画、文化发展进行对比；

第 14、15 周，组织学生系统复习所学知识，并进行考核。

附录 2：

课程设计附表

课程安排	主要授课内容	备注
第 1 周	中国艺术与书画文化概论 中国历史与文化时间线	绘画、书法、雕塑、陶器、装饰艺术、建筑、甲骨文、金文、帛画
第 2 周	书法和绘画基础知识 （历史，风格，工具）	中国书法实践，执笔法，文房四宝介绍，点线练习；篆、隶、楷、行、草书体介绍
第 3 周	先秦、汉	汉文文书（练习写字：一、二、三、十） 《中国艺术》第 5 章
第 4 周	五代十国	佛教的影响； 书法和绘画作品 《中国艺术》第 6 章 （练习写字：木、土）
第 5 周	隋唐时期	书法和绘画作品 《中国艺术》第 7 章 （练习写字：水、火）
第 6 周	实践练习课及期中考核	工坊书画实践 （练习写字：中、金、竹）
第 7 周	宋、元	《中国艺术》第 8 章
第 8 周	清	《中国艺术》第 10—11 章 （练习写字：日、月、天、地、人、才）
第 9 周	民国至中华人民共和国成立	（实践：了解笔、墨、纸、砚）
第 10 周	当代艺术	（欣赏：文房四宝、现代绘画）
第 11 周	体验式学习	欣赏艺术品（欣赏：写字、画山）
第 12 周	知名画廊和博物馆	介绍荣宝斋、朵云轩、故宫博物院、中国博物馆等 （练习写字：荣、宝、云、馆）

续表

课程安排	主要授课内容	备注
第 13 周	中国艺术品市场简介 中印艺术比较	（欣赏：古董、文玩、字画） 中印艺术比较
第 14 周	复习课程内容	/
第 15 周	考试	/

Complementing Language Teaching with Art: Sharing Teaching Experiences of Integrating Chinese Language Learning into Calligraphy and Painting courses

Chang Weipu[1]

Abstract Chinese painting and calligraphy are closely linked to Chinese characters and Chinese language. The teaching of calligraphy and painting or Chinese language usually involves each other. This article introduces the author's experiences and thinking of promoting Chinese language by interating Chinese language learning into Chinese painting and calligraphy classes in India, specifically through art lectures, calligraphy and painting exchange exhibitions, workshops, etc. As Indian culture also has calligraphy and painting traditions, students have shown a strong interest in this, and thus the teaching has been achineving good results.

Key Words Chinese learning; Calligraphy and painting art; Teaching; Sino-Indian

I am a PhD candidate at business school of O.P. Jindal Global University, and a lover of calligraphy and painting from China. Therefore, I have been assigned to occasionally teach Chinese calligraphy and painting art in the university. I tell my students in class that learning Chinese language is an indispensable part of

1 A PhD candidate of Business School of O.P. Jindal Global University, India.

learning Chinese painting and calligraphy. Many Indian students who are the new learners of Chinese language often ask whether it is difficult to learn Chinese or not and how to learn the language well. Since I was living in a Chinese speaking environment before, I didn't think deeply about this question. Now that I am in a foreign country and have been asked about this question for several times in the class, I have begun to think about this question from multiple aspects. There is no doubt that Chinese is recognized as one of the most difficult languages to learn in the world. While learning Chinese, Chinese speaking and Chinese characters are the biggest obstacles. But at the same time, I also tell the students that nothing is difficult as long as you are willing to strive hard. As Confucius, the ancient Chinese philosopher said: "The one who knows is not as good as the one who wants to know; the one who wants to know is not as good as the one who loves to know."[1] It is not easy to learn Chinese well, but if you study with interest, perseverance, and correct method, then there is no difficulty that cannot be overcome.

Research on Chinese language teaching proves that one-sided emphasis on structure, function, or written language makes the teaching too biased, which is not desirable. In the field of second language teaching, teaching Chinese language involves a structure-centered and comprehensive teaching method.[2]243 Teaching students in accordance with their ability, and interest and proceeding step by step are suitable methods for most language teaching processes. There is no fixed way of teaching, but the most important thing is to seek a right way of teaching. The author has tried to introduce Chinese language learning through the teaching of traditional arts such as calligraphy, painting, and tea culture, and stimulate students' interest in learning language from eyes, ears, mouth, hands, and heart. The author has received good teaching results in language teaching, art exchanges and cultural interactions, and has gained valuable experience. The author aims to make better contributions in promoting Chinese language teaching by sharing his own visions.

1 INCORPORATING CHINESE LANGUAGE TEACHING INTO THE TEACHING OF CALLIGRAPHY AND PAINTING

“Calligraphy and Painting” is the collective term for Chinese calligraphy and Chinese painting. The calligraphy and painting culture have a long history. It is the essence of the world’s cultural and artistic treasure and is a form of art that worth appreciation and preservaction in human history. We often say that “calligraphy and painting are not separated”, especially in the early stage of Chinese writing and traditional ink painting. “Calligraphy and painting Share the same origin” is particularly prominent. At the same time, taking calligraphy and painting as the starting point, not just calligraphy or painting, also considers how inclusive and interlinked it is with Indian calligraphy and painting culture. In the increasing “Mandarin Wave”, it is not difficult to find the role of calligraphy and painting in it.

O.P. Jindal Global University in India where the author is studying at is an international university largely dominated by social science studies. The university encourages interdisciplinary teaching and research. At present,10 colleges have been established in law, business, international relations, public policy, humanities and arts, architecture, finance, environment, etc., with 65,000 students. In such an international university, cross-cultural art courses are more diverse and very popular.

There are teaching requirements for doctoral students at university. The author happens to have interests in calligraphy, painting and tea culture. Based on the current needs of the university, facilities and equipment, and the existing situation of the students, the university occasionally offers Chinese culture courses that focus on Chinese calligraphy and painting which integrate language teaching.

Chinese language teaching through cultural and artistic courses is very common in China and has accumulated considerable teaching achievements and experience, but it is the first attempt at O.P. Jindal Global University in India. This has attracted the attention of teachers and students as soon as it was introduced. After the schedule of each course was announced, many students enrolled for the course, and many professors also enquired whether they can attend the class.

Many students still choose to enroll even when they are burdened by their academic work. Some students still insist on signing up for Chinese calligraphy and painting culture or Chinese tea culture courses even though they have participated in several sessions of Chinese language course or have obtained relevant certificates. It can be seen that these two courses are very popular among students.

2 THE NECESSITY AND SUGGESTIONS FOR THE INTERACTION BETWEEN CALLIGRAPHY AND PAINTING SKILLS AND CHINESE TEACHING

The basic unit of Chinese language is Chinese characters. The calligraphy and painting skills and teaching Chinese as a foreign language have overlapping characteristics but also their own categories. If the two can be combined well, they will complement each other.

(1) It is helpful for learners to deepen their understanding of Chinese language and Chinese characters and enhance Chinese language learning from the basic functions of Chinese characters. Calligraphy and painting are the skills which are most closely linked to Chinese language teaching. Compared with other art skills such as paper-cutting, Peking opera, music, and festival culture, calligraphy and painting, especially calligraphy, are closely related to the development of Chinese language and the teaching of Chinese characters at anytime and anywhere. For learners whose mother tongue is not Chinese, it can be said that if they know the history of the development of Chinese characters such as pictographs and the Six Formation Principles of Chinese characters, and understand the history of the development of calligraphy, then they will have a clear understanding of the development of Chinese characters and Chinese language, which is equivalent to

finding the golden key to open the mysterious door of learning Chinese characters.

Picture 1 Chinese Ambassador Sun Weidong participating in the calligraphy and painting session of Chinese Culture Week at O.P. Jindal Global University

(2) The combination of various ant skills and teaching Chinese as a foreign language is conducive to promoting cultural interactions between China and India. India is an important neighboring country of China. It has common genes or complementary factors in religion, culture, art, economy and many other aspects with China. China-India relations and trends affect the development direction of the two countries, Asia and the world. In today's society, anti-globalization, cold war thinking, and zero-sum mentality have blocked further integration of the global village, and delayed the process of mutual understanding, trust, and cooperation between countries. The worsening environment of the Confucius Institutes and Chinese language education centers and the obstruction of educational cooperation indicate that language teaching has been suspected of being an ideological tool and has been labeled with biases. Art knows no borders, and its communication sensitivity and threshold are even lower. When the surroundings are overwhelmed and chaotic, one needs to promote international cultural exchanges through art, which could be a calmer way of doing it.

(3) Integrating Chinese teaching into the art of calligraphy and painting will

Picture 2 Glimpse of exchanges between Chinese and Indian calligraphy and painting artists

also help increase students' interest in elective courses. Compared with simple language courses, calligraphy and painting art courses have more professional characteristics, and are more beneficial to students' job hunting and pursuing higher education. From the perspective of developing students' interest in Chinese, incorporating Chinese teaching into calligraphy and painting courses allows students to immerse themselves in the beauty of calligraphy and painting before they master the written language, which is more conducive to cultivate their interest in learning and exploring Chinese culture. In the classroom teaching, I also added some contents about the comparison of Chinese and Indian calligraphy and painting to promote mutual learning. I personally saw the benefit from it.

3 TWO THOUGHTS ON INTEGRATING CHINESE LANGNAGE LEARNING INTO CALLIGRAPHY AND PAINTING COURSES

(1) Not all Chinese language learning techniques need to be designed and promoted in accordance with linguistics teaching methods. Curriculum design

should distinguish students' learning interests. If some students just want to pay attention to Chinese culture from a professional point of view, or have a vague interest in Chinese culture and don't want to spend too much time, then it is better to integrate Chinese teaching into calligraphy and painting, tea culture, pottery art and other Chinese art skills. If these students are forced into the linguistics learning track, they are likely to give up learning halfway, or lose their interests very soon due to the difficulty of learning the language. On the contrary, if you integrate Chinese language teaching in the calligraphy and painting classes, one will have more interest and positive motivation. During the course, on the 5th Anniversary Celebration of the India-China Research Center, we organized the "Oriental Star-Glory" China-India Youth Calligraphy and Painting Exhibition, where students could taste Chinese tea, practice calligraphy, recite poems and participate in cultural evening event. Students and teachers who were interested in it could experience Chinese calligraphy and painting on the spot, guiding the students to feel the charm of Chinese art. It also proves that appreciating calligraphy and painting does not require proficiency in language. Since students want to learn more about the beauty of Chinese calligraphy and painting, they will take the initiative to learn and interpret relevant Chinese characters.

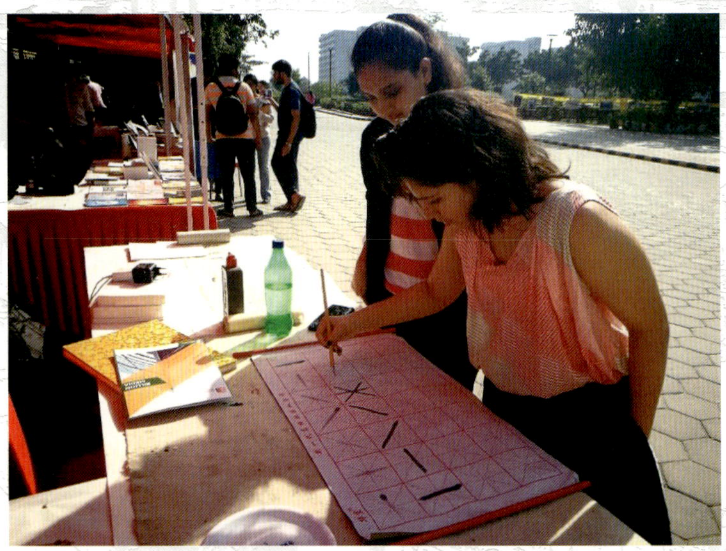

Picture 3 I can write characters—experiencing Chinese calligraphy

(2) Whether it is teaching Chinese language or calligraphy and painting, we should not just focus on output. We should have a perspective of mutual learning and comparative appreciation. In the course, more contents should be added for more comparative appreciation. The requirements for teachers should also be improved. Teachers who are equipped with comparative cultural perspectives are more suitable for teaching Chinese language or Chinese culture courses. In the process of visiting the exhibitions and listening to the lectures, we consciously guide students to conduct comparative research on topics of their interest. This is not only a test and exploration of students' learning, but also a good opportunity to deepen their understanding of Indian culture and art. Without the perspective of knowing each other, and without the awe and appreciation of the culture of the host country, it will be difficult to understand students' learning process, and it is also difficult to summarize the charm of Chinese culture.

Due to the relaxed atmosphere of classes and interesting courses, students recommended the course to their classmates, teachers and friends, and even family members. Many well-known research institutions in China and India, such as the India China Economic and Cultural Council, Institute of Chinese Studies and other institutions also invited me to arrange Chinese calligraphy and painting culture lectures. Although for myself, this art-leading language teaching method is still in trail, but with the interest of learners, good classroom interactions, a good start, and multilateral support, I will keep in mind that "the road ahead is long and has no ending, yet high and low I will search with my will unbending". I would not forget my original intention, and shall continue to explore and forge ahead on this path.

REFERENCES

[1] 孔子. 论语·雍也 [M]. 北京：中华书局，2006.
[2] 赵金铭. 对外汉语教学法回视与再认识 [J]. 世界汉语教学，2010（02）：243-254.

APPENDIX 1:

Introduction to Course Design

Course Title: Introduction to Chinese Art and Culture—Chinese Painting, Calligraphy and Chinese Characters

Class Hours: 30 class hours (15 courses, 1 lesson per week, 2 hours per lesson)

Credits: 2-4 credits

Language of Teaching: Mainly English in the early stage, gradually increasing the use of Chinese in the middle and later stages.

Course description: This course will provide basic knowledge about Chinese calligraphy and painting, and teach relevant Chinese characters, words, phrases or sentences to deepen Chinese learning in the context of art and culture. Chinese calligraphy and ink painting are closely related because they are done using similar tools and techniques. Chinese art (especially calligraphy and painting) is an art of self-cultivation and self-expression, which reflects the mentality and mood of the writer (painter). The similarities and differences between Chinese calligraphy-painting and Indian calligraphy-painting are the unique beauty of oriental calligraphy and painting.

Academic Requirements: In order to get the most benefits from the course, students should fully participate in classroom learning, and be interested and enthusiastic to learn the basic knowledge about Chinese calligraphy and painting. After the course, students should be able to:

1. Understand the basic knowledge of Chinese painting and calligraphy.

2. Learn to appreciate and experience the beauty of Chinese painting and calligraphy.

3. Master some basic Chinese characters and language skills in the field of calligraphy and painting.

Teaching Method:

The course will mainly be taught in class through art appreciation, along with calligraphy and painting practice. Students should read the teaching materials and the assigned reading materials in advance to make the discussions in class more lively and interesting.

Main Content:

In the first two weeks, the main course will be introduced, and a brief overview of the course, an introduction to prehistoric and pre-Qin Chinese art will be given.

From the third to the ninth week, according to the timeline of Chinese history and culture, the development of Chinese characters and calligraphy and painting will be introduced with timeline, including oracle and portrayal notes, seal script, official script, cursive script, regular script, running script, writing style, realism and freehand brushwork, literati painting, etc.

From the tenth week to the thirteenth week, it mainly introduces the development of modern and contemporary Chinese writing, art progress and art market, and compares it with the development of Indian painting and calligraphy and culture.

In the fourteenth and fifteenth weeks, students systematically review what they have learned and conduct assessments.

APPENDIX 2:

Curriculum Design Schedule

Schedule	Main Teaching Content	Remarks
Week 1	Introduction to Chinese art and Calligraphy and Painting culture Chinese history and culture timeline	Painting, Calligraphy, Sculpture, Pottery, Decorative arts, Architecture, Oracle, Bronze inscription, Silk painting
Week 2	Basic knowledge of calligraphy and painting (history, style, tools)	Chinese calligraphy practice, writing method, Introduction to the Four Treasures of the Study, dot-line practice. The introduction of Seal script, Official script, Regular script, Running script
Week 3	Pre-Qin, Han Dynasty	Chinese documents (Exercises: 一，二，三，十) "Chinese Art" Chapter 5
Week 4	Five Dynasties and Ten Kingdoms	The influence of Buddhism, Calligraphy and painting work "Chinese Art" Chapter 6 (Practice: 木， 土)
Week 5	Sui and Tang Dynasty	Calligraphy and painting work "Chinese Art" Chapter 7 (Practice: 水， 火)
Week 6	Practice class and Mid-term assessment	Workshop calligraphy and Painting (Practice: 中， 金， 竹)
Week 7	Song and Yuan Dynasties	"Chinese Art" Chapter 8
Week 8	Qing Dynasty	"Chinese Art" Chapters 10-11 (Practice: 日， 月， 天， 地， 人， 才)
Week 9	From the Republic of China to the founding of the People's Republic of China	(Practice: get to know 笔， 墨， 纸， 砚)

To be continued

Continued

Schedule	Main Teaching Content	Remarks
Week 10	Contemparary Art	Practice, The Four Treasures of the Study, Modern Painting
Week 11	Experiential learning	Appreciate artwork (Practice: calligraphy, Painting)
Week 12	Well-known galleries and museums	Introduce Rongbaozhai, Duoyunxuan, the Palace Museum, Chinese Museum, etc. (Practice: 荣，宝，云，馆)
Week 13	Introduction to Chinese Art Market Comparison of Chinese and Indian Art	(Practice, Antiques, Literary play, Calligraphy and Painting) Comparison of Chinese and Indian art
Week 14	Review course content	/
Week 15	Examination	/

(Translated by Chen Bingrui; Proofread by Aditya Kumar Pandey)

论印度的中文教育政策

王　娜[1]

摘要　印度的中文教育经历了20世纪30年代至60年代的大力发展时期、20世纪60年代中期至80年代中后期的发展严重受阻时期、20世纪80年代末至今的转型发展期三个阶段。该历程显示了中印关系对印度院校开展中文教育政策走向的影响和中文教育的发展规律对印度中文教育最终走向的影响。秉持开放交流合作发展的态度，才能从根本上解决当前印度中文教育面临的现实困境。

关键词　印度；中文教育；汉语；教育政策

印度院校的中文教育一直是在印度的国家教育政策框架内推行的。为了相对全面地了解印度的中文教育政策，本文拟从印度中文教育政策推行的客观状态、影响印度中文教育政策的因素、印度当下的中文教育政策及未来发展几方面进行论述。

1　印度中文教育政策推行的客观状态

中印之间的交流源远流长，古有大唐玄奘赴天竺取经，现有印度20 000多名学生赴中国留学。在整个交往过程中，语言，是不可或缺的沟通桥梁。中印具有“同质文化”特征，中文教育在印度实际经历了怎样的历程，值得回顾和梳理。

谷俊和杨文武提出，印度汉语教学经历了“兴盛时期—停止时期—深入发展时期三个阶段”。[1]102-103 阿西提出，印度中文的教育经历了早期汉语教学的繁荣时期、汉语教学的缓慢前行时期和汉语教学发展的新时期。[2]4 李哲凯提出汉语教学在印度

1　上海政法学院刑事司法学院副院长、副教授，上海政法学院检察制度比较研究中心负责人。

有三个发展阶段，即黄金时代（20 世纪 30 年代至 60 年代初）、停滞时期（20 世纪 60 年代中期至 80 年代中后期）、深化发展时期（20 世纪 80 年代末至今）。[3]16 虽然诸位研究者对不同阶段的冠名不同，但是时间阶段的界定保持一致。也就是说，印度中文教育的发展以“20 世纪 30 年代至 60 年代初”“20 世纪 60 年代中期至 80 年代中后期”“20 世纪 80 年代末至今”三个时间段划分为三个阶段，在这一点上基本达成共识。笔者认为，印度中文教育的发展经历了以下几个时期。

1.1 20 世纪 30 年代至 60 年代初：大力发展时期

第一个在印度境内开设汉语班的教育机构是印度加尔各答大学，于 1918 年开设汉语班。[3]16 20 世纪 30 年代，汉语教学随着国际著名学术大师泰戈尔开展的中印文化交流活动在印度繁荣发展。这个时期，汉语教育在印度大力发展的表现主要有：第一，由世界闻名的学术大师泰戈尔直接推动汉语教育在印度的发展；第二，设立专门的学术研究机构和教育机构，泰戈尔创办国际大学，邀请中国学者谭云山发展汉学教育。国际大学于 1921 年开设汉文系，1928 年将其改为汉语研究中心，同年，中国学者谭云山开设了第一个中文班。1937 年国际大学正式成立中国学院，谭云山担任中国学院的主任。[4]10 中国学院师资雄厚，中文资料充足。来自中国的谭云山直接负责协助印度创建中国学院，并从中国精心挑选文献，由中国捐赠给印度国际大学中国学院。

国际大学中国学院成为印度汉学研究和汉语教育的基地，辐射和带动效益明显。在 20 世纪五六十年代，印度陆续有很多大学开设汉语课程，“如阿拉哈巴大学、德里大学、旁遮普大学等相继开办了 2 年制汉语证书班。此外，外国语文学、中国语文学校的汉语教学也引人注目”[4]10。

1.2 20 世纪 60 年代中期至 80 年代中后期：发展受阻时期

20 世纪 60 年代至 80 年代中后期，受中印关系影响，在印中文教育受创，处于停滞期，其主要表现有汉语学历证书班取消、学习汉语的学生人数骤减、中文学校关闭等。就连国际大学的中国学院，因其地位和受重视程度骤降，也面临师资匮乏、教材陈旧的窘境，很多正常的教学、科研活动没有办法开展。

1.3 20世纪80年代末至今：转型发展时期

转型发展时期也经历了以下几个阶段：

第一，20世纪80年代末期至2005年，随着1979年印度时任外交部部长阿塔尔•比哈里•瓦杰帕伊访问中国，中印关系逐渐回暖；1988年和2003年，时任印度总理访问中国，印度的中文教育逐步恢复。

第二，2005年至2019年，印度中文教育快速发展时期。2005年，温家宝总理访问印度，中印两国签署了《中华人民共和国与印度人民共和国联合声明》，确立了面向和平与繁荣的战略合作伙伴关系。中印友好合作交流迈向新阶段。2010年，印度政府宣布，计划将汉语课程引入印度初级教育课程体系。印度人力资源发展部（现更名教育部）部长凯皮尔•斯柏表示："中国是我们的强大的邻国。将汉语引入印度的初级教育，可以激发孩子们对中国的兴趣，也可以加深他们对中国的了解。"[1] 2011年4月，印度中等教育中央委员会将汉语纳入中学生教学大纲，这标志着印度官方大力支持汉语教育。这个时期，印度的中文教育呈现出的特点是：官方支持与民间投入合力促成积极发展的局面。印度的私立汉语培训机构不断涌现，且已经有超过20所高校开设汉语课程或支持汉文化研究。在政策制定层面，基本上形成了汉语教育在整个教育系统的全覆盖。但是，这种可能性并没有转变成客观现实。

第三，2019年至今。2019年10月，印度政府要求所有与中国签署合作备忘录的学校和科研院所必须接受印度政府的审查。2020年，随着新冠疫情的暴发和中印边境问题的出现，印度的中文教育再度受到影响。同年，印度发布的新教育政策将汉语从政府推荐学校可开设的外语种类中删除。

1 据2010年9月15日印度《印度斯坦时报》报道。

2 印度中文教育的现实困境

2.1 日益增长的“汉语热”催生的中文教育需求与中文教育供给严重匮乏的矛盾

2.1.1 “汉语热”在印度持续增温

第一，开设汉语课程的大学越来越多。

尼赫鲁大学狄伯杰教授从事中文教学多年。他提出，印度原来只有尼赫鲁大学、德里大学等几所高校有中文系，近几年，很多学校都开设了中文系，学习汉语的人越来越多。以尼赫鲁大学中文系为例。2015 年，该系有中文教师 12 名，本科生、硕士生、博士生共 150 余名。而当年他进入尼赫鲁大学学习时，中文系每年只招收 10 名学生。[1]

根据 2018 年李哲凯的统计数据，目前印度共有 40 所大学开设了汉语教学课程。其中，尼赫鲁大学、印度国际大学和锡金大学有本科、硕士和博士专业课程，贝拿勒斯印度教大学有硕士与博士课程，杜恩大学、锡金大学、古吉拉特中央大学、贾坎德中央大学有本科和硕士专业课程，孟买大学有本科专业和业余制班文凭课程，德里大学有全日制班文凭课程和业余制班文凭课程。孟买大学今年刚开设汉语本科专业课程，其他 30 所大学只有一年、两年、三年制业余汉语文凭课程。业余制班每周有 2 ～ 3 节课 4 ～ 6 小时的课程。现在，印度不少公立和私立学校鼓励学生将汉语当成英语、本土民族语言以外的“第三语言”。印度最著名的印度管理学院（IIM）为了使学生在未来获得良好的工作机会，也开设了汉语教学课程。

第二，私立的中文培训机构发展速度快。

汉语是印度私立外语培训班中最热门的课程之一，有如下特点：首先，私立中文培训机构越来越多，在分布区域上，逐渐从大城市向小城市扩张，如纳西克、拉敦等地的大学也开设了一些汉语课程。其次，私立的中文培训机构自身不断壮大，以印华中文学校（YEH CHINA）为例，“印华中文学校是伍莎在 2010 年从新德

1 央广网，发布时间：2018-04-26。

里移居到孟买之后创办的一所私立中文培训学校。学校从开班时仅有 6 名学生，到如今已在新德里、孟买、古尔冈、浦那 4 个城市开设了 18 所分校，拥有 30 多名专职汉语教师和 1000 余名学员的汉语培训学校”[3]57。最后，私立中文培训机构针对不同的学习对象开设汉语初级口语速成和商务汉语等课程。如设立所谓的“精品小班”，汉语老师会定期到某家公司进行定制培训。印度领先企业，如信诚公司、塔塔公司、印度软件公司等，都专门聘请汉语老师为员工进行汉语培训。[3]67

上述中文教育在印度的发展充分表明“汉语热”在这个文明古国正持续增温。

2.1.2 中文教育供给严重不足

即使如前所述，印度的中文教育在不断发展，印度的中文教育始终面临着教育资源供给严重不足的问题，即师资力量匮乏、教材陈旧、教学方法落后等“三教”问题，专业教学水平亟待提升。

第一，印度师资力量匮乏表现在数量不够、来源单一。

就数量而言，以潘卡基 2013 年的统计为例，在 16 个开设汉语课程的大学中，共有 45 名汉语教师，其中本土教师 42 名，外教 2 名，外聘讲师 1 名。[5]20-23 李哲凯 2018 年的统计数据显示，印度共有 89 名印度籍汉语教师，分布在全国 40 所大学和语言培训机构。汉语教师数量最多的尼赫鲁大学共有 12 名汉语教师，印度国际大学、德里大学和都安大学分别有 7 名、6 名、6 名汉语教师，其他学校的汉语教师数量基本上为 2 ～ 3 名。[3]

就来源而言，印度的中文教师主要是本土教师，而且主要是印度自己培养的 20 世纪八九十年代毕业于印度国际大学和尼赫鲁大学的学生。如锡金大学、奥朗加巴德大学、旁遮普大学、英语与外国语大学和杜恩大学的教师都曾经在尼赫鲁大学攻读汉语硕士学位。

第二，中文教育专业水平需要在教师专业能力、教材更新、教学方法等方面提升。基于印度对教师的基本要求，印度本土教师的个人素养很高，均需要获得硕士或者博士学位。但是，他们攻读的专业方向大多是翻译或者国际关系，主攻汉语教育的寥寥无几，并且他们缺乏在中国的研修和专业培训的经历，在教学方法上比较单一，倚重于翻译法，由于不了解中国汉语教育发展的实际情况，与中文教育的发展脱节。印度中文教育使用的教材主要有两方面问题：一是从中国引进教材数量少并且内容过于陈旧，落后于时代发展；二是自编教材比较随意，没有规范性要求。[5]20-23

这种矛盾给印度的汉语教学带来了消极影响，从学生的角度来看，体现在以下几个方面：一是学生退课率比较高；二是年轻人学习汉语的热情高，但是学汉语的机会很少；三是学好汉语以后，有机会找到高薪工作，不愿意再做汉语教师，导致印度本土汉语教师的队伍无法持续壮大。

2.2 印度中文教育政策前后矛盾的态度与中文教育发展客观规律之间的矛盾

如前所述，印度的中文教育政策经历了“弱化学习汉语重要性”，改变“弱化学习汉语重要性”，防范、打压中文教育的基本历程。印度人力资源发展部前部长凯皮尔·斯柏对印度的汉语教学给予关注，他认为“中国不仅是印度的邻国，也是全球资源的最大潜在消费者之一，学习汉语也可以加深对中国的了解。学汉语要从儿童做起，这是培养孩子们对中国的兴趣的方法”[1]。这是尊重客观事实的基本判断。多年来，赴印任教的中国教师人数匮乏的主要原因是印度签证申请获准难的问题。

“汉语热”在印度是一种客观事实，是中国和中国文化逐渐被世界广泛感知、认识的征兆。一方面，伴随全球化发展的趋势，中国的产品给世界各国人民带来了美好生活；另一方面，随着美国在全世界范围内对中国启动贸易战以及一系列的遏制战略，使得很多不关注中国的人开始关注中国。世界格局在发生变化，中国的国际影响力在全世界范内正在持续增强。因此，中文的吸引力也在不断增强。

印度中文学习的市场很大，一方面，得益于20世纪80年代后期不断增强的中印交流合作关系，已经在经贸、人文等领域形成了中印互来互往的基本状态；另一方面，更多的印度人对中国感兴趣，希望了解中国，印度政府部门的工作人员也有学习中文的需求。

中文教育的发展规律决定了印度中文教育的最终走向，印度中文教育政策的制

1 http://oversea. huangiu. com/article/9CaKrnJoDyo. 检索日期：2020年10月28日。

定和执行，应当尊重中文教育发展的客观规律。

3 印度当下的中文教育政策及未来发展

3.1 印度当下中文教育政策的改变

2019年10月以来，印度的中文教育政策发生了重大改变，主要表现在两个方面。

第一，文本表述方面的改变。2020年，印度教育部正式发布的《国家教育政策2020》中，明确“除了提供高质量的印度语和英语外，还将在中学阶段（14岁至18岁的9至12年级的学生）提供韩语、日语、泰语、法语、德语、西班牙语、葡萄牙语、俄语等外语课程，让学生根据自己的兴趣和愿望了解世界文化，丰富他们的全球知识和流动性”[1]。与之前的草案相比，在外语列举中删除了“中文”。

第二，操作上的改变。2019年10月1日，印度大学教育资助委员会发布通知，要求大学在与任何中国机构合作开设课程之前，必须得到中央政府的批准。此外，教育部还计划审查包括印度理工学院在内的多所著名教育机构与中国院校签署的54份谅解备忘录。

综合上述变化，可以清晰地看到，印度此次新教育政策的文本变化，是从原来的政策鼓励走向了政策限制。

3.2 印度中文教育的未来发展

基于上述印度中文教育的现实困境和印度中文教育政策的改变，如何展望印度中文教育的未来发展是两国教育界共同关心的问题，尤其是印度学者，提出了不少建议。

潘卡基认为，印度大学汉语教学存在问题的原因包括来自大学本身的原因和来自社会的原因，大学本身的原因是“专业目标不明确，各专业培养方案特色不鲜明，导致课程设置泛化”“本土大学教师学历背景、专业背景各不相同，导致教师教学

1 4.20. In addition to high quality offerings in Indian languages and English, foreign languages, such as Korean, Japanese, Thai, French, German, Spanish, Portuguese, and Russian, will also be offered at the secondary level, for students to learn about the cultures of the world and to enrich their global knowledge and mobility according to their own interests and aspirations.(National Education Policy 2020)

水平参差不齐”“认识上的问题及资金不足等原因造成印度大学的汉语教学环境以及教学手段落后”，以及来自社会的原因。在此基础上，他提出全面启动孔子学院建设，完善大学汉语课程与教材建设、优化师资结构与教学方法等建议。[5]27-31 岳亚骏提出，印度政府应当努力解决中国教师办工作签证难的问题，给中国教师提供较好待遇，吸引中国教师来印度教学；开发独立教材，引进最新教材；创新教学方法等。[6]32-33 李哲凯提出，要加强中印文化交流，建立孔子学院，构建语言环境，优化课程和教材设置，巧用对比法，提高针对性，探寻全新的汉语授课模式，培养高水准的本土教师队伍，助力汉语教育可持续发展。[3]116-119

笔者认为，印度中文教育的未来发展关键在于尊重中文教育的客观事实和客观发展规律。政府支持两国院校积极开展交流合作，丰富在印中文教育的供给，满足印度“汉语热”的基本诉求，响应印度新教育战略的发展要求和目标，推动印度的中文教育发展是未来努力的方向。中印毗邻，这是事实；中印是快速发展的世界大国，亦是事实。两国文化在世界上均有独特的影响力，中印应携手共同迎接亚洲和东方引领的未来世界。

参考文献

[1] 谷俊，杨文武. 印度汉语教学的发展状况、问题及对策思考 [J]. 南亚研究季刊，2011（1）：102-108.

[2] 阿西. 印度汉语教学历史与现状分析 [D]. 上海：上海师范大学，2012.

[3] 李哲凯. 印度汉语教学历史与现状研究 [D]. 西安：陕西师范大学，2018.

[4] 木克士. 印度汉语教学的问题及对策研究——以 Doon 大学为例 [D]. 济南：山东师范大学，2012.

[5] 潘卡基. 印度大学汉语教学现状研究 [D]. 沈阳：沈阳师范大学，2013.

[6] 岳亚骏. 印度大学汉语教学的“三教”问题及对策研究——以德里大学初级综合课为例 [D]. 大连：辽宁师范大学，2015.

Chinese Language Policy in India

Wang Na[1]

Abstract Chinese Language Learning in India has experienced three stages: the period of great development in the 1930s to 1960s, the period of serious obstruction in the mid-1960s to late 1980s and the period of transformation and development from the late 1980s to the present. This shows that the relationship between China and India more or less affects the trend of Chinese Language learning policy in schools and colleges in India. The development of Chinese Language also determines the final trend of Chinese Language learning in India. It is necessary to follow the path of open exchange, cooperation and development, in order to fundamentally solve the current problems of Chinese education in India.

Key Words India; Chinese education; Mandarin; Education policy in India

Chinese Language learning in schools and colleges in India has been implemented within the framework of India's National Education Policy. In order to understand the Chinese language learning policy of India comprehensively, this paper discusses the objective state of the implementation of the India's Chinese language education policy, the factors that influence the Chinese language policy, the current Chinese education policy in India and its future development.

1 Deputy Dean and Associate Professor, School of Criminal Justice, Shanghai University of Political Science and Law; Principal director of SHUPL's Comparative Research Center of Procuratorial System.

1 THE OBJECTIVE STATE OF THE IMPLEMENTATION OF THE CHINESE LANGUAGE EDUCATION POLICY IN INDIA

China and India have a long history of cultural exchanges. In ancient times, Xuanzang, a great scholar and traveler during the Tang Dynasty, went to Tianzhu (ancient reference to India) for learning Buddhist scriptures. At present, more than 20,000 Indian students are studying in China. In the whole process of communication, language is an indispensable bridge of communication. China and India have the characteristics of "homogeneous culture". It is worth reviewing what Chinese education has experienced in India.

Gu Jun and Yang Wenwu put forward that the development of Chinese language teaching in India has experienced three stages: "The prosperous period, the period of interruption, and lastly the period of extensive development." [1]102-103 Ashish Ahuja proposed that Chinese language teaching in India has experienced the prosperous period of Chinese language teaching in the earlier times, the slow forward period of Chinese language teaching and the new period of the development of Chinese teaching in India.[2]4 Li Chekai summarized three stages of Chinese language teaching in India: the golden age (1930s to early 1960s), period of stagnation (mid-1960s to late 1980s), period of in-depth development (late 1980s to present).[3]16 While the researchers have different titles for different stages, the timeline of all the stages is consistent. Therefore, the development of Chinese language education in India can be divided into three stages: "1930s to early 1960s", "mid-1960s to late 1980s" and "late 1980s to the present times".

1.1 1930s TO EARLY 1960s: PERIOD OF VIGOROUS DEVELOPMENT

Calcutta University was the first institution to offter Chinese language lectures in India in 1918.[3]16 In the 1930s, Chinese studies flourished in India with the cultural exchange activities of Rabindranath Tagore, a famous international academic scholar. The main achievements of Chinese studies during this period in India are as follows: firstly, Rabindranath Tagore, directly promoted the development of Chinese studies in India; and secondly, setting up special academic research institutions and educational institutions. Tagore founded Visva-Bharati University and invited Chinese scholar Prof. Tan Yunshan to develop Chinese studies in India. The Visva-Bharati University established the Department of Chinese Language in 1921 and changed it into a Chinese language research center in 1928. In the same year, Chinese scholar Prof. Tan Yunshan started the first Chinese language class. In 1937, Visva-Bharati University formally established the Cheena Bhavan, and Prof. Tan Yunshan served as the Director of the institute.[4]10 The institute had excellent teachers and abundant materials on Chinese studies. Prof. Tan Yunshan was directly responsible for assisting India to establish Cheena Bhavan, and carefully selected study materials from China which were later donated by China to the institute in India.

Cheena Bhavan at Visva- Bharati University became the base of research and Chinese education in India. In the 1950s and 1960s, many universities in India offered Chinese language courses, "for example, the University of Allahabad, University of Delhi, and the Panjab University have successively started two-year Chinese language certificate courses. In addition, foreign language literature and Chinese language teaching in Chinese language schools are also striking".[4]10

1.2 MID-1960s TO LATE 1980s: THE PERIOD OF INTERRUPTION

From the mid-1960s to the late 1980s, influenced by the Sino-Indian relationship, Chinese studies faced stagnation. The main outcomes were the cancellation of Chinese Diploma programs, a sharp decrease in the number of students learning Chinese, the closure of Chinese schools, etc. Even Cheena Bhavan at Visva-Bharati University faced the dilemma of lacking Chinese language teachers and outdated teaching materials, and thus was unable to continue the daily teaching and scientific research activities.

1.3 LATE 1980s TO PRESENT: TRANSITION PERIOD

During the period of transformation and development, there were several stages:

First, from the late 1980s to 2005, the visit of Shri Atal Bihari Vajpayee (the former External Affairs Minister of India) to China in 1979 resulted in gradual recovery of Sino-Indian relations. In 1988 and later in 2003, the Prime Ministers of India visited China. After that, Chinese education in India gradually recovered.[1]

Second, from 2005 to 2019, there has been a rapid development in the field of Chinese studies in India. In 2005, when the former Premier Wen Jiabao visited India, the two countries signed the Joint Statement, establishing a strategic partnership for peace and prosperity. This development brought China-India friendly cooperation and exchange to a new stage. In 2010, the Indian government announced plans to introduce Chinese language curriculum into the Indian primary education curriculum system. "China is our strong neighbor," said Kapil Sibal, Minister of Human Resource Development (now renamed as Ministry of Education). The introduction of Chinese language into primary education in India can stimulate Indian students' interest in getting to know China and deepen their understanding about China. In April 2011, India's Central Board of Secondary Education (CBSE) included Chinese language in the curriculum for secondary school students, which marked a strong official support for Chinese language education in India. During this period, Chinese education in India was characterized by official support and active participation of the people to promote its positive development. Private Chinese language training institutions were emerging on a large scale. There were already more than 20 universities in India offering Chinese language courses or supporting the study of Chinese culture. At the level of policy making, there has been a primary attempt of covering Chinese language education in the school education system. However, this attempt did not turn into promising outcomes so far.

Third, from 2019 till present date. In October 2019, the Indian government required all the schools and research institutes that had signed a memorandum of cooperation with China to be reviewed. In 2020, with the outbreak of the COVID-19 pandemic and the problems along the Sino-Indian border, Chinese

1 According to the report in India's Hindustan Times, 2010-09-15.

education in India was again affected. In India's New Education Policy released in 2020, Chinese language is removed from the types of foreign languages that government-affiliated schools are suggested to offer.

2 THE REALITY OF CHINESE EDUCATION IN INDIA

2.1 THE CONTRADICTION BETWEEN THE DEMAND FOR CHINESE EDUCATION AND THE SEVERE SHORTAGE OF CHINESE EDUCATION RESOURCES

2.1.1 "MANDARIN WAVE" KEEPS INCREASING IN INDIA

First, more and more universities has been offering Chinese courses.

Prof. Deepak, Chairperson of Centre for Chinese and South East Asian Studies at Jawaharlal Nehru University, who has been teaching Chinese for many years mentioned that in India, only Jawaharlal Nehru University, University of Delhi and other few universities have Chinese language department. In recent years, many schools have established Chinese Language department. More and more people are learning Chinese language. Taking the Chinese Language department of Jawaharlal Nehru University as an example, he said that in 2015, the department had 12 Chinese language teachers, and more than 150 undergraduate, post-graduate and doctoral students. When he started learning Chinese at Jawaharlal Nehru University, the Chinese Department recruited only 10 students every year.[1]

According to Li Zhekai's in 2018 data, 40 universities in india have offered Chinese language courses. Among them, Jawaharlal Nehru University, Viswa-Bharati University and Sikkim University offer Undergraduate, Master and Doctoral programs. Banaras Hindu University has Master and Doctoral programs. Doon University, Sikkim University, Central University of Gujarat and Central

1 China National Radio, 2018-04-26 07:50。

University of Jharkhand provide Undergraduate and Master degree programs. Undergraduate and Diploma courses are available in University of Mumbai. University of Delhi has full-time and part-time Diploma courses. University of Mumbai has just started Undergraduate courses in Chinese language this year. The other 30 universities have only 1, 2 or 3 years of part-time Chinese language Diploma courses. Part-time courses offer 2-3 lectures per week, which is 4-6 hours per week. Nowadays, many public and private schools in India encourage students to use Chinese as a "third language" other than English and their native languages. India's most famous Indian Institute of Management has also offered Chinese language teaching courses considering better job opportunities for the students in the future.

Second, private Chinese language training institutions are developing rapidly.

Chinese language courses are in huge demand in private foreign language training institutes in India. In this regard, more and more private Chinese language training institutions are being established in big cities as well as in small cities. For example, universities in Nasik and Dehradun also offer Chinese language courses. Additiorally, private Chinese language training institutions are growing. Let's take Yeh China as an example, "this is a private Chinese-language training school founded by Ms. Usha who shifted from New Delhi to Mumbai in 2010. The school started with only 6 students, and now has established 18 campuses in four big cities like New Delhi, Mumbai, Gurgaon and Pune. It has more than 30 full-time Chinese language teachers and more than 1000 students."[3]57 Moreover, the training contents of private Chinese language training institutions are structured according to the needs of different learners. It includes contents from elementary Chinese speaking courses to Business Chinese courses. These institutes are the so-called "small sized, high-level content" centres. Chinese language teachers regularly provide customized language training for companies. Some of the leading companies, such as IT companies, Tata Group, software companies etc., all hire language teachers to conduct Chinese language training for their staff. [3]67

The development of Chinese language education in India mentioned above fully shows that the "Mandarin Wave" is increasing in this ancient civilization.

2.1.2 THE SHORTAGE OF CHINESE EDUCATION RESOURCES

As mentioned earlier, Chinese studies in India is constantly developing, but it has faced the problem of serious shortage of resources, such as a lack of teaching faculties, obsolete teaching materials, and outdated teaching methods. These "three teaching" problems are prominent. Also, the professional teaching level needs to be improved urgently.

First, the lack of teaching faculties in India is manifested in several aspects.

Speaking of quantity, taking Pankaj Sharma's statistics in 2013 as an example, there are 45 Chinese language teachers in 16 universities offering Chinese language courses, including 42 local teachers, 2 native teachers and 1 external lecturer.[5]20-23 According to Li's statistics in 2018, there are 89 Indian local teachers in 40 universities and language training institutions throughout the country. The largest number of Chinese language teachers is at Jawaharlal Nehru University, and there are 12 Chinese language teachers. Viswa-Bharati University, University of Delhi and Doon University each has 7, 6 and 6 Chinese language teachers respectively. For other schools, there are basically no more than 2-3 native Chinese teachers.[3]

As far as the sources are concerned, Chinese language teachers in India are mainly local teachers, and most of them are trained in India. As for their educational background, the teachers most graduated from Viswa-Bharati University and Jawaharlal Nehru University in the 1980s and 1990s. Chinese teachers in universities such as Sikkim University, University of Allahabad, Panjab University, English and Foreign Language University, and Doon University all tudied their Master degree in Chinese language at the Jawaharlal Nehru University.

Second, the level of Chinese language education needs to be improved in the aspects of teachers' professional ability, textbook updating, and teaching methods.

Based on India's basic requirements for teachers, local teachers ofter have high academic qualifications, whith either master or doctorate degrees. However, most of their majors are translation or international relations; a main focus on Chinese language education is very few. Also, due to the lack of research experience and professional training in China, they rely on. In the simple teaching methods such as translation method, and they do not understand the actual situation of the development of Chinese studies and Chinese language education. There are two main problems of teaching materials used in Chinese education in India: first, the teaching materials introduced from China are insufficient and the contents are out-dated, which lags them behind the present times; second, the self-compiled teaching materials are casual and have no normative standards.[5]20-23

This contradiction has had a negative impact on Chinese language studies in India. From the students' aspects, it shows that: first, the students' withdrawal rate is relatively high; second, young people are enthusiastic to learn Chinese, but there are few opportunities to learn the larguage; third, after learning Chinese well, there is a chance to find a well-paid job, and thus he/she will be unwilling to be a Chinese teacher. As a result, the number of local Chinese language teachers in India could not continue to grow.

2.2 CONTRADICTIONS BETWEEN THE INCONSISTENT ATTITUDE OF CHINESE LANGUAGE EDUCATION POLICY IN INDIA AND THE DEVELOPMENT OF CHINESE LANGUAGE EDUCATION

As mentioned earlier, India's Chinese language education policy has experienced the basic course of "weakening the importance of learning Chinese" — a change in "weakening the importance of learning Chinese" preventing and suppressing Chinese language education. "China is not only a neighbor of India, but also one of the world's largest potential consumers of resources. Learning Chinese can also deepen understanding of China," said Kapil Sibal, the former Union Minister of Human Resources Development. Learning Chinese should start with children, which is a way to cultivate their interest in China.[1] This is the basic judgment of respecting objective facts. For many years, the shortage of Chinese teachers to teach in India is mainly due to the difficulty of obtaining visas.

"Mandarin Wave" is an objective fact in India, and it is a sign that Chinese language and Chinese culture are widely perceived and recognized in the world. On the one hand, with the trend of globalization, Chinese products have brought a good life to people all over the world. On the other hand, with the United States launching a trade war against China and a series of containment strategies, many people who did not show interest in China earlier, have started paying attention to China now. The world is changing, and China's international influence is growing around the world. Therefore, the craze for Chinese language is also increasing.

Thanks to the growing exchanges and cooperation between China and India in the late 1980s, India has formed a basic state of exchange between China and India in economy, trade, humanities and so on. Moreover, more Indians are interested in China and want to know more about the country.

The development of Chinese language education determines the trend of Chinese language education in India. The formulation and implementation of Chinese language policy in India should respect the objective development of Chinese language education.

3 CURRENT CHINESE LANGUAGE EDUCATION POLICY AND FUTURE DEVELOPMENT IN INDIA

3.1 CHANGES IN CURRENT CHINESE LANGUAGE EDUCATION POLICY IN INDIA

Since October 2019, India's Chinese education policy has changed significantly, mainly from two aspects.

1 http://oversea. huangiu. com/article/9Ca Krn JoDyo, accessed: 2020-10-28.

First, changes in documentation. In 2020, the *National Education Policy 2020*, officially released by the India's Ministry of Education, made it clear that "in addition to providing high-quality Hindi and English, foreign language courses such as Korean, Japanese, Thai, French, German, Spanish, Portuguese and Russian will be offered at the secondary level (students aged 14 to 18 years in grades 9 to 12) to enable students to learn about the world culture and enrich their global knowledge and mobility in accordance with their interests and aspirations".[1] Compared with the previous policy, the word "Chinese" was deleted in the foreign language options.

Second, changes in operations. On October 1, 2019, India's University Grants Commission issued a notice requiring universities to obtain approval from the central government before offering courses in cooperation with any Chinese institution. In addition, the Ministry of Education planned to review 54 memorandums of understanding signed between a number of prominent educational institutions and Chinese institutions, including the Indian Institute of Technology.

Synthesizing the above changes, it can be clearly seen a change in India's new education policy, from the original policy support to policy restriction.

3.2 FUTURE DEVELOPMENT OF CHINESE LANGUAGE EDUCATION IN INDIA

Based on the practical difficulties of India's Chinese language education and the change India's Chinese education policy, how to look forward to the future development of Chinese language education in India is the common concern in the academic circles of the two countries, especially among the Indian scholars, and many suggestions have been brought up.

According to Pankaj Sharma, the problems in Chinese language teaching in Indian universities are caused in the universities themselves and the society.

1 4.20. In addition to high quality offerings in Indian languages and English, foreign languages, such as Korean, Japanese, Thai, French, German, Spanish, Portuguese, and Russian, will also be offered at the secondary level, for students to learn about the cultures of the world and to enrich their global knowledge and mobility according to their own interests and aspirations. (National Education Policy 2020)

As for the universities, "the professional objectives and the characteristics of the training programs are not clear, which leads to the generalization of the curriculum", "Different academic and professional background of local teachers lead to unevenness in their teaching level", "The problem of understanding and the lack of funds lead to the outdated teaching environment and teaching methods of Chinese language studies in Indian universities" and reasons from the society. On this basis, he put forward suggestions on constructing Confucius Institutes in an all-round way, perfecting the construction of Chinese language curriculum and teaching materials in universities, and optimizing the structure and teaching methods of teachers.[5]27-31 Yue Yajun proposed that the Indian government should strive to solve the problem of getting work visas for Chinese teachers, provide better payment and environment for Chinese teachers to attract them to teach in India, develop independent teaching materials, introduce the latest teaching materials, and innovate teaching methods.[32-33] Li proposed to strengthen cultural exchanges between China and India, establish Confucius Institutes, construct better language learning environment, optimize curriculum and teaching materials, use comparative methods skillfully, improve pertinence, explore a new Chinese teaching model, train local teachers to improve their teaching skills, and promote sustainable development of Chinese language education.[3]116-119 The author believes that the key to the future development of Chinese language studies in India lies in respecting the objective facts and progress of Chinese language education. The active communication and cooperation between colleges and universities in the two countries should be supported and the supply of Chinese Language studies in India should be enriched. It is the fact that China and India are adjacent neighbors. Both countries are rapidly developing to be world powers. The two countries have unique influences in the world. China and India should join hands to meet the future world led by Asia and the East Asia.

(Translated by Sun Meixing; Proofread by Bhavana Kumari)

REFERENCES

[1] 谷俊，杨文武. 印度汉语教学的发展状况、问题及对策思考 [J]. 南亚研究季刊，2011（1）：102-108.

[2] 阿西. 印度汉语教学历史与现状分析 [D]. 上海：上海师范大学，2012.

[3] 李哲凯. 印度汉语教学历史与现状研究 [D]. 西安：陕西师范大学，2018.

[4] 木克士. 印度汉语教学的问题及对策研究——以 Doon 大学为例 [D]. 济南：山东师范大学，2012.

[5] 潘卡基. 印度大学汉语教学现状研究 [D]. 沈阳：沈阳师范大学，2013.

[6] 岳亚骏. 印度大学汉语教学的“三教”问题及对策研究——以德里大学初级综合课为例 [D]. 大连：辽宁师范大学，2015.

Part 5

第五部分 特辑

Special

Youth: The New Force of China-India People-to-People and Cultural Exchange Mechanism China and India have the largest similarities than any other country in the world: The Power of Chindia

Himadrish Suwan[1]

2020 marks the 70th anniversary of the establishment of diplomatic ties between China and India. Guided by the important consensus reached by our two leaders, China-India relations have achieved stable and sound development and tapped deeper into the potentials for over decades of bilateral cooperation. Since time immemorial, our area has been an inspiration for scientific, spiritual, and cultural progress for the whole world. Since Emperor Ashoka and Tang Dynasty, Hiuen Tsang and Kasyapa Matang, Buddha and Confucius have nurtured this region like the Yangtze and the Ganges rivers. In a way, we were magnets to attract the finest minds and scholars of the world. In times of social divide, where countries are battling for front row seats to the show, we tend to lose sight of the larger picture of mutual correlation. In reality, our origins are all the same and we come up from the same lineage of humans, thus making us closer to each other and much more psychologically connected than we care to admit. China and India, on these very lines, share much of their background. Not only because they are geographical neighbors and are so closely linked by international borders, but because what today stands as two different nations came from the same bare beginnings.

I have had a deep interest in Chinese civilization since I was a student. China's

1 Chairman, Confederation of Young Leaders (CYL).

spectacular history deeply appealed to me and when I was a student researching Asia, I had a dream to visit China in person. China is the country with the largest population in the world. India is the country with the largest youth population. In history, the youth were the driving force to enhance cultural exchanges between China and India along the ancient Silk Road. The eminent Chinese monk Xuanzang, at the age of 27, came to India to study the Buddhist Sutra. Dr. Dwarkanath Kotnis, a young Indian doctor went to China to fight together with the Chinese people during the World War Ⅱ. In contemporary China, people appreciate Indians. Once again, in the 21st century, it is the youth destined to shape the vision for a shared future between China and India.

Many visitors from China had written about India in ancient times that have been adopted in their art, technology, and philosophy. Xuanzang's visit to Ancient India is of importance in the history of China-India relations. He was indeed an ancient ambassador of peace between China and India. His praise of Harshavardhana and the Indian people in his travel accounts deeply influenced Chinese pilgrims. India is much indebted to this Chinese traveler for the valuable accounts he left behind with many details of political, religious, economic, and social conditions of those days.

Last August, in Beijing, I boarded a taxi to the airport. The driver asked me: "Where are you from?" I said: "India."—He started playing with his mobile phone, and a familiar song grabbed my attention. Most of the older Chinese generation is familiar with this Raj Kapoor's 1951 popular Indian song called "Awaara hoon" (a wanderer but still happy even though nobody is waiting for me). By a strange coincidence, the driver started singing another popular Indian song, "Aankhen khuli ho ya ho band" (whether eyes are open or closed, I just see her whom I love) from an Indian movie released in 2000. Indian cinema resonates with the Chinese audience because they connect emotionally with the common. Indian actor Aamir Khan is very popular in China right now. His movie *Dangal, the Secret Superstar* got a substantial box office in China. Chinese movie stars such as Jackie Chan are household names in India. Hopefully, the two great nations can leverage the power of music, cinema, and dance to boost their cooperation.

Coming to some societal and family dynamics, it has always been observed that China and India follow a very similar structure of placing domestic bliss above ambition and mostly consist of deeply connected families with solid foundations. Chinese and Indian society are highly complementary, interwoven and interdependent; they are just on different timelines. Listing out the similarities, Chinese and Indian cultures are the most ancient living cultures in the world and both of them are more family oriented as compared to western societies. Social functioning is also starkly equivalent in regards to education, where both countries place an extremely high priority on their students' seriously investing time in schools, colleges, and universities. Attitudes toward teachers, education, and child upbringing are the same. Philosophical and religious ideas match with each other. Beliefs in traditional medicine have been shared. Music is based on pentatonic scales in both countries.

The most important indicator of twinning cultures lies in the way they treat their guests. Both nations have a rich tradition of making their visitors feel at home and make them enjoy themselves to the fullest, exposing them to everything their country has to offer, from rich cultural heritage to historical monuments. This is most visible in the adapted cuisine of India, which shows deep influences from Chinese flavors. On any given day in an Indian metropolis, foodies are spoiled with choices. There's now Peruvian cuisine, French patisserie, Mexican tacos, and more. But all these choices haven't taken away the crowds inside the scores of Chinese restaurants that dot every city, with names like China Bowl, China Pearl, Chung Wah, Wangs, or Zhangs. Although India has tweaked the basics to her needs and tastes, the subtle clues of nostalgia remain. Both countries have several dialects and languages in them unlike the stereotype that Indians speak Hindi and Chinese Mandarin. There is a lot of diversity that exists in both countries. The older generations in both societies are more traditional and orthodox while their younger generation is more accepting and open to new ideas.

Perhaps, China has emerged as a new yoga superpower. It is estimated that there are millions of practitioners in China and over thousands of yoga schools &

trainers nationwide. The interactive history that has been shared between China and India for a long time makes it easy for yoga to be understood by China's vast population. Just like other countries, China has also been influenced by yoga, the physical and spiritual practice originated in ancient India. The Yunnan Minzu University of China became the first university out of India to award a Master's degree in yoga and I was awestruck to observe the admiration for yoga during my visit to the university.

A strong India is the best thing that could happen to a rising China and vice versa. India and China are two of the largest and fastest-growing economies of the world. India in the global playground has a rich prologue to speak of. It has emerged from tumultuous times to become a country not to be trifled with. Charting a history that is sporadically dotted with conquests, it is no surprise that India has established a stronghold in every sphere of diplomatic capabilities today. From being the pioneers in medical sciences to producing world-renowned sports persons, scholars, scientists, and doctors, India occupies one of the highest pedestals in the global framework.

On the other hand, the contribution of export-import of linguistic cooperation has been paramount in enhancing communication and increased people-to-people exchanges. Language is the spirit of civilization, just like the soul of a country. The Chinese language has the largest chunk of people consummating it as a mother tongue. Chinese is not just a popular language; it is also a scientific language. Modern Chinese people can understand theories written 2000 years ago by Confucius; Chinese students can read poems written by Qu Yuan. In sharp contrast readers in modern days have difficulty in understanding Shakespeare's masterpieces. Just like the undiscovered charm of its language; China has a great amount of undiscovered literature. It is monumental to read about them, not just to understand the culture but also to dissolve the misnomers.

Rabindranath Tagore, the first Asian recipient of the Nobel Prize in literature visited China in 1924 and was adorned with the name of "Zhu Zhendan". During his stint, he said, "I do not know why coming to China seems to me like returning to my native soil. I always feel that India has been one of China's extremely close relatives, and China and India have been enjoying time-honored and affectionate brotherhood." Certainly, there's no fundamental contradiction between the two countries whose great civilizations stress on the concept of harmonious development in the spirit of "vasudhaiva kutumbakam" (the world is one family) and "*shijie datong*" (world in grand harmony).

Since the ice-breaking visit of Indian former Prime Minister Rajiv Gandhi in 1988 and Chinese former Premier Wen Jiabao's visit to India in 2005, China-India cooperation in the areas of economy, soft diplomacy and politics significantly expanded. However, the trio of socio-cultural-educational and people-to-people understanding between China and India is still stagnating as a result of an absence of language familiarity. Language promotion and development at the non-governmental level must be enhanced to build a great wall of people-to-people cooperation. Hindi and Chinese scholars have put forth significant attempts; however, it is challenging for Chinese and Indian academic institutions to expand the bandwidth, mainly due to the substantial deficiency of established language experts. The absence of in-depth mutual understanding in the areas of linguistic cooperation is one of the key factors affecting the potential of our bilateral relations.

It would be wise to recall the comments of India's former Minister for External Affairs, Late Smt.Sushma Swaraj on the contribution of Hindi in the India-China friendship—"When two friends sit together, what do they want? They want to talk their hearts out to each other, share what they feel. And for that, we need a language. I should be able to understand Chinese when you speak, and you should be able to understand Hindi when I talk," adding that an interpreter sitting between two friends may not be able to convey the feelings. It is paramount for the Chinese and Indian government to heed substantial attention to the export-import of linguistic cooperation to supplement the dragon and elephant to dance together.

The West tends to have the misinterpretation over the Asian century as it believes it would be a China-centered century. But late Chinese paramount leader Deng Xiaoping articulated long ago that no genuine Asian century would come without the development of China, India and other regional developing countries. China and India share similar historical and political experiences from the early 19th century. China has been calling for "peaceful development" for decades, and India has been a champion of the Non-Aligned Movement, a group of countries that are not aligned with or against any major power bloc. The past 70 years have proved that friendly cooperation, which has dominated most of the time, is the general trend and the mainstream, far more prominent than differences, confrontations and frictions.

The collective vision and leadership of our leaders have laid the strong foundation of building upon the bilateral ties of our two great nations. Both our leaders had promised each other and our people to build a great wall of amity: full of hope, trust and progress of diverse and cutting-edge cooperation, and joint endeavors & shared successes. Such a promise flows as much from the natural affinity and friendship that has linked us for centuries as it does from the compelling win-win case for engagement in almost all spheres. Young people from both nations are going to be the strong pillars on which the success of this initiative would stand.

Over the past years, the two sides have set up a lot of interaction platforms for youth between our two countries. Every year the two sides organize two-way exchanges of socio-cultural-educational delegation. Members of the delegation are young men and women drawn from diverse institutions and include doctors, engineers, management graduates, business people, entrepreneurs, journalists, musicians, and students. The role of youth in fostering development partnership between China and India is of immense and utmost importance as it is only when the youth of the two nations ideate; the outlook and aspiration alter. But these are not enough. We need more concrete measures to enhance youth-to-youth cooperation between China and India including expanding the scope of exchanges amongst the youth with a focus on specific groups such as interaction with movies, education, press and sports.

Concerning cooperation and partnership, the 4 "E"s would have the potential to contribute effectively to the people-to-people ties between both our nations.

(1) **Education.** This would involve active partnership and cooperation between young students, faculties, academia, and institutions in the fields of academic research, culture, arts, language, social sciences, etc. Organizing digital training programs, skill development workshops, webinars, creative and essay writing contests, social media campaigns. The objective under this pillar should be to bring young people from both nations closer through educational partnerships and cooperation. The two sides can shortlist resource persons for carrying out joint training programs and keep on expanding the list of trainers as the initiative progresses. The resource persons/trainers can be nationals of both our countries and should ideally be people who are practitioners and have had a considerable amount of professional success in their respective fields.

(2) **Entrepreneurship.** Both India and China have been giving immense attention to boost the "Start-up Ecosystem" in our countries because we have a whole new generation of entrepreneurs emerging in the region. This start-up revolution is being led by young people who are breaking away from the traditional notions of jobs, careers, and employment in general. China has one of the finest start-up ecosystems in the world and with a population as large as India, entrepreneurship is extremely vital to us here. Both Indian and Chinese entrepreneurs are full of optimism about the future trajectory of our countries. Under the larger spectrum, a dedicated Youth Entrepreneurship platform could be established which shall aim to enhance the communication, increase mutual understanding, and deepen business cooperation among the youth entrepreneurs of both India and China. Young entrepreneurs face several challenges in their journey to launch high-impact and high-growth enterprises. Yet when they succeed, entrepreneurs can act as powerful agents of change — reducing inefficiencies, creating jobs, and boosting economic development. Entrepreneurship is not only about taking companies public but a lot of entrepreneurial activity in the two countries is in the exercise of getting things done more efficiently and creatively. And we as growing nations should try

our best to give them all the help and support and make things easy for them in the market.

(3) **Entertainment.** Entertainment can open the windows of our cultures to each other's youth. Be it through music, dance, movies, yoga, tai chi, food; entertainment has the potential to bridge physical distances and bring people closer through joint digital movie screenings, music performances, art workshops, yoga, and tai chi sessions, and even talent shows wherein young amateur artists from India and China converge together to showcase their talents in performing arts.

(4) **Exchanges.** There is much to explore and know about each other's nations for young impressionable minds in both countries and people-to-people exchanges and connection is the bedrock of strong, vibrant bilateral relationships. It is the young people on both sides that would lead both India and China to have deeper and closer cooperation in the years to come as these young people occupy positions of eminence in sectors like Business, Academia, Research, Culture, and Scientific communities. Informal groups on the lines of "Friends in India" / "Friends in China" can be established with a dedicated section where young Indian and Chinese nationals could reach out to each other for any assistance while traveling to each other's country. Instead of just relying on travel portals and online forums while traveling to either country for information regarding places to visit, food, hotels / homestays, camping, safety, and security, etc., young people from both nations can then make real connections with each other and might even find travel companions/hosts. This suggestion would have the potential to contribute effectively to the people-to-people ties between both our nations.

Mahatma Gandhi once said that an ounce of practice is worth a thousand words. We must seize the opportunities, take concrete actions, and march together on the path of pursuing the Chinese dream and building a new India. As the only two large developing countries with a population over one billion, China and India have the largest similarities than any other country in the world. All these dimensions help us understand the importance of letting go of our differences and work in collaboration towards building the 21st century as Asia's century.

青年人：中印人文交流机制的新生力量
中印力量所在：极大的共性

苏万焕[1]

2020 年是中印建交 70 周年。几十年来，在两国领导人达成的重要共识指引下，中印关系实现了稳定健康发展，双边合作潜力也在不断挖掘。自古以来，中印一直是全世界科学、宗教和文化发展进步的灵感源泉。从阿育王时代到唐朝，玄奘、迦叶摩腾（Kasyapa Matang）、佛陀、孔子的思想滋养了长江流域和恒河流域。在某种程度上，我们是磁铁，吸引着世界上最优秀的思想和学者。在社会分化的时代，各国纷争，往往忽略了相互合作能够带来更光明的前景。事实上，我们有着同样的起源、相同的血统，这使得我们彼此的联系更加紧密，情感上的联系也比我们愿意承认的要密切得多。从这些方面来说，中印有很多共同的背景，不仅仅是因为两国从地理上来说是邻居，被国界紧密联系在一起，还因为在今天，作为两个不同的国家，我们有着相同的起源。

我从学生时代就对中华文明有着浓厚的兴趣。中国波澜壮阔的历史深深吸引了我，当我还是一名致力亚洲研究的学生时，我就梦想亲自访问中国。中国是世界上人口最多的国家，而印度是青年人口最多的国家。历史上，青年是推动两国沿古丝绸之路文化交流的驱动力量。中国高僧玄奘 27 岁时来到印度学习佛经；第二次世界大战期间，年轻的印度医生柯棣华来到中国与中国人民一起战斗。当代中国人也对印度人赞赏有加。21 世纪，打造中印共同未来的美好愿景注定还要靠年轻人。

许多访印的中国人写过关于古代印度的文章，并将这些内容融入艺术、技术和哲学中。玄奘的古印度之行在中印关系史上具有重要意义，是古代当之无愧的中印和平大使。他在旅行记录中对跋摩王朝（Harshavardhana）和印度人民的赞美深深

1　印度青年领袖联合会主席。

影响了中国旅行者。印度非常感谢这位中国旅行者留下的关于当时政治、宗教、经济和社会状况的宝贵详细记录。

2020年8月在北京，我坐在一辆去机场的出租车上。司机问我："你来自哪里？"我说："印度。"他开始拿出手机，这时，熟悉的歌声吸引了我的注意。年龄略长的中国人都熟悉拉兹·卡普尔创作于1951年的流行印度歌曲"Awaara hoon"（《拉兹之歌》，"一个流浪者，尽管没有人在等我，但仍然很快乐"）。巧合的是，司机开始唱另一首印度流行歌曲："Aankhen khuli ho ya ho band..."（无论眼睛张开还是闭上，我都会梦见我的所爱……），这首歌是2000年上映的一部印度电影的插曲。印度电影往往能够引起中国观众的共鸣，因为它们在情感上与普通人息息相通。印度演员阿米尔·汗现在在中国很受欢迎。他的电影《摔跤吧！爸爸》和《神秘巨星》在中国获得了可观的票房。成龙等中国电影明星在印度也是家喻户晓。希望这两个伟大的国家能够借助音乐、电影和舞蹈的力量来促进合作。

谈到社会和家庭动力学，不难发现，中印两国人民的家庭观念都非常重，都秉持家庭幸福胜于雄心壮志，而且两国社会通常由基础牢固、关系紧密的家庭单位构成。中印之间是高度互补、交织、相互依存的，只是在不同的时间线上而已。两国的共性有许多，中印文化都是世界上现存最古老的文化，家庭观念重，这与西方社会不同；在教育方面，社会职能也不尽相同，都重视学生在学校的时光，都尊师重教，注重孩子的成长；哲学思想和宗教思想相互吻合，对传统医学有着共同的信仰；另外，两国的音乐都以五声音阶为基础。

中印文化最重要的共通点在于二者的待客之道。两国的待客传统是让宾客宾至如归，尽一切可能向宾客介绍丰富的文化遗产和历史遗迹。这在印度菜肴口味改进中体现得最为明显，印度菜肴深受中国风味的影响。秘鲁美食、法式糕点、墨西哥玉米卷……每一天，在印度的大都市，琳琅满目的美食让你无从下手。但这并不影响遍布各个城市的中餐馆顾客络绎不绝，例如中国碗（China Bowl）、龙凤大酒楼（China Pearl）、中华（Chung Wah）、王氏中餐（Wangs）或张氏中餐（Zhangs）。尽管印度人根据自己的需求和口味调整了菜肴中的基本元素，但原版菜肴的细微痕迹依然存在。中印两国都有多种方言和语言，并不是印度人只说印地语，中国人只说普通话。两国都高度多样化，老一辈更传统、正统，而年轻一代更能接受并愿意拥抱新思想。

也许，中国已经成为一个新的瑜伽超级大国。据估计，中国有数百万人练习瑜伽，涌现出成千上万的瑜伽学校和瑜伽教练。在中印两国的长期互动下，瑜伽被中国广大民众接受。就像其他国家一样，中国也受到瑜伽的影响，瑜伽起源于古印度，是一项关于身体和精神的练习。云南民族大学是第一所印度以外可授瑜伽硕士学位的大学，在我访问该大学期间，人们对瑜伽的喜爱，让我深感震惊。

对于正在崛起的中国来说，印度的强大应该是一件好事，反之亦然。两国都是世界上最大和增长最快的经济体。全球舞台上的印度有着良好的开端。它已经从动荡的时代走出来，成为一个不可轻视的国家。历史上，印度偶尔被征服，但如今已在外交的各个领域都占据了重要位置，这不足为奇。从成为医学科学的先驱到培养出众多世界著名的运动员、学者、科学家和医生，印度在全球体系中占据着最高的地位之一。

另一方面，语言的双向合作对加强沟通和增进人文交流至关重要。语言是文明的灵魂，也是一个国家的灵魂。以汉语为母语的人数最多，汉语不仅仅是一种流行的语言，它也是一种科学的语言。现代中国人可以理解2000多年前孔子写的理论，中国学生可以读屈原写的诗。与之形成鲜明对比的是，现代读者很难理解莎士比亚的杰作。就像莎士比亚的语言有未被发现的魅力，在中国还有大量未被发现的文献。阅读这些文献至关重要，不仅是为了了解文化，也是为了消除误用情况。

罗宾德拉纳特·泰戈尔是第一位获得诺贝尔文学奖的亚洲人，他于1924年访问中国，并获赠中文名字“竺震旦”。待在中国的那段时间，他说：“我不知道为什么来到中国对我来说就像回到了我的祖国。总觉得印度一直是中国极其亲密的亲人之一，中印两国一直有着悠久而深厚的兄弟情谊。”当然，两国之间并不存在根本矛盾，两个伟大的文明都强调“天下一家”和“世界大同”的和谐发展理念。

自1988年印度前总理拉吉夫·甘地首次正式访华和2005年中国时任国务院总

理温家宝访印以来，中印在经济、软外交和政治领域的合作显著扩大。然而，由于缺乏对彼此语言的熟悉，中印在社会文化教育和人与人之间的了解方面的合作仍然停滞不前。必须加强非政府层面的语言推广和发展，以建造人民之间合作的长城。印地语和汉语学者对此进行了大量尝试，然而，对于中印学术机构来说，扩展语言合作的“带宽”具有挑战性，这主要是由于现有语言专家的严重不足。在语言合作领域缺乏深入的相互了解是影响两国双边关系潜力的关键因素之一。

这里有必要回顾已故印度外交部前部长苏什玛·斯瓦拉吉针对印地语对两国友谊的贡献所做出的评论——“当两个朋友坐在一起时，他们想要什么？他们想倾诉彼此的心声，分享彼此的感受。为此，我们需要一种语言。你说中文的时候我应该能听懂，我说印地语的时候你也应该能听懂。”她补充道，坐在两个朋友之间的翻译可能无法传达这种感受。对于两国政府来说，重视语言双向合作，为龙象共舞保驾护航至关重要。

西方有对亚洲世纪误解的倾向，认为这将是一个以中国为中心的世纪。但已故中国领导人邓小平很早以前就明确表示，在亚洲，没有中国、印度等发展中国家的发展，就不会有真正的亚洲世纪。中国和印度从19世纪初就有相似的历史和政治实践。几十年来，中国一直呼吁“和平发展”，印度也一直是不结盟运动的倡导者，不结盟运动是一个不结盟、不对抗的国际组织。70年来的实践证明，与分歧、对抗、摩擦相比，长期以来的友好合作才是大势所趋，是主流。

双方领导人的远见卓识和领导才能为建立两个伟大国家的双边关系奠定了坚实的基础。两国领导人向彼此以及两国人民做出承诺，建造一座友谊的长城：充满希望、信任，推进多样、前沿合作，携手努力，共享成功。这种承诺不仅源于两国在几乎所有领域的合作中令人信服的双赢案例，也源于几个世纪以来将双方联系在一起的天然亲和力和友谊。两国的青年将成为实现这一诺言的中流砥柱。

多年来，双方为两国青年搭建了许多互动平台，每年都组织双向交流的社会文化教育代表团。代表团成员来自不同机构的年轻人，包括医生、工程师、管理专业毕业生、商人、企业家、记者、音乐家和学生。青年对推动中印发展伙伴关系能够发挥巨大的、举足轻重的作用，因为只有两国青年积极构想，前景才能得到改变。但这些还不够。我们需要更具体的措施来加强中印青年之间的合作，包括扩大青年之间的交流范围，重点关注特定领域，如电影、教育、新闻和体育方面的互动。

关于合作和伙伴关系，从以下四个方面努力可以对加强两国人民的联系做出积极贡献。

（1）教育。这将涉及青年学生、教师、学术界与学术研究、文化、艺术、语言、社会科学等领域的机构之间的积极伙伴关系和合作。组织数字化培训项目、技能发展研讨会、网络研讨会、创意和文章写作竞赛、社交媒体活动。这旨在通过建立教育伙伴关系和合作，拉近两国青年之间的距离。双方可以列出开展联合培训项目的培训人员名单，并随着项目的进展不断扩大名单。培训人员可以是两国的国民，最好是在各自领域有大量专业成就的从业人员。

（2）创业精神。印度和中国都非常重视优化“创业生态系统”，涌现出新一代的企业家。这场创业革命是由年轻人领导的，总体来说，他们正在打破对于工作、职业和就业的传统观念。中国拥有世界上最好的创业生态系统之一，拥有与印度一样多的人口，创业精神对中国来说至关重要。中印企业家都对两国的未来发展非常乐观。在更大的范围内，可以建立一个专门的青年创业平台，加强中印青年企业家之间的沟通，增进相互理解，深化商业合作。年轻企业家在创办影响力高、发展快速的企业的过程中面临一些挑战。然而，他们一旦成功，就会成为变革的强大推动者——提高效率，创造就业机会，促进经济发展。创业不仅仅是让公司上市，两国的许多创业活动都是为了更高效、更有创造性地完成工作。作为发展中国家，我们应该尽可能给予青年创业者所有的帮助和支持，让他们在市场上更容易地开展活动。

（3）文娱活动。文娱活动可以为两国青年打开文化的窗户。无论是音乐、舞蹈、电影、瑜伽、太极还是美食，文娱活动有潜力通过各种方式缩短物理距离，拉近人民之间的距离。例如通过联合数字电影放映、音乐表演、艺术工作坊、瑜伽和太极课程，甚至是两国年轻业余艺术家汇聚一堂展示、表演艺术才华的才艺表演活动。

（4）交流。对于易受外界影响的年轻人来说，中印都有许多值得探索和了解的地方。人文交流和联系为强大、充满活力的双边关系打下了基础。两国的年轻人将引领中印在未来几年进行更深入、更密切的合作，因为这些年轻人在商业、学术、研究、文化和科学等领域所起的作用越来越大。可以建立诸如“印度朋友”（Friends in India）或“中国朋友”（Friends in China）之类的非正式团体，设立专门的部门，让两国青年在前往对方国家旅游时提供帮助。这样，两国年轻人可以借此建立真正的联系，甚至可以找到旅行伙伴或东道主，而不是仅仅依靠旅游门户网站和在线论坛来获取关于旅游地点、食物、酒店 / 家庭住宿、露营、安全和安保等信息。这个建议有可能为加强两国人民的联系做出积极贡献。

圣雄甘地曾经说过，细微的实际行动抵过千言万语。我们必须抓住机遇，采取实际行动，在追求中国梦和建设新印度的道路上携手前进。作为仅有的两个人口超过 10 亿的发展中大国，中印两国有着最大的共性。所有这些都有助于双方明白，放下分歧、携手合作，将 21 世纪建设为亚洲世纪的重要性。

（孙美幸 / 翻译；汪美岑 / 校对）

后　记

这本《汉语心桥——汉语在印度的传播与发展》，汇集了中印两国对印汉语教学领域的专家、学者和教育工作者一线汉语教学和研究的宝贵经验，回顾和总结了印度汉语教学的发展历程及对两国人文交流的关键作用，较为全面地反映了新世纪在中印两国人文交流大发展的背景下，在印汉语教育的发展现状。本书的编纂旨在梳理在印汉语教育的发展脉络，探讨在印汉语教学的理论和方法，通过汇集和整理来自中印两国汉语教育工作者的第一手资料，为在印从事汉语教学的两国教育工作者提供最真实和具有操作性的汉语教育教学理论和实践指导。

语言是人们相互沟通的桥梁，是了解一个国家最好的钥匙。历史上，中印沿着古老的丝绸之路进行了深度的文明交流。唐代高僧玄奘西行求法，精通梵文，回国后翻译了 77 部佛经，为佛教在中国的传播做出了巨大贡献。他利用语言优势走遍印度，深谙印度的风土人情和传统文化，撰写了著名的《大唐西域记》，成为人们了解印度历史的重要文献；印度高僧菩提达摩东渡中国，熟悉汉语，在少林寺创立禅宗一派，深深影响了之后千百年的中国佛教和中国文化。正是语言的交流，极大地促进了中印两国的人文交往，加深了两国人民的友谊。泰戈尔、谭云山携手创办国际大学中国学院，培养了一批又一批知华友华的印度青年，他们学成后奔赴印度各地，把中印友好的种子撒遍印度各个角落。徐梵澄侨居印度 30 余载，在繁重的教学工作之余，著书立说并从事翻译工作，把中国和中华文化介绍给印度，把印度古代吠陀经典《五十奥义书》由梵文译成中文。柯棣华医生不顾个人安危，在中国人民遭受日本侵略蹂躏的关键时刻毅然决然奔赴中国，用流利的汉语与病患交流，凭借高超医术挽救了无数生命，他却积劳成疾，英年早逝。正是无数先辈的呕心沥血为中印友好奠定了坚实的基础，这不仅是两国人民的共同财富，也是我们在面对任何困难时仍保持信心的不竭动力。

本书从征稿、审核、翻译，到校对、编排，历时数月，最终得以成功出版，离不开各界人士的大力支持，在此谨致以深切的谢意。中国驻印度大使孙卫东先生历来高度重视中印人文交流工作，特别是中印语言教育交流合作，拨冗为本书作序，并大力支持本书的出版工作。郑州大学国际交流与合作处、南亚研究中心研究员孙鹏先生，曾担任印度第一所孔子学院——韦洛尔科技大学孔子学院中方院长8年，在任期间积极推动在印汉语教学和汉语考试点的建设工作，主持中国中外语言交流合作中心主干教材《汉语乐园》《快乐汉语》《跟我学汉语》泰米尔语版的翻译工作，积累了丰富的对印汉语教学经验，为本书撰文一篇，分享宝贵经验。清华大学国际关系研究院南亚研究中心特聘研究员包吉氢博士，先后在巴基斯坦和印度生活多年，访问了驻在国的各类学校并广泛与师生交流，组织过学生赴华夏令营及教师赴华汉语培训。她撰写的《百年未有之变局下的在印汉语教学——困境与破局》一文，在百年变局和新冠疫情双重背景下，剖析当前中印关系形势，审视在印汉语教学面临的困境，以创新视角提出了突破困局的实用建议。

本书的出版，也得到了许多印度友人的积极响应和支持。印度青年领袖联合会（CYL）主席苏万焕先生，多年来致力推动中印人文交流合作与两国青年交往，多次亲自带队赴华参访，与中国结下了深厚情谊，百忙中为本书撰写特辑。印度知名学府国际大学中国学院院长阿维杰特博士，专门撰文描述中国学院创办历史和在印汉语教学发展。此外，本书的翻译和校对工作也得到了在印留学的中国学生和印度青年汉学家、留华毕业生的大力支持和广泛关注。

本书还得到了云南民族大学、江西宜春学院、上海政法学院、石家庄市第九中学、印度那烂陀大学、金德尔全球大学、尼赫鲁大学、杜恩大学和印华中文学校，以及长期从事在印汉语教学工作的专家、学者的大力支持。

本书由中华人民共和国驻印度共和国大使馆文化处汇编，在此向为本书的出版工作付出辛勤劳动的所有机构和人员表示诚挚谢意！

顾问：孙卫东

执行主编：孙美幸

编委会成员：余贝贝　蔡育靓　赵　阳　甘露婷
爱　德（Aditya Kumar Pandey）
白婉娜（Bhavana Kumari）　汪美岑　白万丽　陈冰睿

中华人民共和国驻印度共和国大使馆文化处

2022 年 6 月

Epilogue

This book *Bridging Hearts Though Chinese—The Dissemination and Development of Chinese Language Education in India*, brings valuable experiences of China and India in the field of teaching and research on Chinese language by the experts, scholars and educators of the two countries in India. This book reviews and summarizes the development of teaching of Chinese language in India and its key role in cultural exchanges between two countries. It comprehensively reflects the development status of Chinese language education in India under the background of the significant development of cultural exchanges between China and India since the beginning of the new century. The purpose of this book is to sort out the development of Chinese language education in India and discuss the theories and methods of teaching Chinese in India by compiling and collating first-hand information from Chinese and Indian educationists, who are engaged in teaching Chinese. This book provides the most realistic and operational guidance on the theories and practices of Chinese language education and teaching in India.

Language is a bridge of communication between people and is the best key to understand one country. In history, China and India have had carried out in-depth civilizational exchanges along the ancient Silk Road. Xuanzang, the famous monk of the Tang dynasty who went west to seek Dharma, was proficient in Sanskrit and after returning to China, he had translated 77 Buddhist scriptures, which has made the outstanding contribution to the spread of Buddhism in China. He used his language to travel across India and had a deep understanding of Indian customs and traditions. He wrote a famous book named The Great Tang Records on the Western Regions which became an essential document for people to understand the history of India. The Indian monk Bodhidharma went to China and studied Chinese language and further established the Zen school at Shaolin temple. It has profoundly influenced Chinese Buddhism and Chinese culture for thousands of years. Language-communication has extensively promoted the cultural exchanges between China and India and has deepened the friendship between the people of the two countries. Rabindranath Tagore and Prof. Tan Yunshan co-founded Cheena Bhavan in Visva Bharati University trained several young Indians who, after learning the language, they sprinkled seeds of Sino-Indian friendships all over India. Xu Fancheng lived in India for 33 years. In addition to the solemn teaching work, he was engaged in writing books and worked on translations. He introduced China and Chinese culture to India, also translated the ancient Indian Vedic scriptures Fifty Upanishads from Sanskrit into Chinese. At the critical moment when the Chinese people were ravaged by Japanese aggression, Dr. Dwarkanath Kotnis ignored his personal safety and resolutely determined to go to China. There, he communicated with patients in fluent Chinese. He saved countless lives with his superb medical skills. Unfortunately, having been ill from extensive workload, he died tragically at a very young age. It was the painstaking efforts of countless forefathers that laid a solid foundation for China-India friendship. This is not only the common wealth of the people of China and India, but it also give us confidence and serve as a powerful driving force when the two countries are facing any difficulties.

From soliciting contributions, conducting reviews, translation, proofreading and designing layout, this book took months, it got published successfully at the end. This work could not have been possible without the strong support of people from all walks of life. We would like to express our deep gratitude to H.E. Mr. Sun Weidong, Ambassador of China to India, who has always given great importance to China-India cultural exchanges, especially the language and education exchanges and cooperation between the two countries. He took out time to write a preface for this book, and strongly supported the publication of the book. Prof. Sun Peng is currently working at the Office of International Exchange and Cooperation of Zhengzhou University and is also a researcher at South Asia

Research Center at the University. He worked as a Dean of Confucius Institute in Vellore University of Science and Technology, the first Confucius Institute in an Indian University, for 8 years. During his tenure, he actively promoted the construction of teaching Chinese and Chinese examination points in India, hosted the translation of the main teaching material complied by Center for Language Education and Cooperation such as Chinese Paradise、Happy Chinese and Learn Chinese with me into Tamil language. Therefore, he has accumulated rich experience in teaching Chinese to Indians and gave comprehensive guidance to this book. He has also contributed an article for the book to share his experience. Dr. Bao Jiqing is a distinguished fellow of South Asia Research Center, Institute of International Relations, Tsinghua University. She has lived in India and Pakistan for many years, visited several schools where she stayed and had extensive exchanges with teachers and students. She has organized summer camp for students and language training for teachers to China. She wrote "Chinese Language Teaching in India under Unseen Changes in a Hundred Years" which analyzes the current situation of China-India relations and examines the difficulties of teaching Chinese in India under the circumstances of unchanging situation of hundred years and the new novel corona virus epidemic situation. She puts forward useful practical suggestions to break through the difficulties from a new perspective.

The publication of this book also achieved the positive response and support from many Indian friends. Mr. Himadrish Suwan, chairman of the Confederation of Indian Youth Leaders (CYL), works hard to promote cultural exchanges and cooperation between China and India and carried out youth exchanges between two countries for many years. He personally led team to visit China several times and had deep friendship with China. He wrote an appendix for this book by taking out time from his busy schedule. Dr. Avijit Banerjee, the head of the prestigious institute Cheena Bhavan, Visva Bharati University in India, specially describes the history of the establishment of Cheena Bhavan and the development of teaching of Chinese language in India. In addition, the translation and proofreading of this book has also received strong support and wide attention from Chinese students studying in India and young Sinologists and graduates of India.

Also we are appreciated the supports from Yunnan Minzu University, Jiangxi Yichun University, Shanghai Institute of Political Science and Law, Shijiazhuang No.9 Middle School, Nalanda university, Jindal Global University, Jawaharlal Nehru University, Doon University and Yeh China Education, where Chinese language programs have been taught for a long time .

This book is compiled by Culture Office of the Embassy of the People's Republic of China in India. We would like to express our sincere thanks to all the institutions and people who have worked hard for the publication of this book!

Consultant: Sun Weidong

Executive Editor：Sun Meixing

Editorial Board Members: Yu Beibei, Cai Yuliang, Zhao Yang, Gan Luting, Aditya Kumar Pandey, Bhavana Kumari, Wang Meicen, Bai Wanli, Chen Bingrui

Culture Office of the Embassy of the People's Republic of China

June 2022